CYRIL CONNOLLY
Journal and Memoir

Cyril Connolly
Journal and Memoir

David Pryce-Jones

Ticknor & Fields NEW YORK 1984

First American edition 1984

Copyright © 1983 by David Pryce-Jones and the Estate of Cyril Connolly 1983

Library of Congress Cataloging in Publication Data

Pryce-Jones, David, date
Cyril Connolly: journal and memoir.

Includes bibliographical references and index.
1. Connolly, Cyril, 1903-1974—Biography.
2. Connolly, Cyril, 1903-1974—Diaries.   3. Authors,
English—20th century—Biography.   4. Editors—England—
Biography.   I. Connolly, Cyril, 1903-1974.   II. Title.
PR6005.0393Z83   1984   820.9 [B]   83-24282
ISBN 0-89919-280-7

Printed in the United States of America

S   10   9   8   7   6   5   4   3   2   1

ACKNOWLEDGEMENTS

Cyril Connolly was a hoarder of everything he had ever written. While still a schoolboy he had begun the habit of corresponding with friends, who were subsequently asked to return his letters. Most of them obliged. It was as if a total autobiography were always in preparation. Nothing in the past could be let go, in case it might fortify or vivify the present. People and places, and the record of them, were set up to be recollected and revisited, sometimes sacramentalised.

When he died, this mass of material was left to his widow, Deirdre (now Mrs Peter Levi). Nobody had previously read his many travel notebooks and diaries, nor the journal kept between 1928 and 1937 in a large and handsome leather-bound volume with a gilt clasp. When Deirdre Levi invited me to edit this journal for publication, she also made available Cyril Connolly's entire archive. Generally speaking, letters and poems and passages from manuscripts and notebooks, which I have quoted, are from this main source. Punctuation has occasionally been tidied or rectified, notably by replacing dashes with full stops. A number of small excisions have been made from the journal, mostly to avoid repetition, but in a few instances to spare the feelings of living people. The chapter-headings one and all are Cyril Connolly's, borrowed or rather adapted to my purposes from pieces which he had either written in part, or more often, projected.

Without Deirdre Levi's permission to have unrestricted access to all this material, and to make of it what I could, this book could not have been undertaken, and I am naturally immensely grateful for such encouragement.

In his lifetime, the papers had all been in a chaos too daunting for Connolly himself to sort out, whenever he tried. A preliminary tidying-up was done by Andrew Rossabi. John Byrne, of Bertram Rota Ltd, then sifted through everything, reducing piles to files, which he passed over to me in due order. Without his expertise, the random reading of so much material might well have remained too daunting.

Cyril Connolly's library, and with it lengthy runs of letters from some of his more famous friends and contemporaries, now forms part of the collection at the McFarlin Library at the University of Tulsa, Oklahoma. Dr David Farmer allowed me access to this, and I should like to thank him and his staff, not only for their help but for permission to quote. Letters from Connolly to Patrick Kinross are now in the possession of the Huntington Library, at Pasadena. Again, the librarians there went to great trouble to provide all possible material from an archive so recently acquired that it had not yet been catalogued. Once more I am grateful for permission to quote these passages which are to be found on pages 75, 76, 88, 94, 103, 104, 108, 110, 111, 121–2, 123–4. Mrs Lola Szladits kindly provided such Connolly documentation as there is in the Berg Collection of the New York Public Library. When it came to printed books, the London Library was exemplary, as usual.

Among those who generously provided me with personal letters from Cyril Connolly were Mrs Patrick Leigh Fermor, Mrs John Strachey and Mrs James Teacher (letters addressed to her father, Sir Henry d'Avigdor-Goldsmid). Anne Davis, Jean Connolly's sister, and her husband Bill Davis, gave me all help where Jean and her papers were concerned.

I am grateful too to Professor Quentin Bell and David Gascoyne for allowing me to quote from letters they wrote in answer to queries of mine arising out of the journal.

Very many people showed a spontaneous interest in this book, which made the researching of it a pleasure, as well as the sort of tribute to Cyril Connolly which he would have been the first to appreciate. I should like to thank the following for the kindness they showed when answering letters or giving interviews, or for help and hospitality; Sir Harold Acton; Sir A. J. Ayer; Lady Antrim; Sybille Bedford; Noel Blakiston (whose book *A Romantic Friendship* proved invaluable); Mrs Mungo Buxton (née Racy Fisher); Lord and Lady David Cecil; Lord Clark; Lady Cooke (née Diana Witherby); Lawrence Durrell; Lady Elwes; Mr and Mrs Carl Foreman who had me to stay in Los Angeles; Lord Gladwyn; Mr and Mrs Philip Glazebrook; Anthony Hobson; Lord Jessel; Dr Maurice Keen of Balliol College, Oxford, for providing information about the college; Arthur Koestler; William Le Fanu; John Lehmann;

Patrick Leigh Fermor; Peter Levi who checked the classical quotations; Professor Sir Roger Mynors; Stanley Olson; Mrs Janetta Parladé; Tom Parr; Alfred Perlès; Mrs Catherine Porteous; Alan Pryce-Jones; Peter Quennell; Kenneth Rae; John Sparrow; John Sutro; Mr and Mrs Christopher Sykes; Dr Patrick Trevor-Roper.

A great debt is owed to many authors and publishers. In particular, I should like to thank the Estate of David Garnett; Virginia Woolf's Literary Estate and The Hogarth Press; Mrs M. T. Parsons and The Hogarth Press; John Sparrow, literary executor of Maurice Bowra; A. D. Peters, literary executor of Evelyn Waugh; Dr Dermod MacCarthy, literary executor of Desmond MacCarthy; the executors of Enid Bagnold; John Russell, literary executor of Logan Pearsall Smith.

Green leaves on a dead tree is our epitaph —
green leaves, dear reader, on a dead tree

(from the Journal)

Shade Those Laurels

My parents had known Cyril Connolly long before I was born. His name, his reputation, were mentioned in ways inviting curiosity. 'It was no accident, Pryce-Jones, that you have lived near three royal palaces.' I must have been about thirteen or fourteen when I read this sentence in Cyril Connolly's *Where Engels Fears to Tread*, that famous parody of the Thirtyish mode. The surname looked so very exposed on the page. Was the joke friendly or not? The parody had the tone of a man talking in a circle where the most subtle and minute social and literary references could be taken for granted. So Cyril Connolly fixed himself in my first impressions as a character both comic and minatory, and that was no accident.

Then there was *Enemies of Promise*. To a boy at Eton, as I was, living experiences very similar to those described in the book, its impact was unforgettable. Mysteries were revealed in this Guide for the Perplexed. Something called 'character' was apparently much valued for its own sake by adults, and had to be shaped to ends preordained by custom. The process had to be gone through with, and the element of knowing-your-place was confused with the challenge to the individual in a way which was simultaneously comforting and sickening. Evensong in chapel, playing-fields, elms, Tudor brickwork, certain books and texts which were almost sacred, and correspondingly unvarying attitudes – Connolly had formulated all this in his Theory of Permanent Adolescence, whereby he in common with the larger part of the ruling class remained through upbringing, 'adolescent, school-minded, self-conscious, cowardly, sentimental, and in the last analysis homosexual'. But which came first, the ego that couldn't fit in or the institution that wouldn't budge?

'I have always disliked myself at any given moment; the total of such moments is my life.' So opens the confessional chapters of *Enemies of Promise*. Only three pages later comes, 'Already my life was a chain of ecstatic moments.' A contradiction, for who could dislike himself as part of an ecstatic moment? Dislike was here converted into fascination with ego. Again it comforted and sickened to accept that he was the way he was, as though without exercise of will on his part. The passive agent could not turn active. He was not going out to govern New South Wales, or to become a general or a tycoon or even to write the masterpiece which he professed to be the object of his ambition. *Enemies of Promise* carried to its conclusion the debunking of high imperial virtues, it explained why there would be no eminent moderns to succeed the Victorians. Its great hidden theme concerns loss of will-power and failure of nerve among the English, which makes it exemplary, one of the case-books of the century, to be remembered as long as anyone is still interested in the people who once coloured so much confident red upon the map of the world.

In the summer of 1953, when I still had my last year of school ahead of me, my father took me to the Bayreuth festival. There I met Cyril Connolly for the first time. An American lady had a large car with a chauffeur, and she generously drove us about in it. I recall Cyril in the party visiting a great baroque house in the neighbourhood. Among much lavishness were silver double-eggcups at breakfast, so that perhaps a hundred boiled eggs were lined up in rows on a sideboard. ('Which tastes best? The first or the second?' he had asked in *Enemies of Promise*. 'The first finger of toast or the last little triangle dug out from the bottom with a spoon? I don't know but I do know that one should never have a third egg, and I remember the sensation of not wanting to eat it yet hating to let it go, and finally forcing myself to dispose of it.') I picture us as well in the Nuremberg museum, where a broadsword, reputedly Charlemagne's, was on display. 'Isn't it dreamy?' the American lady asked. Cyril took her up, doing a turn about the two-handed swing, the heads falling, blood in the runnel – he rarely laughed out loud but had a way of gleaming with the pleasure of anything funny, and meanwhile his shoulders heaved.

He was fifty at the time. He seemed like someone from a more expansive age, a survivor stepping through postwar debris. The presence was powerful. At first sight this was a question of physique. Trouble was taken about his appearance – a long soak in the bath, expensive clothes. Yet he always looked ruffled, more bohemian than he was, someone who could not have peered into the mirror. A double-chin, jowls, discoloured teeth, straggly hair, a figure tethered by its weight and shape. Anything more strenuous than a short stroll in a park seemed inappropriate. Far from being a genial old party, he was evidently dissatisfied at having let himself go, but not so dissatisfied that he was prepared to do something about it. 'Imprisoned in every fat man a thin one is wildly signalling to be let out.' The sentence, from *The Unquiet Grave*, had already become an everyday tag, had entered the language, although often misquoted. It was an autobiography.

'A fat, slothful, querulous, greedy, impotent carcass; a stump, a decaying belly washed up on the shore.' In this vein he could write easily about himself, and no doubt believe the rhetoric too, with some part of his mind at least. At times he certainly imposed a broody, oppressive and even angry self. But self-reproach was enjoyable; the pleasure latent in the vocabulary is unmistakable. This was suicide by aphorism. Long before suffering any real abuse or hurt, the inner Cyril had begun rising in opposition, signalling to be let out. He was not going to deprive himself either of the joys of excess or of the atonement which topped them off. A whole theatre of mood ensued, and other people might very well experience difficulty about deciding at which point they were stepping into the play. Physical clues to the inner self could be observed in the child's snub nose, the eyes alive with humour, a touch of mastery in the features. That inner self had natural creativity and charm, much fantasy, some poetry, and enough sense of reality to insist upon writing regular journalism.

Paradox began here: the depiction of himself as some sort of royal failure was the foundation of his success. Above all else he had wanted to be a great writer. Such a writer ought to produce a masterpiece, a book to endure ten years. *Enemies of Promise* and *The Unquiet Grave* both met this arbitrary standard. That was not enough. Both books were offered as evidence of how much more he might have done, ought to have done. Guilt was one thing, though, and blame another. Circumstances had conspired against him. Nobody could argue the if-only case more plausibly. If only he had been born in another age he might have been an elegiac Roman poet, a classical English wit and essayist, a French *philosophe* or *poète maudit* – if only he had inherited an estate and a fortune to free him from drudgery – if only he were handsomer, lived elsewhere, with someone else.

In his company, it was impossible not to speculate that perhaps he was right – but not for long. It was a matter of observation that he was the centre of attention wherever he went. His comments carried, his silence was feared. Then there was too much glee in his pleading guilty to the seven deadly sins. Could he not remedy what he criticised so savagely? This was surely a complicated parody of someone with the same name as himself whose brilliant new book each year set the whole world talking. Playing the leading part in this comedy of his own devising, he was imitating failure.

Advantage came from it. Here was the way to avoid making hard choices or sacrifices, here was the way to have everything all at once and all the time, to be artist and critic, powerfully realising ambition while claiming not to be doing so. From 1952 to 1974 he was the main book reviewer on the *Sunday Times*, writing a good deal of occasional journalism in addition. He used to say that if he went overboard for a book in his column, then four hundred more copies were sold; so much for literary opinion-making. The Theory of Permanent Adolescence had settled down to having one's cake and eating it.

Disadvantage arose as well, from the risk that this tale of failure would be treated at face value. He was often sloppy, insistent on getting his own way, bad-mannered, and these characteristics reinforced the woeful figure he could cut. A huge wake of comic anecdote and malicious gossip trailed after him. Stories were told in which Cyril always came off worst, for instance borrowing books and either not returning them or marking their pages with bacon rashers or pieces of spaghetti. Stories of Cyril borrowing other people's houses, and in one of them stuffing a half-eaten plate of food into a drawer where it was discovered six months later, or bunging the case of a grandfather clock with things usually discarded in the bathroom. Stories of Cyril tipping wet tea-leaves over his carpets to clean them. Slapstick stories of extravagances, jealousies, petty venalities in which he was bound to be caught out – little or none of it, needless to say, can be verified. On one of the occasions when he was staying with Somerset Maugham, he is said to have picked two avocadoes which his host was specially cultivating, was rightly suspected of the deed, and obliged to unpack his suitcase in order to hand the avocadoes back.

No encounter with Cyril was free from its fictions. He encouraged lapses into comedy, and even self-parody, as though he were the sum total of all the characters he would never invent in novels. No motive could be as it seemed. Yet taking up a subject – Africa, gardening, silver hallmarks, wild animals, a particular landscape, connoisseurship – he was immensely scholarly, studying for the sake of studying, until he could hold his own with the experts.

Puritans, kill-joys, class-warriors, were his natural enemies. A coterie was his natural habitat, in which he was witty and clever, a man of the world, fluent in the main European languages. 'What does Cyril think?' was a valid question for forty years and more in English life and letters. In the guises of dandy, dilettante, glutton, stoic, cynic, clown, Milord, he made himself a ringmaster personality, uniquely prominent and vulnerable.

Something else I remember him repeating, 'Always be nice to those younger than you, because they are the ones who will be writing about you.'

2

Narcissus
Complete with Pool

By the time that Cyril came to write *Enemies of Promise*, the Thirties were upon him, and he had surrendered to the cultural police of the day, only too willing to aid them in their inquiries. Intimate Confessions of a Bourgeois, Down among the Rentiers: he was condemned in advance. In mitigation, he wanted to complete the dossier against him.

He had been a good boy until his grandmother had spoiled him. His great-aunt had been the Countess of Kingston. Aunt Mab, his mother's sister and a favourite, was rich. Kindly disposed but limited parents had brought him up to be a certain kind of Englishman, in the shadow of Kipling and Newbolt, the kind no longer required. The three forcing-houses of his education, St Cyprian's, Eton and Oxford, had unmade him. 'Character' had him in its reactionary grip. A gentleman is not a comrade. No wonder he could not take leave of himself, throw away his chains and his prose-style, join the modernists and write like them.

It was everybody's fault but his. Class had determined every step of the travesty. He was less his own subject than other people's object. The commissar and the Freudian couch-master alike were certain to approve this stance. 'Its engagingly simple left-wing militancy,' he wrote of the book, in the preface for the 1961 Penguin edition, 'breathes the air of the period.'

With some part of himself, he managed to believe that his head-start and his many privileges really had been handicaps. But it was hardly more than a Peter Pan urge not to grow up, not to have the burden of translating so much promise into achievement. For conscious realisation of his predicament did not reconcile him to it, as it is supposed to do. The past was not to be put behind him but on the contrary wallowed in, every precious scrap of it. Prose-style immediately and intimately revealed where his heart lay. Former luxuries, sensuous tastes, castles where once his boyhood had been passed, provided memories so poignant that he still enjoyed reliving them. By contrast the future was a snare. He adored what he was doing his best to denounce, and this flavours *Enemies of Promise* with his ambivalent personality, making a document of it. None of the autobiography is untrue, but most of it pulls towards the fiction of Cyril as victim of circumstance, as orphan of history.

Actually the decorous and comfortably ordered Edwardian background into which Cyril had been born allowed him to make what he chose of it. On all branches of his family tree were large houses and private incomes. 'The surnames of my eight great-grandparents,' Cyril wrote, 'were Connolly, Hall, Kemble, Catley, Vernon, Bowles, Graves and Brinkley. The Vernons had no Irish blood, the Connollys, at any rate since the early eighteenth century had never been there, and now despite my early infatuation nothing infuriates me more than to be treated as an Irishman.' The Protestant Ascendency was well represented – through these forebears Cyril was connected to Robert Graves and Elizabeth Bowen.

Later in life, a favourite fantasy of Cyril's was that he would buy some exquisite house, turn over a new leaf, and settle down to greatness and happiness. Several of these dream-houses were in Ireland, and one of them was Castletown, built by William Conolly, Speaker of the Irish House of Commons early in the eighteenth century. It is likely that Cyril was related to the Conollys of Castletown, but the link was not definitely established either by Cyril or his father, who were both in old age keen antiquarians and genealogists.

Cyril's father kept a bound notebook in which he recorded family pedigrees, most of which have been further annotated by Cyril. The first Matthew Connolly to be mentioned was apparently a Captain in the Second West India Regiment, and he died in 1790. Cyril jotted down a number of suggestions about him; that he had run away to sea, possibly from some Irish Catholic family which could expect no advancement; that he had been taken by the press-gang; that his tombstone had been defaced because it denied him his officer's rank; that he was illegitimate. At any rate his five sons all received commissions in the army or the navy: one of them fought at Trafalgar and his name was spelled Conolly on the Army Lists.

The eldest of the five sons, another Matthew, was born at Chatham, and after a lifetime at sea, made his home in Bath, where he died in 1853. 'Commander,' Cyril noted of him in the pedigree book, 'was a kind of Master of Ceremonies at Bath, a social arbiter in Regency times.' There had been a chased silver claret jug inscribed 'To Captain Matthew Connolly late R.N. from the citizens of Bath in recognition of his invaluable services at the Winter Assembly 1831.' The note discusses the Connolly arms, adding, 'This jug regrettably lost in person by C.C. who finally bought a silver-gilt tankard, also 1831, for £120 as a replacement.' And in a different ink, the conclusion, 'Which he sold'.

This Matthew Connolly did not marry. His nephew, naturally if confusingly, was another Matthew (1816–1901), an admiral and a grandfather described in *Enemies of Promise*, 'with a great reputation for good looks of the genial, bearded, crusty, open sort, charm, gallantry, temper, and bad language'. The admiral married Harriet Kemble, eldest daughter of the Rector of Bath at the time. Of all the eight great-grandparents, the Kembles alone had been rich on a large scale, with a fortune from tea-planting. Cowbridge, their country house, was near Malmesbury. The Rector donated what was then the enormous sum of £50,000 to restore Bath Abbey, so that the main inheritance left for his Connolly descendants was a negative one of regretting what might have been theirs.

The one son of the admiral and Harriet Kemble was born in Bath in 1872 and christened Matthew William Kemble Connolly. He seems to have been grounded in dutiful conventionality. Of his own early life he wrote in the pedigree book: 'Educated at Folkestone, 82–85, Haileybury, 85–89, Paris, Bonn, and Sandhurst. Gazetted 2nd Lieut. King's Own Yorkshire Light Infantry at Guernsey, 7-11-1891. Alderney 1892. Promoted Lieutenant 92. Belfast, 93. Pontefract, 95; Mullingar, 97; Dublin, 98 (District Signalling Officer). Promoted Captain 26-7-99. Sheffield, 99; Buttevant, January 1 1900; Limerick Feb 7 1900.' Tall, he had a military bearing, with a somewhat shut-in and nondescript face and a heavy period moustache. Writing to Cyril in his old age, he would occasionally drop his parade-ground style and reminisce about childhood days in the Kemble house at Cowbridge, or about various cousins.

While stationed in Ireland, he had met Muriel Maud Vernon, and they were married in 1900. She was Maud to her family and friends, but 'dear little Mollie' to him. Connollys, according to *Enemies of Promise*, were 'a frugal, blue-eyed, long-lived, quiet, tidy, obstinate race', while the Vernons of Clontarf Castle were 'a fiery race, proud of their Anglo-Norman descent, their sixty-three quarterings and their position among the sporting Church-of-

England Ascendancy, the landlords of the Pale'. Edward Vernon, Maud's father, was High Sheriff, a member of the dashing Kildare Street Club, and would spend thirty pounds on a gun dog but begrudge his daughters their evening dresses, so Cyril recorded in the family pedigree book. Small-boned and attractive, Maud had a way of knowing how to please, but Edwardian lady that she was, she threw her hand in easily, leaving things to take their course, which, with Matthew Connolly, they were likely to do anyhow.

Officers of the period tended not to own a house but to rent one wherever duty lay, at home or in the empire. Matthew Connolly was no exception. Newly married, he was seconded in April 1900 as adjutant to the Second Volunteer Battalion of the Royal Warwickshire Regiment. Their headquarters were at Coventry. The house there which the Connollys came to rent had as its exact address Whitley Villa, Whitley, which afterwards came to sound a little too agonisingly suburban to be altogether funny. It was there, on September 10 1903, that his son was born, Cyril Vernon Connolly; only child of an only son. That week the *Illustrated London News* carried an article about the Volunteer Battalion, with an accompanying photograph of four senior officers, all mounted, in patrol uniform, with swords. Credit for the battalion's performance on the rifle range, the text stated, was due to Captain M. Connolly, 'who has done much to stimulate interest in musketry throughout the corps'.

'You are a Connolly,' Matthew Connolly was to write to Cyril, in 1945, 'and I imagine fairly typical of the race – we are all ever wanting to be on the move, never staying long in the same place and ever disagreeing with our superiors – and employers.' At the time he was advising Cyril not to buy one of the many houses to have caught Cyril's imagination, for it might be 'a source of continual, everlasting worry and anxiety such as has been the curse to Mummy and me throughout our married life, which has otherwise been *so* happy'.

To the end of his life he refused to admit what had become plain all too soon, that he and his wife were not at all happy but extremely ill-matched. So much was repressed that they found themselves without emotional resources. Complete Edwardians, they expected sentiment to fuel itself without much reference to experience, preferring to say too little for fear of saying too much. Letters which have survived from either of them are almost entirely practical in content and tone, devoid of heartfelt expression – though Matthew Connolly developed an idiosyncratically abrupt line when it came to giving orders. He also liked to append his name and rank to the bottom of letters, even to his son.

Enemies of Promise depicts nothing that can be considered family life. No such thing apparently existed for Cyril, which he thought was the explanation of why he had taken so naturally to feeling lonely and sorry for himself. Dissociation from his upbringing was carried as far as it could go, though he admitted to devotion to his mother. She had written for him a childhood story called 'Grass-Haired Peterkin', she did water-colours and filled albums with prose about rosebuds and fairies, or with verse in this style:

> Rest my baby, God says you may
> Rest once you start on Life's weary way.

Quite early Cyril understood that his parents' neglect of him was overshadowed by their neglect of each other. As he grew up, he resented it, and tended to mock his parents to his friends, for instance claiming (quite untruthfully) that as a matter of course he never opened letters from his mother. He was pretending to have outgrown them more than he actually had. When eventually his parents separated, he found it easier to become a dutiful son, sorry for them at last. They were to retire from each other under cover of face-saving devices: in his father's case, to a London hotel where he lived alone on grounds of economy; in his mother's case, to South Africa on account of a delicate health which in fact saw her well into old age.

No family life, no home. Whitley Villa was given up in February 1906, when Matthew Connolly was posted to Gibraltar – 'Commandant North Front', as he put into his entry in the pedigree notebook. That September he was appointed Commandant of the School of Signalling in Pretoria. Maud Connolly and Cyril lived with him there, on Roberts Heights. In the following year they sailed to England via East Africa, but in October 1908 returned to Wynberg, where Matthew Connolly was now District Signalling Officer for Cape Colony. Out in the veldt, he first became interested in snails, laying the foundations for the career as a conchologist which was to occupy the second half of his life. (His publications include a work of 660 pages called *A Monographic Survey of South African Non-Marine Molluscs* and also *The Distribution of Non-Marine Molluscs Throughout Continental Africa*. Snails in the collection of the Natural History Museum were named after him. In another sphere, foreshadowing his son, he also published 'Pottery', a brochure for the Wine and Food Society, about potted foods, meat and fish pastes, and savouries, all of which he treated as matters of the strongest conviction.)

Cyril's earliest memories were of Wynberg. 'There were chameleons in the garden and squashed apricots; on Sundays the Regiment had church parades and there were smells of pine and eucalyptus, paint blisters and hot tar. I had already grown accustomed to being an only child and enjoyed playing by myself. I had a dog called Wups, a cat called One-Eye and a crowd of other animals, some real and many imaginary. I derived enormous pleasure from animals and something approaching ecstasy from the smells of flowers and fruit and from the arid sub-tropical scenery.'

In 1910 Matthew Connolly was promoted to the rank of major, and posted to Hong Kong. This was judged too unhealthy for Cyril. Accordingly, he was sent to England with his nurse. On the way they stopped to join Grannie Connolly and Aunt Tottie or more usually Tots (Matthew Connolly's sister Harriet, later Mrs Blake) in Corsica where they had taken a villa. A visit with them to Tangier offered more exotic sights and smells. If nothing except the senses could supply information worth having about the world, then the self-sufficient aesthete had already been conditioned. Loneliness, the other necessary ingredient, was experienced through the parting from his parents. Like Kipling at a comparable age, he imagined his return to England to be an unloving rejection by his parents. In his memory this loomed almost like an orphaning, so much so that towards the end of his life, checking the facts, he was astonished to realise how short a time he had actually been separated from his mother and father.

Passed on to relations, he stayed in Ireland with his Vernon uncle and aunt. The romanticism of all things Irish, as described in *Enemies of Promise*, overlaid the sensations of Wynberg. At Clontarf there was a two-handed sword which was said to have belonged to the legendary Brian Boru. Mitchelstown, the house of his great-aunt Lady Kingston, was 'an enormous eighteenth century Gothic affair'. Aunt Mab (Dorothy Mabel, to be exact, and married to Walter Summers, a regular soldier who was well off), encouraged him. The house which she and Uncle Walter rented evoked 'security and romance, fires and potato cakes, footmen, horses, and soft aquatinted Irish winter'. Quite simply, 'The appeal her wealth made to an imaginative child was irresistible.' Aunt Mab and the Vernons, Irish castles, holidays, riches, Upper Class, were equated into a desirable whole. England, by contrast, entailed Grannie, Lodgings, School, Poverty, Middle Class. He felt that he had to make sure of being indulged. That was what he meant when he declared that from the age of seven his character had begun to deteriorate.

In charge of him, Grannie Connolly had to answer to the unusual accusation of not disciplining him. She lived in Bath, at 17 The Vineyard, a terraced house. 'Critical, impatient and sparkling' as he then grew, he took advantage of his grandmother. She was helpless. She allowed him not to have to make a hard choice between alternative toys in a Bath shop, but bought him both. Here was the Original Sin, with consequences as rigorous as those deriving from that first bite of the apple in the Garden of Eden. Why had she so misleadingly taught him that wishes came true? Normal loving instincts in a grandparent seemed in retrospect to have been a deadly tactic for revenge upon her own son for insults suffered long ago. Such a first-generation Freudian cliché was not much softened when he added another drawn from Darwin, 'My grandmother, lonely, religious, and unselfish, was only playing her biological role.' Indecision, Ingratitude, Laziness, Impatience, Cruelty, and Giving Way to Moods had been cultivated in him, Cyril concluded, simply because small faults had been allowed to pay off. But if the blame for these faults of his was properly hers, why after more than thirty years of clear-sighted introspection could he still not correct them himself?

She had spoiled him in the most literal sense. She addressed notes to him as the Duke of Vernon KCMG, signing herself the Duchess of C. She also sent him off in the autumn of 1910 to his first school, St Christopher's, North Road, Bath. He had a red cap, a snake-buckled belt, a cricket bat. Fifteen years later, Grannie Connolly could still be wistful about it. 'How I wish I had my darling little Redcap grandson again, sitting on my knee and making out a lovely tour for me on the map. Do you remember going to bed for me in your red cap and tie the first night you wore them? I really cried when I went in and found you asleep in your cap and tie, it seemed so touching to me.'

St Christopher's absorbed its observant new day boy. 'My favourite exercise was to take a short piece of pointed wood in my hand and meander for hours through the long summer grasses round the playing fields, calling at imaginary ports, tunnelling through the hay, chewing sorrel, and following my faint tracks in the silver grass as a liner follows a trade route. Inside my desk a cardboard shoebox perforated with holes supported a brood of caterpillars. Who can forget that smell of caterpillars, the smell of wet cardboard, drying leaves and insect excrement, the odour of northern childhood? It was on one of those long summer cruises, in a patch of cow-parsley, that I realised my own identity; in a flash it came to me that my name and myself were something apart, something that none of the other boys were or could be, Cyril Vernon Connolly, a kind of divine "I am that I am."'

In his memory he had always been a reader, grounded in natural history, in Mark Twain, Stephen Leacock, Burnand, Lear, Anstey, Ernest Thompson Seton, not to mention boys' comics. Aged nine, in December 1912, he was writing to his mother, 'I want to ask you how to spell Brian Bru [sic] that is how Granny told me it was spelt because another boy and I have got up a thing, that he talks Scotch to me and I talk Irish brogue to him . . . I called myself Brian Bru and I thought I ought to know how to spell it. For Christmas I would like a book called "Barrack room Ballads" by Kipling and a box of conjuring tricks.'

School reports repeated that he ought not to fall below top place in his form. The headmaster, Carrick Trask, was the first to strike the note of enthusiastic expectation, in a final report at Easter 1914. 'We shall miss him horribly, in the past year he has grown into one of the bigger boys and developed in every way. He is of course a boy *quite* out of the ordinary with many most interesting and unusual traits, not at all the usual type of schoolboy. I should have loved to watch the maturing of all his character and we do regret losing him. He has been perfectly well and strong the whole term and full of fine spirits. He will do well wherever he goes.'

3

Discovering Eden

At St Christopher's Cyril had suffered from recurrent malaria caught in South Africa, and Maud Connolly had been worrying about his health. She also disapproved of Grannie Connolly's increasing influence. For these reasons she selected a well-known preparatory school, St Cyprian's at Eastbourne, almost at the other end of the country. Moreover Matthew Connolly had suffered a serious setback after his posting in Hong Kong. As he expressed it, succinct as ever, in the family pedigree book: 'Placed on half-pay, owing to an attack of rheumatic fever, 11-12-1912, and retired under Para. 564 R.W. 2-5-1914, but volunteered for service on the outbreak of the Anglo-German war and was attached to the 7th (Service) Battalion K.O.Y.L.I. at Woking, 8-10-1914.' Failure to play an active part in the war made a disappointed man of him.

Home on his half-pay, Matthew Connolly decided to buy The Lock House, some three miles outside the village of Frimley, set in the heart of the Surrey countryside of heath and pine and military training camps. The house was isolated, surrounded by woods which were dark and melancholy, capturing the imagination. The name derived from the lock on the Basingstoke Canal which had been cut through the trees close to the house. There were latticed windows, gables, tall chimneys and tiled roofs, in part old, in part stockbroker's Tudor: a muddle, but quite imposing. Round the house ran a terrace, and lawns. Connolly and Kemble possessions were assembled, for instance furniture from Cowbridge, silver, pictures, prints.

In one of his earliest notebooks at St Cyprian's, the twelve-year-old Cyril made a gratified inventory of the house down to its beams and panelling. 'Lounge, Dining Room, Drawing Room, Smoking Room, Cloak Room, a Bedroom with a Queen Anne Grate'. Six bedrooms not counting one more in the attic, he noted, as well as 'Stables, Garage, Farmery, Barn, Granary, Poultry House and Run,

Garden'. Also, 'Outer Circle, New Field (½ orchard) . . . Fallen Apple and Tennis Corner'.

A 'Map of the Canal' accompanied the inventory. Every feature within a private topography had been named, The Wood and the Bush Veldt, with three bridges across the stretch of water, Woodland Pools, Rush Swamp, Alder Island, Great Willow, Myrtle Reach, and far away beyond Third Cataract lay The Big Karroo, marked 'Unexplored'. Solitary only-child games were played out here. Certain trees served as way-stations on a railroad, and he would time himself round the circuits, keeping elaborate charts. Or he would act out another South African fantasy of hunting by throwing assegais, either real Zulu ones given to him by his father, or some he had fashioned for himself out of hazel. In the Fallen Apple and Tennis Corner, knock-out competitions were devised and also recorded in notebooks, the captain of the winning team and the world-champion being C. V. Connolly, sometimes alias C. V. Vernon.

The Lock House and its impact have been suppressed from *Enemies of Promise*, heightening the impression that there never had been anywhere to call home. Yet his boyhood was associated for ever in his memory with the place, in spite of, or more probably because of, the tantalisingly short time that he had spent there. With the summer term of 1914, he departed for St Cyprian's, and by March 1915, Matthew Connolly, in uniform again, moved from Woking to Harrogate, to the 11th Service Battalion of the King's Own Yorkshire Light Infantry. Two months later he was transferred to work as an army Record Officer in London. There the family lived with Granny Vernon in 18 Brompton Square. Holidays in 1915 were spent in Harrogate; in 1916 his parents took Cyril on a visit to Oban on the west coast of Scotland. By July 1915 their address was Gresham Cottage, Brentwood, in Essex. From the summer of 1917 to the summer of 1919, they lived in Hampshire, at Ewshot Lodge, Ewshot. The Lock House remained let meanwhile.

When Cyril returned after the war, first as an Etonian and later as an undergraduate, his emotions about the house remained at childhood pitch. His recreations were still the throwing of assegais or going for long runs over the hills across the railway track with a favourite Congo spear. 'I have secret places here which rival the Oxus,' he wrote in one letter. He was proud of a poem written in his first year at Oxford:

[23]

Disused, the Basingstoke canal
mirrors the birches, water quiet,
white shadows in still pools –
over the slow stream
the blue ray of a kingfisher
flashes, and is gone. A moorhen
eddies, towards the reeds
soft with the furry glow
of evening coming on.

What the house continued to mean to him was explained in a letter to a friend at Eton, dated December 1924, but probably never sent. 'I prowl round the empty rooms or turn on one light or all the lights when my father has gone to bed and go out to the end of the garden to see the golden shafts shining through latticed windows and stretching over the grass to where I stand by the dark yew hedge listening to the soft splashing of our stream, my feet in the dead leaves. I do not know if it is really lovely or if I love it because I have been a child here or because I must love something or because one day it will be mine. It is not a "place" but rather a large small house, mostly 18th century but skilfully added to and with a lovely garden now rather run to seed, abiding in a hollow by still water and encircled by protecting trees. My father does not like it because it is damp and because it is out of the way, but my mother loves it more than me. It is full of nice creatures, birds that my mother knows all about, squirrels and rabbits.'

Hope and happiness there were left unfulfilled, replaced instead by consistent feelings of loss and of the transience of things. *Paradise Lost*, when he read it at Oxford, seemed to confirm what he had experienced at first-hand at The Lock House, and its images, once referred to himself, stayed powerfully dominant. 'It was as a boy that I discovered Eden, and it was at first a world of my own before I discovered it had other worshippers, not only all who could agree "*nobis placeant ante omnia silvae*" but a chosen few who seemed to exist as chanting priests to immortalise the tragedy of our first parents and the beauty of the forsaken garden.' Written while he was an undergraduate and preserved among his papers, this was among his earliest impulsive efforts to recapture what was past. The fragment was just as true for him fifty years later.

The Lock House was never to be his to live in – life all too soon realised the myth for him. Early in the Thirties, his father disposed of it, and many of the contents too. The golden age there had been brief, quite beyond recovery, coinciding as it did with the final year of Edwardian England, the close of an epoch.

4

The Path of Duty was the Way to Glory

Photographs of Cyril during the St Cyprian's years show him in a sailor suit, or astride his pony, or out on the school playing-fields in knickerbockers and boots and a cap, with large fur gloves to keep off the cold. Had that slender bright-eyed reliant child been as vulnerable as he said? Had St Cyprian's really been nothing but adversity, physical discomfort, nasty food, bullying, pruriency about sex? Did it deserve an aside like 'Though Spartan the death-rate was low'? Was he recalling it in such vivid detail through genuine hatred, or from sentimentality, or even perhaps because of something positive owed to it but which he had repressed? The self-dramatisation in the relevant chapters of *Enemies of Promise* have put these questions beyond answering.

By coincidence, moreover, Cyril's exact contemporary there had been Eric Blair, otherwise George Orwell, who was quite his equal as a fantasist, as well as something of a genius. Almost thirty years were to elapse before Cyril invited Orwell to corroborate the horror of the past they had once shared. Orwell was only too eager to oblige. His essay *Such, Such were the Joys*, published in 1952, happens to be one of the most brilliant polemics in the language, in which the school and all its works stand, in miniature, for every-thing that Orwell thought most wrong with England. Whatever St Cyprian's had actually been like in the days of Orwell and Con-nolly, its future was ever after assured, like Dotheboys Hall or the Slough of Despond, in the landscape of myth.

Parting with him at the school, Cyril's mother had wept. Homesick, Cyril cried night after night. His early letters to her were preoccupied with concerns of home. Could she put the scarlet tigers on the little hawthorns by the Cape Pond? Had anyone tried to take Gresham Cottage yet? 'Will you get Daddy to write me a letter some

[26]

time as I like his ones so much, and he has not written to me this term (this is not meant to insult you but his letters are so funny).' A year passed before he could write, in September 1915, 'I like St Cyprian's very much though I feel rather homesick sometimes. I know the names of nearly all of them [the new boys] there are 11. There are lots of things more different as we have to unpack our own bags and get things out ourselves, and we get up at 1/4 past seven and then have a cold bath then get up and have breakfast and about 5 boys have baths at a time. I like the chapel very much, we go there directly we have dressed before breakfast.' Adapting further, by the summer of 1916 he was able to write, 'I am not homesick any more as I am always more excited about when I come back than sorry about when I was last there. The grammar of this is rather groggy but you know what I mean. I wonder if I will be able to sleep out at Brentwood like we used to when I stayed there with German measles, if it is hot. How is the pond and the water lilies and the slime?' Still, he told his mother, he dreamed of her every night. Her letters back to her 'Dear Sprat' or sometimes 'Dear old Bean' were mostly about plans, and discouragingly listless.

The owners of the school, Mr and Mrs L. C. Vaughan Wilkes, were known to all as Sambo and Flip respectively. They were responsible for the tone, for the worship of success, for the simple message of 'character'. Flip, according to Cyril, was able and ambitious, 'we learnt with her as fast as fear could teach,' while Sambo seemed cold and business-like. 'She was a stocky spare-built woman with hard red cheeks, a flat top to her head, prominent bones and deep-set suspicious eyes,' Orwell wrote of Flip, who despatched him to be beaten with a crop by Sambo. 'When angry Flip would slap our faces in front of the school or pull the hair behind our ears, till we cried.' Both ex-pupils compared her to Queen Elizabeth I in her dealings with the boy-courtiers. Boys were in or out of favour with her; Cyril plotted his position on a graph. 'I was in a world,' concluded Orwell, 'where it was *not possible* for me to be good.'

The cold and business-like Sambo was, however, writing to Matthew Connolly with this report in December 1914: 'I am *very* pleased with your boy. I consider that he has made an admirable start in his new surroundings. He has good abilities – works well and is very pleasant to deal with: and I feel sure he will be a credit to us. He has kept fit and well all the term and is popular with both masters and boys. I have nothing but what is nice to say of him.' A few months later he was observing, 'I hope to take him up into my scholarship form as soon as I get a vacancy.' Consistent advance, a good term's work, excellent progress, good at all problems requiring original thought – out poured the schoolmasterly praise. Conduct was also often singled out as admirable or excellent.

He became an algebra enthusiast thanks to Mr Ellis, 'gruff and peppery with an egg-shaped bald head', the one member of the staff mentioned in *Enemies of Promise*. Mr Ellis, known as Daddy, thought the Germans deserved to win the war on account of their greater efficiency; he built up for Cyril a personality as Tim Connolly, Irish rebel, in back-handed tribute to the events of 1916. 'My new personality appealed to me. I changed my handwriting and way of doing my hair, jumped first instead of last into the fetid plunge-bath, played football better, and became an exhibit . . . I remember my joy as the upward curve continued, and as I began to make friends, win prizes, enjoy riding, and succeed again at trying to be funny.' Flip and Sambo never called him anything else but Tim; even his mother copied them for a while.

Orwell could already think things out for himself, apparently; he had Intelligence which was better than 'character', he realised that whoever won the war, 'we shall emerge a second-rate nation'. By contrast Tim the Irish rebel was unreal, juvenile, a concoction. Cyril wished to please. The notion of living in a world in which it was not possible to be good would have alarmed him. Actually nothing outside the normal run of schoolboy experience happened to either of them. Nor did they disparage or patronise any of the values of the school, especially not those which were resumed in its lengthening war-time Roll of Honour. The very first poem Cyril chose to preserve must have met with the approval of Flip and Sambo, who had provided its patriotic theme. It was called 'Kitchener'. (On June 5 1916 Lord Kitchener had drowned in a ship which hit a mine.)

> No honoured church's funeral hath he,
> The silent hero of a nation's fame.
> No drone of muffled drums can greet his soul,
> No last post blown in sadness o'er the sea.
> The time-worn rocks alone can mark his tomb,
> His epitaph the roar of the breaking waves.
> No human mourner follows in his train.
> The wailing seagull chants his deathsong through.
> None but the lonely curlew on the moor

Bewail a mighty empire's tearful loss
. . . Bury him not in an abbey's shrine
Midst tablets of stone and coffins of pine
But let him be where no light can shine
And the north sea waves rush in.

To which, on the page of his notebook, has been appended in a careful hand, '*Dashed* good. Slight repetition. Scansion excellent. Meaning a little ambiguous in places. Epithets for the most part well selected. The whole thing is neat, elegant and polished. E. A. Blair.' Self-consciously Cyril then drew attention to the '*Dashed* good', writing below it, 'My dear Blair!! I am both surprised and shocked.' Pleased with his poem, he told his mother that he had had it criticised 'by a chap who is considered the best poet, he did a poem on the other side and sent it to a local paper where they took it'. (Orwell's version was published on July 21 1916 in the *Henley and South Oxfordshire Standard*, which paper had been responsible for his first appearance in print, two years earlier, with a poem called 'Awake! Young Men of England'.)

A letter postmarked November 5 1916 described for Maud Connolly a visit of King George V to a local camp for convalescent soldiers. The boys formed a guard of honour, but it was 'rather a failure . . . We stood at attention for over an hour in the rain. I could hardly move my legs, they were so stiff, then the King came passed [sic] in 3 taxis at about 60 miles an hour. I saw someone's hat in one of them. The wounded soldiers, there were about 1000, all leant on a fence when they saw him, so that it broke and they all fell down a bank into the road. But the worst part was when the fat ass Sammy suddenly took us all away home because our uniforms were wet! The other schools shrieked with laughter as we passed.' That morning, he explained, Flip had lectured them about discipline, in particular that a sentry could not leave his post for fear of rain.

St Cyprian's values were further reflected when Cyril informed his mother that 'this term we have an awful lot of Nobility . . . 1 Siamese prince, the grandson of the Earl of Chelmsford, the son of Viscount Malden (who is the person who will inspect us) and who is the son of the Earl of Essex, another grandson of a lord and the nephew of the bishop of London.' Class-awareness bit into the soul, and Orwell at least was to remain unbalanced by what he considered favouritising of the rich and well-connected. A Russian boy had calculated how his father's income was two hundred times greater than Orwell's father's income, and bitterness about this incident afterwards overcame even his adult reflection about what must have been the fate of that rich Russian. One of the two boys with real English titles, according to Orwell, was a wretched drivelling little creature, 'almost an albino', which in normal circumstances he would have been the first to recognise was unworthy as an epithet of insult. Orwell's fees were paid by Sambo, but any motive of generosity was discounted. The sole purpose apparently was to have boys who would win scholarships and bring credit on the school. Matthew Connolly paid Cyril's fees but had made it clear to the Wilkeses that without a scholarship Cyril (like Orwell) would not be going on to Eton. On one occasion Mr Wilkes allowed Cyril's fees to be paid late, and his letters to Matthew Connolly frequently contained reassurances about finances and prospects. Though it would be a great test of a boy's character as well as his brains to hold his own in College at Eton, Mr Wilkes wrote, 'You will find the school a good financial investment – the fees being only £7.10.0 a term!' When later Cyril emphasised Orwell's resentments and traced them back to St Cyprian's, he was touching on anxieties about status which were close to his own.

Besides Orwell, his friends were Frank Wright, Colin and Nigel Fitzpatrick, Cecil Beaton the future photographer, and Terry Willson (in *Enemies of Promise* called Tony Watson, 'the boy whom I loved for the last three years I was at St Cyprian's'). His mother could be told all about one escapade with Terry, he wrote, because he knew she would not tell Flip as some mothers would. 'This morning I heard a clock strike six (it was 1½ hours fast but I did not know it), it was pitch dark but I got out of the dormitory and then I lost my way and wandered through dormitories. I went into the matron's bedroom but I did not find it out till afterwards, luckily I did not make much row. At last I thought I was in a dormitory at the other side of the house till someone suddenly said "So you've come back Tim!" It was my own dormitory. Then I went out and fell down the common room stairs. This woke up another boy in my dorm. And I was guided to the top of the stairs by him with a luminous watch as a signal. Then I went down to the pantry, got some buns, rewarded my guides and went along to Frankie Wright, where I spent ¾ of an hour in his bed according to custom.'

The desire for the brother or sister whom he did not have, he wrote in *Enemies of Promise*, was so strong 'that I came to see existence in terms of the couple; in whatever group I found myself I would inevitably end by sharing my life with one other,' thereby achieving his destiny as one half of a pair. There were four types to which he was susceptible in the search for his so-called Pair System, the Faun, the Redhead, the Extreme Blonde and the Dark Friend, and all four had appeared by the time he was twelve. (What other types were left?) Fauns, he thought, were to get him into trouble all his life, and Terry Willson remained a prototype.

Eight years later, after he had left St Cyprian's and Eton too, he filled in a lonely Christmas at The Lock House by delving into the papers which he had already begun to hoard. At once he grew maudlin, prisoner of fugitive moments which in other people would have been long forgotten. Initials scribbled in old notebooks, his set of Ernest Thompson Seton, one or two letters, he wrote to a friend, 'have rejuvenated Terry Willson from the limbo of my private school . . . Terry was more faun-like than anyone else I have seen and remains now the one reality of my private [i.e. school]; small and brown and wiry, with an untidy fringe and a small and wonderful mouth and superb brown eyes. He had a green overcoat and we used to get far ahead of the walk and come back together alone. He was a beautiful boxer and runner and diver and played football very well and I used to coach him for the Common Entrance and he used to grin at me when I went up and received prizes at the end of the term. We used to rag among the pegs in the passages at night and sometimes climb out of a window and run out on the lawn but most of the time he would sit drawing which he did beautifully and making me tell him stories which if I did well would lead to a lovely picture of a fox howling or Lobo or Krag the Kootenay ram or a Cossack huntsman [references to Ernest Thompson Seton's books] being deposited on my bed, always lovely living animals . . . He was in far lower forms than me and left a year before. He led a double life and used to smoke and learn swear words and make strange jokes to loose companions but he never was a bad influence on me who was thought to have reformed him nor were we anything but sentimental and chaste. He was very fond of me and knew what was the matter with both of us, which I did not. I told you, I think, of my fatal repression our last night in the bathroom and how I was shy and blundered when he tried to kiss me, wearing a towel round his waist, his brown skin shining, his hazel eyes very soft and his little lips parted. (I can't help "little", they were so.) After that we never met though we wrote a lot for two years more, two years of Eastbourne and two of absence – ill-spelt letters in faded ink. "The Priory, Repton, Derby. My dear Tim . . . I must end now, love and

[31]

what shall I say? Terry." Fancy getting a letter like that on a cold evening in the war and hugging it through tea of bread and margarine and plopping gas lights, and the smell of stale foods.' For weeks after the proffered kiss had been refused, he said, he lay awake at nights, angry and miserable.

The secret with Terry Willson, with everybody, was to be amusing. ' "Connolly's being funny," the word would go round and soon I would have collected a crowd. I revelled in this and would grow funnier and funnier till I passed quite naturally into tears.' At least he showed off how clever he was. 'This grisly process was part of my defence mechanism,' and he continued with it until he was seventeen. 'How to be popular. By being funny' – the tactical advice to himself was even written into a St Cyprian's notebook where it was designed to be read by friends. In several such notebooks were schoolboy jokes, spoofs and parodies which already came spontaneously. One was about Mr Ellis, for instance, supposedly rising to become prime minister, but exposed as a sadist by former pupils. 'Loss of Temper in Cabinet. Premier calls Sir Vernon Connolly A Stinker.' There was also a balance sheet of finances 'obtained by devious means' and 'acquired by kleptomaniacal means', with a halfpenny conscience money paid to the victim. Never tell lies, he counselled, except in two cases, '(i) To avoid punishment on myself (ii) To damage the character of a friend.' What could be more worldly? (Another sentence in the notebook uncannily prefigured the adult Cyril: 'Found. Something very nice but I shan't say anything else about it as I want it myself.')

By 1916, Greek phrases were appearing in his letters home. That summer he won the Harrow History Prize, a cramming contest of dates and names which was open to preparatory schoolboys all over the country. Orwell was runner-up, and among others selected in order of merit were two future Eton friends who both became professors, Steven Runciman and Roger Mynors. That December Cyril starred in the school play. The review in the St Cyprian's magazine read, 'The two scenes from Pickwick showing the ambitious designs of Mr Tracy Tupman and Mr Alfred Jingle to secure the affections and wealth of Miss Wardle, proved one of the big events of the evening and revealed an artist of most exceptional merit in Connolly as the much desired and quite undesirable matured spinster. His acting was of the highest quality and more than deserved the recognition it obtained: his entire performance was exquisite.'

Of course he won his scholarship, in the early summer of 1917, placed thirteenth on the list to Eton. 'My heartiest congratulations on Tim's first effort,' Mr Wilkes wrote to Matthew Connolly on June 7, following up a week later with details. 'The examiners tell me that Cyril did a very fair Latin prose, very good Greek unseen, very poor Latin unseen, an excellent English paper and fair French.' In case Eton could not accommodate as many as thirteen new scholars in the autumn, he sat the Wellington and Charterhouse exams, and was awarded scholarships there too. But boys were leaving Eton early to join the army and there was little or no hesitation about Cyril's place. 'My dearest Sprat,' his mother wrote, 'I am simply off my head with joy . . . All this lovely weather I have been thinking you would love the river at Eton and how nice you would look in their colours.' No other school, she thought, would have meant so much to him.

Letters home now portrayed him on the crest of the wave. 'I had a very nice day yesterday (blackberrying at a farm 10 miles away going by tram, back and had tea at 7. Sausages and bread and honey, then Mrs Wilkes told me Neddy and Nigel to slip out, get boots on and come to the cinema. Not back till 10.30).'

'Mrs Wilkes took her form to see the "Scarlet Pimpernel" last night at a theatre, it was simply spiffing. We did not get back till 1 o'c at night.'

'Yesterday Mrs Wilkes took some of the boys to tea and to bathe at Pevensey. I went as I had come out top of the school in the history exam and as I had improved a lot at classics.'

Evidently the Wilkeses had been consistently well-disposed towards Cyril, and to some extent made a favourite of him in their delight at his performance. Within their capacities, they had done their best for a boy much cleverer and more sophisticated than usual. The accusation that they had forced 'character' harmfully upon him boiled down to the reluctance of a gifted and extraordinary man to admit that he owed anything much to people so conventional and ordinary. Put in terms of the prevailing orthodoxy of the Thirties, Cyril was under obligation to invert his successes, substituting guilt for enjoyment, and mockery for achievement. He hoped that he had made himself not with the Wilkeses, but against them, and in this romancing the Theory of Permanent Adolescence could bloom.

After the publication of *Enemies of Promise* had made open grotesques of Flip and Sambo, Mrs Wilkes wrote to Cyril – a diminished Mrs Wilkes to be sure, for her husband had died and St Cyprian's had burnt down in a fire. The book, with 'the serious psychological damage' done to the school's founders, rendered her almost incoherent with distress. 'Other damage too – which I find hard to think you did deliberately to two people who did a very great deal for you, one of whom at least always defended you against all detractors and understood your particular difficulties tho' you did not (like most small boys) realise this at the time and who has always been your friend in spite of what was said against you later at Eton and Oxford. I suppose that is why your book got me rather badly . . . Your apparent opinion of me is so far removed from all I have ever tried to be and do and which credits me with motives which never even occured to me! Think back a little Tim and try to revise it; you will "justify my optimism" (I need it very badly now in a very difficult world).'

In a *Sunday Times* article, in 1967, Cyril did have revised thoughts about the school. His repentance drew a letter from A. S. F. Gow, then a fellow of Trinity College, Cambridge, but previously a master at Eton, where he had been Orwell's tutor. Orwell's essay (and by implication Cyril's book), Gow began, had been grossly and even ludicrously unfair. For years he had had professional contact with the Wilkeses. He held no brief for them but they had been decent people. 'If some of their methods at Eastbourne now seem out of date, I should doubt if they were much different from those of other prep schools at the time.'

5

The Time of the Lilies

In the summer of 1918, Cyril became one of the seventy or so Collegers at Eton. Already fourteen, he was older than the average new boy. Collegers lived in College itself, in other words the oldest buildings dating from Henry VI's original foundation. In Eton slang, they were collectively called 'tugs', as distinguished from 'oppidans', the large majority of boys without scholarships who were spread over the houses comprising the rest of the school. Collegers were set apart in other ways as well; they placed the initials K.S., for King's Scholar, after their names; they wore gowns over and above the usual uniform of tails; they played in their own teams, and were obliged to specialise in the Wall Game unique to Eton. That they were an elite, with careers already well under way, was assumed. In charge of them was the Master in College, then J. F. Crace, a bachelor at the time, far more penetrating an adversary than Flip and Sambo.

As if the competitive spirit was not already keen enough, College was divided within itself into annual intakes, known as Elections. Each Election tended to be judged as a whole, as good or bad, depending on performance. Fraternisation between Elections, in Cyril's day at least, was rather discouraged. Like all boys at Eton, senior Collegers had rooms of their own, while junior Elections were in the so-called Long Chamber, a medieval dormitory of forbidding gloom, divided into cubicles. The list of boys above Cyril in his Election were L. R. Delves-Broughton, J. O'Dwyer, R. N. Christie, A. R. D. Watkins, J. G. Foster, R. L. Coghlan, C. D. Buckley, R. S. J. C. Wayne, G. Meynell, C. E. Minns, W. C. Milligan, C. G. Eastwood. These, then, were to move up the school in a somewhat artificial bloc of rivals unable to part company, and some of them, whether they liked it or not, were destined for the pages of *Enemies of Promise*.

'Period of complete nonentity,' Cyril wrote of his first two halves (or terms) at Eton, in a notebook containing some of the progress charts he liked to keep. 'Chamber games – Armistice. Dim and bullied.' Beatings were frequent and unnecessary. There was bullying. This was the worst of St Cyprian's all over again, and to describe it Cyril resorted to metaphors drawn from the feudal system, serfdom, the Dark Ages, even the Gestapo. At one point he likened himself to Caligula, at another to Tiberius.

'I felt quite lost and friendless in this world and sought out Meynell, the boy selected by Sambo to keep an eye on me . . . Nobody would have believed that he could make me stand on a mantelpiece and dance while he brandished a red-hot poker between my feet and said: "What is your name?" "Connolly." "No – what is your real name? Go on. Say it." "Ugly." "All right, Ugly, you can come down."'

Such was the power of the nickname branded into the memory by scenes of the kind that contemporaries sometimes continued to refer to 'Ugly' Connolly afterwards, attributing to his looks not only a lifetime's lack of self-confidence but also the obsessive need to be constantly testing quite how much others loved him.

His nerve was ruined. For his first two years he remained at the bottom of the form in almost everything. His mathematics master, A. E. Conybeare, later vice-provost of Eton, wrote a report at the end of the Michaelmas half, 1918: 'His work like his hair is always unkempt, and like his hands and face, frequently dirty. Indifference to personal appearance is no doubt a virtue but I cannot think it is good for a boy to be so grubby.' *Enemies of Promise* bears this out. 'I was now fifteen, dirty, inky, miserable, untidy, a bad fag, a coward at games, lazy at work, unpopular with my masters and superiors, anxious to curry favour and yet bully whom I dared.'

Unpopular with masters was true only up to a point. His classics tutor, J. C. Butterwick, for instance, was writing after that same half, 'An extraordinary boy of great individuality and a way of looking at things at once quaint and amusing and unexpected. Had the division been placed on its feeling for good English or for any aesthetic qualities it possessed he would be near the top, as he is something of a writer himself, something of a humourist and a lover, too, of literary beauty. But as a writer of Greek and Latin prose, he is for a K.S. a perfect scandal . . . he is friendly to a degree, cheerful, good-tempered and amusing, so that he has added much to the gaiety of this singularly nice division.'

Crace, the Master in College, saw him in much the same light.

'The boy certainly has a vein of great originality,' he put in his report for Michaelmas 1918, 'he is very quick to see a point, thinks for himself with independence, criticises and comments well, and has a really remarkable gift for "occasional" verse – so there is no lack of promise: but it is all very undisciplined at present.' Startlingly he concluded, 'If his ability is to grow up to something better than cheap journalism, he must tackle the training of it in habits of thoroughness and accuracy of thought.'

In December 1919 Cyril was confirmed. 'I hardly know what to say,' Crace commented about this, 'he has a keen and sincere mind but not one to which reverence comes very naturally.' The usual arguments of belief versus scepticism in fact reverberated in Cyril's notebooks and correspondence until he left Eton. In common with many, he had his Christian phase, and for a time toyed with Catholicism but was never quite able to bring himself to renounce a rationalist universe. 'The danger,' Crace continued, 'rather is of his trying to get on alone, just by the light of good sense, without aiming at very much more than that . . . And he has not got any very romantic ideals – intellectually, for instance, his point of view is more that of a journalist than of a scholar or scientist . . . I should like to know of his having some real enthusiasm or worship for *something*.' At the end of the next Easter half, he was repeating the theme, showing some prescience. 'Someone of course has got to be last, but I do not feel sure that Cyril need have been by so wide a margin . . . He is in danger of achieving nothing more than a journalistic ability to write rather well about many things.' However, there was real candour and honesty in him. 'I cannot help being won over to sympathise when he protested – at the end of a dispute I had been having with him – against my "being so beastly right!"' The threat to force Cyril to apply himself by depriving him of pocket-money was averted at the last moment.

In July 1920 he obtained his School Certificate, passing with credit in Scripture Knowledge (Greek Text), History, Latin, Elementary Mathematics, and satisfying the examiners in English Essay. Now he could give up the classics as a study and specialise instead in history. Once the obligation had been removed, he devoted himself to Latin poets, to Juvenal, Catullus, Martial, for the sake of literary pleasure. Several former Collegers have recalled how he had his copy of Propertius bound in black leather to look like a prayer-book for use in Chapel every day. By the end of 1920, Crace was assuring Matthew Connolly that it would be a mistake to press Cyril to go into the army, for it would be so entirely against his inclinations. Prospects of an Oxford scholarship, however, began to brighten.

Metaphors from the Renaissance now became suitable. Brains, especially in the form of 'Connolly's being funny' once more, won their time-honoured revenge over Brawn. 'I made him laugh and revealed my capacity as a wit.' So the alarming Godfrey Meynell (posthumous winner of a Victoria Cross on the North-West Frontier) was disarmed, even recruited to the side of the aesthetes. By the summer of 1919, Cyril's label for himself had evolved into 'cynical and irreverent'. That Christmas he could draw a line, 'Last half of bullying'. Taking stock early in the new year, he approved of the outcome. 'I am becoming quite a Socrates in the Lower Half of the College, I do want People to like talking religion and morals, to read good books, like poetry and pictures, and think for themselves. I think my ideals have deteriorated. I used to think Perfection the aim of Life, now I think it is Perfection in Happiness.' His final two years at Eton were to be spent under that motto.

The intensity of the experience is reproduced in *Enemies of Promise* but it is not made clear there how precociously and suddenly his complete personality had emerged. The College setting exactly suited his capacity for talk, curiosity about personal relationships, tastes, and ambition for intellectual supremacy. In this restricted club, the members came to know more about one another than was perhaps good for them. Nothing remained private for long. All manner of insider's knowledge lay behind ostensibly day-to-day decisions, for instance, with whom to have tea (the Eton custom of 'messing'), or with whom to exchange signed photographs and embark on Christian-name terms. Intrigues and manipulations about who entered whose room and on what pretext, or who was 'gone' on whom, substantial or insubstantial as these might be, were compared by Cyril to those of Versailles and Yildiz. In another image, College was 'our strange monastic society, a religion invented by sensitive boys under hard conditions, and which existed to combat them'.

Friends in Elections above or below his included Terence Beddard and George (known as Dadie) Rylands, Denis Dannreuther the captain of the school, Roger Mynors and Robert Longden, Denys King-Farlow, Peter Loxley, William Le Fanu, Freddy Harmer, Noel Blakiston, and they feature in *Enemies of Promise* under their own, or lightly disguised, names. As they rose through the upper divisions of the school, they acquired certain privileges, such as administering corporal punishment or ordering fags about, as well as duties to join the Corps or to play games. As a result of attitudes adopted to these temporal and parochial matters, Cyril divided Collegers into 'reactionaries' and 'progressives'. Even after a lapse of twenty years he could still reproduce each nuance of these splits, still taking sides, writing as though manifestoes of high social and political importance had issued from them. What had actually been storms in College tea-cups were exaggerated into grandeurs and miseries. Passion had not abated a bit in what had long since become a Sleeping Beauty landscape. Every cause still remained his to judge, every verdict his to execute. In reality, nothing much had happened except the discovery that his abilities were equal to everyone's around him, indeed superior in almost all cases. Vistas opening on the ego and the world, the intoxication and power of it, had stamped his imagination quite as traumatically as that occasion when Grannie Connolly had showed him a miraculous way out of the dilemma of choosing between two toys he wanted. He could go through the mill after all, and still come out on top. Where Eton is concerned, *Enemies of Promise* fuses contradictory impulses, that the formative moment of his schooldays had been far too shatteringly rich and complex and should never have happened, but he wished it could have lasted for ever.

In his Eton notebooks he wrote about his emergence into the school limelight as something already historical. 'To this early period belongs much doggerel verse written under the pseudonym of Percy Beauregard Biles [an echo of Percy Bysshe Shelley, mercilessly mobbed by Etonians a hundred years earlier?] mostly parodies and skits of the Literary Society, various rag erotic verse, and much doggerel on the respective merits of N.H.B. (Noel Blakiston) and F.E.H. (Freddy Harmer). Also a good macaronic verse about J.O'D (Jacky O'Dwyer) in the metre of *Cygnus expirans* – all this has happily been lost to posterity.'

On the back of an envelope, also preserved, was a listing of moods and motivations from that same moment.

Why ?
no money ?
too lazy
trying to be original and pose
annoying Crace etc
Grossness and hatred of late nights

fear of being bored
jealousy at not being in ??
love of emptiness of College
desire for peace

Crace might very well have been more annoyed by the newly fledged Cyril than he had been by the grubby boy at the bottom of the class. Not that Crace was an unfair or ungenerous observer. Grandson of a notable art collector reared in pre-Raphaelite circles, Crace was not a philistine, nor particularly puritan. Signing his initials on school essays, he formed a flowery butterfly *à la* Whistler, emblem for aesthetic pretensions of his own. He was to marry a sister of John Maud, then a boy in the Election below Cyril's, and later Lord Redcliffe-Maud. Crace lived at Farnham, and on several occasions during holidays Cyril bicycled over there from The Lock House. Once Crace invited him to design and then print some Christmas cards for him.

What aroused Crace's suspicions were Cyril's further searches for the ideal Pair among the Fauns, Redheads, Extreme Blonds and Dark Friends. 'To say I was in love again will vex the reader beyond endurance, but he must remember that being in love had a peculiar meaning for me,' Cyril elaborated in *Enemies of Promise*, leading into one of his more disconcerting thrusts of self-knowledge. 'I had never even been kissed and love was an ideal based on the exhibitionism of the only-child. It meant a desire to lay my personality at someone's feet as a puppy deposits a slobbery ball; it meant a non-stop daydream, a planning of surprises, an exchange of confidences, a giving of presents, an agony of expectation, a delirium of impatience, ending with the premonition of boredom more drastic than the loneliness which it set out to cure.'

Those who did not care for these proceedings were rewarded with mockery, with limericks and lampoons for general circulation, and then written off as 'bleeders', 'reactionaries'. Those irrevocably 'gone' on someone else, and therefore in some Pair System of their own, were the object of exhaustive analysis. Some were prepared to watch the puppy's slobbery ball being deposited at their feet, and to enter into the spirit of the thing, to confess or invent secrets. It was a ritual, flaunted in order to cut a dash and to be a nuisance to Crace. No public school ever discovered how to deal with the dilemma inherent in cooping up together large numbers of male adolescents: the pretence that sexuality did not exist among them involved much hypocrisy and repression. In either case, romantic fantasies

[40]

flourished, and Cyril was perhaps fortunate to enjoy such sheltered circumstances in which to be a fantasist. 'I would give anything to be consistent,' he wrote in a letter to a friend during his final year, 'but I get everything in such a craze that a reaction always follows – with people my career has been a succession of attempts to find the one person who will make all others superfluous – the nearest was Terence who left before his glamour, you (never Farlow), Charles, Jacky, H.N.B., Freddy, over 20 more people I've tried.'

Homosexuality in his case ultimately proved to have been misfounded, a completely erroneous assumption about himself. That it was possible to be so wrong about his true nature, and that it had taken so long to realise it, underlies the tragi-comedy with which these emotions were sustained.

The school's inner culture, he decided, had created the whole misconception. Average Etonians could no doubt have an ordinary education, but exceptional boys like him were at the mercy of a tradition as peculiar as it was deadly. Those who handed this tradition on were akin to high priests. 'There were only five real teachers,' is one of the *obiter dicta* of *Enemies of Promise*, and these were C. A. Alington the Headmaster, C. M. Wells, G. W. Headlam who was nicknamed 'Tuppy', C. H. K. Marten (a future provost of Eton and tutor to the royal children at Windsor Castle), and Hugh Macnaghten. They were in the best humanist tradition, he acknowledged – the quality of their minds was not in question. But their stubborn defence of classical forms trivialised or sentimentalised living language and poetry. Beauty was admirable to these latter-day Pre-Raphaelites only when it was safely dead or out of reach, and therefore they made of it something mysterious, almost evil. In combination they dragged a clever boy back to 'the culture of the lilies', inculcating timidity, pessimism, the inevitability of injustice, fear of standards other than their own. More subtly, they were promoting an aestheticism which was unreal, festering, within it the very vice they abhorred. The more upright and spartan they were personally, the more deceptive their humbug. 'For there was no doubt that homosexuality formed an ingredient in this ancient wisdom.'

Macnaghten taught Cyril in the Easter Half of 1920, and in his report he quoted Cyril as having written, 'It is really a disadvantage of Christianity that the arts, painting, music, poetry and sculpture, are given no place at all either in the Old or New Testament.' Upon which Macnaghten commented, 'A boy who can write like this is obviously far from negligible.' But he added, 'Whether it might not be better for a boy to continue childlike in his views on such questions is another matter.' Rather admiringly, he continued to puzzle over Cyril, concluding in the summer of 1920 that 'he is a real good fellow in the background,' and a year later, at Michaelmas 1921, that 'his English composition has real merit. Let me illustrate – "Stoke Poges is greater than Slough, the Asopus at Thermopylae than the Congo at its widest." I like that.'

In Headlam's eyes, Cyril 'at first seemed to be alive usually, and to have an idea or two'. Then, 'he shows some ambition as a writer,' but 'he does not really like any drudgery, and thinks he can excel without it.' Cyril ought not to rely on 'fireworks' just because he had a ready pen and could make a phrase and quote with some effect. C. H. K. Marten, also at Michaelmas 1921, reported, 'I was astonished at the improvement in Connolly since he was last "up" to me. He is now really *good*; and his writing has that indefinable quality – composed of knowledge, originality, style – which Oxford historians look for in their History Scholarship candidates and label "promise".'

That Michaelmas half he won the Rosebery History Prize, which was open to all history specialists, following it up four months later, in March 1922, with the Brackenbury Scholarship to Balliol. Whereupon the tone of official comment altered. 'I was not at all surprised that he got a Balliol scholarship,' wrote Headlam, 'he has acquired early the power of reading and digesting what he reads.' Alington, the headmaster, was not surprised either. 'He has a very alert mind, and I think he is one of those people for whom intellectual success will be good. I much like all I see of him.'

On April 3 1922 Crace weighed in with praise to Matthew Connolly. 'About his scholarship I should like to say that the credit of it is due almost entirely to himself, and this mainly in two ways; he has developed and cultivated an alert and vigorous interest in a wide range of subjects with a critical and intelligent appreciation always alive, and he has done a very great deal of reading.' Crace went on, 'His election to "Pop" yesterday is another distinction, of a rather different kind: but it is a testimony to his personality from his own contemporaries which is striking because it so seldom falls to boys who (like Cyril at present) have no athletic distinction to bring them to public notice. For better or worse the position this boyish distinction gives him will make much difference to him next half – and it rests with him to use its responsibilities wisely.'

Pop, formally known as the Eton Society, consisted of twenty or so boys, who elsewhere would have been prefects or monitors. At Eton, they elected themselves, which gave them independent standing and cachet. To be elected on account of social or intellectual status, and not for athletic prowess, was unusual in the Eton of the day, and a testimony to Cyril, as Crace had acknowledged. These school heroes were much admired, easily identifiable in the clothes they alone were permitted to wear, coloured waistcoats and sponge-bag trousers, and a flower in the buttonhole, if they so chose. There was Pop-room, like a club, complete with newspapers and stationery with 'Eton Society' engraved upon it in light blue, and postal facilities. Members of Pop could levy fines for minor infringements of school rules.

Cyril had worked to secure his election, deliberately cultivating the votes of those already in, almost all of them oppidan grandees who very well might pay no attention to a Colleger. Some of them are named in *Enemies of Promise*: Lord Knebworth, who was killed in an aeroplane crash in the mid-Thirties, Edward Woodall, Robin Gurdon, Maurice Bridgeman, Nico Llewellyn-Davies who was one of the boys adopted by J. M. Barrie, Teddy Jessel, Lord Dunglass (Sir Alec Douglas-Home, the future prime minister). Anthony Powell, then a young oppidan who knew Cyril only by sight, has recorded in the first volume of his memoirs, *Infants of the Spring*, the reaction of Hubert Duggan (brother of Alfred Duggan, the historical novelist) on hearing of Cyril's election, 'Is that the tug who's been kicked in the face by a mule?' A no less typical example of the envious politicking inspired by Pop elections was recorded by Cyril himself, when he quoted Teddy Jessel as saying to him in the hour of his triumph, 'Well, you've got a Balliol scholarship and you've got into Pop – you know I shouldn't be at all surprised if you never did anything else the rest of your life. After all, what happens to old tugs? If they're clever they become dons or civil servants, if not they come back here as ushers; when they're about forty they go to bed with someone, if it's a boy they get sacked, if it's a woman they marry them. The pi ones go into the church and may become bishops. There goes Connolly K.S., a brilliant fellow, an alpha mind, he got the Rosebery and the Brackenbury, and all the other berries, and passed top into the Office of Rears!' (Jessel and Knebworth proposed and seconded Cyril's election to Pop. In an interview Lord Jessel could still recite the parody of Gibbon which Cyril had written fifty years earlier: 'The depravity of the time can be judged by the fact that the Empress Eudosia preferred the titillation of her favourite eunuch to the more ponderous credentials of the Roman Emperor.')

A number of oppidans had a part to play in Cyril's future social and literary life, not only Anthony Powell, but Brian Howard, Harold Acton, Robert Byron, Henry Yorke (the novelist Henry Green), Oliver Messel. At the time, it would have been up to Cyril to have made the running, and on the whole he chose not to; he parodied the efforts of the Literary Society, or publications such as *Eton Candle* to which he might otherwise have contributed. His immersion in College and in Perfection in Happiness certainly had something stand-offish about it.

In his last year at school, he took to corresponding regularly with chosen friends – the letter-writing habit was never to leave him (until later telephoning took its place). Bravado, indiscretion, kite-flying, fantasy, were all discharged on the spur of the moment. To one friend he wrote that he was house-hunting for a way of life. 'Learning to appreciate the first rate and know the same, learning to look for Beauty in everything, sampling every outlook and every interest (bar stinks and maths) – trying to stop people being luke-warm and liking the second rate, trying to make other people happy but not doing it at the cost of my own happiness.'

Then he went on to gossip about a letter he had received from Eric Blair, quoting part of this 'curious communication' with commentary of his own added in brackets. 'I am afraid I am gone on G (naughty Eric). This may surprise you but it is not imagination, I assure you (not with shame and remorse) . . . I think you are too (to the pure all things are pure), at any rate you were at the end of last half. I am not jealous of you (noble Eric). But you, though you aren't jealous, are apt to be what I might call "proprietary" . . . Don't suspect me of ill intentions either. If I had not written to you until about 3 weeks into next half you would notice how things stood, your proprietary instincts would have been aroused and having a lot of influence over G, you would probably have put him against me somehow, perhaps even warned him off me. Please don't do this I implore you. Of course I don't ask you to resign your share in him, only don't say *spiteful things*.'

Cyril was in his element. 'Rather a revelation of course. I have been much too busy with [he names two others] to look on G as anything more than an exploitable side-line.' In conclusion, 'Of course I like him very much and shall steal him from Blair who deserves no commiseration. When gone on someone you do not ask for a half share from the person you think owns the mine. It is not business. Anyhow G has noticed it and is full of suspicion as he hates Blair.'

A spell was cast even upon those who saw much to criticise in skilful manipulation of emotions of the sort. A letter from one Colleger to another survived in Cyril's papers, in which the effects of accommodating to such a personality are described. Cyril had reduced someone else to tears; it was simply astounding. 'After the way Cyril has treated him, and after the wholehearted way in which he has hurled himself into a quarrel with Cyril last half, it would seem impossible. I don't know what the power is that Cyril has got over other people's emotions. I suppose it's animal magnetism; anyhow it is very disconcerting.'

Holidays were dominated by the absent Eton scene. 'I heard from my people that I had a very good report so Crace hasn't voiced his nameless grievances – he is brooding; a sinister figure among the frowning beeches and black moorland of his ancestral home – there in the massive hall walking up and pacing down at times emitting soft trills and squeaking with compressed lips, the Master in College plans plans plans to secure it from the abyss to which it is rapidly plunging – demons of filth, preciousness and epigonatics flock round him – Delves-Broughton troubled by his body and furtively promulgating sickly theories of hedonism that creep like stealthy weeds in the dark – Blair amid a litter of cigarette ash drinks tea from a samovar which hisses insidiously to Eastwood and Watkins who try to run away but a horrible magnetism detains them – he oozes distrust from Miss Oughterson [the dame in College, or matron] – tracts flutter round his head and in the seclusion of an upstairs room Connolly lies – not alone – in his armchair.'

Crace, Cyril suspected, stopped letters in order to break into this private intelligence service; the grievances were not always nameless. On the other hand the eighteen-year-old Cyril was capable of sounding thoroughly public-school in spirit. Denis Dannreuther, the austere captain of the school, was in Pop and Cyril could not afford to offend him, so that no more than superficial irony was intended when he wrote, 'Yes I am going back to what I hope will be the happiest year of my life – but I do not care whether it is that – I will make many enemies I've no doubt – but what is a man if he tries to please everyone? And besides, I suppose I am very stupid and sentimental . . . I hope to do my little bit to make a purer, nobler

[45]

College, free from all petty jealousy, all evil talk, all namby-pamby preciousness ... we run our race and hand the torch on to our successor, and please God I will finish my lap. And when I too leave it will be enough if I can feel that there is a spirit; it may only show itself in little things, a new deference to the serious, a new recognition of privilege rightly obtained – an obedience to the letter of the law which shows a deeper obedience to the spirit and tradition behind it.'

His last word about himself as an Etonian was in a self-portrait in one of his notebooks. 'Works selfishly and unscrupulously for his own ends, name generally mentioned in scorn – overdoes sentiments in general too – coldly shudders – is bored – is wrapped up in fresh fields and pastures new – is bored by gossip – is inky Christ – is absolutely unjust, affirms it to be true more than once – is not congratulated, is too frank to observe ordinary decencies, is in Provence or Buda-Pest by now – found DSD [Dannreuther] useful for it (has no use for DSD), is purely cynical and selfish, is cold-blooded, his selfishness and jiltings, his theory of selfishness, Schopenhauer-Hollis [a reference to Christopher Hollis, also a Colleger] three parts sensuality in his idea of friendship, only feels the need for sensual attachment, can explain his inconstancy by excellent psychology, pulls the last petal from a sad sad rose – his jewels sparkle but are dumb, needs a closet but flies incontinent to a bosom – is available for a stroll, is trusted to be found in his bedroom – loses his braces – his manners are atrocious – is much too learned – an excellent young man, may be crucified, taught to expect bad manners, grins and says Hail, seems to have a decent sort of time, doesn't put his foot in it, might have to act in play, a pretty act of condescension on his part, against sentimentality, prefers lust – descends from a pedestal of lofty unworldliness – evil gossip about himself and his dealings with the smaller boys – takes a queer kind of pleasure – is angry.'

There followed a similar vignette of Noel Blakiston. 'Unintentionally anxious, daredevilry of, pseudo-immorality of, bored with Cyril, pushingness of N.H.B., an unwanted third, back to childhood ideal, receives prestige from Cyril, becomes insupportable, rather a strain, not taken seriously by F.E.H., has a birthday tea. Family nice as can be – a good fellow but a little spoilt, a very fascinating person in a way.' And of course Crace. 'Something specially bald and crude about his writing, does not honestly like the Headmaster, is quite content with that, has a fairly large finger in the pie, his miserable luck, Mr Milligan thinks no saint, his effusion returned, his imagination, imperative to get out of his way, obviously no scruples about stopping letters, shows the best side of his nature, too childish, bids farewell to his old pupils, no Xmas card from same, fit of sympathy, thinks family Xmas cards a bloody thing to print, his absurd initials, utterly unable to write straight, a chance intruder.'

Confidence in his righteousness was reflected not only in words but in deeds. In his final summer half, according to *Enemies of Promise*, he was a law unto himself, a dandy in a black dinner-jacket and panama hat, reading Pater and Huysmans and Aristippus of Cyrene and the new Huxley novels, admiring white Frau Karl Druschki roses so intensely that he always had some in his room, playing *l'Après-midi d'un faune* on his gramophone.

These languid sensations had to be enjoyed in the melancholy knowledge that they were doomed to stop in a matter of weeks. The world beyond Eton did not offer comparable rhapsodies of egoism. 'Rancid with boredom', he called himself, but this was romancing once again. He was not bored, but deeply enthralled by the brief spell in which he could do just as he pleased, responsible to nobody and nothing. Self-indulgence of the kind was so absolute and voluptuous that the idea of giving it up was unbearable. Could such a thing ever be recovered again? Instead of asking himself why he had been so utterly immersed in what had been really rather immature illusions, when he came to write *Enemies of Promise* he inverted cause and effect. Rather than examine his own essential character traits, he chose to reproach Eton for having granted him circumstances in which to indulge himself without restriction; the school, like Grannie Connolly in an earlier day, should have disciplined and educated him in some quite different fashion (though had that been the case, he might really have had something to complain about). This inversion of the truth neatly allowed him to lay the blame for his own faults on Eton, and also to claim a rebellion against the place which he had never made. Quite simply, he had got much too much out of it, Perfection in Happiness indeed.

By the end of the half, he wrote to a friend, he felt less afraid of leaving than he had done in June. 'However much one tries to be glad at leaving it is bloody hard if you think how very free one is from money troubles – even if one hasn't any – how one has absolutely one's own friends and more power than I suppose I will ever have again. Still, I don't honestly think I would go back for another half if I was allowed to – unless for the fags . . . I think any more Eton would be very bad for me as you've no idea how easy it is to get into the way of A) believing others think you are what you would like to seem to be and B) thinking you are what you would like to seem to be to others.' Jumping to conclusions about Oxford, he already thought he would be a recluse there. 'I can't face all the pushing, bleeding, jealousy, selfishness and intellectual intolerance with which Balliol apparently swarms.' Which was only another way of saying that these were all the things which he had mastered at Eton, and could not relish starting all over again elsewhere.

The annual Corps camp proved his last Eton occasion, likened to a long operatic farewell. The camp was held at Mytchett, not far from The Lock House. He was able to share a tent with another Colleger, to whom he could make a declaration of love. The puppy's slobbery ball had come to rest again. 'I like to abdicate all my personality into someone weaker than myself really – that is the theory of being gone on someone as opposed to hero worship incidentally,' he wrote to this Colleger once the camp was over. 'With you I could reveal every thought of my aesthetic soul as well as my intellectual (e.g. I could read a good patch to you in some book which I would never have done with anyone else) and it was only when I found myself frantically jealous of the soft murmurs borne on the night air to where I lay and mused on my white roses that I realised how fond I was of you.'

As a result of sudden high emotions, Cyril as a brand-new Old Etonian declared that on the first night of the holidays he had cried himself to sleep, not merely silent dripping but making noises like a child. 'I miss you frightfully now,' he wrote, although self-knowledge compelled him to continue, 'and when you miss me next half I shall probably be far more interested in Oxford.' Plans were impossible. 'My God, if Crace caught us sleeping together! I think sleeping together could be expected ad lib for we can never recapture the ecstasy of Tuesday, but the contentment of Wednesday we can always have.'

What had taken place at camp was described, with whatever degree of truth or fantasy, to yet another Colleger. 'Thanks ever so much for your short but passionate note – though it came in a batch of seven from present Etonians it easily went to the top. Most people don't realise that it is very hard to like a person too much through the post – it is a pity we can't get married as you say. I am very sensual but I don't consider any sins of the Flesh though I loathe the sins of the world. I think Apathy is a state not to be complained of

[48]

because it releases you from worldly temptations so much and makes it so much easier to appreciate stuff that isn't worldly . . . personally I found that since I lay with [him] at Camp (don't repeat that to anyone, still less to [him] but I know that the caution is unnecessary) I liked him twice as much for the unselfishness . . . I have no hesitation in saying that it was the happiest night of my life – and [he] agrees. I did not do him or anything and I was not gone on him but in the dark one face is very much like another and it was the perfect understanding which arose out of such close embrace that I valued so much and has lasted ever since after all.' This letter ended in orthodox loyalty. 'Personally I give the Oppidans about 1,000 to 1 against the Collegers. I mean 1 Colleger = 1,000 Oppidans.'

6

Non Sum Qualis Eram

'Somewhere in the facts I have recorded lurk the causes of that sloth by which I have been disabled, somewhere lies the sin whose guilt is at my door.' How was this prize-winning and pace-setting member of Pop plausibly to be connected with disabling sloth? And what sin, what guilt? If the innuendo was that he had been directed into an enfeebling pseudo-homosexual persona which did not fit him, then how was this to be squared with the cloying sun-set brilliance with which this past had been evoked? Only through the Theory of Permanent Adolescence, with its catch-all definition that anyone who had experienced its morbid romanticism could never be free from it – to understand all was to forgive nothing, and not even to forget.

'For my own part I was long dominated by impressions of school. The plopping of gas mantles in the class-rooms, the refrain of psalm tunes, the smell of plaster on the stairs, the walk through the fields to the bathing places or to chapel across the cobbles of School Yard, evoked a vanished Eden of grace and security; the intimate noises of College, the striking of the clock at night from Agar's Plough, the showers running after games of football, the housemaster's squeak, the rattle of tea-things, the poking of fires as I sat talking with Denis or Charles or Freddie on some evening when everybody else was away at a lecture, were recollected with anguish and College, after I left, seemed to me like one of those humming fortified paradises in an Italian primitive outside which the angry Master in College stood with his flaming sword.'

The school swell who cannot adjust afterwards is a stock figure of pathos. It was alarming, odious, for Cyril to have to live up to the high expectations which masters and contemporaries alike had of him. *Enemies of Promise* marvellously anticipated and rationalised his own and other people's disappointments that what had been good enough in College might not turn out good enough elsewhere.

Eton had also concentrated those emotions which had not been released at home. His parents wondered whether they could keep up with him, they complained that he was 'difficult', reinforcing his view of himself as an only child left to his own devices. During school holidays Maud Connolly was often away, so that at The Lock House father and son had to entertain each other as best they could. On August 24, 1920, for instance, she wrote to Cyril from a liner taking her to South Africa, 'I am dying to see all the new walks you have discovered. I wonder if you have been riding.' Or again, 'You don't know how I hate missing your holidays – all the walks we might have gone on.' Cyril's poems had been sent to Mr Sitwell (presumably Osbert) and she was anxious to learn what he had said about them. Then during another holiday, 'The Addisons asked us to a very small afternoon dance Wednesday at Tanglewood. They were very sorry you would be away.' Worries about money were raised. Her allowance no longer went far. 'It was all right when I had it to dress myself but of course Daddy having none now it does not leave much for you and I together.'

Demobilised after the war and therefore quit of the army, Matthew Connolly became an unpaid volunteer on the staff of the Natural History Museum in South Kensington. His studies of South African snails and shells had already earned him the nickname from Cyril of 'Major Conchology, the poet's father'. Opposite the Museum was the Naval and Military Hotel, and there he took a room; eccentric resident scholar and boarder. As his arthritis worsened over the years, he limited his exercise to the walk from hotel to museum, sometimes wearing shoes and no socks, which embarrassed his son. Every January and February he liked to go by himself to some hotel abroad, often the Hotel Savoia, at Alassio. If there were pretty girls in such places, he liked to describe them rather suggestively in his letters to Cyril.

There were reasons for travelling. The pound was exchanged at favourable rates in France, Austria, Italy and Spain. German currency was inflating to the point of worthlessness. If The Lock House could be satisfactorily let, the Connollys could go their ways in the style to which they had been accustomed in army days before the war.

In the summer of 1921, his parents took Cyril for his first impressions of the continent. In Paris they saw the usual sights, the Venus of Milo and the Folies Bergère and Notre Dame. 'Superb' was his favourite adjective of praise. 'The place teems with Americans in the day and *filles de joie* (I think that is the French for them) at night – they are a very smart crowd and I never have the heart to be rude to them ... I found myself clutched by one of these lovely ladies – beautifully dressed and more beautiful than pretty. I said I had only tobacco and asked her if she spoke English. The next moment I saw my pater coming out of the corner of my eye while a husky voice was telling me that her flat was only a minute's walk. I said I couldn't as my father was here and resisted further entreaties. She chucked me under the chin and moved off only a second too soon.'

Matthew Connolly wanted to tour the recent battlefields of Amiens, Albert, Arras, Douai, Lille: 'Some of the French landscape was nothing but waste ground and leafless trees.' At the Belgian resort of Knocke-sur-mer they put up at the Grand Hotel de l'Europe, from which Cyril sent postcards. 'This is the eighth night running I have danced till after *minuit*.' Also, 'I have to shave every day now, hell take it – I hoped to postpone this till I was 18 but it is no good – I wish I was an albino or something.'

At Christmas 1921 the three of them were together in a hotel at Mürren, in Switzerland. 'Terrific precipices, glaciers, and snow masses of the Eiger and Jungfrau.' With some pride he complained of the numbers of boring girls with whom he had to dance until the small hours.

After this he was allowed to go abroad unsupervised, at Easter 1922. His travelling companion was Charles Milligan. He was determined to flirt and if possible to fall in love, he told Dannreuther. 'I write this in one of London's battered caravanserais – Charing Cross. There is a lovely view of the embankment and the lights of the river. I have just returned from a low cinema where I have been – I stood it for an hour or so and finished my cigar to the featuring of Clacton-on-Sea. I am cheering up enormously and have just bought the "Diary of a Disappointed Man" – Freddy's letter was a good omen for my travels. I am absurdly excited at going to Paris, I who have twice been to the Cape, and six months in Gibraltar and Corsica ... Tomorrow! Tomorrow the gates of the world open, hinged on seasickness and I go in ... I am a great believer in unconscious influence on character and my early voyages of which I remember hardly anything make me adore travelling and any sort of country which resembles the veldt. If I had my heaven now it would be to go on a yacht to New Guinea slowly with you and Freddy and a few others – tomorrow – murmurs and scents of the infinite sea. My God what am I drivelling, usual quarrel between the member for Cynics, sceptics and other issues, and the member for Romance-Sentiment, Adventure-Melodrama, in fact Grand Commander of the Beau Geste.'

First stop after the Charing Cross Hotel was Eastbourne, where he returned to St Cyprian's in all his Etonian splendour, to teach an admiring class and to hear Mr Wilkes say, 'Don't forget, Tim, a Balliol scholar has the ball at his feet.' Then with Charles Milligan, he crossed to Paris, revisited the Folies Bergère, doing nothing more than shaking the gloved hands of two prostitutes but afterwards wondering whether some fresh mosquito bites might not be syphilis. *Enemies of Promise* glowingly recounts that journey's sequel, in Provence and the Pyrenees, sacred places, the cradle of his civilisation. But in the meantime, 'I was getting school-sick for Eton.'

One last family holiday began early in September 1922, when Cyril came straight from Camp and was writing to his correspondents about his conquests there. On September 6 he was explaining from France, 'We are now a terrific party here, myself, mother and father, *General*, a friend of my mother's who brought her out here, her sister (my aunt I mean) and her daughter.' General Christopher Brooke, then aged fifty-three and much decorated for bravery, had been Colonel of the King's Own Yorkshire Light Infantry and a friend of the Connollys since early soldiering days. His wife did not die until 1925. It is not clear when his affair with Maud Connolly started, nor whether he had been obliged to resign his commission in 1920 on account of falling in love with a brother officer's wife, which is what Cyril long afterwards came to believe. From 1924 to 1929 General Brooke was Conservative Member of Parliament for Pontefract.

Matthew and Maud Connolly parted from the others on this occasion to escort Cyril through France and Germany, to the Black Forest. 'We are only abroad because my people cannot afford to live in their house and keep me at Oxford,' Cyril wrote. Travel-notes to his friends were filled out with criticism of his parents, instancing 'the usual bickering with one's people – due really to complete lack of common outlook and the eternal jealousy of the young and old. I know when I used to stay at home for the holidays it was far worse over exactly the same kind of points – present-day manners etc etc. I used to be ticked off and sulk and mope and be bloody and wait for the natural reaction of parental affection. I and my father completely lost our tempers yesterday because he swore Mynors had red hair, well reddish-yellow . . . and with my mother today because she

[53]

said that a friend of hers, a Captain Cernalli of the Italian navy was to all intents an Austrian because he came from North Italy. They are such bloody silly points but one can't help trying to put one's people right over them, I'm sure they think me a horrible pedant.' They were all by a lake, and 'my mother compared Titisee (unconsciously) the same day to Switzerland, Scotland, Deepcut Surry and Wynberg South Africa and Roscommon Ireland. I added Eastbourne and the Pyrenees.' When he quoted his mother saying 'she wishes she had never been born', he was probably revealing the true state of her feelings.

From Titisee, he wrote to Jacky O'Dwyer, 'Every night here I try to buy a white rose (Kaiserin Augusta, not as nice as Frau Karl Druschki though it smells stronger). My people think me mad but every night the old man comes straight to me and presents his best white rose . . . we all read while waiting for our things to be cooked . . . my mother is deep in the Odyssey which she deserves and my pater is struggling with the Greek lyric poets (I have provided the literature).' After this rather superior assertion of his education, he went on, 'I want overhauling badly mentally, my philosophy of life has almost passed into the quiet security of a religion from lack of persecution.' No sooner said, though, than recollections of self-inflicted persecutions returned. 'It's extraordinary the number of people I have introduced into society and then got tired of and they've forgotten it . . . Still it is not a thing to worry about and feel the benefactor who is forgotten and surpassed by his protégés, as it was about as much trouble for me to do as it was for them to remember – but it does give me the right to dislike them afterwards after all.'

Between September 21 and October 12 he was away by himself, keeping a day-by-day diary. From Donaueschingen he travelled down the Rhine, learning German but not enough to enjoy the Passion Play at Oberammergau. He had his mandoline with him. Most of the English people he encountered were 'bloody'. Munich was enjoyable, Salzburg bloodyish. At the Hungarian frontier, customs officials viewed with suspicion his many letters from Eton friends, which he explained were 'lieber briefs'.

Budapest looked as if it had been built on a slag heap of slate and sand but his spirits perked up nonetheless. He bought a dictionary as well as *Manon Lescaut* and Baudelaire's poems, and picked up a purposeful Hungarian who showed him cafés with gypsy bands. On his own at Lake Balaton, he 'walked round Tihany through vineyards where I picked bunches of grapes and ate them and maize ditto – got stuck in a bog and went to sleep in a haystack. I must say I have been extraordinarily happy on my trip so far.' The highlight was the plain west of Budapest, the Hortobagy, 'quite unique – very dark green turf stretching in every direction – no hills, no fences, one or two acacias and those spiky wells – occasionally herds of oxen, sheep, etc but I saw no horses'.

Back in Budapest, in the company of another Englishman, he found himself taken to a bar. Two women arrived. 'I was not drunk but feeling very dauntless à la Cyrano.' After some dancing, he retired with one of the women. 'Was very passionate and took her stockings off – she enjoyed it, I think. I love it, I must say, and said I had never been so happy before – tried several "ways of love".' Limp the next day, according to his travel diary, he nonetheless decided that he looked as fresh as ever.

The train journey home was broken by writing long letters about these adventures, mostly in the purplest prose. 'I want only the Romance and Peace of the Mother Church and can't really believe any more than before. My Gods are Pan and Apollo, Nemesis and Fortune. My genius is the King of Kings . . . I worship the frail plants who bud and bloom and die in the Garden of Mortality and Beauty that wounds and fadeth, and Truth that allures and hideth, and Goodness that blossoms from the manure of Pride.'

On arrival in London he had tea at Gunters with his mother. Leaving her, he dined alone with his father. Both preferred not to take him into their confidence, but evidently they were already estranged on account of General Brooke. Maud Connolly was installed in a flat of her own in St George's Square. Within a few weeks she was to write to Cyril another of her letters regretting that she would have to be away from The Lock House that Christmas. 'I think it would be fun to let the house sometimes and for you and me to wander through Italy and Corsica and Greece and have each holiday different.' This was never to happen. It was wishful thinking. When Cyril caught the train to take him up to Oxford on October 14 1922, his family life, such as it had been, was over and done with.

7

Old Before our Time

If Cyril's published views about Oxford are taken at face value, then he had a wretched time there. 'To me Oxford was no celestial city but a place where I was unhappier than I had ever been before. I could have got a good first in nervous breakdowns.' The hero of his subsequent novel *The Rock Pool* was speaking for Cyril when he 'tried to convey something of the gloom, the boredom of college halls and sitting-rooms, the Sunday luncheons, the plates of anchovy toast in the fender, the quiet afternoons spent running up bills in shops, which formed his only exercise, the autumn evenings with their interminable church bells, and fallen leaves. Against this stood out moments of vitality, the rude scholarly jokes, the princely entertainments, life rushing by outside with its murmurs of careers and appointment-boards, while within the frowning walls of the medina all was intrigue and languor.' Several drafts of a poem called 'Oxford' exist, probably written five or six years after he had gone down:

> When days are long and sunny
> the flower of youth is blown.
> We waste our parents' money
> and time that is our own.
> The days grow dark and colder
> beyond the summer's prime.
> We, before time is older,
> are old before our time.

The trouble was that he could not superimpose himself upon Oxford as upon Eton. What he called 'the affectation of laziness and indifference that was considered the Balliol manner' in fact veiled 'the urge to achievement'. Achievement was defined in a banal and even philistine manner, moreover, by means of prizes and promotion. Balliol took its academic distinction seriously. A Brackenbury scholar was expected to work hard and to get a first. A. L.

Smith was Master until his death in 1924, when he was succeeded by A. D. Lindsay, who was no less worldly. The Dean, Francis Fortescue Urquhart, made it his business to see that undergraduates such as Cyril did themselves justice. In 1922, Urquhart was 57, a long-established Oxford character, known universally by the nickname 'Sligger', apparently a corruption of 'the sleek one', according to his biographer Cyril Bailey, another fellow of Balliol. Few other college tutors received a kind word from Cyril Connolly.

Overlapping with him at Balliol were Graham Greene, Walter Oakeshott, the future Rector of Lincoln College, Peter Quennell and Anthony Powell. In other colleges were Harold Acton, Brian Howard, Henry Yorke and dozens more whom he had known as oppidans at Eton. Some among these had already begun to publish verse and prose in magazines in Oxford or even in London. At Oxford, as at Eton, Cyril took no part in such activities, though among his close friends he still liked to circulate lampoons and doggerel. He published nothing, he joined no clubs or societies, he shunned anything organised. Several accounts of him can be read in memoirs written by Oxford contemporaries, and all of them more or less correspond in outline: Cyril was accepted as a significant personality, somebody whose opinions had to be reckoned with, but playing out in the touchlines an unnecessarily woebegone comedy, famous for not being as famous as he thought he ought to be.

Kenneth Clark in his autobiography *Another Part of the Wood* described how he had first met Cyril during their scholarship exams the previous year. Already determined to study the history of art, Clark was at Trinity, where he had just made the acquaintance of another freshman, Robert Longden, whom he had noticed was inseparable from Cyril. 'It was an attraction of opposites. Cyril was not conventionally handsome, and he was certainly not a man of action; but he was without doubt the most gifted man of his generation.' The label 'brilliant' did not suit Cyril, in Clark's opinion, partly 'because his voice had a curiously matt banality, partly because he never attempted to shine or to assert himself'. Cyril had arrived with the millstone of promise round his neck. 'It couldn't be helped. The young Cyril Connolly really was extraordinary.'

Thanks to the presence of half a dozen old Collegers, he could try to reproduce former circumstances. On October 18, after only four days at the university, he had wanted to slip away to Eton, but could not, and cried about it all evening to the embarrassment of Dannreuther, 'but got better after a visit to Duggan who usually has a crew of queer oppidans – Clonmore, Messel, Harold Acton and William – and unlimited drink. He is the centre of "Life" in our lot and one usually has to assist in putting him to bed.' [Hubert Duggan had thought Cyril's face had been kicked in by a mule; Clonmore, later Earl of Wicklow, was at Merton College; William was Harold Acton's brother.]

'If it was a monastery it would be all right,' Cyril was writing a few days later to a friend still at Eton, 'a sleepy place where we could follow the advancement of learning peopled only by Bobbie, Roger, Miles and Randy [i.e. Longden, Mynors, Clausen, Delves-Broughton respectively] with books and fires and nice food and dreamy dons. But it bristles with acquaintances, bridge, tea-parties, debts and people who gloat with joy like John Wilkes and Chris Hollis, who ask Bobbie to lunch and dinner and bridge. I have never been to Randy and his gramophone and found anyone there, nor Roger in his eyrie or Miles in his panelled room or even Teddy (Jessel) in his atmosphere of golf, gambling, and superiority to the same – but Bobbie is whirled into a round of gaiety which is rather awful.' His own current theory, Cyril explained, was to have no acquaintances, and to confine himself to the Middle Ages about which he was accumulating an immense library, mostly in French. Marginal additions showed how a mood could disintegrate in several directions all at once. 'I have cried since seven o'clock and had no dinner,' he wrote, as well as, 'For every boy that becomes a man, *Criez jouvence ou la chimère.*' There was also a quatrain:

> No pain can equal
> > that reserved for me
> living in the sequel
> > of what used to be.

To the same correspondent he described exactly how sentiment was pulling him backward. 'I do not miss College with any special regret for lost power or even lost youth – I have been much younger since – but because it is such a gorgeous setting for the jewels of my pedestal to flourish in.'

One of his ex-College friends was indispensable, Cyril explained, at the start of another letter to someone still at Eton. 'He is particularly good on my latest affairs, comes into my rooms, looks at me for a little and says, "Quite so, the complete bugger, or

sodomy for the millions" – and is altogether cheering. Denis
[Dannreuther] I would never look at if he was in another college but
he is the only man in this whom I know well enough to sit up with
after midnight. Roger [Mynors] usually never goes to bed at all.
Meals here are ghastly – we sit at Tables like in Hall and every single
person is quite bloody bar Roger (& Denis). If they have not bloody
voices they have bloody faces and if they haven't those they make up
by their conversation. Of the Etonian freshmen I loathe Turton,
Ferguson, Martin, Heygate [Sir John Heygate, who in 1930 married
Evelyn Gardiner, the first Mrs Evelyn Waugh], Duggan, and any
others whose names I can remember bar Wilkes, Kerr and Hardy.
Of people in other colleges, I see a great deal of Bobbie, dicker a lot
with Paul Wilson – play Randy's gramophone about 2 or 3 times a
week and see Jessel quite a lot and Miles and Nigel who is still gone
on me. Strickland-Constable also functions now and then. I am not
actually bored and feel that after College this is about the best
substitute nor would I be in another college. And our dons are of
course the best.'

This theme he took up again. 'I am glad to find I have not lost my
capacity for hero worship and lay it on fairly thickly on dons here –
especially Urquhart the Dean, MacGregor my old tutor, Stone my
new one and Cohn. "The man Cohn" obtained a brilliant first in
History and is now lecturing on social life in the Middle Ages,
medieval law etc. He is repulsively attractive, brilliant to talk to and
utterly selfish and cynical. Sligger seriously believes that he is a
personification of the devil. I, Denis and Roger and curiously
enough Jessel have all been worshipping him from afar (John
Wilkes has been introduced to him 7 times but not yet recognised)
but I got him worst last night. I was introduced to him (only my 3rd
time) and listened to him and Urquhart having an epigram fight
(Sligger from the idealist point of view but was utterly squashed).
Afterwards he invited me to his rooms and we had a *tête à tête* till ½
past 3. He sometimes gave me advice and sometimes pumped me
and sometimes explained his views of life (which are revolting). I
went down quite well and kept my end up and have scored a lunch
to meet the only other Balliol freshmen whom I have felt any desire
to meet . . . I have contrived to drop all my former rash acquaintances among the freshmen without any actual fracas and maintain
an aloof silence at meals except to Roger. Urquhart is wonderfully
refreshing after ushers – a Dean whom you can pinch, put your arm
round his neck and call Sligger with no self-consciousness at all is

surely a good turn after Crace . . . I am getting rather Oxfordised –
at present I have not had enough intellectual companionship to
develop much but a little more Cohn will make me rather a *mot
juster* – must finish and go to tea with Messel now.' (Not all former
acquaintances appreciated being dropped. Teddy Jessel wrote him a
note of rebuke: 'Although at Eton I was more or less superior to
you, up here it was not worth your while talking homo sex and
getting drunk with a person not up to your intelligence.')

His first term over, he spent Christmas 1922 alone with his
father at The Lock House. Immediately afterwards Matthew Connolly left by himself for Alassio, and Cyril joined a party consisting
of Mynors, Dannreuther and Longden, 'the pack of freshers', to be
escorted by Sligger on a tour of Sicily, with stops on the way through
Italy. On a postcard dated January 2 1923, Cyril told his father that
he was on the train from Girgenti to Syracuse: 'Sicily so far has been
superb – we are two days at Syracuse – one at Taormina – two at
Rome, three at Florence, and one at Pisa and one at Chambéry,
Savoy.' He did not think it worth his while to call in at Alassio. 'I
have got you a small bit of Roman marble mosaic from Agrigentum
but the snails here are very big and dull. Longden is superb, Mynors
very good, Dannreuther not so and Sligger in fine form.'

Another postcard of the same date, carrying the message 'I still
like you very much!', opens the correspondence to Noel Blakiston
which has been collected in *A Romantic Friendship* – Blakiston was
then in his last year as a Colleger. Two days later he was describing
the temple at Segesta as 'very good and my opinion of the Greeks
goes up – also for having the theatre at Segesta on top of a hill where
they would see the sea instead of sheltered. The Romans however I
think were bloody, the Coliseum is a consecrated charnel house . . .
the Pont du Gard in Provence alone redeems their architecture and
also some of the aqueducts in the Campagna.'

The Sicily tour marked the moment when Cyril could enter
'Passion for R.P.L.' in his self-addressed calendars. It was the
puppy's slobbery ball all over again, but this time more extreme
than ever, hero worship, a feminine identification on Cyril's part
with a self-confident masculine personality. 'Good-natured and
cheerful, has a mind like a well-kept allotment,' Cyril had commented about Longden in an Eton notebook, continuing, 'always
very tolerant and susceptible and flattered at the attention of anyone
else.' In *Enemies of Promise* Longden appears among the liberal-
minded Collegers in the Election ahead of Cyril's, as a well-

intentioned member of Pop, 'one of the angel-faced Athenians'. When the book was reprinted in 1961, Longden was singled out in the Introduction as 'the mainstay of my existence during the seven years after leaving Eton'. This was true. Cyril was unremittingly possessive about Longden, grudging whatever social or family demands came between them. Longden's father was an admiral. Like the Connollys, the Longdens had moved from one posting to another, but the family was close-knit. When an embargo was laid on Longden at one point by his family, to stop him going out, Cyril interpreted it as an attack aimed at him.

'Longden was that rare and irresistible combination, an intelligent extrovert,' Kenneth Clark wrote in *Another Part of the Wood*. A scholar of Trinity, where he was reading greats, he was very much an all-rounder, keeping himself fit at the Oxford athletic grounds, running the quarter-mile in fifty-four seconds, as he once wrote to Cyril.

In his letters to Longden, Cyril was usually informative and neutral in tone, eager to provide amusing descriptions of people and places. Now and again he sounded suggestive, although in his case joking is hard to distinguish from wishful thinking, or indeed from facts. In a letter written towards the middle of December 1924, during a moment of depression at The Lock House, Cyril seems to have declared what his feelings were. 'Anyhow please don't sleep with Ronnie, he is too tall for you. Smith would be better (this is the page of a letter that one's parents always find). Yes I think it was a very good term,' he went on. 'I always want to sleep with you more than anything but it is not very practicable at Oxford and the way we manage keeps me quiet (put on its lowest footing). I get awful ποθος here [in this connection he invariably used the Greek word for desire], not seeing a soul all day and having a nice bedroom with a fire and if you did not want me to think about you it would only be about someone else.' Some days after that, he was writing, 'I think you are morally (in broad sense) far and away above anyone I know. I mean if I did something you despised or thought mean, you could make me quite incredibly ashamed if you became indignant.' In reply Longden committed himself to nothing more than 'I think of and admire you a lot.'

On the tour of Sicily, Sligger had taken the two of them under his wing, and he was to devote a good deal of his time to keeping Cyril on an even keel. In Sligger's rooms a dozen or so undergraduates would gather in the evening for a drink, and to listen to music and what might be called high-table conversation. The son of the celebrated pro-Turkish polemicist David Urquhart, Sligger had inherited a small estate in Ireland, and a chalet at Saint-Gervais in the Savoy Alps where he liked to invite parties of these selected undergraduates for some serious reading and some mountain walking. A medievalist, though no very profound scholar, he believed in the old adage *mens sana in corpore sano*. As a young man he had nearly become a Jesuit, and remained a pious Catholic, prone to end his letters, even to someone like Cyril, with God-fearing exhortations and blessings. Although scarcely ever moving outside all-male society, he was a natural innocent, and if he had suspicions about the Connolly–Longden relationship he was certain to keep them to himself. Cyril often acknowledged his benevolence, though when in his last eighteen months at Oxford he came to read Proust, he compared Sligger to Françoise in *Le Côté de Guermantes*, 'because he is jealous really and difficult, unaccountable, and faithful and using his own language'.

Evelyn Waugh in his autobiography *A Little Learning* drew the contrast between Sligger's 'sober salon' and the Hypocrites' Club consisting of his cronies, 'a group of wanton Etonians', notorious for drunkenness and a flamboyance which in some cases was patently homosexual. Sligger regarded the Hypocrites' Club as a source of corruption and successfully set about closing it down. Waugh's revenge was to enter Balliol late at night and shout in the quad, 'The Dean of Balliol sleeps with men!' Cyril's first memory of Waugh, as recalled in a broadcast in 1967, also concerned late-night shouting in the college. 'Why do you make so much noise?' Cyril asked Waugh, then still a stranger to him, to receive the answer, 'I shout because I'm poor.'

The Aesthetes, then, so distinct from the Hearties, were further divided among themselves. Cyril and his friends sought shelter in their ivory tower, Waugh and his friends liked to be seen and heard carousing. It was – and in many ways it remained – a question of how much noise each was prepared to make. 'Cyril was too fastidious for the company I kept,' Waugh concluded, speculating that Cyril would have been happy in Peckwater (where the richer Christ Church undergraduates had rooms) with an allowance of £750 a year – which happens to be what he would have recommended for himself.

On the endpaper of a 1923 Oxford notebook Cyril drew up a list of 'bad-hats', to use his phrase, with Waugh, Alfred Duggan and

Harold Acton among others on it. A second list included other members of the Hypocrites, such as Waugh's friends Terence Greenidge, David Talbot-Rice and Robert Byron. A complicated network of arrows in red and blue ink mapped out how Cyril perceived various enmities or friendships among them. (In the map's margin is the throwaway remark, ' "Barrenness and not birth control makes me a sterile poet," said Mr Connolly.')

Richard Pares was a member of the Hypocrites, and his name was joined on the map by a red arrow to Waugh's. Where Pares was concerned, Waugh is supposed to have said, 'I was cuckolded by Connolly.' At any rate Pares was inveigled away from the Hypocrites and into Sligger's sober salon, or as Waugh chose to express it in *A Little Learning*, 'rescued from bohemia and preserved for a life of scholarship'.

In a letter dated March 23 1923 Cyril was writing about Pares. 'I had been rather gone on him ever since Wednesday night – enough to wander round the quad looking for him especially after Bobbie went – this time he produced my most dog-like devotion and infantile mood – what Sligger would hasten to call childlike not childish. He took me round for the rest of the morning to banks and things, taking my arm outside the London County and Westminster (thrill), then we played Chris's gramophone and I lunched off oranges as per usual. That afternoon Gradwell took me sailing which was cold and long.' On the Sunday of that week, 'when it was dark we walked round Trinity and Balliol together and I dined with Chris, Gradders, and Hilary Belloc (who has failed History Prelims) – we talked till twelve, then I went to bed but found a note from Sligger – we talked till one.' Next day, the term being over, Cyril and Pares went to London, to Westminster Cathedral. 'A service was going on with candles and droning prayer, just light left to look up to the sombre vaults of the roof. I took him along to the font and we had a fine mutual soul-storm. Richard wept profusely in the puritanical atmosphere while I pretended not to notice.' Pares, Cyril concluded, was a nice odd childlike boy. 'I know the fate of all my sudden enthusiasms, and of course Bobbie is Bobbie.'

That term Cyril won a distinction in History Prelims, 'the only one so far and I was congratulated on my "good work indeed" by the lady examiner'. At the start of the vacation, he called on his mother in her flat, then on his father in his hotel, himself spending forty-eight hours in a bed-and-breakfast place. Then he set off on a bicycling tour of Holland with an old Colleger, whom he decided to ditch on the very first day. 'The real reason was an attack of unsociableness as I want to be alone except for my invisible companions.' So on a train via Angoulême and Bordeaux, he reached Saint Jean de Luz, and eventually Pamplona, in time for the Good Friday processions. In Burgos, next day, watching another Easter procession, he wrote in a travel diary that he 'felt homesick, for buttercups and water meadows and quiet sunsets, rectory lawns and people who talk the same language. Missed Eton and everyone vaguely.'

Once back at Oxford, however, in May, he received a letter from a Colleger asking him not to write any more, because however much he might explain things to the Eton masters, 'it worried these poor men'. The mother of one boy at Eton had sent Cyril an imploring letter: 'Keep him from those things which though beautiful might bring him to evil thoughts.' Cyril was finally warned off by Headlam, his old tutor, in a letter dated June 27, saying that it would be wiser and kinder on his part to stay away from Eton, and College in particular.

Social life at Oxford was expanding. He had at last attained tolerance, he said, by adopting an attitude of genial superiority which could be altered to disarming humility when necessary. At Trinity with Kenneth Clark was Patrick Balfour (who in 1939 succeeded his father as Lord Kinross), and they took Cyril to lunch with Maurice Bowra 'who was very nice and when they were gone dropped his manner . . . he seems very keen on us but thinks Bobbie knows too many people . . . Patrick thought our friendship marvellous and did not think such inseparability had been possible after one's public school. Kenneth thinks it wonderful and us the luckiest of people he knows in that we still have plenty to talk about to each other – they all expect us to go on all our lives. Maurice says we ought to dig in North Oxford where we cannot see anyone but will accept Bath Place as not too near Trinity and near him – he will make us both Fellows of Wadham . . . Thank God Philip's little set [Philip Ritchie, then also an undergraduate, became a boyfriend of Lytton Strachey's, and died prematurely in 1927] is going out of College next term but I agree with Maurice about Philip and his jealousy, sentimentality, bloatedness and growing affection for Bobbie . . . Bobbie should develop odd and that set makes him dislike oddity.'

Maurice Bowra was then twenty-six, and had been a Fellow of Wadham since 1922. As an infantry officer, he had served in the trenches. Compact, blunt-featured, he spoke in a booming and hectoring manner which invited riposte rather than contradiction. Learned, confident of his opinions, in the swim, he was accustomed to enjoying the last word, and the first as well. Generous and hospitable, he was prepared to entertain almost anyone, but not to suffer fools. All was well with the world, in his view, except that the wrong people were in charge of it. It was a duty to push aside the Old Guard (a favourite term of abuse), so that he and his friends could replace them – in which, over the coming years, as Warden of Wadham, Vice-Chancellor of the university and a virtuoso of jobbery, he was generally gratified.

Cyril was one of a number of people who modelled themselves perhaps more than they knew on Bowra: Evelyn Waugh was another. Humour derived from conversational thrust. Gossip, enjoyable in itself, served the deeper purpose of laying bare the foibles and vanity of all men. If disobliging jokes could not be made to someone's face, then behind his back would have to do. Since Bowra and his imitators could not easily imagine being wrong, they naturally chose to put others right. In no time at all, Cyril was writing that he and Bowra presented a front of untroubled loyalty, 'but rejoicing in our unity we slander everyone else so little good is gained'. This was known as making bad blood, in an expression much relished by Bowra.

When Cyril came to write Bowra's obituary (reprinted in *Maurice Bowra*, a collection of essays edited by Hugh Lloyd-Jones), he declared that Bowra had drawn him out and saved him from despair. 'He would introduce me to one of his older friends like Philip Ritchie with a genial, "This is Connolly. Coming man (pause). Hasn't come yet –" and he introduced me to modern literature.' In his *Memoirs* (published in 1966, when Cyril could not only read but review them), Bowra described how he had come to know Cyril through Harold Acton and Brian Howard and their set. 'He was slim and slight with a rather large head, a fine forehead, eager questing eyes, a face that registered every change of feeling, and a soft hypnotising voice.' He was quick to notice changes of mood or small betrayals of character. Cyril at Balliol, it seemed, had reacted strongly against his earlier career and no longer wanted a rich social life. But the judgement 'poorly armoured against shocks' was not a compliment, coming from Bowra. The one chink in his own very complete armour arose from the fear that his homosexuality might be exposed.

Far too social by nature ever to have withdrawn into genuine reclusion, Cyril was indulging in that special selectivity which is a devious form of self-assertion. Only the very best, like Bowra, could be good enough. He need have no truck with anyone average. The pose had the advantage of excluding external challenge. It was not worth pitting oneself against those whom one did not condescend to treat seriously. Nemesis lay ahead in the form of the final examination. Either he had to do so brilliantly that his contemporaries would forgive him whatever had been insufferable in his show-off, or he would be exposed as no more able than the next man.

Cyril resolved this dilemma by ducking it. One last academic effort was to write an essay in his second year for the Gibbs Scholarship, for which he received a note from the Senior Censor at Christ Church, saying 'sadly it was only *proxime*.' Otherwise he made a point of reading only what was outside the syllabus, and ornamental, Mallarmé, Proust, Rimbaud. '*La chaire est triste et j'ai lu tous les livres* – Bobbie is rather the same and we read Whistler, Wilde, Beardsley and Max and glean news of the Nineties,' he wrote during his first summer term, 'of course we are in no way decadent beyond the way we are all decadent now. Brooke and Fletcher and de la Mare . . .' Perhaps unexpectedly, Bowra was in the orbit of Sligger's sober salon, and through him Cyril also met J. D. Beazley [at Christ Church, as from 1926 Professor of Classical Archaeology] and Professor R. M. Dawkins of Exeter College, distinguished equally as authorities and Oxford characters. To himself, Cyril appeared to have such approval as was worth having, and saw little or no reason to change anything.

At the height of his Oxford career (February 1924 was pencilled on the top of the letter forty years later) he gave this satisfied portrait of himself. 'All last vac I was brutally anti-intellectual and anti-Oxford but I like it more than I have before now – if only my vitality would not decay under this dead sky. I have four friends, two Etonians and two Wykehamists, their names are Longden, Mynors, Clark and Balfour, two are in Trinity and two in Balliol. Whenever I am unable to be with Bobbie, I go and see one of them, so life is quite simple. I glory in being exclusive and am rapidly forming a small but intolerant clique who can ignore or more often, comment on, the surrounding scene, which is what it comes to – and when they aren't scum it is more fun commenting on them still.'

An analysis followed of 'C. V. Connolly, his moods'.

'high vitality – quiet and hearty, OR hard and crashing
low vitality – quiet and thoughtful, OR sulky and refined
no vitality – dim and industrious.'

'I have a gem of a room – it is small, painted nominally primrose
yellow, in reality burnt orange, and remedied [?] this golden background hang 6 sombre young men of the 15th century, all in black
frames. The fire-place and mantel are white. In one corner there is a
small bracket with a 16th century angel I bought in Italy in it. The
bookcase is let into the wall with a curved top, it is packed, and a
Florentine candlestick bears an electric light which illumines the
gold and kid of chosen volumes and casts a warm golden glow over
the remaining walls. The windows face south over grass. In one
corner on a table stands one of the New Columbia Grafenlas that
are supposed to be the greatest improvement in gramophones since
their discovery. Underneath the table are five albums of records and
about 30 loose ones.' He had written nothing except a Greek
epigram in a copy of Hérédia's poems, which he had had bound for
Bobbie. He strongly recommended Eliot's *The Waste Land* which he
had been reading: 'sterility disguised by superb use of quotation and
obscure symbolism'. To complete the picture, 'I am myself lying on
the floor by the fire with some tea in my real Chinese tea set bought
from Canton – I wear slippers I had made for me in the market of
Gabès, in the Syrtes major. O what a good fellow am I!'

8

Seven Lean Summers

For the long vacation of 1923, he first returned to Spain. By the middle of July he was writing to his friends about a prolonged walking tour, about gypsies, a night in a monastery, hill towns with names worthy of a ballade, La Poble de Lillet, San Juan de las Abbadeses, Camprodon. 'I bathed in the Blue Med in the Bay of Roses – Bahia de Rosas, and got burnt on the back on the sand of San Cristobal de la Roda – "for the rest the sin made me an Arab but never warped me to Orientalism!" – no Mr Crace it didn't really.'

Abroad he was 'Catholique et Irlandais', he informed Longden. 'I am rather a masterpiece of the picturesque at present if people wouldn't mistake me for a "booscot". I have my Hall's hat [i.e. from the Oxford outfitters] and Basque beret in reverse – my new Blazer, very cool, a white shirt and O.E. tie (for towns only), Pop shorts [these are khaki] marvellously cool but I wish my knees weren't so hairy, delicate lady's stockings (grey khaki) on my feet – a brain wave, that, as the trouble of shorts is that all stockings are so thick – these cost about 5d a pair – Hall's socks over them and folded down over thin canvas boots with rope soles, noiseless and light and perfect for mule tracks – the socks exactly match the rope too. Add a Corps haversack (with 2 clean shirts, washing things, foot soap, eau de cologne, Baedeker, clean socks and stockings, jumper, silk scarf, 1 spare hat and a straight ash plant with spike, thong[?] and knobs, as high as my shoulders, and you have a complete outfit.' Inconveniences of the walking tour included thirst, heat, fatigue, hunger, solitude, dirt and pains of various kinds, but still he was covering an average twenty miles a day, in mountains where Englishmen had apparently not been seen before.

On the way back from Spain, he met up with Longden at Avignon, where in celebration he spent a month's allowance in five days. Sligger's house, the Chalet de Mélèzes, to which they then proceeded together, was high in spectacular scenery above the village and railway station of Saint Gervais, on a mountain called the Prarion. Cyril and Longden had an attic with a sitting room to themselves. In the woods above the chalet they found a ledge of rock on which to spend the days reading. On September 2, Longden left. In an instant decline, which he described in a long letter to Longden, Cyril went upstairs to bed, in order to write out of his system the melancholy of being alone, whereupon Sligger came up too, and sat on the bed. 'I should think myself an awful shit if I didn't weep – and would be too – and I do not mind weeping – only wanting to weep and having to play chess. I got much worse after Sligger went away and went and lay on your bed. Sligger urged me to pray for you if I was miserable again but it sounds rather like a medicine! I told Sligger I had done so once already but didn't tell him it was "Please God make us good and keep us together and we *would* like that yacht!" ' Soon he felt heartier as other guests arrived, Mrs Blanche Dugdale, niece of A. J. Balfour, as well as Richard Pares, though he seemed 'menacingly' under Sligger's influence. Others in the chalet included Christopher Hussey and Gladwyn Jebb, future architectural historian and diplomat respectively.

On September 9, which he made sure everyone knew was the last day of his teens, he walked into Italy in a party comprising Sligger, Jebb and Hussey and David Balniel (future Earl of Crawford). Instead of catching a charabanc back, as expected, Cyril and Lord Balniel returned on foot, spending Cyril's birthday on the top of Mont Blanc. 'It was very good indeed especially at dinner in a hut at 10,500 feet and we start over the glacier with lanterns at 3.30 next day with sunrise to watch.' Other descriptions of his Mont Blanc walk sounded more melodramatic, as in retrospect he grew prouder of his feat. At the end of the holidays, Sligger considered him 'a sociable little person'.

'I only tolerate Oxford because I couldn't be with Bobbie otherwise,' Cyril wrote at the end of the year. By means of the fantasy of subservience to Longden, he was making the Theory of Permanent Adolescence come true, concocting a romance of loss and failure, narcissistically rejoicing in what he seemed to be mourning. He quoted Verlaine, '*Pas de couleur, rien que la nuance*, not a splendid creed and we will outgrow it but good for us now I think – it is *la nuance* which intoxicates to the verge of weeping.' He complained of 'Tristesse d'Automne' and of his steady deterioration since the age of seventeen, going bad two years earlier than Rimbaud: 'The Rosebery, my scholarship, and Pop being stages in

[69]

the decline with their ever-increasing publicity, advertisement and solace of the world, and Bobbie only in the year that follows to keep me from sheer ruin.' A maxim followed. 'Life should be lived wildly and furiously within – outwardly with absolute calm and composure – nor ought one's true opinion to be given to anyone.'

At Christmas 1923, staying with his father in a hotel in Alassio, he had what he called a social rest, dancing all night and spending the morning in bed, as he wrote to Patrick Balfour. 'I have wanted to be abroad every term, and simply loathed coming back each vac and never perhaps was I so glad to leave England as when I smoked a cigar on the Havre boat and reflected that I was crossing for the 15th consecutive time.' He continued, 'My love of travelling is a consuming passion that, wedded to my friendship with Bobbie, is the basis of my existence – so much so that I want only to go alone or with him and couldn't bear other companionship.' Balliol and its undergraduates were 'the great sty'. History he liked only in those patches 'that catch the morning sun of beauty or in those faded and decaying corners where the last rays fall'. Books were not much of a consolation; he was reading nothing that he had not read already. For the next two years he proposed to escape from the present by travelling.

Purposeless flight was actually part of the hysteria from which he thought he was escaping. Here was one beginning after another which was merely arbitrary, which could lead nowhere and could have no ending. No effort was required either, beyond marshalling the requisite funds from his father or his mother.

The travelling was within the ancient classical world. From Alassio he went to Sicily, seasick en route, and then to Tunis, which had its moments. 'You look down on the crowded turbans and fezzes and blaze of colour, blues and reds and browns in the dresses and babel of voices, and smell of scents as they go by, Turks, Arabs, Jews, Maltese and Americans, boys very pretty and lively, grave old men, veiled women, and a jostling crowd on donkeys or feet – at first it is very frightening.' A fortune-teller flattered him by saying, '*Ne pensez pas. Vous pensez trop.*'

It proved a mistake to buy a third-class circular railway ticket to Gabès, Tozeur, Kairouan and back to Tunis. When he found the ragged orientals rushing into the carriage, in his own words, he funked it and paid the first-class supplement, only to find that at Gabès he was running out of money and could not complete the journey. From Gabès he rode out along a river bed into the *bled*, 'marvellous country, a fresh green stream running along between high red gorges, cliffs of about 80 feet of sunbaked earth and 3 swaying palms standing up against them . . . higher still a grassy upland of young palms and laurel roses all over the ground and the water rising in a quiet pool surrounded by grazing camels and sheep and goats with lambs bleating and shepherd boys'. Some Bedouin lived in nearby caves, and one woman grinned at him so that he took off his coat and combed his hair for her. 'I loved the primitive style of showing off to please the lady and got up and strutted round as gracefully and elegantly as I could, then sat down again like a mannequin.'

To return to Gabès he had to pay a share in a car. The car stuck in the mud, he missed his boat and had to endure three penniless days in Tunis. In a public place, the Garden of Allah, he picked up someone by the name of Tayeb bin Ahmed who arranged credit at the hotel. Longden forwarded him a much-needed pound. By the time he was able to board a boat home, he had decided that Araby was 'gruesomely sordid when there is no sun'.

Each Easter he revisited Spain, for more walking and train-rides mostly in the south. Once he crossed to Ceuta and Tetuan in Spanish North Africa, with 'white streets with eastern smells and Arabs and Berbers and mosques and dervishes'. In the summer of 1924 he had his first experience of Greece. The approach to Athens excited him to the point of satiety. The Parthenon was 'absolutely shattering', and he told Longden that at the sight he had burst into tears, 'undesirably, incomprehensibly'. On inspiration, he continued to Constantinople, where he spent a fortnight. The Cyclades islands, especially Paros, Cos, Naxos and Santorin, were pretty but by the time he returned to the Palace Hotel in Athens, disenchantment had set in. 'The Mediterranean population are all Americanising, straw hats, suspenders, bars, sweat, football and Mr Eugenides!' Vulgarity reigned everywhere, and the South was more thorough about it. He implored Longden not to tell anyone that he was not enjoying things much, 'for it is best they should think I am'. Loneliness even made him wonder whether this might not be his last trip. 'Nearly all my vitality of any kind has been concerned with missing you – which I do all day and all night without stopping, sometimes badly and mostly quietly but always a lot. I know you don't like it – but what else can I do?' A visit to Crete killed another week before the two of them could meet on August 8 at Sligger's Chalet.

No sooner was he at the Chalet, however, than he wrote to Noel

Blakiston that Bobbie was rather tiresome. 'He is so very florid and worships his own comforts, arranging cushions for about 5 minutes before sitting down and always swinging golf clubs about and chortling and guffawing from his arm chair. He has very little idealism and is rather self-satisfied and tepid.'

His twenty-first birthday at the Chalet was celebrated dismally. Sligger brought up from the cellar some Burgundy with which to drink his health. Meanwhile he had begun to plan and even to start his first attempt at fiction. It was to be a historical novel, set in 500 BC and concluding with the battle of Marathon. Some surviving pages introduce the protagonist, Gorgias, son of a rich merchant in the corn trade, and his young friend Tamanis – idealisations of Longden and himself. Invention fizzled out once autobiography was exhausted. The plotting confused him, he admitted. Restlessly he rushed off for one more excursion through Italy, to Naples and down to Taranto and 'lonely Doric calm Sicily'.

Mishaps on almost all his journeys flustered him and constantly wasted time. In the Basque country he had lost his passport, and in Granada his luggage was mislaid. In Avignon he had earache and on one occasion at the Chalet he had to descend to Geneva to find a dentist for his toothache. In Athens he caught a fever, and his hands grew so hot that he could not bear to touch his skin with them. He had sunstroke in Rosas; he was ill in Gandia. In Florence he had a boil so 'enormous, conspicuous and painful' that it had to be lanced. Money ran through his fingers. Extravagantly he could not resist the best hotels; he bought the most expensive presents for his friends. Often he was unlucky, for instance in Naples paying a taxi with a five-pound note worth 500 lire, when the fare was 25 lire, and realising too late what he had done when the taxi quickly drove off. By the end of his second year at Oxford, he was complaining of debts of £60. His father could be counted on only for £40, and Cyril resented him for not providing more.

Some chance encounters were diverting. On the boat to Sicily he had listened to the headwaiter, a communist, denouncing Mussolini. 'I started a great argument by saying that I did not want to marry, that I wanted to go to South America with a friend of mine and when I had made money we would be explorers (I am known on the boat as the Signorino from my tender years). The Captain sided with me against the married couple and the claims of Liberty and Solitude were long compared.' On a train from Paris to Marseilles he met a dancer called Chiquita who looked about twelve and smoked cigars. The father of her two-year-old baby, she said, was Augustus John. Cyril was impressed when she joined her lover to work a system in the Monte Carlo casino. Catching the boat to Athens, he found among his fellow passengers an impressive old Arab called Mahmoud who liked to hold his hand while they sat in silence; in a Constantinople café he sat with a tubby little Spanish novelist who admitted to writing deliberate rubbish but wanted to dedicate his next book to him. A young French boy who made advances was repulsed, he assured Longden. His letters from abroad contained story after story of assorted English bores, spinsters, clergymen, Oxford chaps, whose often comically misdirected good intentions he had made a point of thwarting.

There were formative moments too. In the National Museum in Athens he recognised two men as Professors Buschor and Woodward. At Oxford he had already been introduced to Greek painted vases by Professor Beazley. Buschor, head of the German School in Athens, conducted him round the collection of vases, sculpture and steles, forcing aesthetic judgements out of him, 'rather nerve-wracking but I got them all right'. Greek art had been ruined by Plato, according to Buschor, whose purist tastes were for the seventh and fifth centuries BC. 'At present I am very influenced by him,' Cyril wrote to Blakiston. 'He is a wonderful man, ageless, attractive, frightfully brilliant, frightfully industrious, Spartan and always laughing like one of the first Franciscans.' Buschor also showed him over the Acropolis.

Professor Woodward, 'the worst kind of pompous, worldly, well meaning usher', nonetheless invited him to dine at the British School. Since Cyril was planning to go on to Crete, Woodward gave him a letter of introduction to Sir Arthur Evans, then engaged on his famous excavations at Cnossus. Sir Arthur's assistant, Mackenzie, was off-putting. A house-boy eventually fetched Cyril up to the house. 'Evans gave me lunch – he is a terrifying little man, very old, 73, and very lively and nice. He offered me Burgundy or Chablis and Minoan water and was rather amusing – Mackenzie an untidy old fossil rather like an Eton maths don – also a young man who seemed very like a clerk in a Cook's office abroad, dapper, unemotional, with rather a cockney accent. After lunch Evans showed me round the house and the new frescoes which were rather thrilling.' These consisted of flowers, some baboons, and birds. 'I will say for the Minoans that they gave freshness to their paintings and did like nature for its own sake but otherwise they seem to me to be singularly uninteresting.' For a while he toyed with the idea of becoming an archaeologist.

Then in April 1925, just before Easter weekend, he arrived at the Washington Irving Hotel in Granada, close to the Alhambra. His spirits were low. He had a cold, his luggage had been lost. He was greeted with cries of '*Señor de los Pantalones*' on account of his surviving plus-four suit and baggy grey trousers. Worse, he had no money. 'My father has scored by not sending me the £15 he promised me or indeed any letter at all – and as I spent my last penny on an orange I am completely broke till he does.' Five letters received from Blakiston, one from Piers Synnott and one from his mother, alone relieved the dreary prospect. The guests in the hotel would not do at all but 'there are some people who look like the Sitwells who are known to be in Spain, certainly they are extremely humorous whoever they are. I have just been listening to them in the smoking room drowning some Americans from Palm Beach who were discussing the "routine" here (a round of golf in the morning, lunch and a si-es-tâ in the afternoon etc) by arguing loudly whether they could afford a week in a first class residential hotel at Scarborough for £10.7.6 or whether they would have to do with second class accommodation and third class railway fare.'

The Sitwells were kind to him, he wrote to Piers Synnott. 'Edith is rather terrifying, a kind of Ottoline [i.e. Lady Ottoline Morrell] – Osbert and Sacheverell witty and cultured and kind. They echo each other completely but Sacheverell is rather nice-looking and Osbert rather bloated, both very tall and speak in a distinguished voice very like Philip Ritchie.' (*Façade*, first performed in public two years earlier, had maximised Sitwell publicity. As a result Edith Sitwell had taken to giving regular tea-parties in her London flat, and on her return, in May, she invited Cyril to one of them. With the shadow of finals upon him, he nevertheless attended.)

The one and only university vacation when he did not go abroad but stayed at home intending to work was Christmas 1924. It was no pleasure to be alone at The Lock House with his father. Every day, sometimes twice a day, he wrote long letters to Longden or Blakiston, to Roger Mynors or Kenneth Clark. Some of the letters were headed 'Outre Tombe' and 'Everywhere the Feast of the Babe'. He had fantasies. 'Listen, when I am rich and older and this house is mine we will come down in summer, you and Noel and William and Freddy, Charles and the rest . . . We will be met by a motor punt at North Camp and glide along the waters to dinner here.'

But he had complaints too. 'Damp has got into this house *ke jadis fust si mignonne*. We have no servants properly speaking as my father can't get them, partly because he won't let me, partly because they find this lonely. We live in squalor, no sheets, no soap, no washing, and meals seem never cleared away. We have no means of getting about and know nobody in the neighbourhood and are absolutely cut off. I have not spoken to any person at all since I left Oxford except my father and four days ago a piano tuner, five a grocer and seven a man sent to see about our dying bees. Did you know bees died? My father is unbearable and being always alone with him is almost more than I can stand. He gets very drunk usually after dinner. By himself; on port – in which case he may come in here. When finding speech difficult, he gives up the attempt and goes to bed. Otherwise I hear him hiccoughing and curse and talking to himself. Oaths out of the darkness. He is vulgar and snobbish and mean and greedy, deceives himself and tries to deceive me. He fusses the whole time and is irritable and ready always to think he is a martyr – from vanity and self-pity chiefly. He would read my letters if I gave him the chance, and worse than most of his faults are the noises he makes eating and far worse digesting, so that evenings are inconceivably harrowing. All that might be bearable if it wasn't for πoθoς for Bobbie. This has got worse and worse, largely because he did not write to me for a fortnight.'

His father did the persecuting but suffered from persecution mania. Cyril did not like to leave his mother alone with such a man. 'My mother and I are both very sensitive people and perhaps rather easily appalled.' She was due to arrive at the house only on Christmas Day, not that her presence would alleviate much. 'The worst will be over but she and I do not really trust each other as she is convinced I do not love her, though I do – and she has a good many prejudices contrary to mine which clash, as the more I love people the less I make allowances for them.'

As soon as he could, he left for a reading party organised by Sligger in the house of some relations of his, at Minehead, in Somerset. Among others there was Bowra, 'in magnificent form, he really is most amazingly witty and keeps it up very well, as well as coping very well with Sligger . . . When Maurice and I are alone we talk seriously and I find him incredibly fine. He really is a very great man and a very good one too, not merely in the ethics of the intellect. I find my devotion to him grows a lot and now I cannot bear to see him hurt or pained.'

[75]

In the eyes of someone else in the party, Cyril thought he detected a gleam, he confessed to Bobbie, but 'I will try and not sleep with him.' Whereupon he wrote to Patrick Balfour the exact opposite – the kind of letter for which he had once mocked Orwell at Eton. 'I want to be frank with you – would you mind awfully if I slept with him? You see, we are going to be alone here for several days and I could weep for loneliness on these nights when the wind howls and the rain beats on the window and it is very cold . . . I long for that approximation of bodies which can give me confidence again . . . if it would cause you pain Patrick, write and tell me and I will do my best – only don't write to him about that as it would not be fair to me . . . I would not make a practice of it at Oxford as I shall have Bobbie there . . . I suppose it is the same as you and me "doing things" after you were gone on him, without asking him . . . I know it is a lot to ask and even so it is likely that he will not have me.' A letter of apology followed instantly. His mood had passed. Besides, 'I daren't do anything with him because I would have to tell Bobbie and he might well use his right then to have other relations too, and that could be the end of all things.'

Not even at the last moment did he make an effort to catch up with the required reading, and cram. A few days before his finals, he gloried in driving out into the countryside with friends, to listen to nightingales in Oakleigh Woods, and to drink gingerbeer in Brill. This was at least consistent. Rather than stand revealed as someone who should have obtained a first-class degree but had failed to do so, he preferred avoidance of the whole issue, displaying instead how void, how unworthy of him, was the Balliol spirit of achievement. The deception might take in others, but he knew the predicament he had made for himself. During the examination, instead of answering one of the questions he drafted out a note actually headed 'In Schools', and continuing, 'These examinations are pretty crashing. I know very little history and haven't read half the prepared books; it is a death struggle between style, intelligence and plausibility, and a stern unknown board of examiners who have none of the enterprise of scholarships and fellowships, only remorseless desire to see if people know their stuff. My ignorance is colossal; I had an easy paper this morning and a hard one now; it is like a cat playing with a mouse. Just as I feel secure and playful a great paw knocks me down with "Outlines of Constitutional History from 1307".

Fear and the pit and the snare are upon thee,
O Inhabitant of the earth
Venit summa dies et ineluctabile tempus.'

After his viva in the middle of July, he heard that he had got a third. Bowra commiserated. 'How horrible,' wrote Roy Harrod, the economist, already a don at Christ Church, but, 'You and others always told me you hadn't worked.' Cyril had already departed for the annual Chalet, and one of his Eton friends wrote to him there, 'I was so sorry about your finals: but what difference can the doddering opinion of a few dryasdust examiners make to your incomparable self?' At the end of August Cyril answered him, 'I don't mind much about my finals. Long ago I decided to make myself an educated man rather than let people make me a historian; and I have no wish to linger at Oxford though I don't know what I shall do instead. I have had a nice vac so far. I went to Cornwall with Bobbie for a fortnight. Then stayed with my grandmother in Bath, then stayed with Noel, and then went to Spain with him which was very nice and then on here.' A meeting was planned. 'I will probably come from Venice and go on next day to Munich to see some Greek sculpture and hear *Siegfried*. But I am uncertain at present. My parents may not let me wander round that way or I may go to Albania instead.' Longden wrote, 'I am glad Sligger took your third so well. I was very anxious about it and trying to think what I could do if he did not. The telegram (sent as soon as I heard) was a sort of vote of confidence which I thought you might be needing.'

The 1925 Chalet was 'disastrous', however, because the who-sleeps-with-whom intrigues of the Minehead reading party had broken out again. Bowra reacted jealously, 'uncouth in his love and savage in his hate', in a phrase of Cyril's. Cyril wrote to appease him. 'I confess one of the consolations of my third was hoping that it would draw a letter from you . . . I hope you haven't done too much goose-cooking.' He described his holiday so far: 'I met Brian Howard by chance in London and we scoured the embankment for νεο γυίον ἥβαν [young flesh] but without success. Philip Ritchie and Sackville-West saw us there.' Since then, five days had been spent in the cult of Bobbie's memory, 'keeping carefully alone, not uttering to anyone and trying to make the Chalet like Wuthering Heights which obsesses me at the moment'.

As for the January letter, he could not honestly remember its contents; he was sorry for having occasioned a *mésalliance*. Those in whom Bowra was interested need not be cause for bad blood. 'I

[77]

am fairly sure they have not slept together or anything except some kisses and some poetry reading and stream-damming. Still all that was squalid enough. I feel as if I was apologising to you for my dog having fought yours.' He also slipped in, 'I suppose I must get a job. Can you suggest what sort of one, and where one asks?' Cyril's goose was cooked, though, and for years to come Bowra represented him as a supreme and quite unforgiveable mischief-maker. (By the 1960s, when the quarrel had long been laid to rest, Bowra was writing to him, 'What you say about Richard Pares is most interesting. I don't think he was really your boy. He was at heart a Puritan and rather a prig . . . Bobbie's snobbery must have been an agony to you, but he had great warmth and sweetness and was not in the least a prig, least of all when he was a headmaster [at Wellington, where in October 1940 he was killed when a German bomber released its load on its way home] and might so easily have become tiresome. I can see that he ruined your Balliol life, but I fear that might have happened without him. You were much too clever and much too young to take that hard road easily.')

After he had left the Chalet, and was at a hotel in Bayonne, he received a letter from Sligger. It was September 10th and Sligger apologised for not having sent a birthday telegram. But he had written to Barrington-Ward then of the *Observer* and Ryan of the *Manchester Guardian* about possible jobs. On the 26th he expected to be at Downside Abbey for a retreat, and hoped that Cyril would be able to be there too, with Longden.

9

A Broken Coriolanus

Two days with his mother in her flat, 80 St George's Square, Cyril decided, were 'worse really than two weeks with my father because she can be so exacting and unfair and I cannot make the same allowance'. There was nowhere else to go, though, when he returned to London towards the end of September. And what was he to do with himself? On September 25, an anxious Grannie Connolly wrote to say that she had given £200 to his father, which he was to pass on to Cyril as and when he judged fit, to help with future prospects. The following day she wrote again, this time with the news that she was also paying a tailor's bill for him. 'I think I shall feel 20 years younger again when I hear you are *really started* on some career.'

A proposal to be secretary to John Buchan, at Elsfield outside Oxford, came to nothing. The Oxford Appointments Board forwarded more of the usual suggestions. 'The Memo on Colonial Appointments has arrived, and seems to contain several things you would like, such as administrative officer in Kenya or Tanganyka, starting at £300 a year, or educational appointments at £400.' Matthew Connolly was reaching the limits of his patience. 'I am also writing to Sir Arthur du Cros about you, but there is no reason why he should worry, except on account of having known me twenty years ago, so you will see that you *must* bestir *yourself* in trying to find work, as I do not intend to keep you after 26th instant.' A second letter rubbed it in. 'We only want you to choose your own career, and, for your own sake, to make very good in it and be *very* successful!'

Cyril continued dithering. Longden, who had in his sights a first and a Prize Fellowship, was reluctant to leave Oxford, and could not spare time for white ties and evenings out and London hotels – expenses, he wrote, which neither of them could afford. On October 17 he was advising, 'I daresay by the time you get this you will have decided upon something to do; I should think a tutorship abroad would be better than England as you will be more in command and will chafe less: though there is this point, that a tutorship is at best only a stop-gap, and if in England, you would be more at hand for seeing about something else. I do feel personally that you should make up your mind not to worry about "becoming cosmopolitan" etc but be ready to go away for any period that may be necessary to get a good job: because you're much more likely to deteriorate by hanging on in England with too little money to live as you would like, which will make you bitter and worldly quicker than anything.' If Cyril had to disappear for a year in order to do something very boring, he ended with a promise, 'Of course I'l! write to you.'

Journalism, as promoted by Sligger, seemed a most precarious and possibly degrading career. With no great hopes, but for the sake of independence from his parents, he would accept a tutorship, and by the third week of October he had the offer of one. He was to sail at once to Jamaica, to coach a thirteen-year-old, Charlie d'Costa, who had been removed from Marlborough after an accident playing rugger.

Sligger's loyal recommendation for the job was dated October 25. 'Mr Cyril Connolly is a young man of unusual capacity. He has a wide knowledge of a number of subjects and he can write extremely well.' Mr Connolly was a gentleman and an honourable man, he added. An interview followed. Mrs D'Costa was on the point of returning to Jamaica, and Cyril agreed to accompany her.

So on November 2, he found himself at Avonmouth, embarking on the SS Patuca of the Royal Mail Steam and Packet Company. A lump in the throat, an exulting Matthew Connolly, banishment to the edge of the universe, tears of home-sickness – departure was like St Cyprian's all over again. On the back of an envelope he scribbled a note to himself, 'One is not sufficiently oneself at 22 to triumph permanently over exile.' It was the first time that he was going of his own free will beyond the confines of Greek and Latin civilisation. In a few pages of a surviving manuscript, he transferred the experience on to a fictional character just like himself, who felt doleful and queasy as he said goodbye to his parents at the docks, but was relieved to find on the second class deck other pariahs as recognisable as he was.

In real life, however, 'the sea grew bluer and the nights hotter till we got really into the tropics with all the crew in white, flying fishes, phosphorus, blazing sun and calm seas and new and brighter stars. I used to sleep on deck, all our party did and one dark night came a lovely smell of wild jasmine and I knew we were near land. The next day we passed Haiti and Tortuga and saw Cuba in the distance.' He had written some doggerel as well:

> 'There'll be some fun tonight; Major Sanders
> has borrowed a uniform of the commander's,
> there's going to be a competition for shelling peas
> not open to Spaniards and Portuguese
> . . . an old Marlburian, but his friend's "not quite"
> he's got a big business not far from Rio
> and is going to play the drum in the new jazz trio.
> It'll be the best crossing we've had for years,
> the band's got the Pirates and the Gondoliers.
> The captain's a real good sort through and through
> he's letting the second class have sports too.
> That Dago's using his napkin like a bib.
> What, not feeling well? You'll be better by Gib.'

A letter of November 16 from his father caught up as a reminder of what was left behind. Lawyers had written to recover £54 in respect of another tailor's bill. Cyril had some shares, and it was suggested that these be sold off to pay such debts (which was in fact done a few months later). 'I am sorry to say that I am more than disappointed at your behaviour during the past year, and especially since you left Oxford.' Cyril had been living free, he pointed out, 'at the expense of your mother and myself, whereas you frittered my present away on useless travelling, and seem to have been spending a lot of Granny's money on still more clothes and gaiety: while you did not speak the truth to us on more than one occasion'. He wondered if Cyril's employers were any relation of S. J. da Costa, who died about 1908, and had been one of the most famous collectors of shells in recent years. Finally he recommended business openings in the West Indies.

The D'Costas lived outside Kingston, at Halfway Tree, 'in a fashionable suburb which looks like the garden of Eden – greenness in every direction to green mountains on one side and lagoons on the other'. As early as the seventeenth century a small number of Jewish families had settled on the island, and the D'Costas were one of the most prominent among them, long since established and prosperous. 'The father is kind and quiet, the mother I like best – she is very witty now I know her and very kind and intelligent. She quarrels with her husband and her daughters and gets sent cables to come back to England all the time and blank cheques, strings of pearls etc, – she rather replaces Sligger for me.' The two daughters were in their early twenties, and when on the warpath, according to Cyril, they made a very fair Goneril and Regan.

As for Charlie, nicknamed Benji, 'He is quite humorous and quite affectionate but that is about all I can say for him. He is incredibly selfish, greedy and conceited, old for his age in the most unpleasant way and young in the nastiest too – he is also a bridge and motor car maniac. I should think he will be a successful business man or possibly a lawyer.' The routine was not demanding. 'We work from eleven to one and read or sleep till about four. From then onwards one plays tennis or bathes or goes to a party and at night we dance or go to the cinema or out to dinner – we often bathe in the early morning too or ride or run. It is a fairly hearty life but doesn't impinge very much.'

Soon he could admit that the social life and even the teaching suited him. 'If only I had someone less bone-idle, conceited and prosaic to teach, I should enjoy it very much,' he wrote to Blakiston. 'Charlie yesterday was rude to his sister, to his mother, was ticked off by his father and rude again to his mother, ran away and went without dinner, refused breakfast this morning, affected earache, refused to kiss his mother good morning or to address his sister at all, the usual family feud raging over enemy action and me being consulted about how one can get one's hair to turn white etc. I enjoy the jokes, secure in knowing I am going to dine and dance tonight and in the possession of nice books to bury myself in.'

His real life, he wrote to Freddy Harmer, was buried in the French language, for Jamaica was altogether too anglicised to be profitable to him. He read Racine, Chénier, La Fontaine and du Bellay, more Proust and more Rimbaud, and imitated them. He was writing alexandrines and light verse – Auburn, in the following example, was the D'Costas house.

> Je suis à Auburn, cruel site,
> ici demeure le roi Mesquite,
> hélas, j'ai été trop piqué,
> me gratter est trop compliqué.
> D'ailleurs c'est une chose indigne
> d'être mangé avant que je dine.
> La danse des Black a lieu ce soir,
> les Black me donnent des idées noires.

[82]

One parody, written on Auburn paper, began,

Dorothée de Lauriston, divine Dorothée,
Dieu m'a mis en exil aux lieux où vous fûtes née.

Dorothy had come out on the SS Patuca and was one of the Jamaican girls whom he liked, finding them as a whole 'cool and competent'. '*Je vous aime,*' he wrote to her, '*pas passionément, ni même à la folie, mais assurément je vous aime,*' but he concluded, '*il ne faut pas tuer les amants: tôt ou tard ils se suicident.*'

Whether or not to womanise, how best to set about it, occupied much of his correspondence. 'This island and I have given up all attempts to conform to the Maurice [Bowra] creed. The result is that I have enjoyed three months of perfect chastity as no woman seems able to arouse the slightest sensation of sex or passion in me, only I find them soothing, decorative and amiable, while men here are dull and squalid and the perpetual spicy breezes and eternal sunshine make any strong feeling quite impossible beyond a mild loneliness on moonlit evenings and the anguish of remembering Eden when the rain falls long. There are three kinds of people here, Jamaicans, Jews, and the upper Kipling classes – the latter, soldiers, officials, tourists and wives of various descriptions are dull in the extreme, the Jews are patriarchal and vulgar and the Jamaicans the most interesting, elegant and languid and cool but able to be aroused to a slow and deep intoxication by drink with the men or dancing with the women, though often they are combined. There are also coloured people, rather disappointing Chinamen, coolies, and quantities of niggers and occasional bouts of planters who arrive for weekends and paint the place red. The tropics are very expurgated in Jamaica; there are no snakes, no wild animals except alligators, no yellow fever, nothing but hills and greenery, endless flowers and palms, scenery like Chinese poems or more often like Christmas carols on a Hawaian guitar. You would never think the lotus could be so real or so insiduous or intellectual, and sexual drowse so thorough and so kind. I lead a very simple life, teaching my *puer* in the morning, playing bridge after lunch and then swimming or playing tennis with more bridge before dinner and often after it or else dancing about three nights a week and going to the cinema which is lit by fire-flies and immersed by saxophones. I get away from the household a good lot and have a fair amount of friends. Tennis is quite pleasant in the rose-filled gardens where your favourite Cattleyas (shades of Odette and my own cousin who named them!) grow fifty on a stem besides hollyhocks and mangos, coronet palms, sweet peas and lignum vitae trees. Swimming is very pleasant indeed, though it is only in swimming baths because of the sharks, but I enjoy the gradual mastery of a new element and the pleasant dissipation of playing bridge in bathing suits on a Sunday morning, stopping to dive in from the roof on which we sit, and dressing to drink champagne and dance and doze in rocking chairs till lunch *à l'ombre des jeunes filles en fleur.'*

What he could not have, he began as usual to miss more and more. 'The elements of life: England, the real greenness, buildings of Bath, something solid and not as alive as I thought: Marvell's England, too good to fight for, with all the dignity and charm and sober melancholy of Bobbie. Bobbie himself whose influence will be restraining and not fertile as I once thought, but who I see now will never change for me from being the finest and friendliest person I know and the best critic and highest symbol in my Platonic scale. Oxford not much of a place really; it puts off the evil day, that is all, and is on the whole a safe place to think of one's friends, under-standable and unchanging. London certainly to be avoided – still it contains my friends also to a degree.'

To Longden himself, he elaborated, 'I like you best as the serious and rather depressed young man behind the mask – and I think we could knock spots off Gray, West, Walpole and Ashton for being good types of young men – and we are both persistent amateurs. I hardly give Oxford a thought . . . but you seem so god-like from here, *o quam te memorem* Bobbie . . . I wish we had lived in Cromwell's England, or rather a bit before it. I remember joking with K [Clark] once about you – "a typical product of the 30s". "The 30s?" "The 1630s." I mightn't have had such a bad time, there was room for Kenelm Digby as well as Marvell, Falkland and Co.'

On April 4 1926 he sailed home to Avonmouth, with Mrs D'Costa also among the passengers. Adventure and escape had amounted only to exile, he assured himself in a classically modelled poem:

O wasted youth among the isles
    that faithless Caribbean surge
and the interminable miles
    of cold Atlantic would submerge
in living death beneath the palms,
    return – before the spirit grieves
no more for woes the sun embalms
    as faint as woodsmoke under leaves.

10

Du Côté de chez Logan

A suspicion that he had been insufficiently missed by his friends was submerged in the urgency of finding something to do. A letter from the Oxford Appointments Board, dated April 7 1926, was offering 'an opening for a man who wishes to take up the career of a Rubber Planter in the Selangor River Rubber Co'. The Asiatic Petroleum Company and British-American Tobacco were similarly proposed, as was Guinness, the brewery. From Balliol, Sligger provided more references. Gabbitas Thring, the educational agency, was approached ('To many an unknown genius postmen bring / Typed notices from Rabbitarse and String' as Auden thought about this last resort of those with poor arts degrees). A literary man, Montague Summers, was hoping to move to Oxford, and he wanted a secretary – Cyril might do. Sligger was not in favour, he did not care for Summers: 'an unpleasant man who had scent and paint and that sort of thing and was very unpopular in College'. He urged Cyril to have something written to show to people – 'You must force yourself to write.'

Longden was successfully pursuing an academic career at Oxford. 'I am afraid our old friendship is of the past and the new one stands shivering on the frontier station in the drizzle of the dawn and has lost its luggage,' Cyril told Blakiston. Of all the letters which he wrote to Blakiston, and which have been collected in *A Romantic Friendship*, more than half date to the twelve months immediately following his return from Jamaica. Noel Blakiston was then no longer in College at Eton, but an undergraduate at Magdalene College, Cambridge. As soon as he could, Cyril went to stay with him there. But Cambridge, and what he called 'the cold radiator types' of the university, tended to lower his spirits. A fantasy sprang up that he and Blakiston would rent cheaply a cottage on the Devon coast, and live there.

Returning with Blakiston's younger brother Jack from Cambridge to The Lock House, Cyril was caught up in the General Strike. Enrolling as a special constable, he spent a week at his mother's flat in London. To some friends he wrote that this was exciting, to others that it was dreary. On May 22, once more at The Lock House, with the strike over, he explained to Synnott, 'Sorry if I lost caste through strike activities – there was little else to do in London, and we had not laid in enough coal to last here. Jack (Blakiston) and I got here with some difficulty from Cambridge and returned with even more. I am chiefly occupied in trying to fix Narcissus on paper but he eludes me with either a pose of artificial elegance or a boring and exasperating sincerity like a schoolboy. How old was he and who were his parents? I think the worst part of spring is over.' That same day he received a note from Montague Summers to regret that arrangements to have a secretary had fallen through.

'My father wants to ship me to the colonies unless I get a job in a fortnight,' he told Noel Blakiston on June 8. 'There is only Sligger between me and the gangway.'

Rescue arrived in the form of a suggestion from Kenneth Clark. 'You must on no account go to the colonies,' Clark wrote. 'Has Bobbie or Sligger spoken to you about Pearsall Smith? He, though a worldly old gossip, is not disreputable and goatish like Summers. He wants a secretary, or rather he wants to keep some young man from journalism, and in return the young man is to do various jobs of scholarship – look up passages in 17th and 18th century authors, mainly in quest of philological quarries. I don't know if such a job would appeal to you: you would find him a trifle pedantic, and very much the slave of polite civilisation.' Pearsall Smith lived at 11 St Leonard's Terrace, looking on to Chelsea Hospital, and a call on him one evening after dinner was recommended. This proved enough. Cyril was employed, at a salary of £8 a week. After the annual holiday with Sligger at the Chalet, he would start in July.

Logan Pearsall Smith was then fifty-nine, not that age had made much difference to someone who had always been so self-controlled and set in his ways, as though born elderly. Large and somewhat ungainly, he was self-conscious about his appearance, and he was soon defending himself with a typical maxim, 'There is more happiness on the other side of baldness than Cyril can possibly imagine.' Clever and ironic conversation was his weapon for holding people at bay. So long as all concerned were indeed the slaves of polite civilisation, he did not in the least mind wounding others or

[86]

being wounded. The only path he would advocate, he told Cyril, was the one leading to the ivory tower. Friendship could go so far but no further; he made sure that nobody had claims to make on him. There were such things as happy marriages, he told Cyril one day, but he could not help noticing that he had always been recommended to marry by women, never by men. To one lady who asked why he had never proposed to her, he replied that he had thought of it but then remembered that she had no central heating in her house except on the ground floor. Relationships which might prove open-ended and therefore unpredictable – not only marriage but homosexuality as well – were spoken of with an abhorrence perhaps suggesting the strength of his repressions.

Puritanism like his reflected a fear of human experience but was explicable in terms of his background. His parents had been Quakers, living in a small town near Philadelphia. The family glass factory there provided their fortunes. Never a whole-hearted businessman, his father evolved into a celebrated evangelical preacher, while his mother became a militant feminist and prolific publicist. Violence of emotion, in both their cases, had self-destructive elements.

Educated at Harvard, Logan Pearsall Smith later read greats at Balliol, where he absorbed *fin de siècle* aestheticism at its purest. What he called 'the unfailing fountain of my little annuity' permitted him to escape into literature as though it were a zone wonderfully free from responsibility of any kind. He went to Paris and wrote a novel which he showed to Henry James, who was tactfully discouraging. It was all of a piece that afterwards he should have immersed himself in baroque writers like Sir Henry Wotton, Jeremy Taylor, Donne. He was a busy anthologiser. In the process of building a curiously antiquarian personality for himself, his dissociation from America became complete. 'I am willing to love all mankind except an American,' was a favourite quotation. In 1913 he took British nationality. Literary celebrity of a rarified kind came in 1918, with the publication of *Trivia*, followed four years later by *More Trivia*. These short collections of aphoristic paragraphs had an impact on account of a distant or introverted pessimism which amounted to distrust of everything and anything. There was no safe refuge in the world, apparently, except in style.

In addition to his house in Chelsea, Pearsall Smith rented Big Chilling, a Tudor farmhouse at Warsash in Hampshire, with a view out over Southampton Water. Rather unexpectedly in so sedentary

[87]

a man, he had a passion for sailing – in June 1926, the month prior to Cyril's arrival, he had been on a cruise in the Aegean on a yacht taken by his friend Edith Wharton.

'I am living a pleasant life here,' Cyril wrote from Chilling at the end of July to Patrick Balfour. 'Pearsall Smith doesn't appear till lunch and is benevolent and amusing and we sail on the Solent. I would like to write but tolerance and sanity make it almost as hard to write as it was formerly to be happy.' Settling in, he told Synnott that he was happy, sailing, feeding, reading, writing and working. 'Logan is a very witty man and sympathetic as well, a blithe old Chinaman with a kind of bleakness that delays always those excessive confidences that win friendship. I have a Tudor attic – I have read nothing epoch-making to tell you about and my French is rusting. I leave here at the beginning of September.' Matthew Connolly was relieved that 'things seem to be going to pan out all right about your staying on in the secretaryship, and hope you will do so; I am glad Mr Pearsall Smith likes chess, as it will be an inducement for him to keep you.'

The pretext for the September travelling was a guidebook to the Balkans which Cyril was intending to write, in the manner of Richard Ford's celebrated book about Spain. Sentiments, rather than practical matters, were to be served, and the whole work was to be a companion, a homage, to Longden who was proposing to travel through the Balkans later in the year. Going out to Vienna, he met up with his Eton friend Freddie Harmer, and they continued down the Danube to the Black Sea ('I am in the smoking room and Freddie is nearby reading Tolstoy in German, there are a few lights at Chanak and Gallipoli which we have been watching till we got cold' – to Blakiston.) So on to Constantinople, staying once more at Tokatlian's Hotel. A letter from Pearsall Smith was waiting there. 'I miss you secretly very much, and often wish you were here for a sail or a game of chess. I find I like being tutored, and hope you didn't find me too tiresome a pupil. You seem to have been giving my address to some of your shady friends – I have had a letter or two of an extraordinary kind. Where do you pick up these people?' The journey then proceeded through Salonica, Athens, Nauplia, Brindisi, and eventually Venice and Munich.

Pearsall Smith asked nothing for himself when he set about encouraging whatever might lead Cyril to write. He recognised intelligence when he saw it, and that autumn he did his best to realise his ambitions for Cyril. Results were expected. Disciplined himself, he was shocked by waste, especially waste of talent. Cyril was to judge him 'conscientious without knowing what to be conscientious about', which was true, but also a rationalisation of his own difficulties in becoming as professional as Pearsall Smith in the straightforward matter of literary production. What with his curiosity, and the demands he made on people, Cyril could never have been merely a disciple of Pearsall Smith's, but he was influenced by him as by no-one else. First of all, he came to perceive the literary life as something complete in itself, enticing and static. Then Pearsall Smith's natural assumption that works of art were destined to last longer than people and therefore took priority over them, strengthened Cyril's innate feeling for elegy, for the dying fall and the inevitability of imperfection. *Trivia* he instantly thought 'supreme'. From Pearsall Smith he learned how to rely on the *mot juste*, and to use the exact quotation from the classics in support of a viewpoint. Also he came to an enduring belief in the divine right to good silver, rare editions, even a yacht, all in all to a life voluptuously free from care. To have had a private income like Pearsall Smith's afterwards seemed to represent the tantalisingly unattainable day-dream. Not to have had such a private income explained and excused everything unfulfilled. In that respect, Pearsall Smith's good intentions proved corroding.

Cyril could be packed off to Chilling but it was harder to oblige him to write. Except for the servants who looked after him, he was more or less alone there for six weeks in November and December 1926, 'practising death' as he told several friends. Pearsall Smith allowed him to use the gramophone and the car, however, and to invite Blakiston, Longden or anyone else to stay. And in fact he managed to slip away to London and to Cambridge to visit Blakiston.

A pointed, rather arch, joke took shape when Pearsall Smith wrote to him on December 7. 'You will not, I am sure, have been long at Chilling without getting in touch with the boys who are being educated there under special conditions, owing to their moral and mental deficiencies. Among these backward or difficult boys there is one, Joe Congothly by name, to whom I stand in the position of guardian, and who is to me the cause of considerable anxiety and care. You have made his acquaintance, no doubt, and have heard, I fear, of the serious trouble he got into a few months ago. I try to believe his story, that he was more sinned against than sinning.' He went on, 'I have, however, decided that he had better be removed at

[89]

the end of this term from an institution where he is exposed to these misadventures.' The remedy was 'to stay with me for a while in London, if he will agree to live quietly here and do his lessons under my supervision, and not bang about London all day in bad company, and come reeling home after midnight from the night-clubs and low haunts which he loves to frequent'. Congothly was 'rather sullen and suspicious but not incapable of responding to kindness'. Initially the secretaryship had been due to last only until January 1927, but Pearsall Smith did not intend to deprive himself of Connolly's company on account of Congothly.

In London, Pearsall Smith was able and willing to promote him, playing the part of a metropolitan Sligger, so to speak. Regulating his social life carefully, Pearsall Smith chose to see only those who uncritically shared his tastes. Bluestocking ladies whom he liked to have tea with, or with whom he liked to stay in their comfortable houses in the country or abroad, included the painter Ethel Sands and her companion Nan Hudson, Violet Hammersley, and Lady Colefax. He liked the Sitwells, and Sir Edmund Gosse. Cyril was flattered to be introduced to Maurice Baring, whose novels he then read and enjoyed, including *Tinker's Leave*, published in 1927. Maurice Baring had had several plays performed, and a vague proposal arose that he and Cyril might collaborate on a script. That he was 'superbly unimpressed by achievement' was one good reason for approving of him. Etonian, Catholic convert, classicist, linguist, amateur pianist, Maurice Baring represented a *beau idéal* of the kind of cosmopolitan figure that Cyril would have wanted to be, at least when man-of-the-world moods were uppermost.

Another influential friend of Pearsall Smith's, and an admirer of *Trivia* books, was Desmond MacCarthy. Since 1920 MacCarthy had been literary editor of the *New Statesman*, where he wrote a weekly column under the signature 'Affable Hawk'. His house in Wellington Square was within walking distance of St Leonard's Terrace, and he dropped round regularly, sometimes to play chess with Pearsall Smith. Anglo-Irish, a successful Etonian and a member of the Apostles at Cambridge, MacCarthy was sociable by nature, disposed to talk rather than to write. Easily distracted by cleverness, he was neither very efficient nor very industrious. However much the articles he had written were praised, the books he had not written were regretted more. As a critic he was open-minded, but with a disposition in favour of classicism which made him sound more conservative than he was.

Cyril responded at once to what he called 'the desert island equality' which MacCarthy produced. In his diary Cyril noted approvingly how MacCarthy, speaking of life in general, one day had said, 'One downward twist, a turn of the wrist and the wound is incurable' – phrasing and sentiment alike might have been his own. Those who impressed him were always examined as models, and MacCarthy was no exception. 'Ask Desmond about himself and he tells me of his life at 23, said he was as idle as I was and it made him eventually ill,' ran another diary entry, after the two had known each other a few months. 'Desmond is really more intolerant than Logan because his is the practical intolerance which resents disagreement as being really too tiresome when you have so little time to state your views. Logan's is merely the pained surprise of a believer, not the angry protest of a shepherd when one of his flock holds up all the rest by refusing to enter the fold.'

Besides, MacCarthy had a wife, Molly, and children, the eldest of whom, Rachel, was then seventeen – 'the family I like best in the world', Cyril was to write in his diary, no doubt seeing a possible substitute for his own suspended family life. During the spell of 'practising death' at Chilling, he had already made of Molly Mac-Carthy a confessor. 'Solitude confirms me in my faults, sloth, untidiness, abstraction, morbid imagining and slothful arrogance,' he wrote to her. A probably unposted draft of another letter provided more escapism. 'It is more or less an open secret that books are all absolute tripe and if there is anything nastier than another lying about a room it is one's own writing – O do let's go to Ireland.' That November Molly MacCarthy presented him with a copy of her memoirs, *A Nineteenth Century Childhood*, which had been published two years earlier, and which he immediately found 'supreme'. (Its opening sentence read, 'I was born in the 'eighties into a sheltered, comfortable, religious and literary circle.' Her father, E. C. Warre-Cornish, had been Provost of Eton, and Pearsall Smith kept a notebook of the sayings of the redoubtable Mrs Warre-Cornish.)

'I went to Molly's party yesterday,' Pearsall Smith wrote to Cyril at Chilling, on November 17 1926, 'all the young lions, or rather the young tom-cats of Bloomsbury were there, a few older celebrities, trembling for their thrones and reputations among those hoping to replace them, and a few ladies of fashion anxious to be in the intellectual swim.' René Crevel, a young French poet and surrealist, had been giving an address, 'an anti-intellectual gospel and attack on reason, chanted and bellowed at us in a kind of figurative and bombastic prose which, though we pretended to follow it, I am sure none of us really understood. The whole thing – the brazen pretentious boy and the anxious pretentious audience, was extremely funny, but I was sorry for Molly, though I hope she didn't realise, being deaf, how absurd the lecture was. Fascism is as stupid in literature as it is in politics but fortunately less dangerous.'

Derision of the kind was only in part idiosyncratic. Pearsall Smith had long observed those who were in the Bloomsbury group, and had taken a careful stance to one side. He acknowledged that they were free spirits, but thought them self-satisfied, too busy with the promotion of one another, and much over-rated. He had rebuked Virginia Woolf to her face for writing for glossy magazines out of opportunism. She reciprocated with judgements about him in her letters, such as 'a little censorious, mildly buggeristical'. His habit of drafting everything eight times exposed his vanity, and not his craft, in her opinion. Eventually they were to declare themselves 'enemies', contrasting, at least over the tea-table, his Chelsea and her Bloomsbury. Virginia Woolf signed off a correspondence on the subject with a statement of her admiration for the delightful people and brilliant gatherings of Chelsea. 'I need only mention, besides yourself, Desmond, Maurice Baring, Ethel Sands, Bob and Hilda Trevelyan, Mr Connolly, Mrs Hammersley, and then there's Lady Colefax round the corner,' but she admitted that she had mocked them all, and her sarcasm was evident.

Some of this was play-acting. David Garnett, Gerald Brenan, Arthur Waley and his friend Beryl de Zoete, for example, were among those who moved without strain between Chelsea and Bloomsbury. R. C. Trevelyan kept a room in 11 St Leonard's Terrace where he used to spend a night or two of the week, but this did not prevent him from publishing his *Poems and Fables* in 1925 with the Woolfs at the Hogarth Press.

Desmond MacCarthy, however, was in a more ambivalent position. In his memoirs Leonard Woolf conceded that MacCarthy was a member of Old Bloomsbury, and so a friend of long standing, but he went on, 'One of the several reasons why Desmond never fulfilled his youthful aquiline promise and never wrote that brilliant novel which in 1903 lay embryonically in his mind was that he thought that he *ought* to write a novel and that the novel *ought* to be absolutely first class.' (Change the name and the date, and exactly the same sentence could be applied to Cyril.) Leonard and Virginia

Woolf alike could not resist the implication that literary journalism of his sort was intrinsically second-rate, an implication which they did not bother to hide from him or anyone else. When MacCarthy was in financial difficulties in 1927, Virginia Woolf helped to raise funds for him, but purse-watcher that she was, her disparagements increased. 'He is worse than a sieve, a drain, a wastepaper basket, and amiable into the bargain,' she was to write a year later, 'so that one gets nothing done, as with a crusty character. Nothing but smiles and promises.' To be patronising him was enjoyable.

'I don't like Bloomsbury,' Cyril had written to a friend at the end of his final term at Oxford. Experience at first-hand confirmed the instinctive dislike. What excluded him from Bloomsbury at the start was the attitude of the Woolfs towards Pearsall Smith and Mac-Carthy, his two generous supporters and sponsors, who between them provided him with a first footing in literary London. When one day in October 1927 the uncharitableness of Bloomsbury towards MacCarthy was being discussed, Cyril recorded in his diary, 'I said it was because they were envious and could not manage to explain him away. I said they tried to think he was a buffer but they knew he wasn't, that they could not forgive him for liking the things they liked, and then liking other things as well – for being a high brow in intellect and a low brow in heart.'

Such a confident expression of his own opinions, when still only twenty-four, was worthy of Bloomsbury, as a matter of fact. Had he been introduced there by unqualified admirers of that circle, he might have become a friend and disciple of the Woolfs, like several of his contemporaries from Eton or Oxford and Cambridge. Much united Chelsea and Bloomsbury, but what separated them were divergent definitions of the purposes of literature and art. To Chelsea, self-expression was a means, the chief means perhaps, to enjoyment of a fuller life; to Bloomsbury, it was more strictly an end requiring no further justification. The Pearsall Smith set looked at Bloomsbury and deplored people who for all their gifts and privileges were stuck in class-conscious and money-conscious attitudes, self-denying people, in short parochial and priggish. The Woolf set looked at Chelsea and envied people who had travelled too widely, who were at ease in foreign languages and settings, treated money and status loosely, self-indulgent people who were, in short, suspiciously worldly.

The Twilight of the Dons

On February 9 1927 Logan Pearsall Smith and Cyril caught the Golden Arrow to Paris, where they spent a few days before continuing to Bordeaux. 'I find it very hard to realise I am travelling as a rich man and find I have a strong inclination to discourage Logan from buying cigarette boxes, or taking rooms with baths,' Cyril wrote to Blakiston. 'Logan is enjoying himself and is terrified out of recognition by the brutal efficiency with which I arrange his travels.'

By February 13 they were in the Madrid Palace Hotel. Then they crossed the Mancha, to reach Granada. 'Tomorrow is going to be a good day, we motor from here in the early morning to Motril over the end of the Sierra Nevada and through the Alpujarras, Durcal, Lanjaron, Orgiva, and then along the coast to Velez Malaga.' They stayed in Seville, Cadiz and Algeciras. A house near the sea at Almuñecar sparked another fantasy to replace the Devon cottage – whenever he felt the need for a fresh start in the future, the idea of a retreat in Spain rose to the surface. Here were over twenty kinds of fruit, the people seemed beautiful and welcoming, the house was for sale for seven hundred pounds, he told Blakiston. 'Logan offered to give it me but he would hold it over me if I did not live there so I said I would rather try it first – the point is would you like staying there, supposing you were a schoolmaster and would Jack? It opens up the whole question of the south.'

The tour was a success. 'I like Logan and get on very well with him,' he wrote to Patrick Balfour. 'I think I could get on with anybody, travelling now so long as I was left reasonably alone.' Also, 'Travel I like a lot, more than anything really, but I don't feel that it is an end in itself or the basis of any real aesthetic, it is just one's peculiarity to find it hard to keep still, homeless since the loss of Eden. With his drear pedantry and morning beard, whether in summer time on Bredon, or in the winter in Liskeard, Cyril arrives, the noisy showman, staring, the sunset's connoisseur.'

For the first week of March he split off by himself for a journey to Morocco, sightseeing in Tetuan and Tangier, and as far inland as Fez, before rejoining Pearsall Smith in Spain. They caught a boat to Naples, where once again they went their separate ways for a while. In Rome Cyril was to meet up with Longden who was then researching at the British School, and together they were to go to stay in Florence with Kenneth Clark and his wife Jane. For the past year Clark had been working as an assistant to Bernard Berenson, the art historian, whose house i Tatti was at Settignano. In order to be within walking distance, the Clarks had taken a house called Chiostro di San Martino. Berenson's wife Mary was Logan Pearsall Smith's elder sister, and family affection ran strongly between them. Pearsall Smith also considered his brother-in-law a modern Goethe, and he was pleased to be in a position to introduce Cyril to him.

Born in 1865, Berenson was then at the height of his fame. His books and his theories had long since been recognised and debated by scholars, but in addition he had done a great deal to enlarge general interest in art history and collecting. A man of the widest tastes and reading, fluent in a number of languages, he was eager to learn from anyone who had anything to contribute. Quick and inquiring as he was, he made not the least pretence of suffering fools, and all too often the turbulence in the house arose from the fact that he could not help pointing out to Mary how much less intelligent she was than the others there. But together they had created i Tatti, more a court than a villa, with its gardens and walks, its library, its pictures. Conversation, food, guests, were all supposed to be rather strenuously perfectionist. One of Pearsall Smith's more sincere maxims maintained that 'it is impossible to be both first-rate and fashionable,' but the Berensons at i Tatti seemed the visible contradiction of it.

When Cyril disagreed with some of Berenson's opinions, and corrected him about the birthplace of Juvenal, he was being a good guest according to the standards of the place. Counter-attack was accepted as defence there. If Berenson chose, Cyril observed, he could be considerate, generous and charming. 'He talks the whole time and downs everybody else, and though he has enormous and universal knowledge and is excessively stimulating, half his remarks are preposterously conceited and the other half entirely insincere.' Cyril added the remark that 'it is like listening to an academic Lloyd George.' Mrs Berenson he found large and broad and homely.

Because he succeeded in pleasing, Cyril was invited by the Berensons to stay at i Tatti. He accepted all the more gratefully because in doing so he could avoid Maurice Bowra, who with John Sparrow, the future Warden of All Soul's College, had also been staying with the Clarks at Chiostro di San Martino. (Bowra, who conceived argument as monologue and found the process of learning to be confirmation of what he already knew, proved a failure at i Tatti. This did nothing to dampen his past jealousies, so much so that afterwards Cyril was to draft him a long letter of challenge. 'I hear you have begun an offensive against me again. Can't you manage to leave me alone for a moment, for, after all, it must be nine months since we last met, and as we are so little in each other's way I don't see how a reopening of your famous crusade will do you any good. I have made a point of not making bad blood about you, but you can't expect me not to retaliate, and between us, we will only succeed in making a great many people dislike us, and very few believe what we say. I realise that to you absence and failure are unforgiveable sins but I am neither wholly absent nor completely failing.')

Longden returned to Rome, and then set off on his projected tour of Greece and the Balkans. Meanwhile Blakiston arrived in Florence, and accompanied Cyril to Sicily, round the sites which four years previously Sligger had shown his party of four undergraduates. Once it was over, Cyril thanked Blakiston for contributing 'to the most sustained ecstasy of my life'. A long round-about journey by himself via Vienna, Prague, Dresden, brought him back to Chelsea at the end of April.

Something of a watershed had been reached. The future could hardly consist of permanent travels. He was dissatisfied but could not settle, could not apply himself. Ecstasy had to be paid for with woe, Pearsall Smith told him. 'Yours is a life of dizzy heights and deep abysses – I envy it in a way, for it is a life of that poignant reality which is the stuff of art.' The remedy was obvious. Cyril had to work. The case was weakened because Pearsall Smith was also telling him, 'I believe in the long delays of art and the nine-years pondered lay.' The tenor of life in Chelsea had no urgency, on the contrary tended to luxuriate.

Desmond MacCarthy took him on to proof-read at the *New Statesman*, and to write brief unsigned reviews. To sit in an office, to linger there late into the night, was enjoyable. But boredom and frustrated ambition were fretting him, as expressed in some aphorisms and ideas very much his own, in spite of stylistic derivation from Pearsall Smith's *Trivia*.

> People need new friends, they are cannibals in affection who eat their own friends, just as others have dramatised themselves and always need new audiences before whom to re-enact the noble versions of their lives.
>
> A best-seller is the golden touch of mediocre talent.
>
> It's a wise worm that knows its own turning.
>
> The five virtues, Pride, detachment, integrity, charm, impulsiveness.
>
> The three vices, Meanness, insincerity and meanness.
>
> The ten tripes, Books, Friends, Sweeties, Theatres, Universities, Sundays, intellectuals, anti-intellectuals, Alps, arguments.
>
> The five possibles, Talk, intimacy, wine, travel, fens.
>
> And if you do not when you can
> you shall not when you would.

In his experience there was already insufficient novelty or variety. Weekends in Oxford or in Cambridge were stale. The MacCarthys had been lent Shulbrede, a house in the country near Haslemere, which belonged to Lord and Lady Ponsonby, and he was sometimes invited there, but if the MacCarthys were away from London, he complained that he had 'nowhere to lay my head and my troubles'. In his letters he mentioned seeing Peter Quennell, Harold Acton, Edward Sackville-West, Bryan Guinness, Christopher Sykes, but in spite of the Bright Young Thing aura, 'I am hating London, estranged from intimacy, and greenness and spending too much money.' When Patrick Balfour proposed that he find a house for the two of them to share, he thought he saw how to turn over a fresh page.

Pearsall Smith had made virtually no demands of any kind on him. All the same, out of contrariness mainly, Cyril had come to feel his benefactor as rather a constraint. It would have seemed a sad and arid fate to have developed into a bachelor of the kind, all passions sublimated. During the first part of 1927, Pearsall Smith wrote out a little spoof to which he gave the title *Handbook of the "Down with Cyril Society"*. Its most revealing remark was, 'Cyril could be a perfect friend – if he loved perfection; but if he loved perfection, where would I come in?' What Pearsall Smith hoped for was a complete identity of views leading to unrealistic devotion at arms' length. Sexuality in general was a danger to be warded off by

[97]

mockery, as in another one-liner in the *Handbook*, 'The act of copulation is an unstable basis upon which to build a life.' Cyril could never have remained for long in the orbit of someone who could really believe that.

On the back of the small *Handbook*, Cyril reacted by pencilling some verses about himself.

> Contrasted faults through all his manners reign –
> though poor, luxurious, though submissive, vain,
> though grave, yet trifling, zealous, yet untrue;
> and e'en in penance planning sins anew.
> All evils here contaminate the mind
> that opulence departed leaves behind.

Penances and plans alike centred upon the long-delayed discovery of the opposite sex. What was happening was only the consequence of the schooling considered right and proper for someone of his kind. Adolescence had indeed been retarded bizarrely, possibly permanently had he stayed with Pearsall Smith. His various romantic friendships had been externalisations of ideals, each the product of his rarified and exclusively male upbringing. Only one or two of his friends proved adult homosexuals, and they were never really to forgive him for what to them appeared an almost treasonable transfer of allegiance. They were to react to being dropped with much the same bitterness as Cyril's Pop friends had done, but whereas the latter had laughed at him, the former might pursue him down the years as a homosexual *manqué*.

The change in himself was no very deep realisation but a simple matter of opportunity. In 1927 he began to keep a diary (in a leather-bound volume, the precursor to the Journal which follows here in Part Two). 'It is both difficult and curious to find oneself suddenly estranged from the male sex and plunged into joy and bewilderment by all encounters with the other; obviously there comes a time when this has to be, especially if one's lot is cast further and further from the academic groove. The main thing is not to fight against this reverse, for this would be impossible, but simply not to lose one's head. It is humiliating to find oneself in a moment subjected to all the painful emotions of a schoolboy, to feel hopelessly optimistic and sentimental, wearily attentive, and ingenuously shy, it is humiliating but it is also refreshing and on the whole pleasurable if one can only keep quiet about it. No convert can be dignified and all must expect to receive the scorn of those whose convictions have not changed, both in the party which they leave and in that in which they now find themselves. To keep the best of my old friends and not to be taken in by my new ones, and to deduce from my symptoms as coolly and quickly as possible what are likely to be my dangers in this unknown country, should become my task. Here I must admit that I am both infinitely fastidious and absolutely susceptible; hence that my experience is likely to be a series of rapid disillusions.'

If only Molly MacCarthy were present, he could ask advice, 'if I am likely to be attractive to women and what one should do to please them'.

At Chilling during the summer, he found himself with Alys, younger sister and part-time housekeeper of Pearsall Smith – in 1920 her husband, Bertrand Russell, had insisted upon a divorce, something to which she could not reconcile herself. 'Trouble with Bertie is two things,' so Cyril recorded in his diary a verdict of Pearsall Smith's on this former brother-in-law of his, 'he must have something to hate so he goes into politics and someone to love so he has to make money in journalism. He has to love and he has to hate and (with gruff satisfaction) that's how *he's* chained to the wheel.' Also staying in the house at the time was Margery Fry, who had recently become Principal of Somerville College, Oxford, and was the sister of Roger Fry, the Bloomsbury art critic. The presence of these two middle-aged ladies drove him to conclude, 'I should like a liaison with a direct and sensible young woman, working in London, sympathetic, Sophoclean, English, we would meet for very late dinners after working late at offices. The blend of tenderness with dignity.' (The ladies had revenge of a sort, for before the visit was out Cyril was noting, 'Talk of nationalities at dinner. I prove anti-American, anti-Semite, anti-Jewish-American, anti-French, anti-Celt, anti-foreigner and more than I will admit of an Anglophobe. Two nights later Margery Fry discerned a strong vein of anti-Indian, anti-Negro, and anti-Anglo-Indian.')

Exactly the type of direct and sensible young woman happened to be on the train taking him on July 15 out to Sligger's chalet. She was on her way to Argentière, down the railway line. Her name was Alex, she was a friend of Jane Clark's, and had a job at the Board of Trade. The haphazard encounter propelled him into a romantic daze. At the Chalet he acted out Byronic solitude, sitting alone, and characteristically observing how he was 'thinking of someone to miss'.

Back at Chilling, and then in London, he wondered how to contact Alex – at one point he took to loitering outside the Board of Trade in the hope that she might emerge. 'This I call rather a victory for her,' he entered in his diary. It was mere idealisation, however, for he plunged straight into an account of what he did next, which was to walk to Charnwood Street, in Lambeth. Chica, the girl whom he was calling on there, was given no surname – any more than Alex had been – according to his diary they had met accidentally through someone called Sandy. He gave Chica an expensive dinner in an Italian restaurant in Brixton. 'I did feel that it was entirely fitting to be existing alone in an unknown world with Chica as the only company I felt up to.' Then, 'We discussed boys and women. She said that the way to manage women was always to ask what they would like to do and then make them do the opposite of what they said and that they regarded being thwarted and contradicted as a proof that somebody cared for them.' Chica and her friend Peggy, he reflected, were girls who had 'a real simplicity and dignity which made me proud to be their companion and I seemed to learn more from them than from anyone in Chelsea or Bloomsbury that I could be with at the time'. He saw himself living out *Sinister Street*. The passage ended, 'Chica has dark red hair, white skin in shadow, and makes love with half closed eyes.'

Bobbie Longden had not really fallen by the way, he told himself, but remained constant, and very busy with his work. 'A girl who really reminded me of Bobbie would attract me probably more than anybody has done yet.' Sexually he was governed by a principle of frustrated incest, he speculated half-seriously, having had no chance of knowing brotherly or sisterly affection.

Conventional young man that he was, he began to brood in the abstract upon marriage as the ultimate end of a relationship with a woman. At the height of the infatuation with Alex, one day he went over the arguments with the MacCarthys and Gerald Brenan, something of a Bloomsbury renegade, who had already fulfilled the ideal of finding a house in Spain, at Almuñecar, to which he could withdraw in order to write. 'Desmond said the reality was better than the idea, Molly said it was a great leap in the dark and the most romantic experiment in life. Desmond said the great thing was to marry someone who was attractive even while you hated them, he said you had to expect to be told unforgiveable things, he said it was not wise to marry early. Molly said marriage was a good institution if you could only find the proper wife. Brenan said he wished he had married at 16 and was a widower. He said he had proposed to a breadseller at Toulon last summer and been rejected. He said he would like to share everything, to darn socks with his wife while she helped with his reviews. Molly said the division as it was was equal, Desmond said the important thing to remember was that men and women were really alike though it was fatal to treat them as if they were so.'

The fact that Patrick Balfour was also claiming to be in love with a girl caused hesitations and misgivings when the moment to move into lodgings was suddenly at hand. There might be clashes, unfortunate meetings, incompatabilities. Self-respect was also involved. Was Balfour good enough for him? 'No man likes to admit that he is about to live with a fool.' Balfour was then writing gossip for the Rothermere Press and perhaps would turn into what Sligger feared, 'that hard thing, a man about town'. It was a *fait accompli*, however, for Balfour had signed the lease for 26a Yeoman's Row in Knightsbridge. 'Rather a slum and hardly more than a studio', in Cyril's eyes, but he was reconciled by its proximity to his grandmother's old house opposite, in Brompton Square. On September 1, while Balfour was momentarily away, Cyril moved in.

Pearsall Smith, who earlier had been teasing him about fleeing the country and being sure to let him know his new name as well as his new address, now wrote on September 6, 'I hope you are happier in your new house – the first settling in is always a time of discouragement.' A few days later he pretended that now he felt shy of Cyril, 'as if you were somehow a new person in your new surroundings'. With the arrival of Balfour, apprehensions subsided, and it was not long before Cyril was earning small sums by helping to write gossip paragraphs too.

Now an outright protégé and no longer even a nominal secretary, Cyril continued to receive the weekly £8 from Pearsall Smith. He lived off this allowance. Meanwhile for much of October and November he was a guest at Chilling. Pearsall Smith's nieces, Ray and Karin, were also staying there. They were the daughters of Mary Berenson and her first husband, Frank Costelloe. Both had inherited the strong family personality. Ray had married Oliver Strachey and was the mother of Barbara and Christopher. Karin had married Virginia Woolf's brother Adrian Stephen, and had two daughters, Ann and Judith. These four children were then aged between eleven and fifteen, and Pearsall Smith, 'Uncle Ogre' to them, welcomed having them in the house, though on rather strict terms. Cyril had hardly ever before been in the close company of children, and pages of his diary were devoted to his observations, as upon a new species. One afternoon, playing croquet, Ann said, 'Look at Cyril, he's given the most exquisite wonk to the elliptical ball,' whereupon he wrote that he would willingly wait seven years to marry her.

To complete the family party, the Berensons arrived. In London they were staying in Lady Horner's house. Approvingly Cyril quoted Berenson's views that Bloomsbury was a comic rebellion, a kind of dandyism compatible only with youth. When they then discussed the state of England, Berenson declared that the real danger to the country came from 'civil servants, the spirit of Keynes', and not in the least from any supposed decadence or American influence.

The people he thought he had been in love with, permanently, since the summer, comprised, 'Nancy whom I hate, Peggy who is a bore, Rachel whose shares go neither up nor down, Alex whom I have forgotten altogether, Bobbie who has become a hearty, Noel who has become a wraith, Ann who is only eleven, and now Racy, divinely English, unawakened, staid'. Highbrow women were exactly what he did not want, he decided, 'all that education does is to deprive them of their own judgement and supply them with a bigoted devotion to Bloomsbury.'

Racy, latest on the list, was Horatia Fisher, seventeen at the time, and as a rule accompanied by her sister Rosamond, otherwise Ros. Their mother, Cecilia Fisher, was the sister of Molly Mac-Carthy, to whom fell responsibility for having introduced Cyril to them in the first place. Sir William Fisher, who had commanded the Mediterranean fleet, was then at the Admiralty, and as formidable a figure as his brother the historian H. A. L. Fisher, Warden of New College, Oxford. At the time the Fishers had a house in Chelsea.

Seemingly an emanation of what he thought he was looking for, Racy replaced Alex in his imagination. He took to calling on her, to writing to her or about her, with all the single-mindedness of which he was capable when his emotions were engaged. He began to tabulate reasons for and against marriage, he exhorted himself in his diary about the need to have a steady £1,000 a year, or better still £3,000. 'How nobly one can love if one is a householder.'

Reality obtruded. 'Cecilia Fisher came to tea on Thursday: delicious, exquisite and charming. She said that she didn't believe children really began to live till their parents were dead.' To him she looked like a Maurice Baring heroine, and he made her sound like one too. 'She talked of the unhappiness of youth, and how unnecessary it seemed, how Ros and Racy were not so happy as she.' Racy had nothing wrong with her but too much vitality, and 'will be a magnificent woman at 40, she said, but it is a long time to wait'. Down to practical matters – 'Cecilia spoke of the importance of money to marriage with which I agreed. She said, "We must find you a rich wife." Molly's identical words on another occasion. They smart.'

Grown-up toleration had limits. He was asked not to call at the house, not to write letters. When he appealed to Molly MacCarthy, she sided with her sister. How-could-you letters were drafted, and one or two were sent. The greater the obstacle, the higher the ardour: no doubt he was gratified to visualise himself as victimised. Day-dream, in a word Racyitis, endured well into the new year.

At Easter 1928, he returned to the Berensons at i Tatti. In a Florence 'riddled with American bankers, snobbery, cocktails and culture', with the Winston Churchills and the Londonderrys, Mrs Otto Kahn whom he thought had an income of £1,500 a day, Laurence Binyon, Percy Lubbock, and King Edward VII's friends the Keppels and their daughter Violet Trefusis, he could still manage to inform Blakiston, in a letter of May 10 1928, that he was 'skewered by the thought of Racy'. To Balfour he was writing of the feeling 'that in losing Racy I've also lost the best part of myself. I shall never be in love so youthfully and innocently again, I feel exiled from the Edwardian world and not hard-boiled enough to fit easily into the modern. With the really smart, the really Bohemian, or the really low, one is not reminded of this respectable English Eden, which is why I choose them but the thought of Racy doing the flowers or some trivial thing which doesn't concern me is enough to shatter it all.' He ended, 'I feel like Satan only without his vitality.' Having passed through Paris on his way out to Italy, and then again on his way back, he thought he might stay there. The sense of freedom, he wrote, had gone to his head. 'I sat in a Montparnasse café in the sun and had a revelation of the joys of modest liberty, surrounded by the banks of American exiles. I should like to live in a garret with a Spanish mistress – instead I met Cecil Beaton.' A pound a day and no ties of any kind might apparently work wonders.

His first visit to Berlin followed (see Journal, page 142) and there he and Longden stayed with Harold Nicolson, then councillor at the British Embassy and always eager to welcome a presentable public-school pair of their kind. Again with Longden, Cyril returned in September to Spain, on what turned out to be the last occasion when they travelled alone together. 'I have been very happy with Bobbie,' he wrote to Balfour on September 28, 'We have had a lovely trip, never seeing anybody but Spaniards, taking photographs, bathing in rivers, sleeping in mountain villages, making absurd jokes. I dread coming back to London.'

Yeoman's Row was too expensive, he owed Balfour money for the rent and was afraid of the resentment that he might provoke. Instead, he tried to come to an arrangement to share a flat with Gladwyn Jebb (see page 174). Christmas 1928 was spent with the Sykes's at Sledmere (page 195), and early in January 1929 he crossed to Paris again, to become involved in his first real affair with a girl. Racy was dismissed from his imagination. As for the male loves which had dominated his past, in tones of some wonder he noted that they had been rendered 'hard to judge in terms of mere duration'.

12

'Nor Could The Muse Defend Her Son'

During the weeks of 'practicing death' at Chilling, Cyril had completed a short story with the title *Dies Irae*. On the Day of Judgement, Aristippus of Cyrene and Ecclesiastes and Po-Chu-I [whose poems had just been rendered into English by Arthur Waley] have risen from the dead and are having a mortal meal in the place where they happen to have foregathered, the country-house of a cultivated American long resident in Europe. They discuss the eternity now facing them. Their reflections were philosophical but the context was essentially comic. This revealed Cyril's peculiar obstacle to finding, and then maintaining, a voice of his own. His style had natural verve in it, with satire just under the surface of his observation of life, but this would never do for the highbrow he believed himself to be. What came spontaneously was not to be trusted. Art enfolded ambitions about which there could be no levity, and to do justice to them he felt obliged to put on a performance, suppressing disrespect and so covering himself from imaginary criticism.

Instead of being a young man's *tour de force*, *Dies Irae* amounted to commentary on the assorted ancient sages, proving Cyril's understanding of his reading. The manuscript bears corrections in Pearsall Smith's hand, and it was posted off to America, to *The Dial*, though it stood no chance with that modernist literary magazine.

Under the immediate Pearsall Smith influence, he completed what he called, 'The sort of book most authors end their literary careers with, a Trivia, a craftsman's handbook, a collection of tropes and felicities, few quotations, and much criticism'. Thirty to forty thousand words long, its purpose was to teach him to write for his own edification, 'a pretty hard job as a matter of fact'. Standing just over his shoulder to direct his thoughts were his modern sages, Proust, Valéry, Rimbaud. But some of the aphorisms certainly derived from his inwardly observant self.

'Enough is not as good as a feast but not enough is better.'

'The worst vice of the solitary is the worship of his food.'

'Privation determines our realities more than possessions.'

'What did you say which has made you so angry?'

In a section with the heading 'Certain Aims in Life Discussed', an inquiry into 'Pleasure' contained the sentence, 'one has to admit that most people who are out for a good time usually succeed in getting it.' As for 'Ecstasy':

> 'All moody and emotional people must live from thrill to thrill, golden moment to moment – this is Aristippus as opposed to Epicurus. Here the difficulty is bridging the gulf from one thrill to another when the most appalling reactions are bound to ensue, unless a high standard of comfort and content is maintained. This rather artistic attitude to life is wholly incapable of supporting any ethical system whatever, and is likely to lead to dangerous sensation hunting. Sensuality is moreover the easiest form of ecstasy, which must be hard put to it to define what thrill is permissible and what is not, unless it supposes that all are.'

But the vitality with which to maintain pagan thrills and inclinations was deficient. Fifteen more years as a sensation hunter were required before this trial run could emerge in an adult form of self-expression as *The Unquiet Grave*.

A more sustained piece of writing among his juvenilia was the Guide Book to the Balkans. He completed it while staying at Chiostro di San Martino with the Clarks and grandiloquently signed off on the last page, 'midnight. 28.3.27'. The original was then presented to Longden, who took it away with him from Florence, consulted it while in the Balkans, and after his return to Oxford, had it typed out. Only the final five pages of the carbon copy appear to have survived. In them, the figure of a traveller is described in the third person, a traveller idealised for the quickness of his responses and the range of his sentiments. In Vienna, at the conclusion of his tour, for instance, 'Here he can still set his watch by Central Europe, and feel, though no longer in the Balkans, that they loom very near him and perpetually are cropping up in a waiter's speech or a dancer's face in a cabaret and here he can go through his impoverished accounts, which is a great pleasure for the traveller and kills time better than any other expedient, and here he can remember his accomplished journey and give prizes for the best sunsets, the best beggars, the best landscapes, the best statues, the best acquaintances, moments and meals.' Consummating this rather orthodox prize essay, quotations in Greek, Latin, Italian and French come crowding one upon the other.

For a while he polished it, and then on August 9 1927 posted it off to David Garnett, who was the only publisher whose address he remembered, he noted in his diary, no doubt to keep up his courage. The novel *Lady into Fox* had already made Garnett a well-known author, and he was also a director, with Francis Meynell, of the Nonesuch Press, which carried great prestige. Friends need have no expectations, Cyril continued in his diary, he could not be bothered any longer with the book. 'If it is rejected, I shall most certainly continue to forget it and it is well to take a pen and stop one of these earths of the wary mind. It deserves to be rejected as I see its imperfections and can not bother to correct them. Once one is tired of a thing one cares not where it is, so long as it is out of sight.'

Had he read the comment, Pearsall Smith would not have approved. He and Cyril were at that moment bothering hard to refine a paralysing sentence, 'Writing, if not actually a disease, is, of all forms of incontinence, the most degrading.' Neither of them believed anything of the kind, needless to say; indeed the aphorism contains concealed pride in the writer's craft, and its purpose was to ward off guilt about not writing more incontinently. Pearsall Smith's pernickety perfectionism was an inhibiting example for Cyril at a moment when he had to acquire confidence and endurance – MacCarthy's inability to deliver was a comparable caution, too close for comfort, that literary impulse was easily diverted into neurosis. Both older men were failed novelists, and more generous energies and application were required if Cyril was to succeed. He had meanwhile picked up his historical novel about ancient Greece, only to drop it again, this time finally.

Instead, a contemporary theme emerged erratically. 'Thought of a novel which would begin with the hero in a waiting-room of Gabbitas and Thring. A good subject for a cynically dreary introduction but it would have to be rather a flippant book.' *Green Endings*, as this novel was to be called, was melodrama, if anything. Sent to the colonies, its young hero was to escape by pushing someone off the rocks at Gibraltar. Mistakenly assuming that he was wanted for murder, he would work his passage to Spain, to Almuñecar, for a romantic affair. Back in London, in Brixton, he would confront his friends. Somehow the General Strike was to provide a conclusion.

Really beginning to write the novel, he found that 'it is a fine repository for spleen and epigrams can hide their heads more modestly among its verbiage. My hero is a wild unhappy boy but behaves like a Michael Arlen young man on paper, so strongly do all the characters run away with me. I doubt if I shall ever finish it or get the parts to hang together. It is humiliating to have to borrow real characters or utilise real situations but how subsequently unreal they become if one tries to invent them. It is really a grotesque daydream nightmare of my own experience in the lean years.' What he could not manage, he perceived, was the invention of a plot. Exploration of his ego and all its works interested him far more. The wild unhappy boy existed only as a form of self-flattery.

Floundering with *Green Endings*, he received a letter dated August 11, from David Garnett, about the Guide Book to the Balkans. Only forty-eight hours had elapsed since the typescript had been posted off, but here already was the news that Garnett was delighted with it and wanted to send it on to Francis Meynell, then away in Dalmatia. 'This I suppose is success,' ran Cyril's diary entry. 'Exuberance at breakfast, then a reaction and since then a vague disturbing satisfaction working under ground.' Immediately Pearsall Smith was 'happy about the whole thing and prophesying fame and money'.

Literary journalism was opening up simultaneously. Cyril's first signed appearance in print had been in the *New Statesman*, on June 25 1927, when he wrote an article on an edition in seven volumes of the works of Laurence Sterne. Now he was invited to become one of the magazine's regular novel reviewers – MacCarthy's letter with the offer capped the first flush of Garnett's praise by arriving in the very next post, on August 12. 'A signed review once a fortnight,' Cyril informed Balfour, with the rent of Yeoman's Row on his mind, 'so now I feel more financially secure. It means I shall have at least £10 a week and some kind of established job which is more important as I don't get much for doing the novels, though of course one can sell them.' While accepting happily, he foresaw rocks ahead, namely that he was too highbrow, likely to be unpunctual and unreliable, and would now have to take pains to keep the friendship of Peter Quennell, potentially a rival man of letters.

A second more expansive letter from Garnett discussed what ought to be done about the Balkans book. 'The fact is that I am tremendously enthusiastic about it: I want to "hail your genius" as the Russians say. I adore the book: I think you are an enchanting, most amusing and very good writer and I want to publish the book.' One of the partners (the only others were Francis and Vera Meynell) was against it, however. A further opinion would have to be sought. If necessary, Garnett undertook to find another publisher. Raising his spirits in his diary, Cyril observed, 'I feel literary power running through me like sap all this August in a way it has never done before.'

Negotiations about the book bogged down. Cyril approached Anthony Powell, who was then on the editorial staff of Duckworth's, with a request to read the manuscript. Powell, according to his memoirs *Infants of the Spring*, had already read 'with a view to publication' the collection of aphorisms, or Commonplace Book, which Cyril had put together to teach himself how to write. From Yeoman's Row he now wrote to Powell, 'Perhaps you could come to a meal next week and take it away with you, if you still want to look at it. I haven't heard from the Nonesuch yet. Would a kind of essay, pamphlet length, on the Future of Travel be any good to you? I have one I thought of doing but did not finish and in my present state of hating fiction – it looks the kind of thing I could do.'

Powell replied on November 30 that not much could be done with the manuscript as it stood. The length was all wrong. He liked passages about sulking, traveller's loneliness, friendship and so on, and felt that Cyril was to be congratulated because the Nonesuch Press was taking on the book – that was the one firm which would get away with it with ease.

In December Garnett at last sent a contract, but also mentioned alterations which were to be made to the manuscript. Probably these were never done; the advance for £30 did not arrive until more than a year later, February 11 1929. Garnett's genius-hailing tone had altered by then. 'We are in no great hurry to publish,' he wrote, and suggested that perhaps it might prove tactically better if Cyril completed a novel which could precede the Balkans book. The advance was 'on the Guide *or* the first book we publish'.

Reviewing, Cyril quickly suspected, was opportunity and hindrance; it restricted even as it launched. In his diary he analysed the several kinds of writing open to him. First, pot-boiling, which he dismissed, and secondly journalism, which exercised the mind and got rid of the recurring need to be competent and adaptable. Finally, writing proper, 'the expression of oneself for oneself with one eye on posterity and the other on old age. This includes all that is written from the desire to create beauty or to discover truth, to preserve the moment or destroy one's troubles, to perpetuate one's ideas and sensations and also to explain them and to give one's best to one's friends.' Few literary projects, and certainly not *Green Endings*, could make headway in the face of definitions like those.

Nor did the schema allow for the kind of writing which came spontaneously. Take this extended passage in his diary – he was pleased to copy it out with minor revisions in a giving-one's-best letter to Balfour, dated May 31 1927. 'I asked Hope Mirlees if she liked a book (I think it was *The Constant Nymph*) and she said, "Dionysiacally, yes, but of course Apolloniacally, no" – "Of course." Or else I say I would rather read a new E. M. Forster than a new novel by anyone else. "Well of course I'm awfully fond of poor Morgan, but I must say I've never managed to finish one of his books." "I agree, he describes people but he can't manage places" etc – "Yes, and poor Bunny (everyone is poor in Bloomsbury) he describes places, but he can't manage people. I thought *Go She Must* . . . George Moore . . . *Lady into Fox* so chichi . . . like a German film . . . like a bull-fight – like *The American Tragedy* – like what poor Virginia is trying to do but fails." "Like what poor Lytton succeeded in doing and failed." "Like what Arthur says Sashie is failing to do but succeeds, like Greek –" "I don't know Greek." "Like *Greek Street* I was going to say." "O was that a good book, I never read it." "It was, but of course it isn't now, of course." "Of course of course of course. Courses and horses. Corps Houses. Horses and houses, and truly what I minded most." "I don't like books, old ones are so dirty and new ones smell." "Well what do you like then?" "I like Latin." "I don't know Latin." "I never thought you did. But you are a Nervalian too?" "Of course!" "Of course of of of of course." "I liked his first book but of course the publishers got hold of him. The priests got hold of him. The Sitwells, Lady Colefax, the critics, the Stracheys, the Dictionary of National Biography got hold of him, and so of course his second." "Of what?" "I said, Of course." "Well, it doesn't matter how they do it as long as they fail." "Or how they fail as long as they do it." "And if it is any good it will blow over –" "Of course." '

A comedy of manners, a *Decline and Fall* of his own, lay in virtuosity of the kind – but for it he would have needed what Waugh had, the confidence to let himself go, and not mind what was said. Reviewing might be the occasion for a turn but all the same justice had to be done to the books under review – in the end what set him apart from other reviewers was the way he reconciled creative and critical demands. To someone of his academic background, however, the whole process of reviewing was instinctively not quite respectable; people like him were not supposed to wander off into Grub Street. As the inexperienced do, he played safe, at first presenting his opinions stiffly and correctly enough to win the approval of any imaginary professor who might wag a finger.

In the long May 31 letter to Balfour he had also said, 'I agree with you that critics are awful but I feel now that everyone goes off the rails when they talk of books, myself included. Usually because they hate to feel that anybody else has written a good book (if they write) or else from party loyalty (the Sitwell dependents) or else from perversity.' Those were the observations of a novelist at heart, drawing attention to the envy and vanity which the critic conceals in his response. Practice developed personality. In the event, reviewing was not a banal exercise in banality and adaptability, but a process of self-realisation.

From September 1927 until October 1929, with infrequent interruptions, he published his fortnightly piece. Wyndham Lewis, Paul Morand, Ford Madox Ford, Hemingway, Dreiser, Rose Macaulay, Elizabeth Bowen, Godfrey Winn, sped down the mill-race. 'There is no tragedy like that of the unintentional best-seller. The early worshippers have left in a body – rats indignant to remain on so unsinkable a ship.' Through such images, the prose became less conventional and more in tune with the way that he was actually thinking and talking. He was picking his way. 'Mr Galsworthy and Mr Walpole are borne down the stream of time, humped anxiously on slabs of property like Eskimo dogs marooned by the thaw on crumbling pack-ice.' E. M. Forster's *The Eternal Moment* was 'full of that demure malice with which the author delights to punish the *bonne élève*'. And, closer to his own experience, 'To write an autobiographical novel is to live on capital, hence only permissible when, like Proust, you know you will not live to write about anything else.'

The Well of Loneliness, Radcliffe Hall's lesbian novel published in August 1928, involved him in controversy. He did not think much of the book but opposed attempts to have it banned. 'The world is perfectly prepared to tolerate the invert, if the invert will only make concessions to the world. Most of us are resigned to the doctrines of homosexuals, that they alone possess all the greatest heroes and all the finer feelings, but it is surely preposterous that they should claim a right, not only to the mark of Cain, but to the martyr's crown.' He continued, 'Homosexuality is, after all, as rich in comedy as in tragedy.'

New books discussed in the column of November 3 1928 included Thomas Mann's *Death in Venice* and Gide's *Lafcadio's Adventures*, as well as two first novels, Harold Acton's *Humdrum* and Waugh's *Decline and Fall*. Setting these last two off against each other, he disparaged Acton the better to praise Waugh for possessing the comic spirit. The critic was grateful for *Decline and Fall*: 'Not a great book, it is a funny book, and the only one that, professionally, he has ever read twice.' Alike in subject matter, but not in style, both novels were rake's progresses of the kind which might have materialised from the ruins of *Green Endings*.

'I am too soft for journalism, too rough for literature.' No doubt he swayed himself with such face-saving formulae when putting them down in his diary, clever at rationalising whatever he wanted to do, and more particularly whatever he did not want to do. Hardly had he discovered Waugh than he was deciding that the English novel was without hope. Dealing with a monster batch of eleven, on February 23 1929, he wrote, 'These books have finished the reviewer — more than he could do for them.'

A farewell to his column, with the title *Ninety Years of Novel Reviewing*, was published in August 1929. The average work of fiction had seemed insupportably mediocre. To make the point, he fantasised Miss Bumfiddle's new *Goosegrass or Cleavers*, with its heroine the beautiful Alimony, and upon it two critics, Tenderfoot and Goo-Goo, expend the full range of cliché. (Over the years a deadly library could have been collected of similar works, for instance those by Hedda Bedales 'five foot ten and a half in her hikers', Miss H. K. Boot's *With Gourd and Gherkin* and *A Weeny Tour in France*, Jenkins's *Cauliflower Ear*, or Christian de Clavering's *From Oscar to Stalin, A Progress*. Also *Flittershins*, *Ramshackle Roger, Armed October, Open The Sky, Fifty Years Down Under*, not to mention the Crutch Foundation with its award of 'The Forgotten Man Prize' and 'The Troubleday Trophy'. *Enemies of Promise* introduced Mr Vampire of *The Blue Bugloss* and Walter Savage Shelleyblake, author of *Vernal Aires*, and *Backstairs and Petticoats*, a chronicle of famous Royal mistresses.) Parody had its serious purpose. 'Like the King at Nemi, the slayer shall himself be slain. Brave and agile, the reviewer enters the ring. He rushes blindly at the red wrappers. He disembowels a few old hacks. But his onsets eventually grow futile, his weapons are blunted, his words are stale . . . eventually the jungle claims him.' The world-weariness was affected. His true voice had been heard in public for the first time, in spite of as well as because of, the despised reviewing.

He hoped to write longer articles for the *New Statesman*, he was in correspondence with its editor Clifford Sharp, he might become its theatre critic. A publisher proposed that he write a book about the state of fiction. *Life and Letters* had been launched in June 1928, with Oliver Brett (later Lord Esher) as its sponsor, and Desmond MacCarthy as its editor. A barley-water magazine, in Cyril's opinion, but he contributed several essays and reviews, in one of which was this paragraph concerning men of letters. 'Trained from their birth to festoon the world with verbiage, to delay, to decorate, to scheme and windify over the reputations which they exist to celebrate, these armchaired adventurers, with their arch humour, their quaint, apologetic egoism, their eminence socially and academically, each in his own right a gentleman and a gasbag, have gone down before the modern spirit and divided their mantle between the professor and the Sunday journalist.' Not the prose of someone closing his eyes to what lay about him.

In August 1928 MacCarthy had been appointed to succeed Sir Edmund Gosse as the leading reviewer on the *Sunday Times*, and he therefore left the *New Statesman*. Soon afterwards he wrote Cyril a letter accusing him of being an opportunist and a sponger. Quite what had provoked him is now obscure, but it may have been something quite as small as the failure to pay a laundry bill at Chilling. The original letter, unsparing, but apparently not preserved, was followed by another which began, 'I lay awake last night thinking of the pain and worry my letter may have caused you.' He tried to sound reassuring. 'You have no idea how quickly the attitude of gossips will change if you determine upon independence and guard against those habits into which fascinating hard-up people slip. And out of your wounds and your capacity for enjoyment will come something which will lead to triumphant recognition – sooner or later. You have got the intellectual daring necessary as well as the indispensable power of perception. I believe in you, and I don't readily believe in people's gifts.' The schoolmasterly tactic of rubbing blame in by apparently withdrawing it suggested that to a considerable extent his heart might not have been in the rebuke.

The letter, Cyril acknowledged, had made him go hot and cold. 'I'm not as bad as you make out – I'm not a scheming cadger, but as to being an *opportunist* one you are painfully right. I'm not disloyal about my friends either, within the margin that conversation allows. I have had a *pariah* sense in a way ever since the Fisher incident last year, a feeling of being a Cain at war with respectable people.' The failure of the MacCarthys to support his suit to Racy had embittered him; he was only just getting over the old-fashioned idea that women were either angels or tarts. Nor could he fit into smart Bohemia. To the MacCarthys he must have seemed 'a house-rat, a life-sponger'. He went on, 'As you say, I like and need affection and admiration, and yet I am always trying to wound others, polemically, while remaining infinitely vulnerable myself. As to my vulgar streak I agree it is inopportune to indulge it now, when I am poor, but on the whole I think it is valuable, there is so much unexploited beauty in sheer hedonism.'

Another good reason for breaking off literary journalism was that during the course of visiting Paris in 1929 he had fallen in love, and naturally he wanted to stay on there – an arrangement considered impractical by the *New Statesman*. To Balfour, he said that Yeoman's Row had now definitely become too expensive. To Pearsall Smith he reiterated that Paris was the one place where he was sure he could write. Pearsall Smith encouraged him to go. While in Paris, Cyril arranged to collect his weekly allowance of £8 at Shakespear and Company, the famous bookshop run by Sylvia Beach (through whom he met James Joyce, see page 203). Appeals to Pearsall Smith, some of them comically desperate and undoubtedly sponging, arrived from the Joe Congothly figure who had made himself out to be such an irrepressible spendthrift. Pearsall Smith never faltered, not even after August 1929, when he began to mention regularly that he himself was getting into low financial water because of the crash on the stock-markets. He objected to outright loans, but not to advancing future weekly payments in a lump sum. This was in recognition of his expectations. 'You seem to be the one person who can express the modern sensibility – the ways of feeling of your generation – and when you have a book to publish you will have a delightful success,' he wrote. In 1930 he was advising an American editor that three new stars had appeared on the horizon, David Cecil, Kenneth Clark and Connolly, 'the latter the most gifted and original of the three'.

In Paris, in the course of 1929, Cyril began another attempt at fiction, his Alpdodger story, referred to in his journal (page 175). As though it were factual, and not wishful thinking, he jotted down on the inside cover of the notebook, 'A novel which, with all the faults of a first book, is greeted with all the indifference due to a second.' Alpdodger was variously described as 'the first casual passer-by', 'a charlatan whose very charlatanism may only be a perfect disguise for genius', holder of 'a lecturership in eurhythmics in Arsover College', and 'Alpdodger *roi de Perse, esclave des tyrans*'. The only life that Alpdodger cared to recapitulate was the artist's life in Paris, saying of himself, with pride and not the least shame, 'I know simply that a life of definite and studied materialism and a philosophy of appetite and cynicism, and a cult of sensual and senseless ease, are bad things for an artist. They narrow the imagination and dull the more delicate sensibilities. I was all wrong, my dear boy, in my life, I was not getting the best out of me.' Once again, there was nothing to plot except mood, and eventually this notebook too petered out in static self-preoccupation.

When another publisher, Wren Howard, a partner of Jonathan Cape, came over to Paris in October 1929, with the aspiration of prising out the Alpdodger novel, or any other work of fiction, Cyril fell back on the contract with the Nonesuch Press. Garnett then wondered what was happening, and Cyril wrote him a long letter full of exculpation. The novel was not progressing because he was too lazy, he could not think ahead enough for ultimate reward. He wanted to be obliged to show up instalments once a month, and to be paid serially. 'Unless someone stood over me I'd always put off going on with my novel. You seem to think that I have a fully fledged novel which I'm trying to dodge you with – all I have is a fragment of a novel which I want someone to make me go on with.' It was no good, he complained, leaving gracefully alone someone who wanted a slave-driver.

13

The Birds of America

Jean Bakewell was eighteen when Cyril fell in love with her. American, attractive, slim, enrolled in an art-school in Paris, and sometimes even attending its classes, she was in a number of ways a freer spirit than he was. In spite of her youth, her experience of life had been wider and more varied. The Twenties were on the turn, and her emancipation led to his.

His journal, between pages 210 and 221, describes the emotional impact of Jean upon him, amounting to a complete change of direction after the long series of adolescent crushes. Jean did not fit into the sort of relationships he had hitherto fantasised, she could not be typecast just as a Dark Friend. Immediately he had recognised her as someone he might marry.

Until he had met Jean, he had fallen in love with people as though he were visiting places in which to set himself off. Thinking of himself as 'the most unlovable mug in England', he could hardly credit that he had succeeded in winning the love of someone with such American glamour and the chance to pick and choose as she liked. In his mind, everything connected with his affair turned legendary as soon as it had occurred. At least it was consistent with the old self to be sacramentalising every scrap of his experience, losing no time in the conversion of life into literature.

There was no real wish to keep the record as such. What was safely stored up in the journal was raw material for the future study of the strongest emotion he had ever known. So he interposed questionnaires, and drew up calendars of events, and provided other so-called documents. Once the emotions had been garnered in, and had become a firm basis, he luxuriated far too much in them ever to be bothered to give them the fresh shape of a novel or a memoir. 'I believe in Montparnasse, in the Kingdom of Harlem, in the voices of infants singing in the Coupole' – the Alpdodger story also grew into a love rhapsody of the kind, until it ran parallel with the journal, even merging when Jean copied into the Alpdodger notebook correspondence of her own. At that point the fiction was abandoned, as though to prove how much of life will not in fact convert into literature. (In 1968 Cyril wondered whether a successor to *Enemies of Promise* might not be extracted from the journal and the Alpdodger notebook. There comes back to me a conversation with him from that time – did I not realise what it had meant to be young and English, in the Paris of the surrealists and in love? It had completed his formation. But all he then did was to add a few annotations to the journal.)

Possessiveness gripped him. He wished he had known Jean earlier – 'I could have foreshadowed a biggish chunk of Jean's past.' He could not know enough about what she had been up to before they met. The Bakewells were possibly distant relations, for they descended from Derbyshire Bakewells who had emigrated early in the eighteenth century to settle on the Pennsylvania–Ohio border. In response, Noel Blakiston, then employed in the Public Record Office, was to be asked to look into family antecedents; in response, Matthew Connolly was to copy the Bakewell family tree into the pedigree album which he kept.

Jean, her younger sister Anne and lastly her brother Tom, had been born in Pittsburgh, where the Bakewells had built the first skyscraper, eleven stories high in brownstone, as well as the first glass factory in America. Until 1918, when her parents divorced, Jean's childhood had been spent in Pittsburgh. Then the three children accompanied their mother, first to New York, later to Pasadena on the West Coast. Their mother, born Gertrude Logan Paxton (with Quaker connections, and distantly related to Logan Pearsall Smith), gave them a jazz-age background in which ease of life was almost inseparable from instability – originally the Paxtons had made a fortune from business and banking in Wheeling, West Virginia. In 1920, when Jean was ten, her mother settled in West Chester, 'at the end of the Main Line from Philadelphia', as Jean put it in a fragmentary diary written for Cyril's benefit and amusement. With the exception of the popular novelist Joseph Hergesheimer, and a local literary critic with the name of Sidney Williams, 'Mother's friends were mostly gay young sparks.' Mother and a friend, Jean also wrote, 'were suffragettes in a giggling sort of way and for the cause gave teas in smart hotels and wore trousers and rode on tractors in farmerette parades'. In West Chester she married again. Her second husband, Daniel List Warner, came from Baltimore, but his family was also from Wheeling, West Virginia. Together they built a house at Woodbrook, in attractive country between Baltimore and Wilmington. Meanwhile Jean's father, William Bakewell, was more interested in golf and fast cars than in his children. The Depression hit him hard. He died in 1932.

Pleading her artistic gifts, Jean was allowed to leave school early and to go to Paris for the first time in 1927. Nominally she was in the charge of a favourite aunt, and she was accompanied by Mara Andrews, a close friend of her own age, from Baltimore. Through Mara, Cyril met Jean (page 213). Jean apparently wasted no time before proclaiming that she and Mara were lesbians. To judge from his reaction, Cyril seems to have been credulous, not to say gullible. Perhaps it appealed to him to let his imagination rip; perhaps the idea that he might be seducing a lesbian consummated the adventure of Paris. And perhaps Mara and Jean enjoyed keeping suitors at bay by means of this diverting exaggeration.

Mara and Jean had shared a flat in the rue de Vaugirard for some months. Their friends included a number of other American girls with similar East Coast backgrounds, some of whom are mentioned in the journal, Helen Ashbury, Annie Gordon Boyce, Connie Gill, Elizabeth Marshall.[1] As a rule they were escorted by parents, and what distinguished Mara and Jean from them was the lack of serious chaperones. They had some pretext of being educated, or presented in European society as debutantes. Like Jean, Mara attended the Colorassi art school nearby, in the rue de la Grande Chaumière. According to Jean's sister, Anne Davis,[2] 'Mara was very ugly, I can see the lesbian angle, she looked like a bullfrog, and had a brilliant mind.' A certain number of letters from Mara to Jean were preserved by Cyril, and they are written in a forceful and entertaining style all their own. Mara and Jean cultivated an up-to-the-minute slang vocabulary. Zippers had just been invented; they wore dresses which zipped up at the back, and so called themselves 'Zipplings'. Men who made passes or were otherwise a nuisance were known as 'butter-and-eggy'. There were scores of them. One night, for instance, it was the turn of Ford Madox Ford,

---

[1] In the words of Alpdodger, 'No social history, I suppose, will find them sufficiently important, those American girls who studied art in Paris for the ten years after the war. Yet their effect on those who knew them was incalculable. These frank, generous, confident beings, economically independent, socially free, had when their youth and beauty was also taken into account, a kind of Amazonian splendour for the male population.'

[2] In an interview.

who 'very drunk, which I soon learned to be his usual state, asked every minute, "Did you ever have a British author in love with you my dear?" He is old and fat and mumbly.'

Maurice, the Count, 'ze Baron', an Italian duke, an attaché from the Czech embassy, white Russians with names like Vladimir Youlgaroff, Swedes with names like Michel Werbloff, and Dodo, Schwenkie, Binx, Mr and Mrs Glück, Paul Hinricks, Abraham Eisenbach – the Mara-Jean circle might have stepped straight from the pages of Scott Fitzgerald. Here was the free and easy population of the Latin Quarter, expatriates mostly, but not exclusively, and either amateurs or bohemians who could well afford to try their hand at the arts, or else professionals who did not expect to be recognised, and occasionally did not even care.

Among the latter was Alfred Perlès, known by the diminutive Fredl. Born in Vienna in 1897, he had been living in Paris since 1920, writing, earning a living by contributing to the Paris edition of the *Chicago Tribune*. One companion of his was Brassai, the photographer from Transylvania, and another was Henry Miller, who in his novels was later to romanticise this Paris atmosphere; also a Hungarian painter, Lajos Tihany, as well as a Roumanian surrealist Gregor Michonze (see page 203). Perlès had a small appartment in the rue Delambre, behind the Dôme, in which café he had probably met Mara. In letters to Jean (which were incorporated into the Alpdodger story), Mara was constantly confiding the latest state of what she called 'Marafredl Inc'. In the opinion of Perlès,[1] there was nothing lesbian about either Mara or Jean. The *Herald Tribune* went so far as to print the news of his engagement to Mara, in a gossipy paragraph about the well-known novelist and the dashing art student, with Miss Jean Bakewell expecting to be their bridesmaid. But this was merely the aftermath of a studio party which had got out of hand.

Describing a long romantic walk with Fredl through the Luxembourg Gardens one night, Mara portrayed herself through a new word, 'boyle', which 'is derived from girl and boy, and signifies, not a lesbian, but a girl who is boyish in a Zippling way, and comports herself as "a gentleman among women". It is a noble title to be worn with pride. So since I was elevated to a "boyle" I have worn only a

---

[1] In an interview. He also said, 'Pointlessly but pleasantly we enjoyed ourselves without being any good at enjoyment.' An autobiographical novel of his, *The Renegade*, captures the whole scene.

dark blue beret, striped sweater, dark blue shirt and coat, and carried a cane, shown no hair about the ears, taken my gin like a man, and become once more famous in Montparnasse, though only on Friday and Saturday nights. Boylishness belongs to the era of the "Trois et As" bar, in the rue de Tournon, which you do not know, and consequently can scarcely realise the greatness of your loss. It is wonderful, beautiful, bawdy, perfect. It is frequented by Donald Duff, now one of my dearest cronies, and by Julius before he got off for Cherbourg and his fairy lover. The barman is Jimmie, the Great[1], of the Parness and the Dingo. The gin fizzes are better than the Vikings'. The music is the Hawaian trio that played at the Académie Moderne ball. Figure it out for yourself. In my character of boyle I can only frequent bars, so Fredl and I, with any boon companions that happen along, always sit at the bar for our bracers, and life is joyous.'

Jimmy and Bubbles Gessner (page 215), as we shall call them, were a young couple with a flat in Paris and a house in Villefranche. Gessner had inherited a great deal of money from a family business in America, and he indulged his wish to be an artist. In the year before she met Cyril, Jean had had an affair with Gessner. Subsequently she had another affair with a Frenchman, and he had made her pregnant, apparently having designs to marry her for the sake of her money. When first she met Cyril, Jean was in the early weeks of this pregnancy, and feeling sick. She was also planning to have a backstreet abortion – it cost her five hundred francs (all of which Cyril records by way of 'additional information', pages 214 and 216).

In February and again in April 1929, Cyril and Jean went on journeys to some of his favourite haunts in the Mediterranean, in Spain especially. In Corsica, that Easter, they met up with Peter Quennell[2] and his first wife Nancy Stallybrass. On May 11, Jean sailed from Le Havre to go home, on the understanding that she would return in the autumn to live in Paris with Cyril, and possibly to marry him. Soon after her arrival at Woodbrook, she developed appendicitis and had to have an emergency operation.

---

[1] Jimmie Charters. For more about him, the 'Trois et As' and other bars, see his memoirs, *This Must Be The Place*, (1934), with an introduction by Hemingway.

[2] In an interview Quennell recalled, 'Cyril turned up with this sulky little girl, swarthy, not awfully *soignée*.' But he liked her. The bill for a mistakenly expensive meal caused a scene, and there was some embarrassment when on a beach Jean stripped naked for a swim.

Cyril meanwhile had set off to Berlin, for a second but even less satisfactory stay with Harold Nicolson (page 207). There, at the British Embassy, he picked up a letter from his mother about Jean, saying that in a novel 'you could not believe such a romance could be real'. If they both liked The Lock House, something could be arranged. She continued, dampeningly, 'You must remember you can never expect to get the same as you felt for Racy again. It is like your first glimpse of the tropics – even much more beautiful places can't stir you the same way.' She wondered whether perhaps Pearsall Smith or one of his friends might not give him money to go straight out to America.

At Chilling for the rest of the summer, Cyril prevaricated. He wanted Jean as she was, but he also wanted her to be different. In the way he had done with Longden and others, he tried to incorporate her past as completely as possible into the present, as it were colonising everything about her. Recovering from her operation in hospital, she wrote him a long letter, dated July 11, in reply to his self-centred approach. She was sorry if he felt jealous, she began, but he was making out that her affairs had been 'serious and shabby lapses', although she had not known him at the time. Regret was not the same as shame. 'There are people no doubt who consider you a mistake, who will consider you even more of a one if by chance we don't marry, but do you think I will regret having known you?' She did not criticise his affairs. 'The very quality which made me go off unhesitatingly with you once I decided I wanted to, annoys you in me. Be logical darling, though I love you so much now, in the beginning you weren't an enormous exception.' In any case, 'I'd rather have my own mess than anybody else's perfection.'

On August 6 Cyril rehearsed his hesitations to Balfour. He thought he would marry in the following spring, but 'I wish I felt surer of myself, most of the time I feel in love but when the actual fuss of getting married crops up in any form I feel a sinking feeling, half trapped and half terror at being talked over and disapproved of.' Home truths mixed with the usual worries. 'The trouble with Jean is that we have all our faults in common, laziness, love of pleasure, extravagance, fondness for good food and drink, for travel, low life, long baths, etc. She would never "run" me – but I don't think now that I would ever suffer being run. And as she says, she can never look reassuring to English women, though good with buggers and men. I think we would live out of England till her grandmother dies and we should have enough money to hold our own in it. I hate the little London ménages, the Waughs, Murrays, Quennells type of existence, there is something so mousy about them. Also Paris is rather Jean's setting, she knows a good many French people and is fond of bummeling [i.e. 'going around and about' in idiomatic German] and can go on with her painting. I don't think she will ever paint really well but she is good at rather amusing drawings . . . if you feel that it would be disastrous for us to marry you must tell me so. We both at present are rather lacking in domesticity . . . gusto with one's friends I still feel to be the nicest thing in life. Still, marriage for me will be the best way to continue with it.'

In favour of Jean was that she had no feelings about homosexuality, and 'she's really a very intelligent and talented young girl, able to dress and with considerable sex appeal, a lot of other nice qualities and very much in love with me.' They would not be poor. 'I had no idea she was rich when I fell in love with her, but I can't be sure how much the thought that she will one day have £15,000 a year may have influenced me since, or else I think it may be only randiness.'

Sailing from New York on August 29, Jean was reunited with Cyril a week later in Paris. How to be discreet had already been much discussed. In the event Cyril made his headquarters on the Left Bank, in the Hotel de la Louisiane, while Jean stayed there or with friends, including Mara, who was living with relations. They visited England, and – accompanied by Mara – the Riviera.

To Desmond MacCarthy Cyril wrote a long self-justification, posted from the Hotel de la Louisiane on October 29 (on page 238 he talks about himself in the same way). 'Obscure, bookish, independent and wintry – I don't think anybody can accuse me of sponging, for I never meet them.' He and Jean had bought four ferrets as pets. They were looking forward to getting married but not to settling down. His mother was in Paris and she approved of Jean. 'Don't say I'm engaged in such a way as will let me in for letters of congratulations. All the pirate gang of London buggers will probably be malicious about it, headed by Maurice Bowra I should think, but with luck I shan't come across them, and though I'm not marrying for money at all they will be right in so far as I couldn't possibly marry without it . . . if I am to marry it's so much better that I should marry someone as literary and bohemian as myself instead of a cultivated English rose who'd gentlemanise me into nothing or else drive me into exile by the correctness of her family.'

Pearsall Smith would object, he thought. 'You know I'm really devoted to Logan, far fonder of him than of my parents.' The allowance would be cut off nonetheless. 'He's taught me enormously how to understand life – but he's sure to feel that I am denying him by marrying even though he feels that I'm unhappy without marrying someone – I can't help being more human than he is in that way.'

What with the crash on Wall Street, Pearsall Smith might have been obliged to stop his weekly subsidy anyhow. And the marriage had his blessing: 'That you won't have to support her is an added piece of luck.' On January 21 1930 Pearsall Smith was commenting: 'It is odd to think that you will so soon be going to America. You may like it – people do at first. It is only after a while that the dreadful monotony and meaninglessness of it all begins to depress you.' Ten days later he hoped that Cyril would write about his American experiences. 'The blacker the picture, the more I shall like it.'

Cyril and Jean sailed tourist-class on a German liner, the *Bremen*, at the end of February. With them was the sea-sick ferret, Rose of England ('who performed her cycle of eating, playing, sleeping and relieving herself and who saw three continents from a warm sleeve' – *The Unquiet Grave*). H. L. Mencken, then at the height of his reputation as a journalist and publicist, invited them up to the first class, because he was a friend of Jean's mother and more particularly of her stepfather, List Warner.

Five weeks had to elapse before the wedding. Cyril stayed at Woodbrook. List Warner introduced him to the exclusive Baltimore Club (of which Mencken was also a member), and it was from there, on March 3, that he wrote to Balfour to say that he liked Jean's family, her mother was amusing and cultivated, and her sister Anne was a sweet American rose. Their house was in the middle of beech woods on the shore of a lake. 'It has lovely furniture, pictures etc which we spend our time surreptitiously valuing.'

Though the letter conveyed novelty and excitement, he claimed to be bored but comfortable. 'I have my own bathroom, and Jean and I our own car and chauffeur, an electric laundry in the house washes all one's clothes as they get dirty and drink flows everywhere. The food is excellent – but no conversation, no intelligence of any kind except at bridge possibly.' Jean would have a fabulous trousseau and £1,000 a year to live on. The Bakewells sounded richer and richer, he said, but he and Jean hardly dared to hope for anything from that side of the family. He thought it showed admirable courage on Jean's part to give up a good time at home in order to live with him in Paris on the money they would have. 'We find the absurd conventionality of being engaged rather refreshing.'

Quite as conventionally, he felt that he ought to express the kind of opinions about America which would win the approval of Pearsall Smith. He and Jean swore that they would not be returning there in the future. For the wedding, which was on April 5, he asked an old Colleger, H. M. O'Connor, to come from New York to be best man – 'a martyr since the world began', Cyril had described O'Connor in an Eton notebook ten years earlier.

For Blakiston's benefit, he put down with bravado what had been achieved by marrying. 'I came to America tourist Third with a cheque for ten pounds and I leave plus five hundred, a wife, a mandarin coat, a set of diamond studs, a state room and bath, and a decent box for the ferret. That's what everybody comes to America to do and I don't think I've managed badly for a beginner.'

This tally had a complexion of insecurity. Even bragging had self-criticism in it. Jean had not been married for her money, but she could facilitate intoxicating day-dreams, so long as he could trust himself to love her. Only a short year before he had met her, he had written, 'I believe one loves the first woman one thinks of after one has loved another.' She was the first woman he had ever really thought of. If it was true, as he had told Balfour, that they shared their faults in common, they also conspired happily in the spending of her allowance.

But happiness was a factor of money. Cyril had no belief that it was possible to be both poor and fulfilled. What price did the rich have to pay for their well-being, and was it too high? With his marriage, questions of the kind rose to the fore. In the Alpdodger notebook he speculated about the changes and compromises which accompanied the new access to inherited money. 'You must be altered, *arrangé* as poor Lawrence called it, and then you can borrow our cars and drink our claret at all our lunch parties and take volumes of Saint-Simon and be given that Guardi you wanted so much – only there is something a little wild and rough, a smell of action and liberty, of evenings unaccounted for, like a tom-cat, and some of us are a little worried by it. It's quite a simple operation, one feels a little removed from life after it, but remember one gets all the pleasures except for the rather vulgar consummation. One enjoys the essence without the tumescence.'

On a premise of money, happiness turned into an idealisation of the simplest sort, with ephemeral pleasures its only dimension. In the words of the Alpdodger story again, '£30,000 from the Grand National Sweep Stake. I invest £25,000 at 5%, perhaps in Columbian 7% even, for they have never yet defaulted. With £1,000 I buy up a Bentley, the large eight-litre tourer that goes 100 m.p.h. With another £1,000 I finance my flight abroad, putting by the remaining three to rent and furnish a small Georgian house in London in the Fall. I go first to Foyot's hotel in Paris, and book the little suite up the staircase, with the corridor looking on the Rue Condé. Then I go south, returning thin and brown.'

Endeavour has been suspended in this fantasy. It is a matter of idleness, chance, whimsical gratification, passivity and escape. On a sheet of Ritz Hotel paper which he then hoarded, he penned a comic formula for someone with these Alpdodger aspirations, beginning, 'I am not a member of any clubs but I belong to a great many exclusive hotels.'

Happiness, so conceived, did no doubt derive from decaying romanticism, as he observed in *Enemies of Promise*. Arguments asserting superiority on grounds of finer sensibilities, hedonistic aptitude, the privilege of the artist to take his distance from a cruel or indifferent world, were at best self-serving, and meanwhile the ensuing conception of happiness had become very incomplete and trivial. What was demanded was an uninterrupted series of ecstatic moments, unrelated to performance, to integrated personality, in the end to reality. Somehow, at hazard, ecstasy was to be distilled out of life as though by alchemy, which of course meant money. The dread of missing a moment of ecstasy was in contrast to the perpetual disappointment of actual events. Excluded from the conception was any mastery of the self with its fears and selfishness, and, still more debilitating, there was no delight in the steady exercise of talent. There had to be neither challenge to accept, nor discipline to sustain.

Keeping this journal which covered his adult self-discovery and then the first and best years of his marriage to Jean, Cyril was manoeuvring narrowly between resentment about not-having and surfeit from not-wanting. 'I feel I am coping with a being called Irony who gives me everything I want at the cost of not wanting it,' already at Eton he had understood this about himself. Jealous gods were on guard to single him out for their sport, to blunt and spoil and deprive. In his homosexual stage, he had seen himself as punished by loneliness and poverty. As a married man, he saw himself punished by company and worldliness.

Egoism alone remained constant, and the journal throughout reveals the ingenuity and contrivance with which he managed to explain it away to himself. Blame was for other people. Hard upon each other follow the inspired starts and guilt-ridden stops of his mind – the phrases and observations, sketches and turns, which might have impelled whole books in someone less self-centred. The journal was a record of contradictions, and it petered out because after a while moneyed frustration proved so similar to unmoneyed frustration. All along, he laid claims to the licence of the exceptional artist while finding it almost unbearable to practice as an artist at all; standing firm on opinions which then made him timorous; craving love and recognition but impatient when he received them. It was far more enthralling to him as man and writer to observe how these tides of ego would ebb and flow than to set up around them struggles which he had no intention of resolving.

The Journal of
CYRIL CONNOLLY
1928–1937

A number of people are frequently mentioned in the journal by their first names only. For instance:

Bobbie	Robert Longden
Christopher	Christopher Sykes
Desmond	Desmond MacCarthy, with his wife Molly, (or Mollie, as spelled by Cyril)
Eddie	Edward Sackville-West
Elizabeth	Elizabeth Bowen
Gladwyn	Gladwyn Jebb
Harold	Harold Nicolson
K and Jane	Kenneth and Jane Clark
Logan	Logan Pearsall Smith
Maurice	Maurice Baring (unless indicated as Maurice Bowra)
Noel	Noel Blakiston
Patrick	Patrick Balfour (as Lord Kinross then was)
Peter	Peter Quennell, with Nancy (first wife) and Marcelle (second wife)
Rachel	Rachel MacCarthy
Racy	Horatia Fisher
Raymond	Raymond Mortimer
Vita	Vita Sackville-West, wife of Harold Nicolson

Went with a note to Racy on Wednesday night, it was cold and the post had gone. There was a taxi ticking up outside her door – thought of Swann and Odette and felt like my own ghost, depressed and jealous and rather wild.

> κυμα το πικρον Ἐρωτος, ᾽ακοιμητοι τε
> πνεοντες
>   ζηλοι. και κωμων χειμεριον πελαγος.
> ποι φερομαι; παντῃ δε φρενων οἴακες
> ἀφεῖνται.
>   ἠ παλι την τρυφερην Σκυλλαν ἀποψομεθα

[Bitter wave of love, and sleeplessly blowing
jealousies, and winter sea of riots, whither am I
carried? The rudders of reason are lost, ah yet
again we are bound for luxurious Scylla.
                    – Attributed to Meleager]

Those Greek lovers put one to shame for passion but they seem never to have heard of intimacy. They really illustrate the limits of emotional distress and joy to be got out of purely selfish love. Love is extremely complicated because it is the result of four conflicting causes – we, the introverts, never realise that it takes two to make a love affair, just as at cards we never realise that our partners may have anything in their hand.

Love composed of the subjective and objective emotions of two people.

| Subjective | loneliness = desire to be loved | 1. | The general need for someone to love or be loved by, two emotions, loneliness or lust. These are short-lived and send him out to seek an |
| | lust = desire to love | | |

object for them and die down when the normal process of hope, attack, possession and satiety has been gone through.

Objective devotion = love for somebody
gratitude = being loved

2. Particular affection for some one person – this emotion is called up by them and intensifies all the emotions of 1. for loneliness and lust cannot be so easily appeased.

Backwards diary. Wed. 21st dined with Maurice [Baring] at the Berkeley. Our party (α +).

Tuesday Wrote my article in the morning, very cold day. Lunch at the Travellers 20th with Gladwyn Jebb, nice, praise of Bobbie. Literature discussed, on to see Sligger off at Victoria but met the wrong train. Back and go on with my article. Maurice arrives, talk to Maurice, send off article and go on to tea with Hilda Trevelyan.[1] Stuffy. George Moore comes, impressive and fussy, on to dress and talk to Leigh,[2] then we dine at the Ivy and discuss being turned down. Nice dinner but Leigh ill at the end. Talk to Steven Runciman,[3] on to the Ritz and write to Bobbie, then go and fetch Nina Seafield. Thrill in the drawing room at North Street, the candles, the logfire, the dull light on my top hat, the taxi waiting in the frost outside. Then Nina's footfall on the stair and delicious *roucoulement* of greeting. On to Lady Cunard's, carol singers drear, dance with Nina and talk to Patrick and Bryan Guinness who arrive. Snobbish thrill at sight of the Prince of Wales walking alone

---

[1] Hilda Trevelyan, then aged fifty and unmarried. 'A flashy actress' according to Virginia Woolf, she had been the original Wendy in *Peter Pan*.

[2] Leigh Ashton, Keeper of the Department of Textiles of the Victoria and Albert 1925–1931, and later the Museum's director.

[3] Steven Runciman, the historian, had been a contemporary in College. Fellow of Trinity College, Cambridge, 1927–1938.

up the wide staircase and shaking hands with Maurice Baring and Diana Cooper at the top. Supper with Patrick and home and talk of Racy. Enjoyed the rich patina of the Cunard soirée, the lovely women, the vacant faces of the extroverts, the expression of envy on Clarence Marjoribanks and the incredible stupid air of luxurious abandon on Lady Cunard's face as she danced with the Prince of Wales. We sat next to him at supper.

Monday Idle morning, [Christopher] Sykes comes. Lunch at St Leonard's Terrace and take Ann and Judy to see Chang.[1] They come back here for tea and are nice and amiable. After that wait ages for Racy and go in and out into the snow outside and change and rechange my tie. Racy comes and we discuss our situation, not arriving at any settlement beyond the general relief of being able to discuss it. Racy very lovely and boyish, wearing a yellow skirt that matched my cushions and altogether brown faced, green eyed, tender and jovial. Ros came to fetch her and we all went to Westminster in the tube and walked to South Ken. through the snow. Feel infinitely happier after seeing Racy – able to do without seeing her again. She liked the diary. I think she really may be in love with me and certainly would not like to let me go. But there is something about her which makes it impossible for me not to discuss everything on a business footing. It was magnificent of her to come. The prospect must have frightened her, poor child. Dressed for dinner and confided joyfully in Patrick. On to Nina Seafield's for dinner – very nice and warm. Nina very attractive and Proustian, on after to the Café Anglais where Bob[2] joins us but we aren't able to discuss anything. Back late with Patrick and talk over Racy whose health I drank several times. Write to her in the small hours.

Sunday Extremely idle morning, lunch about 2. Ring up Rachel[3] who has given Racy the diary. She said Racy would come here on Monday at half past six. Rosemary Wilbraham and friend come for

---

[1] Ann and Judith were the daughters of Karin and Adrian Stephen; Chang, a panda in the Zoo.

[2] Lord Boothby. Elected Member of Parliament for East Aberdeenshire 1924. From 1926–29, Parliamentary Private Secretary to Churchill who was Chancellor of the Exchequer at the time.

[3] Rachel, daughter of Molly and Desmond MacCarthy. 'She is the most beautiful girl with a smooth glossy head like a seagull' – Richard Kennedy, in *A Boy at the Hogarth Press. Memories*, by Frances Partridge, contains a passage dated November 24, 1927. 'Cyril

bridge which we play till after seven. Round to Mummy and say goodbye. Dine with Patrick at his club with Leigh Ashton who is charming. Patrick very sympathetic about Racy and has made all the difference to my turning down.

Saturday Fail to ride, owing to the frost. Lunch with Logan and we go afterwards to Battersea and see a good 18th century church. Lovely sunny winter's day. Logan came back to tea and later Rachel rings up to say Racy has not been allowed to come to dinner. Gloom and misery again. Luckily I had written to Racy in case we couldn't discuss anything there so I took that and all my diary that was about her, and went round. Rather a gloomy dinner with Molly and Rachel. Rachel sympathetic afterwards and we walked out weeping into the snow. Home and slept badly and did not tell Patrick till the morning. Letter from Racy in the morning.

Friday Eastwood[1] to lunch. Read novels. Mummy to tea. Freddie to dinner, nice, walked round to Elm Park Gardens but the house was dark. 'Racyitis' pretty acute I fear. Lovely letter from Racy. Hope springs again.

Thursday Lunch with Logan and dismal tea at Crosby Hall. No Rachel. Round to see Mummy afterwards and on to dinner with Bob Boothby and Gladwyn Jebb at the House of Commons. Excellent dinner and like them both. We hear the prayer book thrown out, all very exciting. Walk back with Jebb. Henceforth I shall be a cad and a careerist. P.C. to Racy who glows like an electric toaster during these last days of the crisis when the will to win has returned again.

Wednesday[2] Bob Boothby, his mother and Nina Seafield to lunch. I like her and she asks me to a cocktail party, nice lunch. Boothby asks me to dinner. Write a good offensive letter to Racy which may do some good and go to Nina Seafield for a cocktail. She has red

---

Connolly has been told by someone how badly he behaves about money, and indeed he used to take poor Rachel out to grand restaurants, order the most expensive dishes, and then suddenly find he had forgotten his wallet. Now he takes every opportunity of paying for Rachel in public, saying in his flat voice: "Oh no, I'll pay, or Desmond'll be complaining." ' In 1932 she married Lord David Cecil.

[1] Christopher Eastwood had been a contemporary in College. Freddie Harmer too.

[2] Paragraphs from here on, and continuing down to the break marked Paris. March–April 1928, were clipped and manicured for an essay 'One of my Londons', collected in *Previous Convictions*, (1963). The comment was then added, 'Even after twenty-five years I cannot read the jottings of this vanished youth who bears my name without discomfort.'

hair, blue eyes, a stubby attractive figure and a lovely stammer and gasping kind of speech. She is so attractive that she must be a Lesbian – very much like Gilberte or the Duchesse de Guermantes Gilbertine. Bob there who offers me a job, exciting. Back and dine out with Patrick at his club. Ring up Racy and hear her voice and write to her again. Mrs Fitz's,[1] a lovely girl called Lily French, v. young and attractive. Back still desperately in love with Racy to a late bed.

Tuesday   The first quire in this diary I tore out and gave to Racy, the days here recorded backwards are leading up to Christmas Eve. Since then, I lost the keys of the diary which remained locked till the middle of February. Then new keys were made and a fountain pen helped me to write in it. The chief events, after a bout of Chilling, have been the new troubles with Racy – who came to a party given in our house by Giana Russell.[2] She and Ros and Patrick and I talked together the whole of the evening, of the perfect evening. The storm brewed over the weekend, and the main fact, out of a mass of complications and rumours, is that Racy and I are at all costs not to meet or write again. As we had agreed ourselves to drift for two years, this is all very silly and shows what fools parents are. Patrick and I were miserable for a long time and now are beginning to recover again.[3]

I am lying on the sofa trying to imagine a yellow slab of sunshine spread thickly over a white wall. When I can imagine it and add the smell of olive oil I shall go abroad and be a free man. No deputations will fetch me back, no envoys will drag me from my tin table under the fig tree, or my carafe of wine. Thin chickens will peck between my feet, lean cats will mince through the refuse, the old woman is not talking to herself, but to the things she sweeps up off the floor. You have come about your fortune? Then I am sorry for you.

> *Hélas, chez ton amant tu n'es point ramenée.*
> *Tu n'as point revêtu ta robe d'hymenée,*
> *L'or autour de ton bras n'a point serré de noeuds*
> *Et le bandeau d'hymen n'orna point tes cheveux.*

---

[1] Night-club proprietor.

[2] Georgiana Russell married Noel Blakiston in October 1929. Rosamund Fisher, elder sister of Racy, married Lord Coleridge in 1936.

[3] A marginal note was added here in 1968. 'Racy (Mrs Mungo Buxton) dropped all my letters, diary etc in the Thames on eve of wedding.'

'O sir, how can you say so. Was that why you left London?' I left London because I was scared. The trams came right up to my window at night, and the trains shunted outside the door. One day a boat came in. I kept so still I heard my beard grow. 'And then, and then?' *Hélas chez ton amant, 'O cruel', tu n'es point ramenée.*

27th. O god Patrick is awful
       O mother how can I stand it.
       Give me strength.

Feb. 27th 28 29 30 31 1 2 3 4 5 6 7 March. Thank God only 10 more days. O sweat.

March
General sense of depression and discontent with usual horror of literature and hopeless uncertainty over Racy
      and I ne can ne may for all this world, within mine hearte
      find to unloven her a quarter of a day.
Leading, superficially, rather a complicated life, almost entirely feminine and based on the complete separation of my atavistic English instincts from my louche Bohemian ones. The *soif* for life has intensified greatly so that to dine out in the evening is not enough and has to be contrasted with a sequel among the centres of vitality afterwards. Nearly every day I street-prowl and feel more and more that cultivated people are shrimps in a rock pool, from whom I can learn nothing. Here are some efforts at documentation.

ROTHERHITHE   Walked one evening round Rotherhithe St. Good docks and bridges but very little life, a few pubs, some wooden houses, and continuous smell of lice which makes one feel abroad.

LIMEHOUSE   Gambling dens suppressed, met a Chinaman in Pennyfields who offered to show me round any evening; he was reading, with a Polish sea captain, a book on psychology. Touching to see the English waitress writing out symbols on bits of paper and learning fresh ones from the proprietor; when she got one right she smiled foolishly and threw it in the fire. B says the café in Limehouse better than the restaurants. Charley Brown's disappointing.

[134]

SHADWELL   Love Lane disappointing. Ratcliffe Highway where there were 1,000 brothels in 1890 is no more. The embankment however is very lovely and the grass beside the shore. Good market in Watney St. (Shadwell Station) Best in evenings.

WAPPING   Good high street (wharves) – waterstairs. Here I saw that strange nocturnal goatish clergyman skip around an alley blinking at the unaccustomed light from the bonfires (Guy Fawkes day) that crimsoned his long white beard.

WHITECHAPEL   Much the best part of the East End, the road from Aldgate E. not so interesting, as the side streets, especially those between Whitechapel road and Commercial Road (markets) round Leman St. and the parallel streets (Wentworth St., Old Montagu St.) on the Stepney side. Here is real Latin gaiety, and crowds and music and colour, rows of cars standing outside obscure cafés and an excellent band in a tiny dancing hall (Levins) – in the East End the people in tenements seem to make more noise and colour than those in the streets, however picturesque they are. The Jewesses are amazingly attractive, especially in a kind of mass bloom that emanates from them in large quantities. They seem to walk up and down the street all night. Men dingy and undersized. Talked to two girls who would not believe I was an Englishman – in all contacts with these classes it is amazing to realise how deeply they dislike the English, even when English themselves, and how impossible it is to convince them that one is English oneself, so foreign does the language sound when spoken well. The English girls of the lower classes like Indians, Italians, or niggers; those of the lower middle seem to despise them, but obviously like them in practice. Good manners and passion of the foreigner are everywhere well spoken of – on the other hand nobody likes the Jews. Bunny Garnett said when one got into one of the big tenements they spoke of it like a house with bugs in – the Jews have got in

there, it won't ever be clean again. Evan Morgan[1]
said the East End was utterly promiscuous and
bisexual. It is amazing to see how extinct the upper
class appears to be becoming, or how its existence
is forgotten by the lower who are also utterly
unlike Dickensian or Victorian conceptions of
them themselves. It is a Jewish-American civilisation and their only conception of paradise is
richer people doing the same things as themselves.
Cinemas, cars, motor bicycles, corner houses,
boys, girls and business seem the story of their
world, and only with these materials can they
imagine any other one.

SOHO   Very little known of the unexploited Soho, i.e. the
restaurants not frequented by ordinary visitors.
Really two Sohos, the first halves of Greek St., Dean
St., etc consisting of semi-fashionable restaurants
and night clubs (Gargoyle), the other of cafés and
clubs and real foreigners, this really North Soho.
Cafés etc so far explored.

New Compton St. Greek restaurant. *Echt.* Café
opposite entirely full of niggers, seems nobody else
there at all, very crowded.

Wardour St. Chinese restaurant, tiny, marvellous
coloured waitress, Tondalaya type, 17, father
West Indian, mother German, name Lydia. Other
waitress also attractive, half Chinese, but both
without any racial quality except appearance.

Broad St. Greek restaurant, more Greek, less
oriental than N. Compton St.

Hopkins St. Café apparently always full of crooks
etc. V. sinister. Kept by Jews. Open all night.

One should be able to live at least three lives concurrently and God
knows how many in rotation. We live in a complex age, so why not
be complicated? Try and associate with all the people one is afraid

---

[1] Evan Morgan 1893–1949. Succeeded as 2nd Viscount Tredegar in 1934. 'A fantasy
who could be most charming and most bitchy' according to Nancy Cunard (quoted in *Ronald
Firbank*, by Miriam J. Benkovitz).

of – choose one's women from the types that inspire one instinctively with uneasiness and fear. It is so long since I have written in this diary because to write in it reminds me of Racy and I have enough to remind me of her without that. I see that I am not really ready to marry yet, but that I would be ready to marry Racy at any time, and cannot imagine marrying anyone except her.

Last days in London characterised by financial needs, desperate anxiety to get abroad, away from Racy's world and a deepening passion for low life. When staying with Logan spent every evening exploring London, mostly Southern suburbs, and East End (good bridge at Canning Town), lovely houses in Southwark. Lives [?] by Hopmarket, Green Dragon Court. Went to Bath and to Sunningdale to see Noel, not a very satisfactory visit but better than nothing – Brixton Monday night, Jebbs Tuesday.

Paris. March–April 1928
These five days seemed very important. Growing affection for Paris and a sense of relief at the spring having been so safely tided into summer (was hating it in London where nothing seemed up to it).

Sevilla first evening. Disappointing. Had a Moroccan, young and v. lovely, but very cold, competent and costly. Haunted several days by another woman there, Spanish looking, lovely skin, who would obviously have been much better, and who seemed to reproach me for not realising it.

Friday. First ideas of greenness, wet and rainy. Thank god I have no associations with Racy of the summer, only autumn, winter and winterspring, to go on. Real sense of release at being in Paris, and of life somehow beginning again.

Florence
Logan said of Hardy's second wife that she had tried first to get off with George Moore – or so he said. 'George Moore would have said that of the Virgin Mary,' said B.B., 'if he'd ever heard of her.'

B.B.[1] said he had asked Lawrence (T.E.) to lunch in Paris and he had accepted and written it down in his engagement book. He never turned up and when B.B. reproached him later, he said that he saw

---

[1] Bernard Berenson was then 53.

him write it down. Lawrence said, 'Well, look at my engagement book!' He had accepted fifteen invitations for that day.

He said a work of art was the conveyance of an ideated sensation, an experience recreated in the imagination. His theory of ideated sensations was the same as Proust's and Santayana's essences. (They aren't.)

Count Potocki[1] to dinner, he came very late in a blue suit, middle aged, reddish haired, charming accent, rather like an elderly Philip Ritchie,[2] he talked modestly & urbanely of art and politics, and though he was probably enjoying himself at being treated as an authority on them, I liked to imagine that he was in reality bored stiff and beneath the most perfect manners, thinking about the next kind of woman he was going to have.

Lunch with the Waterfields,[3] unable not to feel pleasure at hearing Piers[4] addressed as Synnott in his presence, the tutor in his absence, with the general qualification that he is perhaps not quite right in the head. Piers obscure and on the defensive. He said he got more emotion from literature than from life, from Virgil's Italy than Italy itself. He wore two buttonholes.

Princesse Jean de Caraman-Chimay to lunch, young, attractive, *belle laide*, absurdly Proustian, not remarkably intelligent or educated but amazing compared to what she would have been in England. Intolerant and hard outside the circle of writers she has chosen to accept. Amazing elegance and ease of manner but would obviously be a bore.

'Do you feel you miss anything by not going to the theatre, B.B.?'
'As much as by not seeing a blubber fight in Alaska.'
'The next world is a Kind of Foreign Legion into which only desperate characters go in.'

---

[1] Count Potocki was a Polish landowner and magnate. The so-called Count Geoffrey Potocki de Montalk who was imprisoned for publishing obscene poems in 1932, might not have been welcome at i Tatti.

[2] Philip Ritchie, at Balliol with Cyril, had become Lytton Strachey's lover. He had died in 1927.

[3] Gordon and Lina Waterfield lived at Poggio Gherardo, once Boccaccio's house. Since 1921 Mrs Waterfield had been the *Observer*'s correspondent in Italy. She was highly regarded by Berenson. *Castle in Italy*, Mrs Waterfield's autobiography, records a full life.

[4] Piers Synnott had also been at Balliol with Cyril. In 1928, he became Assistant Principal at the Admiralty.

'Nobody ever laughs at an honour, least of all those who say they do.'

Morand is a kind of jazz-bar D'Annunzio.

'Nothing is really good that has a popular success, nothing is right that is the fashion, I hate successful people,' said B.B. and Logan.

One cannot appreciate B.B.'s talk till one realises that it has absolutely no relation to his actions except in so far that it occasionally is generated to conceal them.

Chief authorities for recent years.

1928 First six months. This diary. Letters to Patrick and Racy.

1927 Small diary, red diary. Letters to Noel. (First six months), letters to Bobbie, Patrick and Racy. (*New Statesman* articles.)

1926 Letters to Noel and the MacCarthys. Little diary, black notebook. Letters to Logan.

1925 Lost diary. Letters to Bobbie and Noel, Jamaican and other fragments, black book. Letters to Patrick, Maurice [Bowra].

1924 Letters to Bobbie and Noel, Patrick and Piers, Oxford notebooks. Poems.

Main sources

4 diaries, 2 black books, letters to Noel, Bobbie and (later) Patrick and Racy.

William le Fanu, has in Ireland, some of my Eton letters, otherwise I have as complete as possible a selection of my remoter past, Eton and early Oxford.

'She is drowning. Agenbite. Save her. Agenbite. All against us. She will drown me with her eyes and hair. Lank coils of seaweed hair around me, my heart, my soul.'

Salt green death.

We.

Agenbite of Inwit. Inwit's Agenbite.

Misery! Misery!

On winter sands of Westgate the cold sun, declining, shone. Pearl grey spits, wet fishes on a slab, dully wet, out of the water heaving. The bright wind blew hard across the stone pier. Tweed tailormade the wild haired girls, laughing, their gay eyes, skirts, rough stockings, laughing. Red sunset in wide pools all along the seamed boards, along the pierway. Chill cold, let's go in, tramp, tea tramp, red sunset, grey sunset, streak streaming setting set, how dark how light how winter evening. Green posts sea lapped. Groan wrung from turnstile tramp, coal black high winter waves, sweet girls with salt stung cheeks, bluehanded homing. I with them tramp, impostor, youth drained, I for the last mockery there O Eden. Honey tweeded, fire bright, home was poor exile. Drink this and die for ever, this moment, moment of Margate, the wild white city, the windstreaming.

(Moment of wild white city, sea city, of Margate, the wind streaming.)

June 16th
Chilling again. Strangely like and unlike last year.

Describe your whereabouts, give an account of your travels since last you wrote in this book. Outline your emotions, crises, and state your present scheme of a) the next six months b) life.

Left Florence with guilty joy, and joyless innocence. Went to Venice (about May 10th), walked by the slums, the newest canals and lost my way. Dined alone to oodly music, God no wonder the Bolsheviks despise the sentimental and effete emotions of the Bourgeoisie, *Chanson Hindoue*, *Moments Musicales*, *Solveig's Song*, Tchaikovsky's *Chansons sans Paroles*. Everything tender, everything Kreisler. Faster, please, I didn't ask you for a musical catalogue. Distressed by greenness in Venice, recalling Oxford canal, and Waley's poems. The Sleeping Beauty. Lilac memorial of so many wasted summers. Faster, please. Left Venice next morning and in great haste, hired a motor canoe and just caught train to Zagreb.

What impressed you on the journey?

Cliffs, blue sea and sands of Trieste, scrubby green tableland of frontier mountains, horror of Yugoslavs, and a phrase from Joyce's *Ulysses*, sensation of being on my own again.

What did you do in Zagreb?

Wrote an essay in a café, looked at peasant costumes, strolled about, went to a cabaret, hated the Yugoslavs and missed Bobbie.

You are concealing something. Yes.
What are you keeping back?

After the cabarets were all closed, a taxi driver took me out to a 'road house', a little mountain inn in the hills above Zagreb, there was a sinister fiddler there and two girls of 17; I had a drink and chose the younger; she had a lovely figure, rather sturdy, fair hair, Slav face and green eyes, and was neither made up nor powdered and she was sulky and had been crying. We went off to a little shed and had supper. It was cold and frosty, we had Mosel and ham. The police came in, two plain clothes detectives, and asked us questions, then the manager whom I hadn't before seen rushed in and bundled us out into the night. The girl was called Pepitza and spoke only Croat. I put my coat round her and she showed me where to drop over the garden wall. We climbed down and ran down a path. We were in the vineyard and lay and kissed on the cold ground between the trailing vines. The moon was very bright and I learnt the Slav name for it and for some of the many stars. We saw the lights of a car go down the road and heard a whistle and climbed up again by a path in the moonlight. The police were satisfied and had gone. We went back to our supper. I stuck marigold daisies into Pepitza's hair. She had never heard of London and we had some champagne. Then I had her and she was still cold, but very fresh and young, the whole thing came to under a pound and I walked down to Zagreb with all the nightingales singing in the dawn and the dew wet on the grass and wondered how my friends would see me.

Why couldn't you tell me this at first? Well go on with your story, if you won't answer.

I left Zagreb and went to Nagykanisza in flat Hungary on a sunny day. They charged me fifteen shillings for a transit visa. I was very angry, the train went on to Szombathely where I sent a p.c. to Joyce,[1] and on by the factories of Sopron, black sunset, to Neustadt and Vienna, dined at Sachers, and went to a cabaret, good coloured dancers. Next day wrote to Bobbie, lunched at Sachers, and took a

---

[1] Joyce Turner was a daughter of the novelist Mary Borden, by her first husband George Douglas Turner. In 1918 Mary Borden married General Sir Edward Spears. In the *New Statesman*, December 24, 1927, Cyril favourably reviewed her novel *Flamingo*, a study of the English and the Americans, in his opinion 'probably the two best hated nations in the world'. Mary Borden took him up, hence his friendship with Joyce Turner. Her hospitality continued even when he reviewed her next novel *Jehovah's Day* in quite another tone: 'These are the stock puppets of English fiction.' (*New Statesman*, November 17, 1928.)
For the Spears at Villefranche, see page 172.
'While Tranter Reuben, Mary Borden, Brian Howard and Harold Acton lie in Mellstock Churchyard now.' From 'Dorset' by John Betjeman.

sleeper to Berlin by Prag. I shared it with a toad-like Czech and we never spoke, even to say good night, on the whole journey. Reached Berlin early, went to the Adlon and had breakfast.

Berlin, rang up Gladwyn, went round to him, we talked and read. Lunch with Gladwyn and Harold. Gladwyn and I go sightseeing ineffectively. Back to Adlon and round for dinner, nice, with Mario[1] there too. Bummel after, Ivor Novello[2] and two friends collected from Adlon, dreary round of homosexual places, everybody falling out till only Ivor and I left having supper.

Next day. Lunched with Ivor and we went to the Zoo in the rain, afterwards swimming at the Wellenbad. Dinner with Harold and we all go to a theatre, afterwards to a cabaret, where Gladwyn gives us supper. Very amusing play by Molnar, amazing how the Germans are such good and natural actors. At supper the band played the famous Berlin tango, Ivor raved over it and wrote the music down by ear on a bit of paper. We were impressed till Berners[3] told us that he had looked over his shoulder and seen him get it all wrong.

Ivor Novello

Short, good stocky figure, frightful clothes – good looking, charmless face, black moustache, faintly. Terrible cultivated voice, calls everybody darling, obviously a very nice nature, said suddenly to me in a taxi, 'How nice you are' – I thought he meant a carthorse which we were passing and said 'Yes, he's grand.' He seemed put out. He said he got from three to fifteen hundred letters a week and liked them and found them the most intelligent criticism he got from anyone. He said the *Constant Nymph* scenery had worked up the cast so much that they all fell in love with each other; he said Mabel Poulton spoke pure cockney and was entirely instinctive as an actress. She believed the whole thing and her cry, quite unexpected, when she saw Antonia off made them all weep. He said she fell in

---

[1] Mario Panza, sociable Italian diplomat.

[2] Ivor Novello, 1893–1951. Actor-manager, song-writer.
'The face was too good to be true, with the impeccable nose, the raven locks, the huge eyes, the chiselled lips,' writes Beverley Nicholls in *The Sweet and Twenties*. 'Ivor was not a conceited man. His only weakness was that he was apt, by a sort of instinct, to turn into profile.' Also, 'There were no women in Ivor's life – not in "that" way.'

[3] Lord Berners, 1883–1950. Composer, author, prankster, dilettante.

love with him, and he with Elisa Landi (or was it Benita Hulme). Margaret Kennedy had tried to stop him getting the part, had never been near them, and never written to thank him. He seemed vaguely homosexual, as if he had picked it up as part of a gentleman's education. He worshipped culture and intelligence. His tragedy. For culture (Lord Berners) and Gladwyn Jebb (intelligence) didn't worship him. They found him a bore and said so. Harold explained that he liked success, that Ivor was very good looking and had a heart of gold, if malleable gold, and that when Gladwyn was his age he would be more tolerant. No-one liked his manager. Ivor seemed much influenced by Eddie Marsh. I liked him and got on well with him by hauling my standards to half mast, and practicing a little self-effacement. I said how awful Americans were, he said yes but even if one hated any, one had to admit they all had personality. He had been several times to America, he must have been told that all Americans had personality before he started, and not had the intelligence to let his five senses disprove it. Of such is the Kingdom of Art.

Next day we went over a palace (Sykes, Berners and I) and lunched with Harold. Gladwyn and I bathed in the Wellenbad, tea with Berners at the Westons, went to museum and saw the fine archaic statues, and finer vases (Achilles binds Patroklos), also the Egyptian monuments. Dorothy Warren's[1] picture show and tea with the ambassador. D. Warren very attractive. Mario and a German to dinner, vicious argument on duelling. All the English, except mysterious Lascelles[2] were against it. Tempers just kept, Mario won the day. On to a *palais de danse* with telephones on every table, we played silly jokes ringing people up.

Ivor had a gramophone in his room and played me a very good blues from the German Jazz Opera *Johnie spielt auf.* I went on some cabaret crawls on my own. I remember offering a bottle of champagne to anyone who could guess my nationality. Gladwyn Jebb

---

[1] Dorothy Warren was the niece both of Philip Morrell and of Sir Herbert Warren, President of Magdalen College, Oxford. She ran the Warren Gallery in Maddox Street, where later in that summer of 1928 D. H. Lawrence exhibited pictures which attracted the attention of the police. 'They say she has had every sort of love,' Virginia Woolf wrote of her on June 26, 1926, to Vita Sackville-West. She married an importer of Styrian jade, Philip Trotter, see page 191.

[2] Dan Lascelles, a sombre young member of the Foreign Office, thought by Nicolson to have a brilliant career ahead of him.

took me on a walk and ended up by a statue of Beethoven, without saying anything. When I read the *New Statesman*, 'Portrait of the young Beethoven,' said Harold, 'contemplating his organ.'

Last morning in Berlin spent in packing. Gladwyn and I collided with another car in the Kurfurstendam by the way. Met two young men, Jenkinson and Lancaster, of the Blues, arrived for the weekend with letter for Harold whom they hoped will tell them the best brothels, and where to find a smutty cinema. Depressed by these perfect materialists, their wealth, self-confidence, dandyism, a complete harmony with this earthy life, the children of the world. Lunch party at Harold's. Met the Keelings, pompous ass of a husband, warpy, attractive, cooing, elegant, malicious Latin wife; attractive sandy-haired handful daughter. Donna Sioia, Mario Panza, and Mrs Carnegie there. Mrs Carnegie said, 'So Mr Lascelles has arrived, I don't think I shall like him, I hear his nails aren't always quite clean.' This struck me as epitomising the stupidity of women, their dragging snobbishness and cowardly worship of the correct that has pulled so many husbands down. We left after lunch and motored to Dresden, where we dined at the Bellevue. I found letters there, distressing one from Patrick which put me off living with him. Another from Logan. At dinner we discussed our love affairs, and went out for a walk along the Elbe. This (*nuit de Dresden*) was very important to me. At Berlin I felt life to be beginning again – Harold was so nice to me and I found it a joy to discover someone in whom I could be interested.

Harold Nicolson

Rather a big man, red face, nice curly hair, nice hazel eyes, small mouth, moustache, looks absurdly young, dresses like any casual amateurish Englishman with Bloomsbury ties and shirts. Had a dog but did not seem to like it. Appears a *faux bonhomme*, but is not one really. Gladwyn called him 'a real gent'. I am not absolutely sure about this, but it is certainly what he would like to be and what he really behaves like, very tactful and soothing. Fearless moral courage, intelligent but not up to the real Bloomsbury standard, or that of me and Maurice. A kind and sympathetic man. I got very fond of him. He says he hates femininity, and though he seems masculine and English, it is easy to see why. He is rather protean and slippery, the adaptable diplomatic manner. I like him more than anyone I have met since Desmond and Maurice Baring. His great point *droitesse*, the savage triumph of a love of truth, literature, and intelligence over his highly ingrained and artificial environment. And the defects – vanity, social sense, opportunism – in his own nature. I encouraged him to write more descriptions of scenery. We evolved a man called Peabody who symbolised everything in culture that I hate. Then I like the way he does his work, managing everything with so little fuss, and so much perspicacity, and not being taken in by any of it at all. Beautifully arranged life as a writer, a father, a gentleman, a husband, a friend, and a man of action. I observed all this after being told he was a cad and that one could not trust him. Enjoyed being with men and living as if in digs in Oxford in Berlin. Bachelor rejuvenating existence. Harold – I think only pretending to be in love with me. This year I have made two friends.

'I would rather do the motor trip another time – I have taken notes on it.'

All right – just trace your recent relations with Sd. [?]

At Berlin my load was lightened by appreciation, good living, friends and bachelor society. At Dresden I agreed with Gladwyn that we were too good for whoever we feel in love with, and that the next move was up to her. In the cool evening sunlight of Walsassen, as we glided through the upland forests of Bavaria,[1] I had a real sense of balmy convalescence and impending cure. Gladwyn restored my belief in friendship, and the desire to see more of Bobbie and Noel, especially of Bobbie, came to my rescue again. All these weeks I have lived under his shadow. In Paris, the sense of freedom further strengthened me, as did, infinitely, living with a woman (Olive) for the first time. It shows I can be loved by them, which is important. Chloe a little, and Donna Sioia a lot, helped to strengthen me and now I feel an intolerant, indifferent, almost Bloomsbury young man. I am still in love with her, and want to marry no-one else, but I can afford now not to worry about her, if

---

[1] Gladwyn Jebb's account is in his *The Memoirs of Lord Gladwyn*, pp 35–6. 'Cyril and I left Berlin in my blue Darracq and did a tour embracing Dresden, Prague, Bavaria, the Neckar valley and the Rhineland, finishing at Düsseldorf where we parted.' The beauty of the Jewish cemetery in Prague was singled out. (In the opening paragraph of *The Rock Pool*, the young Naylor finds that the first sight of Trou-sur-mer 'reminded him of the elderberries and nettles of the Jewish cemetery at Prague'.)

'We also visited there a *Nachtlokale* where we fraternized with the local ladies, largely consisting of Russian *émigrées*. Cyril seemed particularly attracted by a (to me) rather hideous woman and, when I reproached him, said in a loud voice, which let us hope was not understood, "We needs must love the lowest when we see it!"'

she wants me, she will get me, meanwhile I can get along very well on egotism, friendship and wenching.

egotism: the necessary conceit of the solitary and the artist: the belief that he is most important when most himself, and most himself when alone.

friendship: the noblest exercise of talent and devotion: to confine myself to very few friends, and old. Bobbie, Gladwyn, Noel, Patrick, Jack [Blakiston], possibly Maurice and Peter, certainly Freddie [Harmer] – but Bobbie, Jack and Noel, Gladwyn and Harold, or simply Bobbie – should do.

wenching: avoiding serious love affairs, and if possible prostitutes, save Mrs Fitz's – but working off one's desire (which is only satisfied if the gratification is romanticisable) by short sharp affairs with any kind of accessible women – avoid virgins, wives, boys, tarts, venereal disease, debutantes, marriage and masturbation. Reduce sex efficiently to a pigeon-holed minimum. First a writer, then a friend, then an inaccessible, cynical womaniser.

Objections:
too flabby to keep my solitude
too suspicious to keep my friends
too poor to keep any wenches, too sentimental to keep them as wenches.
General idea – be a bold bad Bloomsbury tough except with Bobbie.

Back in England feel nothing but an intense disgust at its stupidity. Fatuous newspapers. Still fussing about the prayer book. The wireless with its childrens' corner, reports of tennis matches, lectures on the composition of the cricket team, on the searchlight tattoo, absurd music, jolly, idiotic, or merely oodly. Miss Ivy St Helier beginning, 'Don't be afraid, I'm not highbrow.' Nor she is. All actors and actresses with their frightful genteel Balliol and Tottenham accent. Miss Gladys Cooper married to a gentleman at Dorking. She drew a blank for her profession, dodged the crowd, and gave some money to a charity. He's all right. He's a surname. Really it is the most deplorable country, Americanised without America's vitality, or America's variety of race. Is Ireland any better? Apparently not. The countryside though is at least not destroyed. And this absurd fuss about Shaw and Galsworthy. And all there is instead is the *Nation*, old governess past the age of childbearing; the *New Statesman*, an extremely competent, expert, and philistine man in the street; and *Life & Letters*, august and readable as any late Victorian arsewiper, and as daring and original as a new kind of Barley water. Assets of England, the climate, the countryside, the children, the presence of a few kindred spirits in rebellion, the country houses, the fact that I speak the same language as its female population, that Robert Longden and Racy Fisher live there, that it is in easy reach of the Continent.

Joyce the only man who has really lived in the classical tradition of great writers, a youth of poverty, a journey abroad, exile, penury, and revolt and the production of a masterpiece after ten years, as he promised, 'in silence, exile, and cunning'. He might have been an ancient Greek. 'Irish art the cracked looking-glass of a servant.' O to be more like Dedalus and less like Bloom!

Spent my first two days in England with the Nicolsons, nice journey there from Dover. Liked Long Barn but Knole seemed too big ever to have been intimate or habitable. Vita Nicolson very nice and interests me. I wasn't much impressed by Dotty Wellesley.[1] Good talk at Long Barn which I will try and recall. O Christ Jesus what is wrong with English music? Two half-timbered dances by Edward German. O Albeniz, his Cordoba – out, out, Coromandel – O Eastern spa.

What is C.V.C. going to do about it?

Abuse other peoples' novels; get on with his own.
Be more ruthless, and less flabby, cease being influenced by charmers and gentlemen.
Speak his mind.
You ought to see more of Peter.
Ayant peur de mourir lorsque je couche seul.

Periodicity in men: idea for an essay.

---

[1] Dorothy (Dotty), Lady Gerald Wellesley, 1891–1956. Poet. Close friend of Vita Sackville-West. She edited the 'Hogarth Living Poets' series, though this did little to earn her the good opinion of Virginia Woolf.

Sunday
Visit from Patrick, who is on a yacht at Warsash, he seemed very well, and rather depressed me with all his excitements and gaiety. He said Racy was still cynical and disillusioned, bored by the season, complacent, and out of love. He said Ros [Racy's elder sister] had told him she was in love with him. He had also seen Gladwyn and did not mind me leaving him. He spoke of his money troubles, of his fondness for debutantes, his busy life, his occasional boys, his absence of male friends. It was funny seeing him at Chilling and finding a big Rolls Royce at the door. Now he has gone and I am alone again on this long summer's evening, I feel that he will pass rather out of my life and I am sorry. Maurice told him Bobbie was in love with one of the Guinness girls – Honor I suppose. I wonder if it is true – what time one wastes on debutantes. I suppose because of their vitality – gay, remote, independent, innocent and alert. I wonder if R. would ask me to be his best man, this I feel rather important – who would I ask? Him, or if I married Racy, Patrick. Mollie seems to have told every mortal soul about my quarrel with her, really she has no dignity and no discretion. Possibly she has a guilty conscience, possibly she thinks I am spreading another version, actually I suppose it makes a dramatic sensation for her, and she just can't hold her tongue. I miss Rachel, and must see her soon.

Analysis of 1927
Winter: Snow, London snow, snow at Chilling, holly, tobogganing at Titchfield in the sun – Anne and Judy sliding over the ice on the road by the barn – huge drifts of powdery sunlit snow along by the wood, red and blue jerseys, wading boots, cold feet, warm red faces, all buried in the snow – the metallic argent ringing of broken ice thrown over the frozen pond – the stalactites by the little stream, the crunch of icebound hoof marks, children laughing, arguing, weeping, warm fires at Chilling, baths running, big meals, Christopher's involved conspiratorial whispers, waiting for the post, for a letter, for the letter, cold night of Chilling with games and candles and silence and the sea. Strange hidden arctic sea, dullen leaden stretch of heaving water between the snowed-up stubble field and the ghostly clotted island hills. I have never seen an island before across a piece of water and covered with snow. Inky slush of sleet on the edge of the shore, lapped by the waves, nor snow nor sea yet lasting well beyond the thaw – echoes of our Party – magnificent

dinner with Maurice [Baring] at the Berkeley, champagne, cigars, and caviar – walking back down Piccadilly, the row of coat pegs in our bathroom, Nina's white back, her lisp, her schoolgirl malice, the room slowly filling up, the crowd of white waistcoats and lovely dresses, Maurice, Leigh, Gladwyn, Brian [Howard] – Roddy Henderson rather drunk, hanging over the stairs. The red crowd of masked carol singers crowded into the hall – the candles on our Christmas tree, Oliver's imitations, the laughter, the dances, the floating balloons – sudden vision of the grace of hedonism, the reward of dumb seekers after pleasure, the cold, the crisp archaic carols, the blue noses of the slum children pressed against the tall windows, in the cold slush outside, the winter cold. Next day going down to Chilling, I left a gramophone record for Nina. There was snow in N. Street, on the little Queen Anne roofs, and it was raining as I went by. When I rang the bell on leaving I saw the drawing-room window shoot up and Nina's red Queen Anne head looking out to see who it was. It seemed like a penny in the slot machine, some winter fairytale or a German film, and I was worried by the incomplete meeting, and by missing Joyce's Christmas party and by wanting a letter from Racy and a shave. Rachel crying in the snow after I dined in Wellington Square; she wore Dermod's old coat, and walking down the street we spoke of Racy, of this winter of beauty and anguish and so much snow.

Autumn

Brown and gold – brown chairs and curtains of Yeoman's Row, gold tiles in the fire, the green leaves through the lattice windows, then yellow leaves, then black stems of trees (no leaves at all). The lights of Brompton Road, the newsboys outside the tube station as I come back tired from the *New Statesman* to the gramophone, the warm light, the evening paper and a late tea. Drinking with Patrick on idle Sunday mornings, going to the film society and bringing people back, dinners alone at the Ivy, theatres alone in the yellow fog. When I say suddenly 'autumn' I first see nothing but brown and gold, then I see three pictures rolled into one, the brown fur Kaross on my sofa, the two gold cushions, Racy's brown dress against them, her golden face and hair, a glimpse of the trees through the drawn curtains, the wild excitement in the air – still brown and gold the picture changes, a cold wet afternoon by Battersea bridge, Racy, slim, golden, slant-eyed, in her boy's felt hat and brown jumper looking down the road and tapping with one foot on the kerb – the swirl of the grey autumnal river, the wet embankment, the waiting figure against the trees of the Park, her marsh green eyes and yellow hair. Windy twilight in the Fulham road, the roar of buses, the November dusk, walking away from Elm Park Gardens in the eddy of fast falling leaves, brown leaves from plane and elm crushed close on the rain swept pavement, swirl of the Debussy quartet matching the wide curve of the Fulham Road and the depression in my heart, walking alone on this windy evening, the lamps just lit and wet with rain, alone along the broad street, brown street with lights of gold.

Early autumn in the woods of Shulbrede – white mist from the valley hanging heavy in the air, Rachel dark-eyed, silent, watching me, Molly blinking and purring by the log fire. Dermod [MacCarthy] away at Midhurst, bicycling away alone through the dew damp lanes, into the same mist that creeps over the roses, drowning the smell of woodsmoke with the dank odour of earth and hedgeweeds. Cruel and lovely season, my enemy, my own.

Points from a letter.

North and South, the value of exile, homesickness, and obscurity as literary stimuli. No amount of moving up to it can prevent the South from being unfriendly – except perhaps to a purely detached scientist (Douglas) or the real hard-boiled romantic? Lawrence? Byron (but it killed him) – and are not all romantics essentially soft-boiled?

Homesickness extremely dangerous because the values of the things for which one is homesick become hopelessly exaggerated – if you lived in Newcastle I do not say you would read sentimental books, but you certainly would read all books sentimentally.

Ovid, admirable as a writer when he felt no emotion (metamorphoses) – unpresentable [sic] when inspired to self-pity by exile.

Only the Irish are impressed by exile – it knocks the Celtic twilight out of them – Joyce, Moore, (Yeats a spiritual exile whining after Colonus and Byzantium).

Typical literature of homesickness, the only universal emotion unconnected with love or gain..

The Jacobite's epitaph
The miner's dream of home
Tristia, More Tristia, Ovid

One lovely sonnet and a hundred bad ones by Joachim du Bellay
(*Heureux qui comme Ulysse*)
Grantchester, with a note on the Old Vicarage
Rupert Brooke

Traces only in the Odyssey, Catullus, Virgil, Martial, and the Spirituals.

Taking Grantchester as representative, better than all the ballads, songs, dance tunes on this subject, and worse than the rare flashes of greater writers. Ruth sick for home etc. The general tone is luxurious, broken by occasional facetiousness in the Belloc tradition. Self-pity or a morbid affection for places (variation of self-pity) is bound to creep in. There is no more muck in all literature than is written round innocence in people or in places, by those who have lost it. The word 'little' is a sure give-away —

    hear the breeze
    sobbing in the little treeze

e.g. and was the horrid German grass nasty to you, and those beastly regimental tulips, poor thing, and did you want the little trees to come and tuck you up?
Yes! (bout of masochistic sobbing)

The steady divorce of words from their significance owing to the literary exploitation of their melody detaching them from their meaning is perhaps the most serious cause of the break up of poetical language today. A word like asphodel for instance is used too freely for its sound and now has become a dead symbol – though it will be long before anyone realises it and uses gum cistus or liquorice instead. Every poem must have some trace of effort and intensity either in the emotion behind it (lament for Sidney) or (Lycidas) in the technique. The Georgian poets and the late Humbert Wolfe, now happily defunct, seized on adjectives indiscriminately like shop girls who grab at suspended balls of string to tie up parcels, without raising their eyes.

Poetry, then, largely owing to the mess the Georgians have made of it by using words too big for them, has become a hopelessly artificial search for the *mot juste*.

Possibilities for poetry —

New words	These used without conviction degenerate faster than others. Hardy and Joyce have tried, but their words are not poetical.

[151]

New subjects	The only new subjects can be those hitherto considered unpoetical, i.e. the main bulk of amusements, occupations, and emotions which fill up the lives of the New Democracy. This attempted by Eliot.
New metres	Yeats, old Bridges, many modern poets have tried this, none better, none worse, than the Hon. H. G. Nicolson's Betera. [*sic*. For 'Better 'alf'? Anyhow referring to Vita Sackville-West.] They afford only temporary relief.
New sensibility	This seems a hope but who has got it? Lewis? Lawrence? Quennell? Sitwells have tried to invent one but they can't because they are stupid people.
New language	The only new language is the demotic English of our Tottenham Court Road civilisation – the speech of the Corner House, the Palais de Danse, the Cafeteria and the Sugar Daddy. Eliot has tried to write in this (Criterion) and failed – it is not a poetical language – Joyce is trying to write a book in it and is failing. It is not a prose language either.
Extreme Emotion	Eliot (*Hollow Men*), Joyce (last poem in *Pomes Penyeach*) have shown that it is still possible to write a poem in *quite simple words* under the stress of an EXTREME EMOTION. In both cases it seems to have done them in. (*The Land*, a dodge, an archaistic throw-back)

Demotic English has so spread that a girl said to me, 'I can tell you aren't English by your accent' – another in the Café Royal once said, 'O come and listen, Eva, this boy is most beautifully spoke.'

So poetry looks in a bad way, and modern poets with it, frail children of exhausted loins.

The whole problem raised by the oath of Long Barn is not how to attack the Jewish American gugnunc[1] world, but what ideal of

---

[1] Oxford vogue word, as in:
> G'uggery G'uggery Nunc,
> Your room is all cluttered with junk
> (from *Summoned by Bells*, by John Betjeman.)

equal activity we can put in its place. At present it absorbs almost all the vitality of the western races, and no half-timbered sanctuary, no pagan rock pool, can be substituted in its stead. Again it is at its worst in America, and it is from America that the rebellion will come – we are all too soaked in tradition and culture to create anything outside of it. Green leaves on a dead tree is our epitaph – green leaves, dear reader, on a dead tree.

The wind blows up a ragged mist from the Isle of Wight appealing to my warm love of the unseasonable and the obscure. Don't ever accept a literary judgement of mine unless I can prove it. I am a crank enjoying literary isolation and expecting it. I shall never succeed or wish to succeed as a reliable authority.

Mr Boothby (Turncoat for Aberdeen):
Is the Home Secretary aware that an official in his Majesty's Service has been travelling abroad with an intellectual barley water Bolshevik? A cotton head? A Hans Wurst? A cretin? A man nobody has a good word for?

Mrs Meyrick[1] (From the peeresses gallery): He always paid on the nail.

Mrs Fitz (From the same): My girls have always found him beautifully spoke, and never give any trouble.

Mr Saklatvala[2]: I mean – well I hate to say it – I mean is this fellow a gentleman? I mean is he one of us, has he got any decent clubs, know the difference between a stage and a mantle, all that sort of thing you know, don't you know.

Mr Boothby, reading: The Mustard Club, The Corner House, Lyon's Pop, the Cloven Club, the 43, the Gargoyle, the Adlon Society, the Cavendish Hotel.

Mr Joynson Hicks: Goo'ole Gargoyle, hic, never let ole Hicks hic, down. Jus'say my name – only wish I could say it myself – jus' say – hic – Rosa Lewis – hic – woman in a thousand.

Mr Morley: In a thousand what?

---

[1] 'The indomitable nightclub owner Mrs Meyrick,' writes Michael Davie as editor of *The Diaries of Evelyn Waugh*, 'who, as fast as the police closed one club, opened another. Constantly fined and imprisoned. Two of her daughters married peers.'

[2] Shapurji Saklatvala, a Parsee, one of the richest men in India and consequently Communist Member of Parliament for North Battersea, 1924–29. He died 1936.

The Speaker Order: I believe Lord Balniel knows Mr Connolly.

Lord Balniel: N'no.

Mr Boothby: I told you so; should a government servant, I repeat, travel with an expatriated Sinn Feiner, bearing the name of a man who was most deservedly shot, working as a hack reviewer for a paper whose Editor was recently even more deservedly run in? Where was I? Oh yes! Bolshevik (sensation).

The Archbishop of Canterbury: I am an old man.

Mr Boothby: Bolshevik! (hunting noises from the Conservative benches)

Colonel Faux Bonhomme (aside): I say, look here Bob, damnably awkward, very much afraid. You see this fellow put the labour people up to it; fact is you went to some rather odd places yourself in Berlin, not that I blame you, fond of trumpeters myself, but government expense you know – might make it rather awkward. Then this man Jebb, of course, I know he's a friend of yours, but all the same, sent *Ulysses* – hot stuff, better than Byron's unpublished my missus tells me, banned by the Home Office and all that – he sent it back by the bag[1] – might be very unpleasant, course he probably thought it was a blue book, still if any of those radical papers got hold of it – feel sure you understand – quiet 'im down – how do you feel about a spot of supper tonight?

Mr Boothby: Bolshevik! yes, Bolshevik, he who denies these facts, the low origin, the still lower character of Mr Connolly – but Bolshevik, yes triple bureaucratic Bolshevik he who questions an Englishman's right to travel about with anyone he damn well chooses!

Deafening cheers from all benches, cries of *Civis Romanus Sum*, Hands off Miss Saridge, Tchinovnik, an Englishman's home is his arsehole. Well said, the sort of man we want – what's yours?

The P.M.: I am sure we are all very grateful to Mr Boothby for coming down to address the Political Society on 'Personal Liberty and International Law'. There is just one point I should like to make. Does Mr Boothby, in his admirable summing-up of the present status of the individual, really make allowances

---

[1] For this tease, see page 162, footnote 1.

for the *horesco referens*, the *horrible dictu*, the *je ne sine quoi non* that Mr Connolly, whom he takes as a hypothetical example of the *Lex Talionis* (another good man gone wrong) was actually RABBITED from the CORPS?

Sensation

H.M. the King: I dissolve this parliament.

Parliament: We consider ourselves dissolute.

Three prejudices, two charges, against Virginia Woolf

1. οὐκ ἀπὸ κρήνης πίνω ['I do not drink from the public fountain' – Callimachus] – I read for privacy, and resent, perversely and unfairly, the overpraised.

2. Loyalty to Joyce, her Forster father, who scorns the sympathetic, the presentable, the genteel.

3. She gets in my way, stopping the earths I wish to hide in, female spider by whom I fear to be devoured.

4. She is not really a novelist – she does not care for human beings, her best effects, the mark in the wall, the empty house, are based on the absence of them. This is good, but she shouldn't write novels. Her characters are lifeless anatomical slices, conceived all in the same mood, unreal creations of genteel despair. They are not human beings, but sections of them which portray the doubts, the tenderness, the half-hopes and half-fears of the human mind. From this same misty backwater of the stream of consciousness she fills up all her puppets through a hole in their heads.

5. Considered not as a creator of character (what a paper rose is Mrs Dalloway, how limp is Peter) but as a writer of lyric prose, I found her writing spoilt by (1) carelessness, a fault in the creation of beautiful prose, though less important in the expression of ideas. It is difficult to find a piece of hers that is anthologisable, she repeats her epithets, overlooks dissonances etc then (2) she writes with that lush feminine Keatsian familiarity that comes from being sensually too at home in the world. The fault of all romantic writers, *Dusty Answer* good example. There is a quality in her work that turns my stomach. There is a quality in my own. She grows intoxicated on her language and the suggestion of tipsiness quickly cloys. Then she falls into tricks, her critical essays are full of clichés – almost as many as Lytton's – don't you feel slightly queasy with a title like 'Ramb-

[155]

ling round Evelyn'? 'A society' perversely, I think her best story.

I review novels to make money, because it is easier for a sluggard to write an article a fortnight than a book a year, because the writer is soothed by the opiate of action, the crank by posing as a good journalist, and having an airhole. I dislike it. I do it and I am always resolving to give it up.

Mythology of Homesickness

Adam, natural man, at home with nature.

Existence of Adam based on Grace, Greenness & Security.

Grace = ease with his surroundings in.

Greenness = whatever strikes you as the most thrilling symbol of nature in.

Security = he was looked after, living simply, never straying from his home in Eden, Eden, in Eden.

Effect of the Fall on a) Adam b) Eden

Grace turns to want of grace, sense of guilt and unworthiness, defiance and depression caused by the beautiful – on which man seems an intruder. Hence arises possession, for possession is the destruction of that which puts one off one's ease. Hence the Agenbite of Inwit, romantic, distress and self-expression or the inability to let well alone.

Greenness, or corresponding quality turns to the absence of greenness – physical homesickness for place, exile, emotional scurvy in towns.

Lack of security, or fear.

Thus a longing for grace, greenness and security is the corollary to a consciousness of unworthiness, exile and fear which form the three ingredients of all loneliness, real loneliness, the homesick conviction of straying which drive one to associate with anything at ease in the world.

The pleasure associated with these emotions is because we know that they are important (*dans le vrai*) – because starting, through Adam, as losers, we ought to be unhappy, hence sense of fitness when we are so.

Meanwhile Eden from the Fall to the Flood represents (rather than all that bowery loneliness) the typical desolation that is too strong for man – every conquest of nature over the unwanted occupiers – the Sleeping Beauty's Garden, disappearing islands, revengeful climates, Atlantis, Lyonesse, Hydronil – Milton explains how Eden became a treeless island itself – 'with all its verdure spoilt, to teach thee that God attributes to place no sanctitie, to teach thee the kind of God we have.'

Hence travelling = search for physical
        art   = search for spiritual home of man

All activity arising from distress arising from homesickness. The romantic's fondness for childhood and children or cats, is his fondness for their state of grace; this transferred to fondness for his own childhood – which all romantics associate with grace and security – security found also in pneumatic bliss (bright star).

The lure of empty Eden, acknowledging as hopeless the search for retrieved grace, leads quickly to obscurity, listless renunciation and the love of Death.

Hence all romantics are soft-boiled, because the background/keynote of every romantic is a religious sense. The romantic is a spoilt priest just as the prose writer is a spoilt poet. Awe, capacity for feeling same, seems to me the distinction between soft-boiled and hard-boiled. I am against religion except for simple people, but you are only a tough without religious sense. Of course the soft-boiled should do everything he could to conceal it.

Idea for a vision of judgement. Hell full of toughs, doing everything they want, as in life, the cricket teams come in and out, the football teams go out and in. They are allowed perfect freedom as on earth, and with no diseases, but their maker has also absolutely forgotten about them, and in the course of eternity this will begin to tell. In purgatory all those with a religious sense are collected, they look with eager eyes at Paradise which is separated from them by a sheet of water and a high wall. The trees rise above the wall which is ugly and set with broken glass, it is the only ugly thing there and was constructed from the gaze of the beholders. They catch a glimpse of crab apples, of brier roses and garden flowers and run wild. White petals from unwatched orchards fall and float on the leaden water. At night, and in the evening, noises come from the forest, noises like the zoo. By day harsh, almost malicious squawks rattle up into the metallic sunshine, though reedy single notes of great beauty have sometimes been heard – but no romantic has ever been inside because of their showman promise, the desecration of their worship that proved that the privacy, in their lives, they were permitted to discover, they were unable to respect.

[157]

Tatters of rain streak from a dishcloth sky. I nurse a sore throat and a snivel cold. Soon England will be a slagheap city in a rubble field, stogged bottles in the dingy grass, burdock and peeled hoardings stretching down to a litter of boots and halves of grapefruit thrown up by a bathwater ocean on the insanitary shore.

To make a hero (fiction)

The way is to remove first one set of qualities from one – all those that balance certain others, and so make for stability, and when you have envisaged this lop-sided fragment of yourself, to strengthen the remaining ones, till you have created an intenser being, more and less than you are, then place him, or her, in some situation of your life that you realise now to have been a turning point. Give him a push and he will walk, but down the opposite turning. I call this game 'possible selves', some wander off with academic appointments and end up as desiccated North Oxford K.C.B.'s – others flash quickly into obscurity, slum life, prison, tropic forest, or that goal of so much brave endeavour, the paupers' lunatic asylum – some are country gentlemen, bankers, catholic priests, some clatter over Irish walls on stocky unclipped cobs, others repeat their stories at appalling literary parties, one is a rake and a dandy, one lives alone in an insanitary forest tower, one is wrapped up in the cocoon of marriage, but the best of all die young.

Then imagine your life without one quality, or with one added – practice, experiment, test these new chemical compositions by living for a day absolutely without modesty or absolutely with ungovernable rage, one could surely simulate or subtract any of them for a short space of time until one had discovered the philosophers' stone.

Talk at Chilling – Logan: 'Nobody's ever asked me to unveil a war memorial – perhaps it's a good thing.' 'Nobody's ever asked me to unveil you, Logan, that's certainly a good thing, as there'd be nothing left.' 'At least Cyril, you would have to admit that I spent today improving my mind.' 'There'd be more peace in this house if you improved your chess.' 'There'd be no peace at all, if I beat you.' 'You'd stop playing altogether – well, there's been a good deal of writing done on this side of the table for the last few days – I don't mind unveiling that.'

Visit to London. Recover Racy's letters, dine at Spanish restaurant with Joyce [Turner], exciting dinner, we do not mention R. J. Hall and my paroxysms, see [Clifford] Sharp and lunch with K [Clark] next morning, scour the Fulham Road, bus-naming, pavement-staring, corner-wishing once again. See Gladwyn. He is dining with Bob [Boothby] and Nina [Seafield] and Cynthia Noble as I write this. Back to find a letter from Patrick with the best news I have yet had about R. It leaves me wildly excited and upset. I never thought I could be so distracted again by the mere mention of a name – O hopeless resurrected hoping, returning agony, joy, suspense. The Debussy slow movement played on the wireless, water lifting, lightly but surely lifting the stranded keel. Tidal hope. O RACY, RACY RACY hopeless into this gulf of silence.

July 7th. Late at night got query Vienna on the wireless and heard oh do do do – *quis desiderio*. [*Quis desiderio sit pudor aut modus tam cari capitis?* What shame or measure can there be to longing for so dear a head? – Horace] Considered the whole situation at length, based on Patrick's letter. My article out and reads well – sent Noel a postcard of a mass of cubic wine casks on the quay at Almeria, '*O tu severi religio loci.*' [O thou the divinity of this severe place – from a Latin poem by Thomas Gray.]

Except for poverty, incompatibility, opposition of parents, absence of love on one side and of desire to marry on both, nothing stands in the way of our happy union.

Probably a mistake not to fall in love with handfuls, baggages, Libertina's *fretis acrior errantis Calabri sinus* [ex-slavegirl 'keener than the waves of the wandering Calabrian sea' – Horace] – in fact not to bite off more than one can chew. Are not *Wuthering Heights* and *Manon Lescaut* the only good love stories? Beware of the premature. Bright star, *fessus et viarum*, [tired also of the streets] most most loving breast, insistence on fireside sympathy and pneumatic bliss. The bane of us fundamentally melancholy roman-tics, highly introverted by the gentleman complex. I feel the 'only know I should drown if you laid not your hand on me' spirit to be ominous in its compatibility. One should be trying to tame the high spirited πωλη θρακιης [Thracian filly – Anacreon], not be sponging on them. I would like to fall in love with some unmanageable Kathy who would run away rather than acquiesce under any parental ban. Perhaps, though, I should sooner or later inevitably be seen through. A mistake to borrow anyone's vitality ever – it tires them, it tires you. γλυκυν γευσας τον αιωνα [Having tasted the sweet time]. Harold and Vita are the perfect pair.

[159]

10th. Letters from All Souls (Rowse)[1] and a publisher, not bad for one article. Lovely dinner with Logan in Southampton, passionate Racyitis, good drive back in the glow glow gloaming, Woolston Ferry and Burlesdon, gathered on this beach wryneck, screech-owl, commodious night-jar. Talk of Olive. Feel excited about life and prospects. Elegiac beauty shall be mine.

New letter from Patrick – Racy fallen in love suddenly with a man called Goldman – but there it is. Luckily Bobbie here to break the fall – indeed relief is my chief sensation, for there need be no more uncertainty.

5 o'clock, luxurious flat
in West Kensington

Are you a sadist or a masochist?	Sadist.
Ideal type	Greek *kore*
What do you want to do immediately afterwards?	Eat melon.
How do you feel then to a) friends	Distant.
b) strangers	Affectionate.
What are the oddest circumstances in which you have made love? (Sligger's room.)[2]	open air in bracken, late summer.
4 characters in history or fiction you would like to sleep with. (Countess Walewska. Alcibiades. Nell Gwynn. Princes in the Tower.)	Lady of Elche.[3] Melbourne, Lady C. Lamb [sic].
Views on lesbians	None.
What other emotions do you like with lust?	Pity.
Favourite nationality	English. French.
What spectacle would most excite you?	two girl lesbians.
What form of gratification would you like most?	s f [sic].
Which animal?	pandar [sic].
What general timetable regulates your sexual life?	opportunism.

---

[1] The name was added in 1968. A. L. Rowse was then a junior Fellow of All Souls College, Oxford.

[2] This bracket, as also the one after the next question, contained Patrick Balfour's answer.

[3] A Spanish Gothic madonna much prized by Connolly.

What is your technique with a) men	none.
b) women	improvised.
What qualities in a) men b) women do you prefer?	male characteristics in female and female in male.

Aug 5th.

Wet Sunday afternoon in summer. Timeless abyss of all the year. Harold correcting Vita's proofs, Raymond, Bobbie, Lascelles, reading, all reading. The wind worries the heavy sycamores, rustle of turned pages, crackle of the *Manchester Guardian*; in this stillness I await the first sound, in this blankness for the first image, a cough, a motor horn, the scratching of the dog's leash on the floor. Doors banging in another house. In another country. Cette. The dog fidgeting, the wind rising, the image forming. Cette at midnight, sleepy ride to an hotel near water, the plage de Frontignan, the wide canals.

> *Beau ciel, vrai ciel, regarde moi qui change*
> *après tant d'orgueil, après tant d'étrange*
> *oisiveté mais pleine de pouvoir*

Valéry: cemetery at Cette, Larbaud at Montpelier, Marshal Joffre born, rather absurdly at Rivesaltes, near Perpignan, Roussillon, my first foreign home, lost for so long, soon mine again, found with a stranger and now my cypher is surrendered too. A life spent in creating privacy and in the search for a friend to whom I give all privacy up. So the bee makes honey, yielding it for artificial sugar, so the bee makes honey again. The door bangs, Luna Park. Quarrel over a sea of faces, brisk bitter quarrel in the glow of books, in a racket of noise. Now through fault of pride I mistake physical privacy for spiritual home. Error, after all, why not share Spain, Cerdagne, Roussillon, and I have shared them before – only by escape to altitudes of emotion, to a sensibility too rare for others to breathe freely can real independence lie. To give more vitality than one receives, create more beauty than one borrows, be sought after instead of seeking is to be alone.

Nördlingen May 28.	Questionnaire. Set and answered by Gladwyn Jebb.[1]
Favourite Place	Wherever I happen to be feeling well.
Favourite Emotion	Fear.
Worst Enemy	Eric Lingerman Esq.[2]
Best Friend	H G N [Nicolson].
Religion	C of E, i.e. complete 18th century sceptical Erastianism.
Greatest Ambition	To be thought 'able', in other words to be a reasonably successful man of action with literary leanings and friends.
Greatest Fear	To be thought ineffective and inefficient.
Pet vice	Lack of ambition.
Aim of life in one word	Adventure.
Views on Constancy and Chastity	One can only be constant to a friend or an idea. If one is constant to an idea one's brain becomes rigid, in other words 'on *cesse d'aimer et d'être aimable.*'

Therefore constancy to a friend is the only desirable sort of constancy and this kind of constancy is as beautiful as it is rare. Only fools and invertebrates are sexually constant. Chastity is a male illusion. (It has though a certain retrospective beauty CVC.) Gladwyn chose for the end of the world to be in an English country house with friends.

---

[1] *The Memoirs of Lord Gladwyn*, p 35, has: 'We proceeded to Nördlingen where we sat, this time unaccompanied, in a rather gloomy bar and by way of cheering things up subjected each other to a "questionnaire" – Cyril's favourite parlour game.' The version then published is a little less complete than this one. 'I did one myself for Cyril, but he denies its existence and in any case it was lost. My recollection is that he said that his "ambition" was to "create a work of art", and that he thought that my own "ambition" was dreadful.'

'We were certainly both happy on that trip,' Jebb continued, 'so much so that we agreed that, if we did not get married, we might share a flat when we got back to London. What would have happened if we had set up house together I cannot imagine. Cyril indeed actually wrote a dream piece in which that highly dubious character, Congoly, was accused by the Public Prosecutor of the Establishment of corrupting a well-known member of the Foreign Service by inducing him to send home a copy of the banned work *Ulysses* in the Diplomatic Bag.'

[2] 'A minor Oxford character who popped up at parties' – Peter Quennell in an interview.

Berlin

Cruelty of a) youth b) age

Bobbie, have you noticed how Harold repeats his stories?

Yes.

Do you think he ought to be told?

Not yet.

You can't marry too early, said Harold, for the great thing is to come through the period of fidelity and be still young.

How is it possible to avoid domesticity in marriage, perambulators in the hall, servant discussions etc. I suppose it is all right if you are on the look-out against it? I am afraid it requires a considerable amount of money to avoid domesticity, Cyril.

Sexually, said Harold, I represent a buffer state.

We had some interesting talks. The night Bobbie went we discussed ourselves when young, how we should like to have met ourselves at 18 or 19 and where. Harold described himself motorcycling in Germany and held up two days forlornly at Dortmund. I remembered myself as droll, decadent and rather birdlike among the second-hand book stalls of Cologne. Raymond[1] deplored his lost opportunities and we all admitted that at an age when we were longing for intelligent conversation with people older than ourselves, we had fled from all travellers' advances. I said that this did not really matter, for youth was a period of missed opportunities, they were more rich and significant in their maladroitness than the

---

[1] Raymond Mortimer, then 35. Assistant to Desmond MacCarthy on the *New Statesman*, later its literary editor. Mortimer, 'made it clear that in Harold he had found the love of a life-time', writes James Lees-Milne in *Harold Nicolson*, Vol I 1886–1929, p 236. What had been Nicolson's obsession with Mortimer, Lees-Milne continues, 'lasted throughout 1925 and 1926 before settling into a permanent, peaceful and happy affection'.

On May 16, 1928, Nicolson wrote to his wife, 'Cyril came yesterday. Like the young Beethoven with spots; and a good brow; and an unreliable voice. And he flattered your husband. He sat there toying with a fork and my vanity, turning them over together in his stubby little hands. He tells fortunes. Palmistry. But the main point of him is that he thinks *Some People* an important book.' Nicolson also wrote to his wife that Connolly and Mortimer 'stalk round each other with their hackles up like two poodles'. Cyril probably was toying with Nicolson's vanity; or he may have changed his opinion. At any rate, in the journal which he had been keeping in the previous year, he recorded his first impression of *Some People* in an entry dated July 30, 1927: 'A most unpleasant book, might be written by an undergraduate trying to combine Max Beerbohm and Aldous Huxley with a touch of Beverley Nicholls and a snobbish conceit.' p. 198 below records further approval.

'Conversations in Berlin' was the title of the essay extracted from this section of this journal. It is collected in *The Condemned Playground*.

competent, never miss a moment, grasping philosophy of late youth, and middle age. We later walked in the Kurfürstendamm which was gay and exciting. Raymond said his father had taught him the importance of loafing in any big city. I remember accusing Bobbie of lacking the city sense. I said he did not react to the excitement and glitter and personality of towns at night or their danger and great beauty. This I said intoxicated me, and it was a pity it did not intoxicate him, as scenery did, for cities were as old as sunsets and most of the vitality of modern life was centred in them. Jack has very much this city sense. I thought of Sterne crying, 'So this is Paris! Crack crack crack!' Of course Bobbie has got this feeling and I was adopting my old tactics of accusing him of not having something in order to enjoy the delicious sincerity of his refutation. Last night I asked Raymond if there was any book that could be laid down as a test of intelligence, something that could draw a line between Bloomsbury and Chelsea in its readers. I suggested Proust, because to read it all through must require more than culture snobbery and to have read it all through must improve the mind to a point beyond second-handedness. Raymond suggested *Adolphe*, *Clarissa* and the heavier French classics. Harold said a whole set of smart and stupid people had read religiously every word of Proust and remained as stupid as before. They had probably read Joyce as well. He disapproved so strongly of any kind of culture being made the test of any kind of intelligence that he hardly allowed us to go on with the discussion, which after all, since Raymond and I perfectly agreed with him, was only experimental. We tried to analyse intelligence, and I said all intelligence was criticism of life, the first person to say, 'Life is short, or sad or boring', was using their intelligence and standing outside the atmosphere in which they moved, which was more than an animal or a fish could. Intelligence then proceeded from an ability to comment on life, to an ability to comment on oneself and finally to relate one's experience to other people's and generalise from the particular to general truths about living. Our ability to discuss sexual preferences without feeling sexual emotion was a high proof of our intelligence. Raymond said he thought I was against intelligence or rather against the intellect and I said that I was, for I was really interested in the imagination. He said, and Harold agreed, that the perfect intelligence was an absolutely free mind gifted with an infinite curiosity and able and anxious to grasp and illuminate any non-technical subject. I said that that was just what I hadn't got and that

I believed in and practised incuriosity. I hated well informed people with fluent general interests and vivid curiosity about contemporary problems. I said I respected Raymond's passion for 'actualidades', that he came down to every day as to an examination paper, the hours lay before him like blank foolscap and he was fresh and anxious to answer the questions, whatever they might be. I said I was still writing idle scrolls over those of the week before. I said I was only interested in that part of the present that was relevant to my imagination, with regard to the rest I was absent-minded and bored. Harold said, rather nicely, that it was because there was a streak of scholar in me, both in my nature and my admiration of scholarship and that he respected it. I said that might perhaps be true and Raymond said what insufferable bores were great brains that only exercised themselves on one subject and that people like Whitehead the mathematician were not intelligent at all. I said it was not the scholar in me that was incurious, but the Celt. I happened to have a good intellect and a classical education, but underneath there lay the Celtic dreaminess, incuriosity, and tendency to brood. I said I brooded for hours over the past, going over conversations or ruminating about people and that I could sit for two or three hours engrossed in chewing the cud or in daydreams of the near future, like going to Spain.

Raymond said he had no daydreams, not even sexual, and he supposed this was because he had no imagination, and because he had no imagination he was not really self-dependent and couldn't bear being left alone. We were surprised at this and said we didn't think it possible to have no daydreams. Harold described a few of his which were mostly simple visions of wealth or power or friend worship. 'To find Cyril crying,' he said 'is one of them.' Raymond said he thought these were intellectual masturbations and not at all healthy, though he envied my capacity to be always making use of my mind. Well I am really curious about life, said Harold, and I don't expect you know what has thrilled me this evening most. 'Yes I do,' I said, 'the doctor being rung up from Munich.' I suggested we should all say how that had struck us. Raymond said he had hardly noticed it except to be glad when Harold took us out of the dining room so that the bell did not interfere with our conversation. I had been excited by the call coming from Munich but the doctor having been in today already, I had been annoyed like Raymond, and only deduced a general reflection, that it was like a German to let his

[165]

house and then be continually popping into it with his own key, while an Englishman would scrupulously avoid going back to it once it was out of his hands. Harold then came out with a string of observations, how he had wondered if one of the children were ill, known it was the wife ringing up, wondered how the husband would take it, thought when the phone rang the second time, I shall be able to tell if his child is ill when he comes out by the look on his face, then he had thought this was unpleasant and had bundled us out of the dining room so as not to be tempted to look at the doctor when he had finished – thus doing to spare the doctor what we both thought he had done so as not to bother us. Raymond thought this observation in both of us was the true novelist's gift. I said writing down one's observations really was; anyone could observe. Harold said he thought it was the capacity to keep the bones together and not smother them with digressions and irrelevant facts. I said the thing to do was to write down everything that interested one, skimp, even if it affected the plot, all it bored one to write – then go over taking out what was unnecessary. I said revision should be a question of taking things out and not of putting them in, and he agreed. This may be taken as a fairly typical evening, except that so small a share of it fell to Raymond. Of course I put down more of my conversation than theirs but I do not misrepresent them. Only it is harder to remember what they say than what I did. And after all it is my own diary. I missed Bobbie very much all that day and evening.

We had several lovely evenings. Especially one when we dined by the water in Potsdam. A hot and beautiful night, we had a table in a big restaurant by the water. The talk was mostly of archaeology, but the music, the riverside crowd, the summer night made it seem like some scene in fiction, like the dinners in the Bois of Proust and his friends or C. I wrote a short Chinese poem about it. My throat was very sore and I did not otherwise enjoy it. I liked Bobbie. Two brown half-naked boys paddled by in a canoe, emerging like bronze savages out of the night, and disappearing as naturally into it again. Another evening at home, happiness was discussed and we agreed that Harold was the happiest and most fortunate person we knew (Bobbie was inclined to except Godfrey). Harold was very pleased and said that as a matter of fact he could not remember ever having been so happy in his life as he was at that moment. We all touched wood and laughed at ourselves for doing so. Bobbie said how strange had always been my feeling for τὸ φθόνερον [retribution visited by jealous gods upon those who are happy on earth]. I said I thought most people got it as children, that with me it had been deepened by Herodotus, the speech of Artaphernes about God γλυκυν γευσας τον αἰωνα, giving men a taste first of sweet time. Bobbie smiled back at me. The candles lit up the table, the dark glow of port, the lighter [glow] of brandy, in our glasses. The air was thick with the smoke of our cigars. Raymond's head was thrown back in intelligent meditation. Bobbie was looking at the table. We were all going over our pasts to see if they contained moments as fortunate as this one. I thought of our security here, our comfort, our freedom from worries, our friendship and our free play of ideas and intelligences. I thought of Bobbie so lately restored to me and of our trip to Spain. Yet I felt that real happiness contained more distress and rapture and that Bobbie's slight expression of melancholy and Raymond's silence meant that they too were being slowly forced to refer it to the past. Yes I don't think I have been so happy before, said Harold, and I do not expect, I thought, that we shall be so happy again.

Berlin

Reality of Bobbie. The main feature of this summer has lain in being with him – has been in lying with him. Of course after his letter to i Tatti and the Racy business it was logically unavoidable. He came to Chilling for a week and stayed ten days after which we came out here together, with luck we should only have separated for the inside of three weeks between July and October. At Chilling our chief intimacy consisted in making bad jokes. We were there during the heatwave and life was almost ideal. We would breakfast in our dressing gowns and later in the morning walk down to the sea. The tide was high before lunch and we would bathe and sit on the shore. The water was very warm and blue, the island hidden in a haze of heat, and we would walk back slowly through the green corn. After lunch we would go sailing and play chess and croquet out on the lawn after tea. After dinner we would walk to the wood or down to the sea again and later talk and watch the ships go by. We went over to my cousins at Dibden one Sunday and over to the island with the Hanburys another. Jack came for a night. We bathed and went for a walk, and after dinner drove in the car over to Meon. There was a sunset and we sat on the bridge by the flats of the Meon river. We went up to London for a couple of days, gave Noel lunch at Sovrani's (I thought of us giving lunch to Charly and Nigel at

Martinez) and motored down to Chilling on a lovely evening. I went and saw Bobbie's portrait in Halliday's[1] studio. It is very fine. The gathering Western remoteness of our motor drive as we slid into the Meon valley and the summer evening impressive and I grew eloquent. 'A jigsaw puzzle with half the pieces missing is all that God has given his children to play with,' I remember saying. When we met Jack at Southampton we all had drinks in the South Western Hotel and worked out our bright idea of taking the liner to Hamburg. The general impression is one of perfect simple life, the blue sea flaked with green, the green corn flaked with blue, the flowers and fruit of Chilling and the red brick and grey stone house as it looked in the evening. The heat was incredible, the haystacks and barns and trees shimmered in haze and it rose like a thick invisible weed off the brown path to the sea. I thought of Virgil and the simplest Greek poems, walking back to lunch with Bobbie, with our towels and wet hair seemed 'Camp' or something older than camp. [O.T.C. for Officers' Training Corps, was added in 1968] I suppose because a fulfilment of one's earliest schoolboy daydreams – the summer holidays in which one had one's best friend to stay. Possibly all through life one carries these unrealised equations of boyhood, small things which one had wanted to do, though forgotten themselves, lending a strange glow of gratification to experiences that come later, but still contain them. This walking back from the beach at Chilling for instance has exactly the same appeal and beauty for me as had walking down with Noel to the temples at Girgenti one year before, and that again I connected with the ablution benches at Camp and more so still with the field path to Ward's Mead.[2] I can remember both at Girgenti and Chilling trying to remember an epigram of Rhianus because of its title 'In the Field Path' in Mackail. Both Chilling, Girgenti, Ward's Mead and Camp were all epitomes of summer, in fact of greenness, and there is no greater expression of simplicity, security, and being at home in the world than two friends going down to bathe. Hence the occasion is a fusion of my old trinity, grace, greenness and security, and therefore derived from Eden worship, the first place where two human beings hand in hand took their solitary way. Add the

---

[1] Edward Irvine Halliday, born 1902, portrait painter. Shortly before, he had been at the British School at Rome, as had Longden.

[2] Part of the Eton playing-fields close to the Thames. Athens was a point off which it was possible to dive into the river.

particular Greek element infused into bathing and the Eton summer by the anthology, the Phaedrus, and the chance of falling in with boys on the ways to Athens that we could not otherwise be seen with and the daydreams of their company that one would have if making the journey without them, and the whole is a perfect blend of warm Hellenic paganism, recollected boyhood, and original sinlessness. The best moment on the voyage out (except for a few deckgames a great disappointment) was a wettish afternoon when we worked out the mileage of our tour in Spain, a blend of efficiency, mathematics and all the glow of anticipation. These tours within tours, trips planned on trips, are one of the most elusive joys of travel. Next to that was our luxurious journey to Berlin in a sleeper. Since he has gone, I miss Bobbie more and more. Largely of course as a person, his companionship, his appearance, his jokes, but most of all as an atmosphere, a kind of imagination's weather. The hot dry wind that blows round and about me, in his presence becomes a wet and gentle breeze.

'All Ireland is washed by the gulf stream' I quote, waiting for that melancholy elegiac tide to return. Like the first windy evenings of September, the first drops of blown rain falling in the dark, the first tangle of leaves or sour smell of damp logs, his nature soothes me, excites me and irrigates me, like a dry land at the touch of autumn. And the sense of equality, for I who have made and lost so many friends have only been able to maintain one equal – and now we have known each other long enough to be able to evoke at any moment a parallel in our past, the past that lies behind us in such profusion of troubles, deliberations and moments of vision. For so long our friendship and our youth have run together, like a road by a railway, that we obviously can only reach the one through the other – and only together can we revisit the wilderness in which we once lived and fought. *O tu severi religio loci* tolls through all the memories of my past, spectator of my follies at Eton, partner in them at Oxford. The Mozart fragrance of our Rome journey, the sadness of our first year in exile, the drama of Florence and our first 'chalet', the agony of that Easter term. The tropics of our second chalet, of my Minehead Christmas and last Easter and summer, all culminating in Princetown and in Fowey. The tragic magnificence of the Berkeley, the inadequacy of our friendship, so much more casual, so much more feeble and friendly, that has gone on ever since. And now this relapse, so full of consequences, in the verse [sic] of Spain. And now I have a curious sadistic feeling about Bobbie – perhaps I have suffered so much from him that I need a revenge – perhaps I feel he underrated me and am determined to teach him a lesson out of my neglected pride.

My sadism is very subtle with regard to Bobbie, I do not want to cause him any kind of pain or to hurt him, but I should like to storm him unprepared by a fire and sympathy of conversation, to glow right into his personality by a kind of corrosive imaginative beauty so that he feels he has never lived nor understood anything before as he has on this wild probing caress of words – to give him vitality that is greater than his vitality, to teach him a sensibility finer and surer than his own, to send an intolerable current down to light his heart's globe and to lap him all the time in a gentle warmth of tenderness, humour and understanding, that is my ambition, for if I succeed nothing else that he does will give him back his honeydew, nor will he taste the milk of paradise from other cups than mine. I will have given him the craving which only I can slake, I will have given him an emotional income which I alone can spend. In a moment of worship I will have taught him that only with my vitality can he really live, only with my eyes can he see. There is no finer sense of power than the power of one's own imagination over that of other men, no more exciting and impossible task than that of making oneself indispensable to one's best friend. To snare him in that subtle bondage shall be my revenge in Spain, and when he is there, to love him, laugh at him, and because after all I must preserve my only equal – then to set him free on the branch line to oblivion. Our lives will be a compartment from which all the other passengers have got out. Leave your career to your portrait, let that go from strength to strength while we establish our right to fail. O admirable *veneris idolum*! Gone native in your hut among the broken bottles, white skin in beggar's rags, dull eyes turned upon the coral shore – I will look after you. I will chase away your hula girls, pay off the leper mistress, poke the great crabs that gnaw your mattress. Exorcise the white ants from your bed. I will kindle and glow to your lovely face, a glance of recognition, doing my simple insidious tricks, the rabbit handkerchief, a rabbit, look Bobbie, the cluck of an invisible hen, the disappearing coin, the vixen shadow on the wall. Choza de Indios, reed hut by the sea, last life upon the wild Marquesas, we live in all the beauty of our degradation, for long streaked brown by native drugs, observing all the ceremonies of our relapse, Far away, heads wag, dons groan, friends grieve and gloat, relations and ushers point the moral – the world at their feet, his evil genius, than whom none appeared more full of promise, both of course, not either, yes, yes, I once met him, τον δ' ᾿Ηους ἐκτανε φαεινου ἀγλαος υἱος ['whom the glorious son of Dawn killed' – Homer]. Marsden[1] was right, and Boase and Bailey on the portrait of Robert Longden, this magnificent portrait of a young man is now the pride of the collection. Painted by the great Halliday – the draperies reveal of the subject [sic], unfortunately nothing is known, is known, is known, is known. Holding the coral to my ear I heard the noise of the sea.

Remembering Eden
The hearts chill flutter
O Robert Longden
For what we have done
now shall we be punished.
Fear is lust is fear in one
Though sensibly dismissed
Time is studious to emend
Victim tyrant friend
Actaeon
We are getting on
Birthdays when the year is old
September October
Shade between us and the sun
The palace of La Cuba
A colder day – a day distinct with cold.[2]

Half hours with the great. Villefranche.

Villefranche   * = temporary   out of 10

Guest		Charm	Sex Appeal	Intelligence	Virtue	Guts	50
Bartlett Sir B		4	6	4	2	2	18
Carisbrooke		3	1	2	−N	0	6
*Connolly		−2	0	0	0	0	−2
Lucinge Pce		0	0	1	8	2	11

---

[1] H. K. Marsden succeeded Crace as Master in College. T. R. S. Boase had been an Oxford contemporary, later President of Magdalen College, Oxford. Cyril Bailey was a Balliol don. Boase and Bailey were friends of Sligger.

[2] Written in a paler ink, this poem may have been incorporated at a later date.

Guest	Charm	Sex Appeal	Intelligence	Virtue	Guts	50
Lucinge Psse	4	8	½	1½	5	19
Marsh E	0	0	4	2	0	6
Henley Hon Mrs	0	0	2	8	7	17
Henley	0	0	0	0	9	9
Villiers G	0	0	0	4	0	4
Shaw B	0	−10	−?	0	8	−2
Shaw Mrs	0	0	0	6	4	10
Maurice (Mrs?)	0	0	3	8	6	17
Joy	6	2	8	6	8	30
Mrs Spears	4	4	6	6	6	26
Gen. Spears	1	6	4	1	7	19
Meraud Guinness	5	7	4	4	5	25

At Villefranche 16–24th. Nothing memorable was said.
'And I'll tell you another thing, there was a photographer on the beach this morning, who asked if he could take me diving – take me diving I said, well it's no good me telling you this is three feet I'm going to dive because your newspaper is sure to call it thirty.'

Omnes	:	O Mr Shaw!
Mr Shaw	:	And Charlotte will bear me out, won't you, Charlotte?
Mrs Shaw	:	Tchk!
Mr Shaw	:	That the American papers now think I –
Mr Villiers	:	Most extraordinary. Thlt. Thlt. Uncle Clarendon staying at Borthwick and I can tell you of at least three houses from which I was excluded as an ardent social-ist. Thlock, splutter. Yes, I assure you, as an ardent socialist; oothle.
Mrs Spears	:	Mr Shaw was telling us, Drino,[1] about his experiences bathing on the beach.
Gen. Spears	:	It appears that Mr Shaw has geceived considegable attention from the photo-gwaphers.
Mrs Shaw	:	My husband has been saying –

---

[1] The name by which the Marquess of Carisbrooke was known. Grandson of Queen Victoria, he had been born Prince Alexander of Battenberg. An assiduous and elegant ornament of Café Society, as exemplified by the others in this Riviera party. In 1928 Lord Carisbrooke was 42. Cyril was the guest at Villefranche of the Spears'.

Mr Shaw	:	I was only on the beach this morning and one of them asked me if he could snap, I understand they call it, if he could snap me doing a dive, I have no objection to diving three feet for you I said, if your paper will take all responsibility for calling it thirty.
Omnes	:	O Mr Shaw.
Mr Shaw	:	And now I'll tell you another thing.
Hon. Mrs Henley	:	No that was the youngest sister, Milly married young Tring. Sophie came out in 1908 and Bertina was staying there in 1910, quite a different generation.
Mr Villiers	:	O Thquite. Thquite. Baloodle.
E. Marsh	:	How dreadful! and so unfortunate for – and how did they break the news to Drogo – such a charming boy.
Lord Carisbrooke	:	The Lido . . . Excelsoir . . . The Piazza. The Paratyphoid . . . The Casati . . . The Riva. Charming. Charming. And I so love all the lights and the colour and the water and all the colour and all, and the lights. Lifar. Young Lifar.
E. Marsh	:	Young Woodley! (bursts into tears)
Gen. Spears, arriving with cinema camera	:	Now Mr Shaw!

London reduces all one's friends to snails, whose real selves are never static, but always receding or protruding out of their social shell.

The great problem with women is how to contrive that they should seem our equals – but there are certain equalising factors, the independence of the rich and the smart is almost as levelling as our intellectual independence, and the depth of experience thrust by life upon the underworld is almost as intense as that which we have chosen for ourselves.

October

Back in London after five weeks in Spain with Bobbie: vastly undigested. General dissatisfaction and distress. Gladwyn getting

[173]

married, hence I am homeless,[1] autumn depression. Bobbie at Oxford and no interest at present in literature or work. Talking of his ginger cat, always mewing, Raymond said, 'and she has no cause to, for I pay thirty shillings to get her covered, which is more than I should dream of paying for myself'.

Found another coloured café, near the Shaftesbury hotel, excellent grenadine, smaller than N.C. St.

Impressed by Huxley's new novel.[2]
Unpleasant sense, not only of being just where I was this time last year, but of being practically just where I was the year before. As homeless, futureless, hopeless and unestablished as ever. Shall I live in Paris or the country? If only Bobbie could live in London it would be all right. I am also less interested in literature if anything, and not really so interested in life, at least last year I had a long spell of natural high spirits in Yeoman's Row and the year before I was young enough to stand Chilling, St. Leonard's Terrace etc.

I suppose my happiness is a difficult crop that requires sun, rain, soil, manure and tending to make it flower at all – I need intelligent people, I need smart people, I need low life. I need old friends. I even need respectable people too. I might try and go back to Yeoman's Row but I feel Patrick's world will impose itself more and more upon him, and it is against my principles ever to go back to anything. Thank heavens Bobbie is in England again. The office of the *New Statesman* is the most depressing place to return to that I know, always an irritable atmosphere of nerves and stupidity, nobody ever regarding anything that is written for the paper except as idiotic nonsense or anybody who writes it except as a crank. The motor expert, the city editor, the writer of gramophone notes, explain that they don't approve of what one writes about Wyndham Lewis or Proust, Sharp bullies everyone, and the woman secretary cries, 'And when are you going *away* again?' as one comes in.

State of Literature
The state of literature is pretty static.
Guide to the Balkans permanently held up, whereabouts of copy unknown.

---

[1] For the sake of economy, Cyril had proposed leaving Yeoman's Row, and setting up instead in a flat with Gladwyn Jebb. Nothing came of it.

[2] *Point Counter Point* had been published in November 1928.

Novel nothing written since July, general sense of unreality about it.
Book on novel – No desire to write a book on the novel.
Book on Spain – No desire to write a book on Spain.
Alpdodger story – unfinished.
Joyce article ⎫
Scrutiny ⎪
Spanish article ⎬ unbegun
'Station'[1] ⎪
A. Huxley ⎭
All I can hope to cope with is this diary.

10 October

By some seasonal miracle I seem to be falling in love with London
and recapturing the same exaltation that I attributed solely to youth
this time last year. To feel this jungle come to life all round one in the
evening, the same October mists, fires, lights, wet streets, blown
leaves, to plunge in its many zones not knowing what one will
discover and to return with a growing sense of confidence and
power as a new street or a new district falls beneath one's rule, that
is to be a true explorer, or rather that it is to combine the intimacy of
a wooer with the excitement of an adventurer, to run my fingers
through the town's limp body, to caress the lax pulsating city as
rashly, as apprehensively as a Greek might an Amazon, or a small
spry leopard, male of some great cat. The female spider and the
female mantis, larger than the males, devour them after copulation,
the spider when satisfied, the mantis beginning to nibble her partner's legs in the middle of the act. This is surely symbolic of nature's
attitude to man, of the forest swallowing the explorer, of all the
drivel talked about love and death. The male mantis incidentally
appears to enjoy it, or rather makes the same movements with its
antennae as if it did. Well now boys – suppose that the male mantis
represents the complete expression of the male eros – the desire to
bite off more than it can chew, and the female to represent the desire

---

[1] Robert Byron's *The Station*, about Mount Athos, had just been published, and Patrick
Balfour, for one, was urging him to review it. In vain. On February 8, 1930, Byron and Brian
Howard wrote to propose that he contribute to a book they intended editing as a protest
against 'this disintegration of modern life'. Cyril's contribution 'might express that pagan
feeling that the countryside of southern countries communicates at certain moments'. Also in
vain. His first appearance between hard covers was in a calendar for 1930 called *The New
Forget-Me-Not*, published by Cobden-Sanderson.

to chew more than it can bite off – is not this the '*du bist mein Ruhe*', the 'bright star feeling' – negation of personality through physical contact. In fact the Antonys, the hen-pecked, the physically inadequate, or the Des Sieux are really the manliest type of lovers, because what is closest to nature, must be closest to the nature of man. Therefore one needn't be ashamed of falling in love with ladies of Elche instead of Thracian fillies, with sacrificing oneself to archaic and sinister Kores with their impenetrable reserve instead of strutting round trying to be a bigamist, a he-man – but cocks, cocks of the walk are natural too – and why should humanity not be nearer to the cock than the mantis – so there is room for both classes and room to be both classes.

Friends

Bobbie	Joyce
Patrick	M.M.
Harold	
Gladwyn	

In storage

Freddie	Joan
Noel	Peggie
Jack	? Rachel

The old

Logan
Desmond

à la carte

Brenan[1]	Honor
Raymond	Giana
Bob	Nina
K	Jane

Unsatisfactory, and I have probably left out a lot of people I like. This week, anyhow, I like only Bobbie, Harold, Patrick, Gladwyn and Joyce [Turner] and besides them want only to see Brenan and Raymond Mortimer. Enemies – Maurice [Bowra], Piers, William.

---

[1] Gerald Brenan, born 1894. 'My nightly perambulations of the streets ended in August when a girl called Winny Stafford came to live with me,' he wrote in his *Personal Record* (1974). In a preceding chapter of that memoir, he had judged that 'Cyril's most productive gift has been his curiosity,' which, on the analogy of white magic, he likened to 'white envy'. Also, 'I introduced him to a girl called Lily, whose married name, intriguingly, was Connolly.' She is quite certainly the Lily French referred to in this journal.

Peter and Nancy perhaps. *Au fond je ne crois plus à l'amitié. Mais ça, c'est par paresse. Je pense que l'amitié ne puisse exister en dehors de l'homosexualité ou l'hétérosexualité prodiguée et cynique.* That is to say profound womanisers require their friends less and less except as occasional shock-absorbers. Therefore one can only cut down one's friends if one is to keep up with them.

To lead a treble life without striking a falsetto note, snobbishness, as a disease, does not necessarily attack a vital part, all one's youth one thought it did. 'Shades of the pigeon-hole begin to close about the new-found friend.'

BRENAN brings me upstairs. Winny is here – Winny is wearing a black dress, bare legs, and bedroom slippers – she seems used to being here. A dark fine looking girl of 18 with a pure cockney accent. She gives us tea. I asked about rooms. 'You'll find the flats round here rather expensive, the lawyers make it so respectable.' 'I don't think lawyers are respectable. I think they do things on the quiet.' 'That's what being respectable is, Winny, doing things on the quiet.' 'Well I don't think this street's respectable. I think you drag it down.' They banter on, rather indelicately. Winny was seduced at ten, ran away and made enough money on the streets to have her baby in a hospital. A woman she sheltered for the night stole it all, and she had to have it in the workhouse where she was delivered without an anaesthetic in front of 16 medical students and a sister who told her both she and the child would go to hell. They were immediately separated and she was not allowed to leave the work-house unless she joined the Salvation Army. She refused to sign anything, and ran away to see her child when on parole to go into a convent. She went on the streets again, to keep her child but refused to sleep with men, whom she now hated and only stole their wallets, finally getting in with crooks at last. Brenan found her starving because her corns were too bad for her to walk. He got them seen to and gave her some new clothes but she refused to go on being a prostitute. Margery Fry got her into Lyons and Roger Fry gave her a room. One day she came round to tea with Brenan and asked if she could stay the night. She had stayed ever since. Once when he was away, she had scorched the table ironing, and had been so upset that she ran away to Birmingham, leaving a farewell behind. Otherwise she had never shown emotion or expressed what she felt. She goes out dancing every evening and makes about £9 a week which she spends on clothes, while Brenan gives her her meals. She offered to replace the charwoman. Her dislike of men keeps her absolutely faithful and she tells Brenan everything they say to her when she goes out. I dined with them and was impressed by their perfect relationship, his care not to refine her in any way, and her superb cockney reticence and poise. He said she got on well with Rachel and Frances Marshall,[1] and that he was perfectly happy living with her, though neither of them were in love. Brenan said he had worked as a waiter in Venice but was sacked because his hair was too long. He had begged in Jugo-Slavia afterwards. Raymond thinks he is mad. He seems to me to be a serious writer, rather an earthy Tolstoy mystic and a spoilt priest. He is a further stage of my own equation, hence the charm.

17 Pall Mall[2] Oct–Nov

Visit from Gladwyn and Raymond. Raymond very scathing about Bob's [Boothby] taste. 'Why all these etchings? I can't understand this fetichism – two of Mr Walpole's books are about people who, instead of blaspheming against the Holy Ghost have an orgasm over tearing up an etching and then they're so bloody safe – look at that absurd thing there (a thin black streak across a sea and sky of uniform grey) it's not a landscape but a baby's bottom – and the books, more cowardice – the *Life of Sir William White*, *Where Freedom Falters*, *The Pomp of Power* – otherwise the room is all right, a concession to art is made in these slightly Beardsleyish black cushions, but it might otherwise be any decent private sitting room in a hotel.' 'Well, it's very good of him to lend [it] me,' I said, 'but I enjoy the delicious streak of *mauvais élève* which enables you to spot immediately things like that.' 'But seriously,' said Raymond, 'it shows how bad things are, that the intelligent people like you and me should be sitting here making fun of politicians, it's how the dark ages started.' 'Well I suppose it's how the dark ages will start again.' 'And you're the only person Cyril who would enjoy them, you simply don't believe in civilisation and you don't like it.' 'Yes,' said Gladwyn, 'you are the real revolutionary, the believer in the second coming.' But I don't want the dark ages, I said, I only should

---

[1] Frances Marshall, born 1900. Married Ralph Partridge. Her elder sister Rachel ('Ray') had married David ('Bunny') Garnett in 1921.

[2] Boothby had a flat at this address.

enjoy the transition from one to the other, purely from the point of view of creating something. I think decadence is a fine stimulant, it does people good to feel '*après moi le deluge*', it makes them excited with a dramatic sense of their importance, and they write well – I should like to live on the brink of the dark ages, in a dissolving world that affords more and more scope to individualism. You don't want to create, Raymond, so naturally you prefer a reign of taste. I should fiddle best while Rome's burning, but I don't want to set it on fire. 'Well I don't think you could create even without a guarantee of personal liberty, it's the period before a revolution that's exciting, there's not much individualism in a revolution itself.' 'And it's Gladwyn and his politicians who really want to set Rome on fire – people like this' – Raymond's malevolent fingers shot out and seized a book called *Optimism* which they placed on Gladwyn's lap. 'I'm not a politician,' said Gladwyn, 'but a diplomatist.' 'That is only a more decorative and perfectly ineffectual form,' said Raymond, 'besides, diplomatists get more fun out of a revolution than politicians. Look at the French Revolution, the only people who were absolutely unaltered by it and indeed who had far more scope for making plans were the personnel of the Quai D'Orsay. The only time you aren't decorative is just after a war.' 'That doesn't mean that we arrange wars,' said Gladwyn. 'O no, any more than a surgeon arranges for people to have their appendix out when there's not really any need for it.' 'You mean there would be fewer appendices out if there were fewer surgeons.' 'Of course.' 'But there wouldn't be fewer street accidents, for instance.' 'Come come Gladwyn,' said Raymond kindly, 'we know that your profession is meant for people like Allan Graves, and they aren't really noxious in war or peace, so what does it matter.' 'Well, at least they are decorative.' 'That's just my point about Allan Graves,[1] he's not even decorative – that awful house, and furniture.' 'But his banker friend was worse.' 'I think I disliked Yencken[2] most,' I said, 'a sly bloody arrogant little colonial.' 'The only man Elisabeth Bibesco has wanted to sleep with.' 'The man in her novel?' 'Yes, I don't like him very much,' said Gladwyn 'he probably is rather bogus. I think he suspects Harold rather.' 'O you think he knows he's . . .' 'I think

---

[1] Allan Graves was honorary attaché at the Berlin embassy.

[2] Arthur Yencken, an Australian, was held to be an up-and-coming man in the Foreign Office.

[179]

he's rather suspicious.' 'Well, really Raymond, it was as unfair to make Gladwyn responsible for Allan Graves as if he made us responsible for Hannen Swaffer.' 'I know, naturally, but I adore getting a rise out of Gladwyn.' 'Do you think the phobia of rhetoric in literature is a direct result of the mistrust of politicians in the war?' 'Oh yes, I should think so, what time is it?' But I mean is there a connection between little Belgium, corpse factories, I will not sheathe the sword etc and the instinctive baldness of modern styles? Perhaps the rhetorical writers, Humbert Wolfe, Michael Arlen, Yeats, are just those who didn't come across the war. Half past seven. Good God is it really.

Faits Divers

Romance.

I. Magistrate to married man who was convicted of abduction of girl of 15 – 'Do you think you will have been able to get over your infatuation?' 'Two months in Brixton Prison would get one over any infatuation.' 'Then you promise never to try and see this girl again?' 'Yes.' 'And you, do you promise always to keep away from this man in future?' 'Well, if he keeps away from me, I can't do anything else can I?'

II. 'She is my wife,' he said passionately to a *Daily Express* representative last night.

'She is intelligent,' said Peter, 'in the simian way that women are.' 'You give them something and they hold on to it very tight,' he added, describing the naive ape-like gesture of clutching the handle of an umbrella with his long prehensile hands.

Resolve, having met her, to be absolutely impervious to any impression made by her appearance, and even by her voice.

Waley said *Orlando* was tinsel. Cheers.
Against *Orlando*. Logan, Peter, Arthur [i.e. Waley], Self, Trevy [Robert Trevelyan], Jennings, Squire, MB. [i.e. Maurice Baring], Raymond, Francis [Birrell], Lady Colefax, Todd,[1] Desmond, etc etc.

---

[1] 'Buxom as a badger', according to Virginia Woolf, who had been commissioned to write pieces for *Vogue* of which Dorothy Todd was editor from 1922 to 1926.

A tu cara te llaman
Sierra Morena
Y a sus ojos ladrones
Que andan por ella.

Karin [Stephen] said that at a school in Hampstead that was very advanced, the children were left absolutely to their own devices, and everything they did was taken down and finally they invented a game in which one was head of the form and set tasks and punishments to all the others, and a deputation was sent to the headmistress asking her to beat them.

From cover of *Criterion*. January 1928.
Either
or write for yourself – no public
for other people – no privacy

Literature
1. Crystallization of one's own experience.
2. Creation of a new experience.
3. Profitable exercise of certain faculties.
1. Diaries, letters, notebooks.
2. Stories, novels, experiments.
3. Journalism.

Ideal

To extract the greatest possible value from one's own life. This depends hardly at all on the nature of one's experience so much as on the quality of the instrument used to perceive it – the senses or the mind. One's own life will never be important while one thinks it more important than other people's. The egotist is self-corroded, equally it is fatal to borrow more vitality than you know you can repay. Vitality is tidal.
D'un si doux coeur si longtemps possédé.
Oct 28. ditto
There is a kind of electric malice only generated in the company of tipsy homosexuals that I find really embarrassing, partly because I am not homosexual myself, and partly because it has a kind of metallic esoteric glitter which I rather envy, as I envy any state of society which is carried to the nth term of a series.

The Headmaster of Eton. Confirmation Address.

Romance

Leicester Square on a cold autumn afternoon. The air crisp and smokeless, sky and buildings grey, London looking more like Paris. A fat man, hatless, with an Alsatian on a leash. A frayed woman carrying a parcel. 'Leave me alone,' he shouts to her, 'I don't know you, who are you? – if you don't stop following me, I'll set the police on you. Constable – where's a constable. I wish to give this woman in charge for soliciting.' The crowd collects, the woman gapes, strawy hair wriggles from her hat, the Alsatian runs behind her, entangling them both in the lead. 'Get out you bloody f . . . . . you,' shouts the man – 'you dare come after me like this.' He turns and walks the other way, dazed she follows, silent and hostile. They face each other again. He red-faced, check-coated, hatless, the dog strains and almost pulls him over. The crowd surges round. Accosting. Tart. Broad daylight. Who the Hell. Two girls pass. 'Fancy speaking like that to his bloody f . . . . . wife.' 'Is she a tart?' 'Gawd'struth, she's not a tart, she's his bloody f . . . . . old woman.' 'Can't a fellow have a row with his old woman?' The girls pass, two fat Jews stand beside me, coo, he isn't half giving it to his old woman. 'Constable charge this woman, soliciting.' 'Is he tight. Is he tight?' 'Gawd'struth he's not tight, can't a fellow have a row – he's potty.' 'He's not potty.' 'Yes he is – potty as arseholes.'

Moral

Naomi's sacrifice is one of the most moving things in recent fiction.

Introduced Harold and Patrick. Patrick was telephoning, and waited ten minutes to speak to Princess Bismarck. 'Now that's what comes,' said Harold 'of telephoning to princesses – you'll have to wait another 10 minutes because she's trying on her crown or something. When you get to my age you won't bother to telephone to princesses. There's only one Princess you can always get on the telephone and that's Princess Bibesco, she sits with her ear glued to the receiver. In fact it's impossible to get hold of her off it.' We spoke of the attraction of men of forty to young women. 'I suppose they're more romantic and tender,' I said, 'Women seem to like the air of thoughtfulness and mystery about them.' 'There's not much mystery,' said Harold. 'We take longer, you fellows simply put it in and waggle it – as a matter of fact, though, I used to be able always to stop short and try another way and now I'm over 40 I find I can't do that without a shattering ball-ache that makes one think of cold compresses. The older I get, in fact, the quicker I come.'

The Thirteenth Sitwell and other Caesars

Pall Mall. Nov 1st.

General disgust, especially with literature.

Causes of failure of literature in England

1. 'Gentleman' complex in authors (Gosse)
2. Tittle Tattle about books, the idea that literature is a non-specialised, non-technical subject, and that it is fashionable to know about it.
3. Blighting influence of English materialism and stifling traditions; best sellers, commercial influence. A. Bennett and journalism.

No distinction between the enduring and the readable.

No revolutionary spirit in England, no experiments, no innovations. The weeklies, politically advanced, are retrograde due to the editors assuming that they know more about literature than the critics – besides, labour and advanced thinkers notoriously conservative about art and letters.

Monthly papers

The Criterion Now a pompous quarterly at 7/6, ruined by its dense weight of metaphysic, religion and morality.

The Mercury Conservative and unenterprising – only good point, it publishes a quantity of bad poetry by unknown authors which no other paper will do.

Life & Letters Bitter disappointment, a heavily subsidised paper that could afford to experiment instead determined to pay its way by pleading to a respectable, moneyed and wholesomely English public that is frankly die-hard. The whole tone of the paper that of a literary *Punch*. Pompous editorials addressed to clubman readers. No poetry, no young writers and the contributions of even the good writers lamentably affected by the pretty-pretty appearance and the voguey public – e.g. V. Woolf on snobbishness etc. The Gentleman's magazine.

The public in England:

I The cultivated public.

Favourite epithets, delicious, charming, exquisite, delightful, enchanting, delicious and delicious.

When a book is obscene, or unpleasant, they call it dreary and boring.

When a book is experimental, they call it silly, childish and incomprehensible.

This public forms the active literary world of tea-parties, smart luncheons, cliques, drawing rooms and *chapelles*, their judgements are based on their own cowardice and on the good taste of a few favourite arbiters or procurers. Where insincere their judgements are essentially snob, where genuine, they are based purely on good taste, usually Frenchified, and refinement rather than any particular attention to the ideas of the age they live in. Willa Cather, San Luis Rey, Virginia Woolf, James Laver, various essayists typical of the discoveries of this 'choice' public.

II The plain man – this is the bulk of the English public who read newspapers and are led, and occasionally driven by Mr Arnold Bennett. His favourite epithets are 'pretty good, jolly good, jolly good stuff, pretty remarkable, extraordinary, and very interesting'.

When a book is obscene or unpleasant he calls it 'pretty strong' or simply 'muck'. It depends on Mr Arnold Bennett.

When a book is experimental he calls it mad.

This public forms the passive literary world, the Philistines who are as hostile to new forms of creation as the civilised *dix-huitième* world of Chelsea.

A book in fact must appeal either to Chelsea or Fleet Street.

Thus we have

Conservative Fleet Street, the Philistines
Conservative Chelsea, the Aesthetes
and nobody else who cares very much about anything.

      To be continued.

Nov 2nd.

Last days at Pall Mall. Letter from Bobbie, more Spanish photographs. Visit to BBC. Terrible *envie* for Paris. The cafés of Mont Parnasse. The lights, the crowded, warm interiors, the wasters, the drunks, the artists, the sense of liberty and of rebellion. *Rue Delambre, de la montagne Sainte-Geneviève*, and the cold passage on the Boulevard of afternoon to evening.

Yeoman's Row. Nov 5th.

Almost as depressed and dissatisfied as this time last year and without the inspiration of Racy. My life seems in every way to have retrogressed. Poorer, older, iller, stuck in the same house, the same groove with infinitely fewer friends and considerably less curiosity. Gladwyn, Harold, and the Spears as against the MacCarthys and Maurice. Bobbie, however, much more real.

Ideal. To be more of an artist and a Bolshevik, to write a lot this month and to go to Paris and live in Montparnasse if not in love or otherwise adequately detained here by Nov 1st. *Envie* for Paris continues severe.

When I came back to Yeoman's Row, the children ran up in the dark and said, 'Why it's Cyril, we thought you never were coming back.' I liked this but not as much as I would have once, or as I should have expected.

One cannot really love London. It is unsatisfactory in every way, a foggy, dead alive city, like a dying empty antheap. London was created for rich young men to shop in, dine in, ride in, get married in, go to theatres in, and die in as respected householders. It is a city for the upper class unmarried and the middle class family.—not for the poor.

Every writer or artist must feel an inferiority complex in London unless he is a snob (Browning, Michael Arlen) or in the Reynolds–Johnson tradition of Fleet Street, Garrick, good Burgundy and golfing. Arnold Bennett is the English Bohemian. Of course there are Bohemians but they are afraid to show themselves – they have no quarter and they have no cafés – their only chance is to get rich and voguey and have cocktail parties. Cecil Beaton the struggling artist. Godfrey Winn the starving writer. In Paris they have a quarter assigned to them, and are lords of it. They aren't much better as artists, but they are freer, happier, and harder-working and live in an atmosphere whence great art is more likely to arise.

The more one sees of life, the more one realises it is a hopeless affair without art to synthesize it. 'To love life in all its forms' is like loving ice in all its forms, or lentils: pumice stone, or journalism. Life is only in exceptional cases worthy of being loved, though those cases of course are in no way connected with vitality. To love life is to have the curiosity to search for the occasions when life is lovable – or rather the enterprise to create them – in London they are damn few.

To write on reviewing etc – on Joyce – 2 monologues.
Letters. Bobbie. Montparnasse. M.M. Mummy. Joyce.

First meeting with Ann Chichester, astonishingly lovely figure and complexion, they hurt. Brother, according to Patrick, the most successful man about Kensington.

Contemporary prose is a piano in which half the notes do not sound, they are pressed and don't come up, words that have long lost all their meaning.

What would you take away with you, Patrick, if the Yeo caught fire? 'My hot water bottle and my press cuttings.'

Mrs Jenkins told the laundry that she didn't know where I was but that I would be back from abroad at the end of the week. I'm beginning to enjoy the Yeo more, I said, now that I've definitely decided to come back from Portugal on Friday.

On Youth
Thoughtless and miserable, dull, incompetent, silly.

Overheard in a restaurant – 'This is my idea Gwen. Cinema sermons, five hundred feet, was it worthwhile? Two footballers, one of them is married, one of them has a spite against the opposing centre half, he manages to cripple him and finds afterwards he is married to his sister, was it worthwhile? You get the idea? Two fellows walking down the embankment – beggar – ten shilling note – nothing for you my man – very sorry – one that gave ten bob walks home, other killed in runaway tram. Was it worthwhile? You get me?'

Arthur Waley told a story of the charwoman to Mrs Marshall, Mrs Garnett's mother. Stephen Tomlin[1] had done a colossal bust of Bunny Garnett and left it there. 'That's a rum shaped bit of stone they've got at Mrs Marshall's,' said the charwoman, 'and the joke of it is, it's a little like her son-in-law.' Arthur [Waley] said the only other person who might have made such a criticism was Roger Fry.

---

[1] Stephen Tomlin, referred to as 'Tommy'. 1901–1937. Son of a judge. Married Julia Strachey, 1927.

Odd that there should be a Sickert among the urinary marbles of the National Liberal Club.

In a questionnaire for the ugliest place we knew, both Peter and I wrote Oxford. For the loveliest woman we both chose the Lady of Elche.

Nov 5th

Decision. This evening told Patrick I was going to take up writing. Discussion on people with Patrick at dinner. P. spoke of the preference of his family for sound Cambridge men like Humphrey Mynors and John Maud[1] and asked me what the difference was between us and them. I said the sound men were $\beta+$ and the people like us were $\alpha-$, the gulf was between the first rate and the second rate but that this not an intellectual distinction. The α character depended on developing one quality at the expense of others, in carrying experience in any form to the extreme at which it becomes real. The all-round man never succeeds in this, his ambition is to fit the world, consequently he can never rise above it, or sink below it; in us the love of liberty or truth or pleasure would develop to the exclusion of mere worldly compromise and to take up any independent attitude to life partakes of this α quality, the attitude need not be an intellectual one. Thus the hopelessness of our generation, or of most of it, might be profound enough to be its saving grace. The Spanish word *rancio*, meaning rancid and hence *echt* or genuine, expresses this, for in anything or anyone first rate there is something a little *faisandé* or hard-boiled. It was hard-boiled because it was logical. Another division would be in people whose lives were equations insufficiently resolved $2\alpha = 2$ and into those whose lives were reduced to their lowest forms as $\alpha = 1$. As to the relations between them, just as a virgin does not want to sleep with people through having had no experience, so the second rate, the β, the unresolved, do not wish to be anything else, but once they have had a taste of the other, they find it very difficult to go back. I said I would place Bobbie at the top of the β's – one incident might decide whether he would go over the top. I quoted Mackail, 'to know the best and to have known it for the best, that is success in life', and said that I thought it was the essence of maturity to know what one did

---

[1] Both Eton contemporaries. Afterwards, respectively, deputy governor of the Bank of England, and Lord Redcliffe-Maud, Master of University College, Oxford.

like and what one didn't and that the Mauds and Lubbocks and Loxleys would never get as far as that. We cited Maurice, Peter, Lily [i.e. his friend Lily French, see below], Richard Sykes, Lord Derby and Brian Howard as examples in various departments of this *rancio* appetite for the domination of life.

Laziness is always bringing me to like the second best – just as cowardice is always preventing others from discovering the first. Logan once described the world as a bath of mud with everyone trying to heave themselves out of it and falling in again. If you are proudest of your posterior, says the art of loving, you should arrange yourself in the positions most calculated to display it.

Lily

'O I do like Piccadilly, don't you? I could never stay away from it long. Once I went to live with a man, a nice man he was too, he had a flat in Earl's Court and I stayed down there two months, well one day he sent me up west to get some things and I got to Piccadilly about six o'clock. When I saw the lights and everything I was happier than I'd ever been, I'm not going to lose this again, I said and so I never went back. I left all my clothes there and everything too. I don't know what he must have thought. Well, I got a fiver that night and I walked into Maxim's with it and when the waiter came up I ordered two bottles of champagne. Well, when I'd drunk them I noticed a woman with a red dress on sitting with a man opposite me so I said, "You ought to give me that red dress, it would suit me much better." I suppose I was a bit tight but I just said it to make conversation and she flew in to a tearing rage. "Take this woman out, she's drunk", she said to the manager. "I'll show you whether I'm drunk," I said, "I've paid for this and I've a right to have it," and I hit him on the head with a champagne bottle. O there was an awful row. The band stopped and all the dancing and a detective came and threw me out and they said I'd be arrested if I ever put my head in there again, but I don't mind, I never cared for Chinamen. Well, goodbye, they say the first man you meet after midnight on Hallo-ween means something to you. Not that you're quite the first but the other old drunk was quite impossible anyhow.'

June

'So I cabled to the old gink "send me £100" and he cabled back to New York "you can hardly expect me to finance your amorous adventures" and I cabled back "what can you expect from a pig but a grunt" and do you know I never heard from him again but the day I got back to London he rang me up an' I got £40 out of him to buy a dress. Christ, what are men for except to get money out of, when I feel affectionate I keep it for my cat and my dog – relations, my God, listen to him, one half refuse to recognise you and the other half sponge. I've got two aunts and I got a letter from them both on the same day, one telling me not to dare call myself by the family name considering what I'd become and her sister asking me to lend her £50. And now this old geyser's gone to Biarritz and left me without a penny. Not even paid for my riding lessons. I believe old Fitz has got on to him again, you know I had an awful row with that old bitch. She thought I was taking her men away from her, well what else did I go there for, I'd like to know – she and her Italian countesses my God, I could tell you a bit about Italian countesses, why that girl, at least she's not a girl, used to live next door to me. She used to keep a Frenchman and they'd have the most unholy rows, he used to walk up and down outside her house all night seeing how many men she was getting and I thought he was a detective sent to watch me. I got the hell of a fright until I pointed him out to another girl – Christ, she said, don't you know a ponce when you see one. They have a kind of sly, respectable, well-fed look you know and they always carry an umbrella. Italian countess indeed. Why I'll tell everybody I'm a Girton girl. O yes I'm a Roedean girl, the illegitimate daughter of the Master of the Pytch-ley. But Fitz, you know, she rang up the old geyser and said I kept a man before him, well it was a young barrister that used to keep me – another man said, why June, I thought you were dead.

Fitz told me you'd be run over by an omnibus in Piccadilly – she told someone else I was in prison. So I rang her up ten times that evening and put the mouthpiece to the receiver so she got a shock. It's June speaking you old bitch, I said, I'm coming right round to wreck your place, the next night the police got her and she thinks it's me.'

Moral
'The Honourable Maurice Baring who is one of the chief novelists read by the officers of the Brigade of Guards.' *Daily Mail* Nov. 9th.

Moment of happiness at Yeoman's Row. Amber sunlight through the panes on golden cushion, yellow Kaross, and glass of amber wine. Reading *Ulysses* in the armchair, far cries of children playing.

Pleasant thoughts of last night, Peter and Noel, Nancy and I, and of Lily's momentary cordiality.

Fear of life, hate of self, general misery and intermittent self pity these last few days. *Quando ver veniet meum* [when will my spring come], only gleam of confidence supplied by Bobbie. *Sombra soy de quién murio.* When I was a bully at Eton I made Buckley write a weekly essay for me on Wayne, Eastwood, Milligan and various other boys. At first he hated these essays as much as the subjects, but soon he grew conceited about them and resented any criticism. This suddenly cropped up in my mind. Thoughts of a dry bone and a windy knob. Lost a £5 note at a bad revue, culmination of misery on Saturday night – the most unlovable mug in England. Feel ill unless I drink and depressed when I do. One of the Spanish records sends one off into the wildest fits of mawkish gloom. Genteel canine pathos. The world whips only those who look as if they've just been whipped.

Patrick said of Prince Bismarck that about everyone his wife met he asked, 'Is he a gentleman – I mean is he "in society"?' Princess Bismarck said that every night a glass of beer was brought to him before going to bed which he drank to the Kaiser, and then broke. A French attaché said at Rosita's party, '*Regardez comme ce jeune homme a déjà l'air cocu.*'

> *O douleur, o douleur, le temps mange la vie*
> *Et l'obscure ennemi qui nous ronge le coeur*
> *du sang que nous perdons croît et se fortifie*

21st Nov

Dorothy Warren's party. A hundred people in Boulestin's, an odd mixture from Lady Vita Russell and Lady Witt via Ethel Sands and Arnold Bennett to Anna May Wong.[1] Arnold Bennett tight before it started. Gladwyn introduced me. 'But really,' he said, in his know-

---

[1] Lady Victoria Russell was the mother of Georgiana Blakiston. Ethel Sands, 1873–1962, the artist, often invited him to her house in Chelsea, and later at Auppegard, near Dieppe. After publication of *The Unquiet Grave*, she asked him to explain his intense mistrust of life. He replied, 'My natural states are either *pleasure* or anxiety – boredom – guilt. How does one learn content if one is always dissatisfied, always feeling that one has disappointed everyone and let them down?' (Quoted in Wendy Baron's *Miss Ethel Sands and her circle*, p 254.)

Arnold Bennett had written the script for *Piccadilly*, which was currently being filmed, starring Charles Laughton and Anna May Wong. She had been born in 1907, in Los Angeles, of Chinese parents. The film was released in 1929.

ing falsetto, 'you write damn well, you know as much as me, how do you do it, you know as much as me. I was speaking to Clifford Sharp the other day and I said, tell me, who is this fellow, C.C., who is he? Well there's nothing to tell, said Clifford Sharp, he's just C.C., he said, that's all. Well he writes damn well, I said, he knows as much as I do' – he pointed down the room to where the tables were filling up. 'Gotta go down there,' he quavered, then, confidentially taking the lapel of my coat, he lent towards me. 'Gotta go down there.' Sat next to Lady Keeble at dinner, a strain, afterwards went over and talked to Evan Morgan and back and met the Wongs. Anna May Wong beautiful but really more Malay than Chinese in appearance, rather cold and Hollywood in manner – terrific S.A. but in the hackneyed 'sinister oriental' tradition. Her sister was really more beautiful and wore Chinese clothes. She spoke Florence Mills American, rather like the Blackbirds on their best behaviour. One felt that Chinese faces were as superior to Japanese and in the same relation as their poetry and art. The most beautiful quality of the two sisters was the set of their faces, which were so flat featured and of such water-lily texture that they seemed each to balance on their bodies like a flower on a green stem. It was impossible to stop looking at them and made one feel that they were as remote from contact with one as an animal. They are probably both stupid, childish and spoiled, however, and Anna mercenary as well. Thought of Peter's sunflower. After supper, when everyone was wearing paper hats and banging balloons, a quartet appeared and played the most exquisite Mozart, Byrd, and Purcell, the loveliest and rarest kind of music. Everyone sat back and listened. Dorothy Warren and Philip Trotter lay in each other's arms shamelessly and tenderly and each table basked under the warm music like a man having a shower. Leigh [Ashton] played beautifully afterwards, he and I and Roger Senhouse,[1] Gladwyn, Cynthia,[2] Peter Rodd,[3] Marjorie and Mary Hutchinson stayed on till the end. I have never seen two people look so happy or so in love and liked them so much for it. The party seemed a perfect flowering of the old world and a

---

[1] Roger Senhouse and Lytton Strachey 'would pretend they were David and Absalom, Nero and his slave, a member of Pop (the Eton Society) and his fag, a parent and a child'. This, Michael Holroyd explains in his *Lytton Strachey* Vol II p 548, was Strachey's imaginative method 'of merging more intimately with his loved one'.

[2] Gladwyn Jebb and Cynthia Noble were married in 1929.

[3] Peter Rodd married Nancy Mitford in 1933.

commentary on my conversation with Jacques Blanche that afternoon.

Cham advised a young man not to give his mistress a gramophone record – 'Girls,' he said, 'are replaceable, but you cannot get an American record for three weeks.'

Donegall[1] went to tea with Lady Cunard to meet Virginia Woolf. 'What did you think of her?' I said. 'A nice quiet little thing but terribly shy, poor dear.'

Nina [Seafield] bought a book on Proust. I didn't know you read Proust. Do you like him? 'I don't know,' she smiled sweetly, 'What else has he written?'

And deepest sorrow is a modern ecstasy.

> J'aurai passé ma vie le long des quais
> à faillir m'embarquer
> dans de biens funestes histoires.
> Tout cela pour l'amour
> de mon coeur fou de la gloire d'amour.
>
> O qu'ils sont pittoresques, les trains manqués!
>
> O qu'ils sont à bientôt – à bientôt
> les bateaux
> au bout de la jetée!
>
> De la jetée charpentée
> contre la mer
> Comme ma chair
> Contre l'amour

The poor benefit of a bewildering minute.

1929

With a deepening sense of guilt, failure, loneliness and insecurity, I greet the New Year.

Review of 1928
January	London intoxication.
February	Racy crisis misery. Brixton mornings.
March	I Tatti. Wasted month.

---

[1] Marquis of Donegall, 1904–75. Gossip-writer, close kin to the fifteenth Marquess of Vanburgh in Waugh's *Vile Bodies*.

April	Discovery of *Ulysses*.
May	Racy convalescence. Berlin, friendship again. Entirely satisfactory trip with Gladwyn.
June	Montparnasse, love, art, and liberty. Towards a spiritual home. Long Barn.
July	Heatwave at Chilling. English Pastoral. Bobbie restored (happiest days in year) Berlin again. Hamburg.
August	Villefranche – restoring – Joyce real.
September	Spain with Bobbie.
October	London again, viewed from Gladwyn's and Bob's. Brenan influence on Pall Mall.
November	Patrick and Yeoman's Row.
December	A wild month, intoxication of London as before.

Friends made: Harold, Gladwyn, Raymond, Hyslop[1]
      lost: Desmond, Molly, Freddie perhaps, K and Jane

Friends restored: Bobbie, Noel, Maurice intermittently, Peter

Influences: Gladwyn, Joyce, Harold, Baudelaire

Women: V. Trefusis, Magda Keeling, Olive, Vita Nicolson, Joyce [Turner], Meraud [Guinness], Zara, Lily, C.S., Nina and Maureen.

General reflections: Read and written far too little, Wyndham Lewis review only satisfactory piece of work, increased confidence, however, and aptitude for life – the summer especially May–October admirably satisfactory. Deterioration in dealing with Logan and in highmindedness, generally a year of social success, amorous enterprise, aesthetic Bohemianism and physical, moral and emotional retrogression.

> *O when in my straphanger's heart*
> *will lust and intimacy write again?*
> *With every virgin and with every tart*
> *their horrid dichotomy grows more plain.*
> *O Cain, be able, Abel, be thou my cane.*

The Sermon on the Mount
Nous aimons les femmes à proportion qu'elles sont plus étrangères. Aimer les femmes intelligentes est un plaisir de pédéraste. Ainsi la bestialité exclut la pédérastie.

---

[1] Paul Hyslop, the architect with whom Raymond Mortimer lived for many years. See also p 243.

L'esprit de bouffonerie peut ne pas exclure la charité, mais c'est rare.

La bêtise est souvent l'ornement de la beauté, c'est elle qui donne aux yeux cette limpidité morne des étangs noirâtres et ce calme huileux des mers tropicales. La bêtise est toujours la conservation de la beauté; elle éloigne les rides; c'est un cosmetique divin qui préserve nos idoles des morsures que la pensée garde pour nous, vilains savants que nous sommes!

Last remark unfortunately smacks too much of facetious *galanterie*.

Thou hast led me like an heathen sacrifice
with music and with fatal yokes of flowers
to my eternal ruin.

The poet is referring to the spirit of hedonism.

Resolution: To be altogether more advanced and intelligent, to have more friends and fewer mistresses, to write and read more than I eat and drink, go to Paris again, and win a thousand pound prize with my novel.

'The Spanish and the Negroes are the only two modern civilisations emotionally equipped to resist the Jewish–Russian–American. It is Tottenham Court Road against Seville and Harlem, blues, tango, paso doble, spiritual and sequidilla versus the standardised sentimentality of jazz.' Oscar Slater

England, my not my England.

We have no precedent for an English intelligentsia. Since the battle of Hastings our artists have been occupied with becoming gentlemen, our gentlemen with appearing aristocrats, our aristocrats with being rakes. The flower of our civilisation is a certain splenetic enterprise, an instinctive dignity in living, an absolute grasp of the material splendour of life – a young buck tilting down St James's Street, a clean old man in a club window, a great writer married to an earl's daughter, a country gentleman reading Keats – these are the fruits of our mind and upbringing, these are the images we should preserve, for it behoves us all to respect the types which God seeks to perfect in us, to teach the other nations, as Milton bade us, not how to write, but how to live. No need to awaken latent philistinism, the urbane good taste of our Horace Walpoles, the provincialism of our Johnsonians and Dickensians, like the upper and the nether millstones, will grind all talent away. Writing is a lapse of taste rather than a crime, it is explicit and hence in opposition to our character and our climate. Mothers of Blooms-bury remember your country rather than the massacre of your husbands and lovers, the justice of which the MacCarthy, Sir Squire, Lord Lynd and the Bumboat of Wolfe have kindly consented to explain to you to-day.

The MacCarthy. Before I begin I should like to read you a telegram: 'Simply must have you for lunch, sending car, do tell me what you think of Coventry Patmore, you dear literary thing.'
That telegram is from the Marchioness of Salisbury.
No no, my listeners, sit down, sit down.

The Chairman. I think you will all join with me in regretting that Mr MacCarthy is indisposed and unable to remain with us any longer.

The MacCarthy. Thank you, Seymour, thank you.

A closed car drives up and with bared heads slightly bowed the spectators watch it drive away.

January

Back from Sledmere[1] appalled at my enjoyment of a week in the country. Realised how much more inherently happy I was with people like Richard, Christopher, Angela and Freya than the kind of people I meet in London – also how much better and at ease I felt in this hospitable deep winter party. Richard appealed to all the rake and the oppidan in me. Christopher to the schoolmaster, Angela and Freya to the entertainer and the romantic friend. Enjoyed riding, coping with Adrian and Petsy, so perfectly of the soil, the countryside under snow, the huge warm house, the tobogganing, the shoot, the smell of cartridges, the heavy winging and thud of falling birds on the smoky evening air. Standing in the wet woods listening to the beaters tapping and whistling, watching the farm cart full of birds bowling home over the park, drinking with Richard before and after dinner, making friends with Vermeer Freya over elaborate charades. Tea in Adrian's house, the dogs, the

---

[1] Sledmere, near Malton, Yorkshire, where Cyril spent Christmas 1929, belonged to Sir Richard Sykes, then thirty-four. His brother Christopher, two years younger, had been honorary attaché in the embassy in Berlin, 1928–9. His twin sister Everilda, 'Petsy' had married Adrian Scrope in 1928. Richard and Freya Elwes had married in 1926. Angela Sykes, youngest in the family, was born in 1911.

log fire, the photographs of horses, Petsy's sulky tweeded beauty, the intimacy of the newly married hung like an albatross round one's neck, their gauche account of courtship, their fluent talk of hounds. O the joy of lingering over port and brandy with men in red coats telling dirty stories while it snows outside. Angela especially fascinating, I suppose because she disliked me at first, but mainly because she represents that rude, incurious, exquisitely self-centred phase of youth when even to be in love is a concern of no-one but one's own.

> Où tout ce qu'on l'aime est digne d'être aimé.
> L'innocent paradis plein des plaisirs furtifs
> est-il déjà plus loin que L'Inde ou la Chine?

Failed in this account to bring out (a) deep rooted pleasure of making a new friend in Christopher (b) the peculiar *northern* element of Sledmere, the vast rolling snow-covered fields, the amazing feudalism, only the postman and roadmender in a village of 500 not dependent on the estate, and the grim rich game-pie England of 18th century squires, yellow waistcoats, brown woods, topboots and leather gaiters with the Holdernesse hunt ball and the baccarat room at Tranby Croft thrown in.

Back in London met Princess Bibesco and did not care for her much, her egoism is as tiresome and her appearance about as unprepossessing as my own. My rustic bloom soon wore away for that matter and I have really enjoyed nothing except sleeping with my negress again. She likes to be naked on my chest, resting her head on her elbows and her face on her hands — her black mass of hair and brown skin glow in the firelight and her large eyes looking seriously down at me like a boy reading a book full length on a lawn.

It is curious, looking back, how little I have mentioned Peter in this book, for in a sense he is my only real friend, I borrow most of my ideas from him and lend him some of his, he is after all my only contemporary whose work I can respect, and my only friend who does any work at all.

Idea for a poem, describe falling in love again in terms of rusty machinery clanking into place, of groaning winches, obsolete materials and the whole set slowly in asthmatic motion by a listless donkey circling round an unwilling wheel. The neighbours hear the painfully resuscitated sounds and grin malevolently. They know what these portend.

Fairest Cordelia thou art most rich being poor
most choice forsaken and most loved despised.
Les plis sinueux des vieilles capitales.

Charming evening with Peter and Nancy,[1] Peter muffled up with a
bad cold, Nancy in bed in blue-boy pyjamas. She has a ravishing nut
brown skin, the complexion as Peter says, of a fresh farm egg. We
talked of our future fame, of the Quennell and Connolly period, and
the need to write more notes and letters to each other to give our
biographers something to catch hold of. Peter said Vita had read his
Innisfree over the wireless. 'You mean Procne?', I said, and he told
me he already felt as detached about it as if it had been someone
else's. I explained how I envied their married state and how
debarred I felt from Eden. They said my freedom and lack of ties
stimulated them in their turn. We discussed whether Peter should be
allowed to have prostitutes, and if so when, where and who – Nancy
said she approved because it might stop him from affairs with
anyone else and with them you could never tell where they would
end, with tarts you obviously could. I suggested that a grimly
efficient elderly Frenchwoman who gave him no pleasure and made
him pay double what he intended to would send him back appreci-
ative or that Nancy should suggest that she should sleep with me –
our talk turned, not unnaturally, to diseases, to the inefficiency of
doctors who allowed the King to accumulate 30 ounces of pus, to
the horrors of septicemia, the fact that the law considered a baby
dropped in an earth closet as not a case of manslaughter, and that
the actress Rachel had come to and lived for eight hours without
intestines after she had been embalmed.

What is indispensable to C.V.C.

in music? Debussy quartet perhaps – spirituals perhaps but certainly Flamenco.

in painting – Verocchio I suppose but I could do without all
painting.

sculpture – archaic Greek up to 480.

buildings – Greek temples.

the stage – Blackbirds.

dancing – Spanish dancing.

---

[1] Peter Quennell had married Nancy Stallybrass in 1928. 'Procne' had been collected in his
Poems (1926), and was not much like Yeats' 'Innisfree'.

literature – Greek anthology, lyric poets, Aeschylus, Sophocles, Theocritus, and Homer.
Virgil and Catullus, Tibullus, Petronius, and Horace.
Waley's Chinese poems, Webster, Hamlet, Lear, Romeo, Ford, Donne, Collins, West, Milton, Blake, Tennyson perhaps – but I don't like any of these as much as I used to.
PROUST, JOYCE FLAUBERT BAUDELAIRE RIMBAUD
Eliot, Huxley, Yeats,
Racine, Chénier, Villon, Verlaine, Valéry.
All coplas and romanceros.
Some People – South Wind, Boswell, the Bible too.

in geography – fens, estuaries, islands, creeks, tablelands and woods near the sea. Spain, Greece, Africa, South America and the Indies, China and Burma too, New York and Charleston. Cadiz, Granada, Salamanca, Hamburg, Cologne, Paris, Constanza, Tripoli and Bath, most southern rivers and Mediterranean hills.

in personal relations – intimacy, loyalty, extravagance, tenderness and lust.

in the intellect – first-handedness, wit.

in life – the tragic sense of it.

in death – the fear and facing of it.

in travel – a lyric question based on romance and drink, but everything and nothing are indispensable according to vitality, so who cares.

Rhyming slang etc collected by G[erald] B[renan].

that old geyser
mug = steam tug =, steamer = geyser

on the game
on the town (18th cent)
on the turf
on the batter (on the rag and tatter)
at the race(s)
gonorrhea
  an esod
  an artillery man (gunner)
  packet – tennis racket

screw that god forbid = look at that kid
fisherman's water = another man's daughter
plates and dishes (how's yours = Mrs)
on my Pat Jones, on my Pat, alone
nose = his I suppose
shoes = tippecanoes
heart = jam tart
she's a wide girl
to carry the kosh, to be a twice and once, ponce (Johnie Ronce)
ring, prop, wallet, revolver
puff = bisexual fairy

new American words[1]
to talk blah
to have a yen for (usually inanimate objects)
a hang-over
snooty (high hat)
to have the curse coming or be under the curse
butter and eggs, he gripes me, that gives me the gripes
dumb – dumbular
an E.G. with his London article
and how
so's your old man

'hard work kind o' gripes me even in sex life'
Herbert, Harold, an Englishman.

Advice to a reviewer:

So you wish to take up reviewing – but this is no easy matter. To
begin with, you must be sure that writing is your vocation, next you
must be convinced that reviewing is not writing, hence the conclusion that your vocation is not reviewing. Well, once you feel that,
you can start. Every good reviewer has a subject. He specialises in
whatever subject he has been unable to make into a book. His great
aim then is to down everyone who succeeds. He stands beside the
ticket queue of fame, banging on the head all his rivals as they bow
low before the *guichet* but never stepping in himself. When he has
downed enough he becomes an authority. Suppose he knows about
Spain – what is one book about Spain compared to a critical

---

[1] In 1968 Cyril noted here, 'First appearance of Mara-Jean'.

dissection of at least five? The object of the critic is to revenge himself on the creator, the method will depend on whether the book is good or bad, the work of an enemy or a friend. In the first place the golden rule of the reviewer is 'Never praise' – Praise dates you.

Abroad at least I am interesting to myself, in London I wasn't even that. Wilkinson, literary editor of New Statesman (advanced independent) said he had only once altered his views on anything since he was 16 – he had been a burgundy man, and now he was a claret man.

Arnold Bennett told Francis B,[1] that all his contemporaries Shaw, Wells, Galsworthy, had failed because they wrote for money – whereas he . . . .

Fulco di Verdura[2] objected to Orlando because behind all this exquisite feminine panegyric he always smelt the bidet. Women, he said, could never escape that. That was why Hugh Walpole's Wintersmoon is so much better.

Told Noel I existed to celebrate my sense of guilt.

Baudelaire said human beings were civilised in proportion as they lacked the conviction of original sin.

Richard Sykes, asked why he disbursed all his rents on spectacles in brothels, said it amused him to see how low human beings could sink.

After I came back from Sledmere I went to Paris with Richard. We went to the Ritz in great style and had a cabin on the boat. We had good meals at Foyot's, Montaguet, and the Grand Ecart, and spent some time in the Mosque and Montparnasse. I had a cold and lost my voice after Richard went. Went out one evening with Mara Brand[3] (Bal Nègre) and to tea with Violet Trefusis. Met Mara and Jean, we lunched at the Cremaillière, went across to the Coupole, and Jean and I supped at the Vikings and fell for each other. Next day I went back, hated London and missed Jean and went down to the Tomlins for a bit. Patrick's frightful cocktail party, my Bennett

---

[1] Francis ('Frankie') Birrell, 1889–1953, critic and journalist. 'A most divine man', according to Virginia Woolf's Diary, May 31 1929.

[2] Fulco di Verdura, 1899–1978, Sicilian duke, artist, jeweller.

[3] Jean's friend was Mara Andrews.

article a success. Met Valerie Taylor[1] at Ethel Sands', very nice weekend with the Tomlins – Tommy's ideas particularly illuminating we had some very good arguments (classic v romantic etc). He said promiscuity nearly always arose from a sense of sin, that most homosexuals were in a primitive state of narcissism (hence their passivity), that romantics were made up of the gas of false sentiment and the hard coke of materialism, eye to the main chance etc. (cf. Burlap and his 'devil').[2] We decided that only expatriates were free, since it was not laws that hindered freedom but conventions. The crystallisation of conventions into laws typical of old civilisations – savages have only the former – France in many ways not free – e.g. you can't buy pessaries as in London. We argued much over reason. He confessed to being impulsive and romantic and fighting hard against it. I said I always encouraged my feelings out of a distrust of their genuineness. I was afraid to fight back against myself as I might so easily be beaten, e.g. youthful sorrow and the strategems to keep it alive. Altogether he is the most interesting young person I have met, and I felt I hadn't seen nearly enough of him, like a trial lesson at the Berlitz school.

Back in London grew miserably depressed, persecution mania, loneliness, solitary confinement and missing Jean. Lunch at Boulestin's with Logan, Peter and Valerie Taylor to tea. A good deal at *New Statesman* where I was dramatic critic for a short spell. No answer from Jean which worried me. Sent her a wire on Friday night. The Hallidays to tea. Noel and Francis to dinner on Saturday. Logan had flu, I wrote an article on Montparnasse, and on getting a lovely wire from Jean decided to go that evening. I packed a vast quantity of luggage, rang up Jean in Paris, and had a very nice dinner. I left a note for Patrick. It was raining in London and Noel came and saw me off at St Pancras. We stopped in Piccadilly and said good bye to Marie on the way. The train was a new Midland Express, huge drays kept coming down the platform. I lit my cigar and played the gramophone. It was one of the most pleasant solitary journeys I have ever made. The train slide through Barking and the wet stations of the East End. I played slow foxtrots in my empty carriage and felt that at last I had become an interesting person again. It was very wet and windy at Tilbury. I had a cabin to myself

---

[1] Valerie Taylor, a successful actress, was then twenty-eight.
[2] Burlap in *Point Counter Point*, modelled on John Middleton Murry.

and stood on deck watching the lights along the Thames. I had a perfect moment as the boat moved out. The wind was very cold and the brown water choppy, all the passengers were below and I saw the pilot dropped. As the little tug shot away from the boat in an Ionic curve like the parry of a boat hook I had an exquisite feeling of finality about leaving, of which that seemed such a definite symbol, together with a baffled sense that I could not understand where I had seen that curve before and how to express it in an image – I thought of Kyrle's[1] photo of the fork of roads at Stanton St John's as we saw it from the Church Tower, of young iris leaves and the petals of certain lilies, and of Proust's three trees which made him feel the same. Then I went below. It was very rough and I didn't sleep. We got to Dunkirk in icy cold. Pitch dark and freezing. I slept a little, had some breakfast and with no remorse (how narrow is the line which divides an adventure from an ordeal or escape from exile) played my Da Falla records to the rising sun. It was a beautiful morning, the sky was absolutely blue, I was in a brand new first-class carriage, and the huge black slagheaps of the French mining country looked like African kopjes framed against the red sky behind them.

I got to Paris about half past 10 on Sunday morning, had a shave and found a hotel and went round with the gramophone to Jean. She was lying in bed in a dark blue dressing gown. I stayed with her for lunch and tea, we went out at 8 for a chop, and 24 hours after dining in England I was dancing in the Bal Nègre, to the best jazz in Paris and the most awful collection of Martinique niggers. We decided to go pretty soon to Spain. Jean has short dark hair, green eyes and high cheekbones, olive skin and a rather oriental appearance, like a young man from Indo-China. She wears a dark blue skirt and sweater with a blue handkerchief with white spots tied round her neck and a dark beret. She is 18 and has a good figure. I don't know her very well yet but she is natural and pagan, almost without inhibitions and old-world guilt. Her best paintings are amusing ones of the Luxembourg gardens full of children. She is fond of food and drink, cynical and intuitive about people, rather prosaically well balanced and poised. She has all the good lesbian qualities – frankness, independence, masculinity and an interesting

---

[1] Kyrle Leng had paid court to Cyril in Oxford days. An occasional writer. He shared his life with Robert Gathorne-Hardy, successor to Cyril as Pearsall Smith's secretary.

way of talking about women's faults and figures, hates anything tartish. I feel the difference between us is between English and American, or even old and young rather than one of sex. She is anti-American herself, but won't let me be, she certainly has none of the American womanhood debutante in hard-headed ideas. Not sentimental or over demonstrative.

I went to see Joyce through Sylvia Beach.[1] His flat was rather smart (Rue de Grenelle) and nicely furnished. He wore a white cricketing blazer and blue trousers and at once began to ask me about my family, very very interested in Clontarf – he said he had mentioned Brian Boru's sword in the last bit of his book, and that it belonged to the Vernons. 'I am afraid I am more interested in little things like that,' he said, 'than in the problems of the solar system.' He asked me my age, the date of my birth, which fell in the year he left Ireland and spoke of the lanes round Clontarf. The few cricketing families there were in Ireland, and the beauty of the Dodder river. He asked about my languages and education and said he had read my article on Wyndham Lewis (such a pity he gave up drawing, he added, and showed me one or two). He seemed tired and worried about his wife who was going to have an operation, and about his own eyes, for he was no longer allowed to read – a quiet sensitive, pedantic, tragic, and rather embarrassable man – a lot of the usher about him. He didn't put me at my ease, but I was frightened, and longed to know him better.

Jean and I went to see Michonze,[2] a young surrealist who had fought in the Russian revolution, a very bleak garret studio, no chairs, no carpet, a bed in the corner and a stove, and all hung with fantastic fiery paintings – huge hands, hanging men, red protoplasm advancing down an empty road, weird landscapes, the sirens as two inclined eager long red grubs (like paper snakes that spring from jack-in-the-boxes) yearning out faceless from a brown rock towards a ship tossing on a choppy green sea. *Io son dolce sirena.* Another was of some dull hills of green corn against a black sky, a little like El Greco's Toledo. In front of the picture was a muddy road ending in a scarecrow which had a strange human rather *ighleef* [i.e. mock French rendering of the word 'high-life'] look. Beside the road was

---

[1] James Joyce, then forty-two, had lived in Paris since 1920. Sylvia Beach, publisher of *Ulysses*, was an American expatriate.

[2] Portrayed as Rascasse, the artist in *The Rock Pool*.

an ash tree of the same dull green as the hills, like caterpillar's blood, and tied to a branch of it, like a bunch of cherries, three light scarlet balloons. There is a tree swinging.

I told Jean about Racy one evening and felt better for it. I wish I knew if I was in love with her still. I have never felt so free of ties to England, or so ready to wander in poverty about Europe, since the times I first used to go abroad. I plan to go by Huesca, Teruel, Cuenca, and Murcia to Almuñecar and settle there and write my novel. I feel rather for forests and mountains than the Mediterranean, but Almuñecar as a goal is just what I need. *Ainsi nous errions, moi pressé de trouver le lieu et la formule.* I think Jean is excited, we both want to ride and walk and explore the least known parts of Spain. Brenan might be there. I feel very Hemingway though still haunted by the rhythms of the Bal Nègre. According to Tommy, my capacity to live in the present is my most civilised thing.

So this is your city (*où le spectre en plein jour*).

The dull morning, the slow evening after you came to tea, alone all this time, ting a ling, ting a ling. Thrill, Hullo Hullo. Can I speak to Mr Balfour – no he's out – when'll he be in – will you leave a message – Lady Arse A.R.S.E. Arse is very sorry she is unable : : she's having her : : O yes I quite understand – yes to ring her up on Tuesday. Silence. A man comes for some empty bottles, daylight fading into dusk writing to Peter. Ting a ling. No he's out – yes I will. Another plunge out on the choppy waste of London waters, towards the festering West through the brown streets. Tarts. Lights. Taxis. Chemists' bottles. *Et ego in Arcadia.* And did these feet, lights of the Dôme, noise, laughter, girls' faces, gardens of the Luxembourg in winter, bookstalls on the Seine, the Bois, the Bal Nègre, the Mosque, mediaeval map of Paris brothels drawn to Piscator's erection. Close up of boy's own bleak face, beard blistered, bloodshot eyes dilated with bung longing.

(A great Resolution)

Close up fades. NO! NOT FOR ME! CASABLANCA! O I beg your pardon! Gazes tenderly after the departing cuties – 'Did you see him? must be a puff' – 'O my God what a dial.' The dial passes, face of blank infant's jelly – Brand's Essence perhaps – blue overcoat, black ponce's brolly and a soft felt hat. The dial totters on along the bright mock boulevard – Lyon's Corner House – the new Empire Cinema – the cafeteria. Buy rubber goods. Connolly's opusculum,

Quennell's poems. Rabelais. An English schoolmiss. The works of
Doctor Aristotle.

> I wish I were a pessowary
> On the plains of Bakerloo
> I would eat a micturitionary
> clap and crop and Hope Vere too

Slivers of humanity drip from the bar of the Queen's Hotel, wet
sooty trees. The Café Anglais Leicester Square. Ting a ling. Ting a
ling thrill. Your usual table Mr Balfour, room please for Mr Tossoff
of the Daily Squirt. Close up of a young man of an extreme elegance,
pouting, receding, wherever possible, except at his waist which is
slightly pot bellied. 'Waiter this caviar is cold – bring me the
temperature of the room.' 'O Darling, O I'd adore to – O can't we
all go somewhere sometime and do something – O Darling, O I'd
adore to, Why there's – and there's' – 'He's the dragoman' – 'He's
ipecacuanha Smith' – 'He's our lives from day to day.' 'O isn't he
marvellous – how I hate Rex Evans.' 'Yes, isn't he marvellous, don't
you think it would be fun to, why Darling, I'd adore to, waiter a
clean crab-wrack' – 'Ring up my number and ask if anybody's rung
me up – a Mr Connolly will probably be there.'

(The Daily Squirt)
Well, we were all there, weren't we, at the Café Anglais last night to
hear Rex Evans' inimitable songs and Miss Hopevere's brilliant
imitations. I noticed Mr 'Poke' Balfour (*très chic*) sitting with the
lovely Diana Brassiere, Lady Priscilla Piprag and the Hon Halytosis
and Lady Badbreath, fresh as stilton, where they had had a rattling
day. We were all going, or dying to go, weren't we, answer shitface,
to Mr Balfour's louse-charming party in the Rotherhithe Road. I
suppose talk, I mean good talk, has never been so fashionable as it is
at present, and louse-charming, as Mr 'Poke' Balfour, the lovely
Diana Brassiere, 'Pess' Piprag, and all the cotex crowd were saying
yesterday, is just the most charming and up your arse way of
charming lice. Amen. So Otto Beit. Here ends the Daily Squirt.

The dial passes on, mooningly bulging towards the Café Anglais,
then retreating hastily to Leicester Square. The poor benefit of a
bewildering minute, he murmurs, and makes for the urinal. Men
brush by him, tender flied. These diseases are 'centres of treatment'
rainwater occasionally coagulated into spittle on the wet stairs.
Back among the flamboyant sky signs. Buy Britannia. Go to Egypt

by Cunard. The dial stops opening and closing its messface, alternately, like buried sandshrimps, two beady pink pig's eyes appear. By Russell's lit window a bald preacher screams and flaps in the air. Repent ye, the Kingdom of Harlem is at hand. 'Hullo Billie, where are you off to, in such a hurry?' '*Chérie, tu veux,*' 'darling.' 'Hullo Dearie, aren't you going to speak to me? Why not come back home and have a drink?' The dial's white junket quivers, his knees are loosened, his little red mouth like the rear crystal of a bicycle or the scarlet tongue in a pale rubber ball temptingly appears.

(The poor benefit)

The dial in a dirty room. A slobby Pekingese sprawls by a gas fire. Expert fingers caress his sides. Darling, I tell you what I'll do for one pound more. He rushes out, clutching his wallet. She shrieks, You bloody Ponce, you dirty Nancy, you think you can treat a decent girl like that, you fucking piece of – she rings a bell, a hideous chucker-out appears, carrying a clotted broom and a pail of slops on which some spent French letters float. 'Now then, trying to rob a decent girl wats poorer than yourself (getting suddenly combustible with his own indignation). You rotten little piece of shit, you dirty Nancy. Here!' Blows fall on the poor groping dial, seeping into his suet body, bewildering his metaphysical head so full of gentle musings, so action-flaring for his own bewildering minute. He totters out into the street, runs nervously down an alley and makes uneasy water over the railings, a cat passes, mewing, mange-necked. Here Pussie flutes the Dial. She darts away. Back in Piccadilly he walks hurriedly home. A drizzle falls from the dark sky, rows of sodden houses, silent streets – the canny homes of portbreathed sweetly sleeping people. Dead honeycombs in the rotten hive. The city oozes slowly, like a cesspit, the dial's tired eyelids flicker, a wave of fog seems to bend the houses. Yeoman's Row. He taps his way along the numbers, fumbling his latchkey, wiping the sleep from his eyes. Inside there are no letters for him. At the wedding of and of at and after at Mr Patrick Balfour. Mr Patrick Balfour. Sir, unless we receive. The tinsel gothic furniture, the mock minstrel gallery, the cardboard grille, the quiet, the lonely ache of partial non-existence. ἦ ζωμεν ἡμεῖς τοῦ βιοῦ τεθνηκότος [Or else we live on when our life has died]. The poor dial fumblingly undresses, his blotch face now is shaded by a new day's stubble, his eyes are bloodshot, his paunch is lined with little fatty folds, he lies in bed, yearning against the pillow, hugs it close, murmuring, sighing 'a whole starlit valley

[206]

of leaves and waters' dring a dring dring. Taxis throbbing, bottles clinking, darling how marvellous, darling I'd adore to, a burst of feminine laughter seethes from the street into the room below.

Paris. 29

Remembered the green evening in spring summer when I motored with Gladwyn down the Neckar, the wide and lonely river, the high hills covered with fresh leaved bushes, the trees, the blossom, the meadow sweet in the ditch curving with the curving river down to right in Heilbronn, along the deserted road.

Curious bourgeoisie of Joyce – when talking about his new book and anxious to mention that a phrase was a description of Dublin brothels, he said, 'I refer to – I refer to the lupanar.'

Told Peter that one's attitude to women's independence was essentially that one wished to give them Mappin terraces instead of cages – but nothing more.

Berlin May 29

Discussion on good manners, society and snobbism at lunch. Harold said the best instance of the former was when King Edward had the Shah of Persia to dinner and copied him in cutting off the green tips of the asparagus and eating it from the wrong end. He said how frightened everyone was of King Edward, of the enormous influence he had, and how lucky – since he was becoming so indiscreet and contrary – that he should have died. He described how his death marked an end of an epoch and how everybody felt it, if only because they realised that the Court would no longer lead society but be divorced from it. He said there were no hotels in London before King Edward, except the Grosvenor and the Metropole, and what a relief, in his father's day, taking tea at the Grosvenor was to the dullness of a Sunday afternoon. A discussion on society followed and Harold described the Souls to us. He said the Duchess of Rutland, Lady Elcho, Lady Plymouth and the Wyndhams, Arthur and Gerald Balfour, were the nucleus of it, that they resembled Bloomsbury in so far as the kernel was tough, grand and highly intellectual (the body meant nothing, the mind everything), while the hangers-on of the outer shell, Lady Horner in a sense, and Margot [Asquith], and other ragtag were increasingly affected by the Catholic movement. Rossetti, Burne-Jones and Mr

Wilfred Blunt. He said the Souls really went under over the Wilde scandal (though few of the real Souls knew him) and more so over Harry Cust putting a girl in the family way and having to marry her. Harry Cust and Curzon were favourite young Souls. He said that in the history of English social life the Souls would form the last and most interesting chapter and that he was afraid, as with Bloomsbury, they would be identified with people (I supplied Lady Meux) whom they would never have recognised, and their antipathy to the world and the flesh reckoned by that of their weakest members. He said that for instance the insistence of Margot, and the beauty of the Duchess of Sutherland, would cause them to be given a far higher place than that of the far more important Lady de Grey. He discussed why buggers were such snobs. Was it because they had an inferiority feeling about womanisers or because they were more feminine and attentive to the *petits soins*? Harold said he thought buggers were possessed of more vitality than womanisers, though a second-rate vitality; they were possessed of more energy than women and more dependence than men, in fact they were creepers, and needed something like the framework of society on which to climb. He said in his own case he had only been a snob from 1910–11, and Vita's indifference had soon cured him of it, but with him the parasitic target had been supplied by his work. He spoke of Victorian buggers, how he suspected Greville and knew Yorke, to have been one, and how they flourished at court. He told a story of Gladstone being informed by Cering (?) that a Canon of Windsor about to be made a bishop was one. Gladstone, whom C. had been terrified to tell, only remarked, 'In an experience of over 50 years I have learnt that the pagan qualities to which you refer are frequently possessed by men with the greatest erudition, the most absolute integrity and the deepest religious convictions.' This seemed to me the first memorable conversation we had at Berlin. David Herbert was at lunch as well.[1]

---

[1] Cyril had arrived on May 11th. 'He was not an ideal guest,' James Lees-Milne wrote in *Harold Nicolson* Vol I p 370. Whereas Christopher Sykes and David Herbert did not sponge, Cyril had no 'cigarettes, matches, stamps or soap'.

Marking this second visit's lack of success, Cyril wrote on a sheet of his host's notepaper, and as though in his host's voice, 'I do not receive many visitors, my interests are primarily in scout-mastering and bug-bug-bughunting. It was then that I noticed he had two lobes to his left ear.'

David Herbert, in his memoirs *Second Son*, has described sharing a flat with Christopher Sykes. In Nicolson's apartment, he writes, playlets written by Cyril were regularly acted

A consul at Luanda was found out to have slept with little black boys. They prepared a letter to the Queen (gross immorality) and one to the consul stating cause of dismissal. E. Barrington, Salisbury's secretary, entered in a dreadful panic to show him the documents to sign. 'But my dear Eric,' said S., 'wouldn't it be less trouble to send him to a place where there are no little black boys?' He was sent to Bordeaux (cf. Jowett and the fountain pen).[1]

Harold said no man was so effeminate as the most masculine woman. Vita, for instance, was very much more feminine than Eddie.

> so Adam looked back
> through the new palings
> remembering Eden flowers
> and all the grace of spoilt Eve

Wasted exactly one month at Berlin, in stupid gregariousness and empty bummeling, only two or three interesting evenings, usually those without David, and hardly any memorable talk. All ended in persecution mania and resentment with Harold.

Movements in 1929

Paris – Pau – Canfranc – Jaca – Zaragoza – Teruel – Valencia – Gandia – Alicante – Elche – Murcia – Granada (to March 1st)
Granada (Almuñecar and Motril) till end of March
Cordoba – Algeciras – Gibraltar – Tangier – Tetuan ⎫
by boat to Marseilles and from Marseilles to Corsica ⎬ April
Ajaccio Piana Porto Calvi and Ile Rousse (Corsica) ⎭
Nice (Villefranche) Marseilles again
Paris (May) 1–10 J. E. Blanche. Sylvia Beach. Gide. Walton etc.
Paris – Berlin May 10th. June 11th Paris again.

Paris

Paris in June the true city for the noble melancholy of misadventuring youth. Two important factors for coping with this depression.

---

before a distinguished audience, including the ambassador Sir Horace Rumbold. The Oriental theme was always the same. 'Cyril was the pimp, Christopher the carpet-seller and I was the slave-girl.'

[1] A celebrated story to illustrate cynicism in high places. Suspecting that the religious beliefs of the then Master of Balliol were unorthodox or worse, an Oxford delegation presented him with a copy of the Thirty-Nine Articles and invited him to sign by way of declaring his faith. Jowett at once asked where the pen was.

(1) Always to express your depression in appropriate surroundings – e.g. to avoid London whose gloom is squalid, and which, consequently, squalidifies and degrades the form of depression by introducing an element of despair and futility not proper to the natural melancholy of a historic sense linked by self-dramatisation with a love of beauty. In general, if the surroundings are depressing, feel depressed – the chief cure for depression, drink, is unreliable, it removes the symptoms without curing, it staunches a mood rather than heals it, a piece of premature midwifery instead of letting nature take its way – often too, it intensifies the gloom.

(2) The other cure, people, is equally unreliable. People with a greater vitality than one's own will jar, unless they are so well known that one is not ashamed to be dumb among them – or else so exhilarating to one's snobbery that one forgets everything else in the desire to shine (see drunkenness). People especially with sad voices, sex repressions, or little ambition are usually more depressing than soothing to a melancholy man – contrive instead to make surroundings suit your mood, when the melancholy vanishes as gently as a boil under a hot poultice. Others find self-expression in the form of writing a cure – but what kind of cure is writing? Give me the disease any day, as Alpdodger said. *Important*, when melancholy, to cultivate the 'dying eye' – the minute focus on small things seen closely, as a dying man, a scolded boy, notices the objects around him, so take some place, the Ile Saint Louis for instance, and appreciate it tree by tree, house by house, as if it was your own island and your own garden.

True story of Jean and Cyril.

A diary should be an aid to memory, never a recipient of confidences, but where the confidences are themselves confused and involved the statement of them becomes in itself an aid to memory and hence is legitimate.

> Midas had a secret
> he told it to a tree
> the tender grace of a day that is dead
> will never come back to me.

PART ONE

First period June 1928 Mara

C.C. came to Paris from Düsseldorf where he had motored from
Berlin with Gladwyn Jebb. Lived in Rue Delambre and haunted
Montparnasse, dined one night with a Russian woman, to document his case against the *charme slave*. After dinner in a Russian
restaurant came back to Montparnasse rather drunk. A red-haired
girl whom I had seen several times and thought very attractive was
in the Select Bar, with her was another girl writing a poem. I took
the poem and helped her with the rhymes to it, afterwards we went
and danced. I lunched the next day with the red-haired girl, her
name was Helen Ashbury, she proved very dull. Mara, I saw more
of, we both were rather attracted to Helen, who was mostly, at that
time, lesbian, but both found her dull. I was very much struck by
Mara Andrews, her frankness and sincerity, her boy's clothes and
rather talented unhappiness and we met often and I used to go to the
Bal Nègre with her and see her home from Montparnasse to 30 Rue
de Vaugirard. There was also a very attractive girl called Noah who
made up The Trio. Mara used to fill in questionnaires I set her,
mostly about herself, her tastes in literature, her friends and loves,
her ideas on lesbianism, and on America. As a lesbian, she held
much the same views as I held at my best period (Noel and Bobbie)
as a fairy. She at that time disliked sex very much, she was
platonically in love with an Austrian called Fredl, but her real
romance, so she told me, had been with another girl called Jean
(Ziplings), who was at that time in America. She described the scene
when Jean went to America, and she sat on the pavement and wept.
A taxi driver stopped and asked her to come to the Bois with him. '*Je
n'aime que les filles – je n'aime que les filles*,' she cried. Jean and
Mara and Helen Ashbury came from Baltimore. Soon afterwards I
went to England, and, occupied with Bobbie and Racy, I rather
forgot Paris (the frail and passionate lesbians nobly misadventuring through love and literature and youth; the summer walks
through the Luxembourg gardens to the Rue de Vaugirard).[1]

Interim June 1928–June 1929

I heard no more for the rest of the summer, but in September, at
Cadiz, on my birthday, I got a letter from Helen who was in London

---

[1] Bracket added in 1968.

with Noah asking me to go and see them. Patrick had opened the letter, and I seeing he had read it, felt it was too shaming to read myself, dreading to see which of Helen's *bêtises* he had come across. I never read it till I was living in Pall Mall in October. It turned out to be a very nice letter. Patrick had nearly rang them up instead when he read it. I rushed round to the address they had given, the house was shut up. Finally I found where they had moved to and though they had left, I got Helen's Paris address. I wrote to her and asked for news of Mara. At that time, I was thinking of going to live in Paris myself. Helen answered from Baltimore with information on the cost of living etc gave me Mara's address, said Noah was in Spain and sent me a Christmas card. At the same time (Christmas) I got an amusing post card from Mara and began an answer. At the end of January I went to Paris with Richard Sykes, we wanted female company one evening and searched for Mara all over Montparnasse. After Richard left, I traced her through the Bankers Trust but never got her telephone message, which cancelled the date I had made with her. The three things I reproach myself for, in this period, are all due to my laziness and paralysis of action. If I had written to Mara from England, or opened Helen's letter sooner, I might have carried out my resolve to live in Paris, and in this way I could have foreshortened a biggish chunk of Jean's past, even if Bobbie and I had spent the day in Paris on our way back that we wanted to, or had I been more socially adventurous in Berlin (where Mara was), Villefranche (where Jean was), or Biarritz – where Mara was when I passed through with Bobbie, I might have met them earlier. Then had I answered Mara's card at once or even tried quickly to find her in Paris, we would have all gone out with Richard, and so impressed Mara's mother who tended to think me an undesirable from Montparnasse. This ends the first period of my relations to *la petite bande* – though Mara was the central figure, and Jean but a name. The ones that dictated my actions were really Helen and Noah. Helen was the first to attract me, and after I had seen through her, it was the image of the elusive Marie Laurençin flapper, in London, or in Paris that made me bother to pursue Helen to write to her, and rake, with Richard, Montparnasse. Noah actually was a sly and bitchy girl.

Documents (1) June. Questionnaires. Mara, Helen. Letter (unfinished) to Bobbie. Letter to Gladwyn. Alpdodger story (atmosphere). Letter (I believe) from Mara to Jean. Letter to Logan. Letter to Bobbie (from Long Barn).

(2) June–Jan. 2 letters from Helen, p.c. from Mara. Letter and poem to Mara.

PART TWO

Second Period Jan 1929–May 1929 Jean

The next morning Mara got through to me and left a message for me to ring her up. My voice was very bad. I had a cold on my chest and when I got the number I could hardly speak. Another husky voice answered me, not that of Mara but of her friend (You're welcome). I had rung up to say I could only spare the time to say goodbye on my way to the Gare du Nord, and arrived at the apartment in the Champs Elysées with my baggage. Mara's mother met me at the lift, took me up and said you know, of course, Jean Bakewell, and then went out. Jean explained she had said she knew me so as to vouch for my not being a Montparnassian. She wore a blue skirt and a white sweater; a tall dark girl with a pale oval face, a slightly sullen expression and short boy's hair. We both had very little voice but got on all right and drank *grogs Américains* – rather too many. We talked a lot of books, she was reading *Sorrow in Sunlight* and I had just been planning what to say of Firbank. I was glad to see how much she liked it. She persuaded me to miss my train, and go in the afternoon. She told me (I asked her) that she was a Lesbian and then I realised it was the friend Mara had told me about. It also appeared that Mara had told her a great deal about me, and often spoken about me as the only nice man, besides Fredl, that she had ever met – only she had described me as more of a fairy. Mara then came in and changed into a dressing gown. We went on talking. Jean and I rather drunk, having had so much hot grogs on empty stomachs, and our voices gradually coming back. We all went out and had a very good lunch till late in the afternoon at the Cremaillière. I pretended to be an Englishman and Jean and Mara to be Englishwomen egging me on to brag and boast. I arranged to stay on overnight and borrow my fare back from Jean. Mara had by this period become very respectable, no longer dressing in old and boyish clothes nor going to Montparnasse. In ideas and speech she was much the same, but kept up the appearance of a *jeune fille bien élevée* to a much greater degree. The cause of this was her affair with Maurice, a smart young

Frenchman whom she had introduced me to the year before and whom now she was in love with and anxious to marry. This meant she would not come out with me at night. Jean said she could break a date with another girl, and did. After lunch we all went to the Coupole and danced. I wrote Mara another questionnaire about lesbians, which she answered and also a note to ask if Jean was so much of a lesbian that I could not kiss her. Mara answered not. Then she had to go, and I went back with Jean while she changed. She lived in the hotel which Mara had deserted – 30 Rue de Vaugirard. There we lay down and rested. I kissed Jean, determined for once to be aggressive in my relations with women and was rebuffed extremely rudely. Humiliation gave way to resentment and I was rather unpleasant for a bit. Jean showed me clothes, we talked and argued, I with a fine disdain for time (which apparently impressed her) and we didn't go out for dinner till nearly eleven o'clock. We had supper at the Vikings and danced some more. There we talked sweetly and got on very well, Jean talked of her parents and her past and said how much she liked me. I wrote a note to her, asking if she would spend the night with me if I promised not to touch her (*ayant peur de mourir lorsque je couche seul*). She said, yes, if I really promised and knew 'some place else we could go' – I felt divinely happy and we wandered away. We found a hotel in the rue Delambre after a visit to the Dôme, and slept there. Up to this time my impression of Jean had been of someone very chokey and mysterious with the curious sullen charm of lesbians about her. In the Vikings she had pretended to another man to be Indo-Chinese. It was only later that I realised how masculine and natural she was, and for a long time I felt a sense of disappointment, but as Mara said, compatibility in marriage at any rate is much preferable to mystery, and one should never marry one's 'victims', whether as husbands or as wives. Jean thought my predilection for the '*femme fatale*' extremely stunted and boyish – you should have got through that, she said, by the time you were eighteen. We went to bed and I vainly tried to kiss Jean good night until she relented and asked me to scratch her neck.[1] At that we fell. I had never slept with a young girl before. Jean was only eighteen, and seemed a lovely pagan from

---

[1] Added in 1968. 'Additional information. Jean was in fact pregnant, nearly sick when I tried to kiss her. Father was a champagne merchant, who used perforated French letter as a ruse to get her pregnant and force marriage (financial gain). Afterwards threatened to shoot himself with empty revolver unless she married him.'

Tibullus or the Greek anthology, with her youth, her passive and natural pleasure, her lovely boy's body, her uptilted elastic breasts. We had a sweet night and an adorable morning and rose very late. Jean did not want to tell Mara, and we decided to say we had spent the night with some married friends of hers (the Gessners), she primed me with what they were like, and telephoned to Mara. We had a mixture of breakfast and lunch in the Dôme, we both felt lousy and drank Vichy and ate eggs – Jean very much took command. Afterwards she lent me some money to get back as I had spent all mine the day before. We bought a gramophone record, and bade Mara a short goodbye. It was a little embarrassing, Jean waited outside, while I fetched my bag. Then we went to the Gare du Nord where I caught the four o'clock train and travelled gloomily to London. Jean nearly came with me, but had no luggage. 'Goodbye my sweet Cyril,' she wept and the train steamed out into the winter mist. Luckily we had promised to write to each other, and she said she would come to Spain with me at Easter, though taking separate rooms and paying for herself. I reached London at midnight and found Patrick there. Next day I wrote Jean a long letter, sent back her money. I went down, the day after, to the Tomlins in the country – where no answer came.

Documents Notes to Mara and to Jean.

February 1929

I got no answer from Jean over the weekend and came back on Tuesday, writing articles (*Journey's End*) in the train. I wrote again to Jean, and later wired. The dates here are rather confused – as far as I can remember, I got back to London on Thursday, went on Friday with Noel to *Journey's End*. Patrick, I think had an awful cocktail party that day, I stayed with the Tomlins, Saturday to Tuesday. Lunched with Logan on a Thursday, February had now begun. The wire to Jean on Friday night and answer on Saturday morning. Rang Jean up on Saturday afternoon and suggested coming, she was in bed with flu. Saw for a moment Sheila, and the Hallidays came to tea. Patrick rang up and told me to ask anyone I liked to a party on Sunday night – I could think (that settled it) of no-one to ask. Wrote to Peter and packed. Noel and Francis Birrell came to dinner and after dinner Noel saw me off. (*Documents*: 2 letters to Jean, telegram to and from her.)

Reached Paris on Sunday morning and found Jean in bed, had lunch and tea in her bedroom and in the evening we went out for a chop and on to the Bal Nègre. I think at this period we were about ten days in Paris, waiting for Jean to get well. I wrote my article on Joyce at Sylvia Beach's, sent my guide to the Nonesuch and paid a furious Patrick with the money I got. I can't remember all Jean and I did. I stayed in the Boulevard de Montparnasse and went to the Rue de Vaugirard every day. Jean was in bed most of the time, Mara there a good deal. We went the round of Montparnasse and it was almost a fortnight before we left for Spain. We were very happy and getting to know each other. I wrote my Firbank in the Coupole. We went a lot to a bar called Bateau Ivre and the weather grew quite terribly cold. To cross the street was an adventure and it was an ordeal to get to 30 Rue de Vaugirard. Before we left we had a gloomy evening with the Gessners. We slept together several nights. We very seldom crossed the river. My days were spent writing or talking to Jean who lay in bed; my nights dancing or dining with her, or seeing her off to sleep. When she got some money from America and I from England, we packed up with difficulty and began to go. Our last day we separated, Jean got violent indigestion, the cold was at its height and when we met at the Quai d'Orsay we both arrived too late for the train. We dined in great pain in the station restaurant and caught the next one. Jean forsook her low shoes, blue skirt, blue sailor's sweater, spotted handkerchief and beret and wore a fur coat and a hat. Her indigestion was so bad that she left most of her luggage behind. We caught the late train to Pau, and tucked up in an empty first class carriage, we fled from Paris through the amazing cold of Tours and Orleans, the gramophone playing into the wet Irish weather of the mild but wintry south.

Documents: Letter to Noel from Montparnasse, to Peter.[1]

---

[1] Added in 1968: 'Missing are Jean's very first letters describing the 500 franc abortion which she had just after leaving me. The man (in Montparnasse) said, '*Quel Salope t'a fait ça?*' Or maybe '*vous*' – or was it '*salaud*'? She described the people waiting with usual gusto. This was why she permitted sex from me. She should have gone back for second visit – never did – hence the pains etc.'

PART THREE

Interlude

Original poem begun by Mara and finished by C.V.C. Select Café
2 a.m. 2nd June 1928. This marked C.V.C.'s first encounter with
the *bande*. It is not a very good sonnet.

Sonata on my innocence

> My spirit faints, I trembling sink in sound;
> against my drowning hands the singing strings
> Of this last harmony beat now like wings
> in a fresh ecstasy of flight unbound
> now like the whispered rise and fall, profound
> with sadness of the limpid jets of springs,
> and in my ears, where dies the world, still clings
> the moon-dimmed anguish which the bows have found
> goes through me, through me all that I have known
> the frail lost innocence that was my own
> and never comes again, and never again
> the laughing girls, the steel blue thrust of pain
> that gone for once is gone for ever, and
> runs like a river away, away in sand.

Documents

Jean's telegram. 2nd Feb. '29

Cyril Connolly 26A Yeoman's Row

Telephone Number Fleurus 63–54 how for God's sake do you spell
your name been stinkey sick with grippe and other things one foot
still in grave such cramps you'll never know would adore seeing you
got exp. letter sent Feb 1st but no money I love you very much
darling. Jean.

Mara's postcard. Dec. 28th 1928

What-nots for the season. Haven't been to the Bal Coloniale since I
saw you. Have given up carrying stones for keep-sakes. Helen is in
America and my sweet Jean tromps me blatantly with a Jew. *Quel
malheur* – violently Mara.

C.C.'s Questionnaires.

June 1928 momentarily lost. Mara put F.J.B. [i.e. Frances Jean
Bakewell] as best friend. Fredl as best loved person and companion
for end of the world.

Jan. 1929

Dearest Mara, these questions are from curiosity.

A. Are girls first lesbian chiefly from dislike of sex (college boys, buggy rides, knew at once you were the only girl, and how many! for – pardon my hiccoughs, it's the cold, come closer, for me.) Yes, No?
Answer J.U.N. (abbreviation whose significance I have forgotten).

B. You prefer intimacy to sex – consider them irreconcilable – hence intimacy and loose conversation rather than sex (Noah and discreet conversation?)
Answer I + L.C. [i.e. Intimacy and Loose conversation]

C. Do lesbians who sleep with many women despise women on the same lines (bitches, unintellectual, on the make, snobs, cowards) as men who sleep with many women do? Yes.

D. Is lesbianism a vice of middle classes (shop girls etc) at all? Yes, from fear, not from preference.

E. Can you always tell a lesbian instinctively? Yes.

F. Do lesbians pay women ever? Have never heard of it.

G. What is the future of lesbian girls? Do they generally marry? Marry for a quiet life.

H. Are there as many grades of lesbians as of womanisers? Yes. Lack of competition (what do lesbians feel about fairies?) Eliminates jealousy, lukewarm friendship.

Afterwards Mara told me that she didn't believe in lesbianism except as the passionate friendship between young girls – 'while still in state of grace'. Physically, she said, women excited one more, but could not reach consummation – she supposed scientific *jouissance* was best obtained by beginning with a woman and finishing with a man, in which case her feelings would be for the woman. But most lesbians, she said, are too dumb in youth, too bitchy afterwards.

Lesbianism as the confluence of childhood and adolescence – Mara told me that the favourite *jeu* of her and Jean was to lick their favourite foods and drinks off each other's breasts – especially, she added, 'St Martin's apple jelly'.

February 17th. Document

'We are snowed up in tunnel near Forges D'Abel. Train gone wrong. Love mother, father (2 mothers, 2 fathers, of course implied). Ah been a bad son – Me wicked girl. Us repent. So up your arse with it. Goo'bye Bobbie, Noel. Goo'bye Mara, Ann Gordon. Goo'bye any old place. Goo'bye Maryland. Can't breathe. All over. Can't even play the gramophone. Shit! Floreat Etona! The bar-strangled Banner. Cyril Connolly (sign) Jean Bakewell xxx Feb 17th 1929.' (Banner was a drunk American.)

'Whatever assurance I may derive from the law of probabilities that girl with plump cheeks who stared at me so boldly from the angle of the little street and the beach, and by whom I believe that I might have been loved, I have never, in the strict sense of the words, seen again.'

Yes, but P. had seen her many times like that, and it is the misfortune of C.V.C. that his entire experience of Jean as a mysterious and remote creature whose nature corresponded with her looks has to be telescoped into a morning and an afternoon. In the circumstances, I doubt though if I would have had the energy to fall in love again, unless from the stimulus of some such easy surrender contrasting so favourably with the haverings of Racy, and pouring such balm on my own inferiorities and persecutions from Yeoman's Row. But although it was really the best policy that Jean (whether from idleness or indifference or sympathy) pursued, yet its after-effects were to turn all my normal passion for the adolescent virgin independence and detachment of those I love back to the period of Jean's friendship with Mara, for it was then that for years she was what she seemed to me for only half a day. In giving herself so precipitately she took away a self that I alone, of all the men she had met at any rate, was fitted to enjoy. This explains no doubt the curious thrill I had, the evening I came back from Jacques-Emile Blanche and the visit to Madame de Fels'[1] salon and found Jean, Mara and Elizabeth Marshall all at Mara's mother's – Jean in a blue skirt and a white blouse, and Mara were sitting on the floor, laughing together, and Elizabeth Marshall, though I disliked her, contrived to heighten the impression I had of being 'à l'ombre des jeunes filles en fleur'. Mara at one moment lent over and bit Jean's ear – but of course I may only have enjoyed that evening from the ironical pleasure of seeing Jean and Mara behave as young girls together in front of Mara's mother and Elizabeth while actually

---

[1] Jacques-Emile Blanche, 1861–1942. *Fin-de-siècle* artist, socialite. The Comtesse de Fels was a Proustian *salonière*.

both their lovers were in the room. '*Le plus grand amour c'est l'amour d'autre chose*' but it is sad that in any case my love should be for an adolescence that was over before I met Jean and whose last vanishing remnants I was the first to dispel.

It is so short that radiant morning time that one comes to like only the very youngest girls, those in whom the flesh, like precious leaves, is still at work.

Title for a story or a book (girls by the sea) aesthetic topic, that depressed (the only common one perhaps) both Proust and Joyce.

'I don't dislike England,' the charming wife of Mr Cyril Connolly told me, 'quite as much as my husband' – but then she added with a delicious *moue* and the faintest American accent, 'I haven't seen so much of it.' 'What strikes me most,' she continued, 'is the ugliness of your countryside, the seediness of the men and the dowdiness of the women – and of course,' she added, 'your beautiful policemen – but unfortunately my pip-cramps.' Alas the eternal flux of Lady Punk-yapple's party separated us for ever.

Returned exile

Mr C. Congoly, a returned exile, landed yesterday near Brighton. Tasmanian papers please copy.

Later This evening a correspondent of the *Daily Frig* interviewed the returned exile at the pew where he is staying in St Martins in the Fields. 'What strikes me most about London,' he said, 'is the absence of hansom cabs' – 'And the beauty of your policemen,' he added. 'That reminds me,' he concluded meditatively, 'I have a date.'

Late night special 'London,' the returned exile told a reporter, 'is the gayest city in the world. Its restaurant is nearly as good as a Swiss restaurant and it only wants a cabaret and a brothel to have a night life of its own.' 'What about a casino?' we ventured to ask. 'Well, what about it?' answered the repatriate enigmatically and we felt that the goddess, if such there be, of wit was among us again.

Special late night late special
Suicide of London man. Not Cyril Connolly. Well known club-man returned from abroad was tonight found dead on an asphalt pavement, in which he had deliberately buried himself up to his

neck. 'The evening was a failure . . .' he is said to have said, to have said.

The lesbian's unbitchy contempt of masculine qualities in men and feminine in women.

Montparnasse

A young foreigner and a young American woman. One has a *manual de chymie*, the other a bundle of drawings with her. 'I want you to believe that I am a virgin,' says the young man passionately, 'no woman has ever touched me – we should be going through the adventure together, if you know what I mean.' The young woman tries to look equally virginal, she has her thoughts to keep. Only a variant of the eternal bi-wangle, say Nobsplotch, not God in God whats? Damn your eye – tis very sure he (five letters, fulfils a need of nature) in mine. American homosexuals are best recognised by coonskinned fur coats (fur on the outside), revolvers and cowboy hats. Your invetoroi and heterinverts are (the Kingdom of Harlem is within you) easily distinguished by a rigid intellectual athletic, a drastic aesthetic gymnastic, a reverent cockeye on all mystical experience (towards the idea of a to what). See from Godhead to Paraclete. Ch. 14. The symbolism of the Christchild's navelcord in the apparatus of the Indian ropetrick. A man walks through the café in riding breeches with a knowing smile, a little Japanese in a red sweater and sponge-bag trousers points him out to his girl. *Quel type! t'as vu?*

On to the Bal Nègre, a wooden rackety place full of Martinicans and Guadelupans. The chief instrument in the band is a cocktail shaker full of gravel which is called a Cha Cha – and makes a rhythm like its name. The girls put their arms round the mens' necks, the men round the girls' waists, if expert each keep one hand on their own hip – jauntily, they stay mostly in the same place, frigging.

Transition

Left Berlin and spent a week in Paris. Landed at Newhaven, crossing by the night boat and spent weekend at Rottingdean with Enid Jones and her husband.[1] Riding, bathing and some good talk, chiefly

---

[1] Enid Bagnold, the novelist, was married to Sir Roderick Jones. They lived at Rottingdean and arranged for Cyril and Jean to rent a house during the first summers of their marriage.
'I heard the sort of things that villagers would have said of Rimbaud, after he had passed

about writing. Lunched in Brighton, came up on Monday and saw Logan and Desmond and stayed with Freddie.

Depressed at being back in England – countryside so dirty, sky and fields the colour of corrugated iron. Everybody so weak and knock-kneed, a race of little ferrets and blindworms – only assets the downs at Rottingdean, the comfortable country houses, the green fields by the sea, and the free minds of my friends.

Spain, Morocco, Corsica.

Jean had indigestion very badly the day we started which meant she lay down instead of packing, and so brought none of the things she ought to have had. We both missed the first night train, and met on the platform. Afterwards we had dinner in the station restaurant. It was dark and gloomy and fabulously cold. The air and houses of Paris were the slatey colour of Atlantic breakers in a snow storm, the air so frozen that it hurt one's eyes and made us think longingly of the warmth of the Bateau Ivre, our favourite bar. We got an empty first class compartment in the late train to the south, and Jean lay wrapped in her fur coat. I played the gramophone as we moved off. We had an icy night – but very thrilling – round Tours and Les Aubrais there were great banks of snow, and we waited for hours for the line to be cleared. I got out at Chatellerault and bought some food which warmed us. Jean was in agony whenever she moved. The next morning was wet and misty, but thankfully warm. We went straight to a hotel at Pau, and Jean went to bed there. I had lunch downstairs. We were three days at Pau, Jean in bed for all of them, and all the time it rained. A doctor came (I felt typically the anxious husband) and gave her some medicine and a diet to eat. I meanwhile wrote my last novel review, huggered at a table among a pile of books while Jean groaned from the pillows and the drizzle obscured the mountain views outside. The last evening she got up and we went out and bought some stockings and clothes. Next day was beautiful and sunny, we took the Canfranc train, the mountains all snow covered and Jean feeling almost cured. A pleasant journey

---

through the village,' she wrote to him. Also, 'Yes I know. I said to Leigh Ashton, "Does he like men or women?"' She patched up the ensuing row by observing, 'I said to two people whom I love, Desmond and Vita, that it was on the cards that we might all look rather fools when we were dead if we didn't gratefully harbour you, instead of fussing about faults. And they both agreed.'

up the pass, till the train stuck in the tunnel before Forges d'Abel. We played the gramophone and later walked out into the snow. At Canfranc we had hours to wait and lunched and I taught Jean Spanish pronunciation. We played the gramophone in the waiting room and a lot of Aragonese sang and danced. We got to Jaca for dinner. It was very cold and muddy and we had a stirring night. A mule carriage jingled us from the station to the small hotel and the moon shone on a circle of mountains, but otherwise Jaca is unquestionably drear. Next day we went by Huesca and the amazing rocks of Ayate to Zaragoza. Jean got out of the train thinking I had left it and it went on without her. Luckily there was a station fairly soon. I jumped out at Casetas, telephoned to the station master at Zaragoza to whom Jean had however already been brought weeping and explaining, '*J'ai perdu mon mari.*' She came out to Casetas in a car. We had a reunion on the platform and an omelette together. Then we went back to Zaragoza and had a room with a bath, a good dinner and a good night. Next day we sat in the sun in a café and were warm at last. Jean liked the beggars, the girls and the music and after lunch we took the bus to Teruel. It was a cold but lovely ride and we found Teruel depressing when we arrived. A gloomy mountain town where I got flu and was in bed two days. We left after that and had a superb journey, the gramophone playing and every kind of company in our carriage dancing to it and having their caricatures drawn. Jean, in fine form, danced a solo charleston rather well. Valencia and a lovely room and bath in a good hotel. Lunch, and a lustful afternoon and evening. (5 times.) I'm not sure how long we were actually in Valencia. We drank too much and argued about America a great deal. We had rather bad pâté and caviar in a rather good restaurant, and didn't sightsee at all, except for an amusing cabaret, where we went with the Manager. We went on to Gandia which was gloomy, as was the journey, except for the Cercagente oranges. At Gandia we could not discover any life. Next morning Denia was very much the same, but we lunched there well, and had a good journey to Alicante, especially Calpe and the mountains after it, Villa Sagosa and Benidorm. It was now spring but Alicante is always a disappointing place. The American bar had no barman and we could not get a cocktail there. It is impossible to exaggerate how badly we wanted cocktails all the time we were in Spain. We went on to Elche, which we liked, and by omnibus to Murcia where we couldn't get a bath. The next day we had a long and dreary journey to Granada and quarrelled on the way. We reached the Washington [hotel] at midnight, and were given an annex room.

Granada to be dealt with later.

In love with one of those drone passions in which we really do feel that we have left the best of ourselves behind with them.

London friendship, with its brisk bouts of clique life over a lunch table, the occasional heart-to-hearters at a chance meeting in the street appal and horrify the young man who is used at Oxford to walking into someone's rooms after breakfast and not going away till long after dinner – he is always suspecting a plot or a grievance when people walk out of his life for a few weeks. Yet Oxford past, Oxford friendships, steadily increase in deception as the protagonists drift apart and London ones, more progressive, accommodate themselves to changes of outlook and position.

> *Aunque no tengo la suerte*
> *traslados me a su lugar*
> *aunque no tengo la suerte*
> *ni de besa vi de verte*
> *bodemos vi al mismo mar*
> *Juntarnos a la misina muerte!*

The boy's hat, the foot tapping on the pavement at the windy street corner, October in the park, all swirling leaves and frilled grey pondwater.

What frill of surf on what forsaken sands?

England is a problem – parts of it so beautiful – a few people in it so intelligent and quite a good many extraordinarily nice – yet I can't ever manage to fit into it – the intelligent people are too stranded, detached *defaitiste* observers to make me want to join them, the nice people so stupid, the amusing ones such shits – I hate colonels and I hate the people who make fun of them. The trouble is that those who conform become impossible, and those who rebel only rebel towards a continental snobbery instead of a county one – they are snobs about the successful and the amusing instead of about the well-born and the grand. There is no place in England for a serious rebel. If you hate both diehards and bright young people you have, like Huxley, Lawrence, Joyce etc to go and live abroad. I don't mind being restricted to the friendship of a few intelligent people but I hate the *dépaysé* out-of-the-world onlooker feeling it brings with it. Peter is my only contemporary interesting in himself and not because I choose to make him so. How few people one knows whose attitude to life does not vary in interest with one's own curiosity about it.

Original list of the ten tripes.

Alps, arguments, intellectuals, anti-intellectuals, civics, Chippendale, going to Chartres, gossip, Sunday afternoons, culture and magnanimity.

A restatement:

High-brows, low-brows, sightseeing, nonsense rhymes, gossip writers, Switzerland and Italy, English complacency, American stupidity, Smart Bohemia, and the man of letters.

Never has there existed so large a mass of floating appreciation willing to be mis-directed as to-day.

O niña, mi niña movena
que tu vuelvas un dia
mas que Cristo tengo pena
par la tierra de Maria

derde Zaragoza a Casetas
no es gran distancia
no es en dolor mucha mas
que derde aqui a America

culture = sightseeing in original list
civics came from Rylands
Chippendale from Kenneth Clark
going to Chartres from Noel (Gothic + culture)
magnanimity from Maurice

Newspaper

LET THEM BEWARE!

Once more have or haven't the Conservative party – and unless there is a real effort made there can be no recourse, as someone finely put it, but to the sword or something very like it – like the pen very likely.

WIMBLEDOM

Another Wimbledon has come and gone, and many think it to have been the gayest since the war – we hereby take the opportunity to extend a welcome to the many American visitors who made a long journey to see their country win. England is not only the home of museums and monuments – of Stratford and Stoke Poges – it offers unrivalled fields for sportsmen to see it defeated at its own sports.

SAVE THE COUNTRYSIDE

We must congratulate the Sussex magistrate who ordered ten strokes of the cat to Willie Walton, a child of ten who tied a tin can to a dog's tail. 'It is tins like those,' he owned up, 'that make our Sussex lanes a reproach to beauty traps.' Let magistrates not forget that all three party leaders have signed a pledge to protect the countryside, which should be more in evidence this year owing to the promised improvements on roads and railways. There are several parts of England on no road at all.

WEST END SHOPS RAIDED

Plain clothes men from Scotland Yard yesterday rounded up the West End flower shops engaged in the sale of decadent orchids and obscene suggestive cacti. They arrested a young amorpho phallus and will later make a statement. *Later*: The raid was as a result of private complaints from certain parts, said the Home Secretary. 'I personally have no knowledge whether these cacti are used for immoral purposes – but the shops are kept by aliens – that we do know,' he added angrily.

A FOREIGNER IN ENGLAND

A foreigner, a M. des Esseintes, landed in England to-day. What do our neighbours think of us – what are your first impressions, asked a reporter. M. des Esseintes seemed pale and tired. 'Why I just adore England, Mr Newspaper. I think your old buildings and the quiet of your countryside are just something we haven't got. I think the politeness and courtesy with which I have been treated is marvellous – I'm just dying to see Kew Gardens, Chinatown, the traffic control, and the inside of a lunatic asylum.'

CRICKET & RACING PAGES 2345678

NATURE NOTES

These days shortly after the summer solstice are remarkable for the emergence of the young bats from the nest and often on these gelid summer evenings there is a noise, a whirring in the air – over the clammy stamens, above the flaming pistils of the frondalvias hum these little whizzers, the industrious monopeds, giving voice to their plaintive whipple. Rude peasants fear these little animals and dark superstitions are attached to them – unjustly – for the little fellows have five toes, four fingers and a thumb on their tiny hands and the females, girls, have periods like our own. P.D.W.J.N.S.

ROUND THE TOWN

A sponge and barnacle party in which the guests compete to see who can stay longest is the latest amusement of the Bright Young People – 'We had to invent it,' said Miss Cetera Etcetera, 'to keep out gatecrashers, who are mostly poor people and sooner or later have to return to their work.' The winners were a young married couple – 'It solves our house-hunting,' Mrs Waugh said.

COURT & SOCIETY

Mr Cyril Connolly has arrived at Saint Martin in the Fields. The rest of the Court and Society is staying where it is.

CORRESPONDENCE

UMPIRE DAY

Sir – Would not the British Umpire be a better title for the arbiters of the history of the world? JH

Rather too bright a young man and very self-consciously beautiful in a dark green day suit with golden buttons. He referred to all other American writers by their Christian names to show he knew them and prefixed the epithet 'poor' to show he envied them. Poor Louis. Poor Karl (I agree there). Poor Ernest. Poor Thornton. Poor (presumably) Tunney. [Glenway Westcott][1]

The car was solemnly stopped where the fateful path branched which is now shown like the crossroads where Oedipus was killed near Delphi. The driver posed himself dramatically to reenact the incident and shouted into the undergrowth, 'Edda Edda Edda!' In his khaki shirt and blue trousers, *'comme un pécheur'*, E.M. apparently *'parait un peu fou'*. It was not unnatural that his niece so-called who carried apparently all his money, should bring him to these lonely cliffs all the way from England in order to do him in. *'C'était une femme formidable,'* he admitted, *'et lui, quand le petit Marseillais a télégraphié trois fois, on voyait qu'il était quelqu'un?'*[2]

---

[1] Added in 1968: 'Probably from a letter to Mary Borden.'

[2] A bracket in 1968 explained that this paragraph had in its sights Sir Edward Marsh.

I got no Proustian kick, no Guermantes hangover, from my first salon, but heard nothing but '*il parait que l'ami de peuple a tout à fait bouleversé les élections municipales.*' (Ctsse de Fels.)

An imaginary portrait of Virginia Woolf which made her look like a weepy-eyed ginger-headed Chelsea caravan artist dressed in liberty greens – and another – of more solid flesh called simply 'Mrs T'.[1]

He reminds me of the executed royalties who were always praised for their excellence as fathers or their wit and charm within the family circle. He got more tied up than ever describing something out of his book to me and eventually produced 'woman of the pavement' for the profession he wished to describe – also his petty scheming is very irritating. He sits like a stuffed and martyred animal while people produce lists of clippings, of critics, of invitations, of suggestions for suggestions or reviews within reviews, all the many and various shibboleths for discomfiting the enemy and delineating the faithful. A kind man but too fussy and suspicious – perhaps the malaise of the expatriate – perhaps a canny form of gentleman complex, a great man self-dramatisation.[2]

So few Americans can pity their country and yet feel obligations to it. I suppose because it is a civilised and ironical attitude and Americans are either not civilised or cowed by it into a refined disclaimer of their origin.

Idleness only a coarse name for my infinite capacity for living in the present.

A perfect hopelessness, an inability to act otherwise, and a perfect sense of beauty wasted on a post war world.

I daren't stay more than a night in London, its attractions are too many for me, and end always in disillusion or a deeper consciousness of wasted time.

That sudden glimpse of charm and intelligence among a waste of tourists utterly unfitted to desecrate the Andalusian spring.

Questionnaire

Season   Summer summer

---

[1] '? Jacques-Emile Blanche' added in a bracket.

[2] '? Joyce alas' added in a bracket.

Time	Evening
Place	Brighton
Chap	Connolly
Remarks	People born in this month make excellent literary critics.
Great thought?	Even before it is dark, even before I have come to the bottom of this page, I may have written a phrase that will be immortal and done enough to justify my existence.
Wish of your heart	To be descending the magic river in the Paris Luna Park on a summer night with Jean and Bobbie.
Why?	Dark swirl of moving water, runnel of swift darkness bearing the cockle boat, sudden lights on dark water, on a dark face, glimpses of green plants and painted backdrops, of the switchback from an odd angle then Congo darkness again. Besides I love her.

Would you drink a pint of blood to save your sister?
Would you shoot your sweetheart to save her from a savage?
(Man of colour) – Your wife if you surprised her with one?
Would you – Would you – Would you.

Answers. Salisbury Cathedral, 5 gallons, Sir Joshua Wren, Canberra, Indian hemp, a kind of pancake, 1739.

The New Calendar

December January February	WINTER
March	winterspring springwinter?
April	spring
May	springsummer
June July August	SUMMER
September	summerautumn
October	autumn
November	autumnwinter winterautumn

We thus have eight seasons instead of four – the static periods, summer and winter, remain the same while the two transitional periods, so much harder to define and so beloved of poets and thinkers for their quickening influence on the life of the spirit, become more clearly delineated, and are seen as each containing one pure month and two impure ones that partake respectively of the quality of those that precede and follow them. I don't think we shall have to go back to this again.

> Tiergarten trees blue with rain
> Leaves weep depressed by rainy June
> Sitting at window young man moodily writes
> thinking of horrid things he said to her.

Sir – Is it not absurd that we should continue to call the 9th, 10th, 11th and 12th months (Saptimber, O Tuber, Nova Sembla, and Decent Burial) as if they were the seventh, eighth, ninth and tenth? I suggest a remedy, which both improves the calendar and honours our great men, would be to rechristen them, Galsworthy, Wellsworthy, Shawworthy and Walpoleworthy.

PERSONAL When are *you* going to pay me back? Ile Saint-Louis. No taste is so acquired as that for someone else's quality of mind, but in return, nothing but quality of mind really makes a person indispensable and love of that is the only exception to Proust's rule, *le plus grand amour c'est l'amour d'autre chose.*

Brighton, or Home Truths by the Sea

It is astonishing how much time one can waste, even with no pocket money, on the strength of a general dissatisfaction with one's surroundings. I boil with anglo-phobia – you've no idea how degenerate, physically, the English are. If you take a crowd of several thousands in the front here you notice not only that the women are all ugly and dowdy and the men undersized and weedy but that their voices and gestures express all the hopelessness of the blind mouths from which they issue. Newspaper-fed ignorance, wistful cannonfodder, larvae, they trail round whining out their days' ration of bromides as if cringing from somebody who was going to hit them. So faint, so spiritless, so dull, so dead, so worksore. And not a single creature in holiday clothes, they might be waiting on a tube platform. No trace of rich charwoman cockney, Dickensian vulgarity either, just little ferrety robots squeaking round an empty bandstand. And this huge seaside town without a single place to sit out and take coffee. The road from London passes only a mile of country, the rest villas with red walls and slate roofs. The first view of Brighton, a mass of slate roofs seen through a railway arch, might be inside a factory, each line representing a street between the wall or rather lake of grey slate in front of one. And people pay £500 a year to live in this and Mr T. S. Eliot changes his brown passport for a true blue one! One is perpetually crushed between the stupidity of the old regime and the silliness of its detractors. Perhaps the surrealists are right – the individual artist cannot stand even politically alone.

War and Peace

Distressed on reading *War and Peace* that the Natasha whom Andrey falls in love with should be so unlike Jean and so much more like Ros, Rachel and Racy – and also that Andrey's falling in love should be so like my feeling for them. Again that sense of exclusion from the normal ecstasies of the young but redeemed by the Jeanishness of the conclusion. 'Do you love me?' 'Yes, Yes,' answered Natasha almost angrily. She drew a deep sigh, and another, her breathing came more and more quickly, and she burst into sobs. Prince Andrey held her hands, looked into her eyes and could find no trace of his former love for her in his heart. Some sudden reaction seemed to have taken place in his soul; there was none of the poetic and mysterious charm of desire left in it; instead of that there was pity for her feminine and childish weakness, terror at her devotion and trustfulness, an irksome yet sweet sense of duty, binding him to her for ever. The actual feeling, though not so joyous and poetical as the former, was more serious and deeper.

He Babbled of Green Fields

We went a long walk to Lulworth Cove. For an instant, on the lonely crest of the downs with an old house hidden in a semi-circle of beechwoods that sloped down to the sea below us, I had a moment of love for my country, just as we may suddenly look with passion at someone who has deceived us before the memory of their infidelities swarms in on us again. As we walked further, however, I remembered not so much the beauty of the downs as the awfulness of the people who wrote about them, Kipling's thyme and dew ponds, Belloc's beer and Chesterton's chalk, old Hardy's Dorset and two dreary undergraduates who discuss Schnabel and other rustic topics in the parlour of this inn. They gaze, between mouthfuls of tomato, at the Victorian lithographs around the walls – caught napping – the love letter – the story of a brave end. 'Pretty serious,' grunts one to the other. 'Yes,' replies the culture specialist, 'terrible terrible.' *Glubit magnanimos Remi nepotes* [She screws the great-hearted descendants of Remus – Catullus], I thought, undeterred by a burst of exquisite woodland ride between the cliffs and the valley below. Peter was more loyal to the motherland but talked exclusively of Villier de l'Isle-Adam, when not appraising the landscape around him. We reached a cottage by the sea for lunch. Peter with an air of 'excuse me, poor expatriate, I understand this', flattered the landlady and praised the bread and cheese which was all she had to give us. For this, to my joy, we were charged two shillings each, and I explained that one did not lose much by being a foreigner. I asked if I could bathe from the rocks without a costume. 'But,' she answered, 'there be bobbies' eyes all the way along to Weymouth.'

Eventually we got to Lulworth Cove, through a maze of military reminders that a fatal accident had occurred in 1927 through a pedestrian using the path along the cliffs when the red flag was flying. From Arishmell the sound of church bells was wafted down the petrol-scented English lanes, past the carefully thatched cottages.

> O God to hear the parish bell
> at Arishmell, at Arishmell.[1]

The cove was like a flypaper, people in every direction, and across a space of building lots were parked 12 charabancs. 'I wish I had a camera,' I cried and Peter answered, 'I wish I had a machine gun.' At that, a miracle happened. The helpless bitterness with which he vainly protested seemed to snap something in my head and I felt the relief with which one looks at somebody one has loved and feels 'that face will never be able to hurt me again'.

The deformed and swarming trippers, the motor car park, the wooden bungalows, the tin tea sheds, seemed just a heavy joke at which I could look on with ironic detachment. I felt suddenly free and quit of everything. I saw the Statesman, the Nation, and the Labour government to be just as comic as the conservatives or the yellow press, I had a Santayana feeling of being outside and above it all. My sense of possession, in regard to England, had been finally killed. Besides, even if it is beautiful, I thought, from my point of

---

[1] A postcard of Arishmell church, postmarked July 4 1929, was sent to Jean at Hurstleigh Avenue, Woodbrook, Baltimore. It read:
> 'The downs are rich with close-cropped thyme
> the evening bell from the church doth chime.
> On the squire's flagpole our standard flops,
> God save the countryside from sheenies and wops.'

From *A Whole Day's Hike*, by two young hoboes Quennell and Connolly, 7/6.

view, the point of view of finding things to write about, the English countryside except during a few phases of winter, despite my childhood in it, is a dead form. 'The country habit has me by the heart,' wrote poor Vita, trying to be archly original in dealing with that grantchestered old Trollop – This England, or as the papers call it, 'this England of ours'. I thought of all the ardent bicyclists, all the accomplished couplet-eers, the pipe-smoking, beer-swilling young men on reading parties, the brass-rubbing, Balliol-playing Morris dancers, the Innisfreeites, the Buchan–Baldwin–Masefield and Drinkwatermen, the Squires and Shanks and grim Dartmoor realists, the tramp lovers, and of course of Mary Webb – of everyone striding down the primrose path – Wordsworthian primroses – or down other green rides of this set subject to the glorious goal of an O.M. 'The country habit has me by the heart,' I chanted to the Lulworth trippers and in a schoolmaster's voice of mincing horror '*procul o procul este profani*', but it was Peter, not they, who fled.

Tuesday night (July 16th, same day) Recantation. Went for a walk after tea, a beautiful sunny evening. Over the fields towards St Aldhelm's Head. Met an old farmer of 75 who greeted me, 'You must be the gentleman that's writing a book up at the Square and Compass.' He talked of farming, of Hardy, who had put a mill of his into a novel, of gipsies, horse coping, and riddle women. Went on to Chapman's pool, a lovely unspoilt cove among high cliffs and surrounded by warrens and screes, all covered with flowers and bushes. Met a nice man on a holiday with his daughter, and went round the cove and climbed round the screes above the sea purple in the westering sunshine. Lovely desolate rocky cliffs above me with gulls flying. Caught a sick young herring gull and let it go after. Climbed on up a gap in the rocks and walked towards Worth over the sunlit plateau. The inn bright on the horizon with the church grey underneath. Met a small girl in a red tam o'shanter, walking home by herself to the coastguard station. 'Hullo,' she said, 'where do you live?' Reached the pub about 9 and had a light supper and a pint of cider and afterwards smoked a cigar on the wall outside. Only the conversation in the taproom would have been more interesting in Spain.

Summary:– Saving the countryside must museumize it – you can only destroy the vulgarity of democracy by a principle of equal vitality and we know of no alternative with one. However, there are many months of the year when the English countryside is empty and some when it is empty and beautiful. There is moreover enough countryside, at any rate in Europe, to go round with all our generation and when that is finished people may have learnt to love the towns.

One can only afford to lack social ambition in proportion as one is gifted with social sense.

Seascape

Went down to the cove for a bathe. Warm sunny evening. Pleasant man lent me a bathing dress. Walking back (what a sanctified phrase of English childhood is the 'walk to the sea'), met a man with a motor caravan. Stayed and talked to him and his wife and daughter, green bedspread in the open, a book lying in the grass, some pails and his wife cooking porridge. He had spent his life in the East and was now enjoying the new existence of retirement. Walked up with them to the vicarage garden, where they were going to do some country dances – a few children, one or two villagers, women and farmboys and a couple of bustling women with muddy red faces and fringes of greying hair. They danced on a grass to the gramophone. Now come along – if all the world were paper – siding, turn, siding, slips, take your partner and swing! If all the world were paper? too slow! too slow! too slow! The village women pant round seriously, the fat spinsters dance briskly, giving directions from a little book, the Anglo-Indians skip along with experience, the children look on, the girls breathless and lightfooted, yet heavy with a kind of rustic materialism, their faces and figures a little gauche with the adolescence that hasn't yet finished shaping them. They look like statues still left in the marble and grin and call out to the children in thick sweet voices. Now Newcastle. Now gathering peascods – or is it picking up sticks? The plaintive music so naively vicious, so innocently sophisticated, floats out on the evening air. We want only the best for clergyman's farewell, it's very difficult – single hey, turn, slip, siding, now then double hey, grand chain! I walk away up the road, the distressful notes of clergyman's farewell, the childrens' voices pursue me through the hedges, sad slice of wan little England, a sheep dog is sleeping by the pond, and outside the Square & Compass some boys are playing cricket with a stone. The sun sets over Dorset and the air, the downs, the grey-roofed houses, every flower and every blade of grass unite with the distant archaic music to cry, 'Saul Saul why persecutest thou me?'

Example – Midway between spring summer, and summer autumn falls the old-fashioned month of August come-July, time of gross yellow moons, brown grass and lousy yearnings.

A mood of final emancipation came to me. The next morning I walked into Langton post office, and felt at last an intelligent foreigner, able to appreciate the best in this country, but detached and amused alike by the quaintness and the horror of the modern life in it. A fantastic joke country, a Bali, a Japan. As I was feeling this, I rested by some windows. Suddenly a voice began to bellow inside. 'Very important. Causal conjunctions. We went into this very deeply last week. Read it out.' – 'Causal conjunctions,' quavered a choir of young voices, '*Quippe, qui*, and *quoniam* take the indicative.' – '*Quippe, qui*, and *quoniam*,' bellowed the usher, interrupting them, 'take the indicative.' The rasping voice sounded like a wild animal, as if one had gone by the Zoo on a bus and passed a beast's habitat but the uncouth language blended perfectly with the summer scene outside. Take down this sentence – take it down will you. *Conjectus est in carcerem quod patrem occidisset*. He was thrown into prison on the grounds that he had killed his father *qui eo tempore* who at that time *in Italiam refugiebat* was flying into Italy. *Refugiebat* he thundered and the pedagogic rhythms floated out into the sun and along the dusty hedgerows – *conjectus est in carcere* mumbled the scribbling pupils, *quippe qui* and *quoniam*, causal conjunctions, they chanted till the words were lost across the Isle of Purbeck, a drone above the drone of bees.

Chilling 28th

Thursday 25th. I saw in *The Times* the engagements of Noel and Racy printed next to each other. There would have been long periods when either of these announcements would have had quite infinite power to hurt me, and coming together the cumulative effect would have broken my heart. But reading them on the lawn in the sunshine, I felt only a pleasure. That a period should have been rounded off so neatly that the blow of Nemesis, too late to wound me, should still be deft. It was Proustian, I thought, and felt both glad that Proust had shown me how to get the full flavour from such an incident and that life had provided such an incident to corroborate the greatness of Proust. For this was life in perfection, for once absolutely economical and dextrous in fulfilling itself, it could have made no improvement on this, save the too improbable one of Noel

[235]

and Racy marrying each other. Perhaps I felt a little cheated of a sensation, but then others would get it, I could see Maurice [Bowra], for instance, explaining my Nemesis and gloating over the perils of 'putting all your eggs in two baskets'. Then, too, I felt a slight sense of mockery and waste – how much love, how much of my mind and youth and tenderness had I poured into these now emptied receptacles. Still I suppose any object that incites one to such an expense of spirit, by that alone does good. I wish all the same that my letters to Noel and Racy will be obtainable and safe. In many dormant and unproductive friendships one is prepared to tolerate one's loss of interest provided that most of all the capital one has invested is somehow saved. Then besides being apt, it is an example of divine justice, not the foolish human justice of crime and punishment, but of the lofty impartial mechanism by which life goes on and time passes, all the more surely for our passions spent; the faces that could move us once move other people or move no-one at all, the things we feared slip by unnoticed and many ironic combinations escape us as the past tries ineffectually to pluck us by the sleeve. Time, that uneven artist, plays often to an inattentive audience – but this once it has been appreciated.

φύει τ' ἀδηλα καὶ φανεντα κρυπτεται
τα τερπνα πικρα γιγνεται καὖθις φιλα

[Time gives birth to the unseen and covers up what seemed to be.
 Delights become bitter and then dear again – Sophocles]

– and so I cut out the 2 notices and sent them to Jean.

Or consider. The blow like the lunge of a bull which I have avoided by a lovely veronica of lack of feeling – or perhaps the image should be of the bullfighter hopping behind the slim partition – in this case Jean – to avoid the charging enemy.

Compare the gossip writer to one of those small transparent caterpillars whose digestive processes the onlooker is painfully aware of – the moment being nibbled by the jaws, passing rapidly through some elementary method of absorption and forming a little pellet which awaits the wriggle that will excrete it into print from the retreat so visible at the end of its tail.

Wet Sunday night with much rain and wind, almost enough to keep up that exciting contralto grind through the whole evening. Lately I have been obsessed with autumn, and the day seemed almost like a message from it. The lamps flicker slightly, Logan and Bobbie read their books; the wireless music swells and wanes, the lovely pattern of rain, like sifted gravel, the wind in the chimney, rise and fall. Autumn is my spring, in October my mind floods, my limbs travel, my friend sails. O western wind!

Place	Exmoor
Month	October
Time	After tea
Books	Murasaki Mimnermus
Music	Debussy Quartet
Mood	austere hedonism
Emotion	excited and expectant zeal
Weather	gales with faint bouts of driven rain
Scene	high moorland by the sea — boulders and grey wet pebbles bracken and tough brownstained oaks above them, only the wet heath on top. Puddles look closer and cleaner than they are, for the next moment night will be falling.
Wish	to be tired from a walk and not have far to go, to be coming in wet to the Brendon inn with Jean, or else from riding, to be having dinner of chops and red wine, to be reading and talking with a fire in our bedroom, to be listening to a loud wind, some rain, and a rough sea in bed and not alone in bed.
Moral	*Quam juvat immites ventos audire cubantem*
	et dominam tenero detinuisse sinu
	aut gelides hibernus aquas cum fuderit auster
	securum somnos imbre juvante sequi.

[How good to lie and hear the savage winds, holding a mistress to your soft breast, or when the winter wind drops freezing water, to pursue sleep in peace lulled by rain – Tibullus]

Alas for those who associate with the naturalists which all writers and dramatists are, the setting boards and the killing bottle are always close at hand.

Sep 17. Paris

Autumn is the season to which I am called like a vocation. In these first days of mists and feathery dusk and falling leaves, my mind begins to stir like a boat raised from the mud by the tide. At last the year's vitality has compromised on a parity with my own.

The sweet texture of the day must coarsen into dusk.

Hotel de la Louisiane

I have quite given up the social struggle, I have scratched from the race of life and don't intend to meet anyone unless they want to meet me. *J'ai enfin le goût de l'obscurité, tu sais.* Also I have a room for 400 francs a month and at last will be living within my own and other people's income. I am tired of acquaintances, and tired of friends unless they're intelligent, tired also of extrovert unbookish life. Me for good talk, wet evenings, intimacy, *vins rouges en carafe*, reading, relative solitude, street worship, exploration of the least known *arrondissements*, shopgazing, alley sloping, café crawling, Seine loafing, and plenty of writing from the table by this my window where I can watch the streets light up. Harvey with his Americanised bonhomie is surely the devil. I am for the intricacy of Europe, the discreet and many folded strata of the old world, the past, the North, the world of ideas. I am for the Hotel de la Louisiane.

1930 June

Hotel de la Louisiane. Sep–Feb 13th (Dieppe – Bordeaux, Arcachon – Font Romeu, Puigcerda, Collioure, Figueras, Cadaques, Perpignon, Port Vendres – Sledmere and London.)

Feb 13th. London, New York, Baltimore, Pittsburgh, Washington. Married April 5th. New York again, sailed Mauretania. April 9th. 10 Bury St, St James's (Bath, Newton Ferrers, Chilling, Ridgeway, Swanage, Oxford, Naworth Castle) left for France end of May – Bayonne, Biarritz (Paris) then Toulon and finally took house, Les Lauriers Roses, Sanary, Var, 1st July.

Les Lauriers Roses Sanary CURE DE DESINTOXICATION

Theory that César Franck was a disappointing musician because he couldn't compose except off other people's compositions – inspiration not from life, but from 'playing himself in' off the piano. Similarly I can't write without the stimulus of something already written – old articles of my own, peoples' notebooks, or literary magazines.

The most admirable thing about Aldous Huxley is that he prefers Lawrence.

The real disadvantage of Lawrence is that the nearer one comes to his happy and intelligent paganism, the less one has to write about. Writing is an accident arising out of certain unhappinesses. To write, to walk, to talk, to drink, to have violent exercise, are all alternative forms of self-expression to someone discontented with the present. A philosophy which satisfies man with his lot automatically destroys his imaginative desire to create a better world; a philosophy which encourages normal appetites provides normal satisfactions for the mood which leads to composition. You cure the oyster of making a pearl. Similarly the 'culture pearl', where a piece of mother of pearl is introduced for the irritated oyster to form a pearl around, is detectible by the expert and valued at less than half a real one. Does this not hold good too with self-inoculations of distress and hate? Notice how carefully Lawrence refuses to recognise virtue in anyone but himself.

A reformer can only succeed by refusing to see anything commendable in his disciples. Compare Wyndham Lewis.

Why write, when for a guinea, you can buy the Kum Back, a tennis ball attached to a long elastic and suspended between two posts. The harder you hit it, the quicker it returns. The pen is mightier than the sword, no doubt, but how many such devices are more powerful than the pen.

The biographies of American social queens vie in fascinating casuistry. Each author sets out to prove their family is noble while they deny nobility, rich while they spurn money, and lavish while they bewail all exhibitionism. Mrs van Renselaer thinks New York society has steadily declined since the Revolution. She belittles the claims of Philadelphia, Baltimore, and Boston because they were small and unimportant at the same time as she praises New York for the time when it was small and unimportant. Equally she praises the expensive fêtes of the eighties while blaming the expense of the present day ones. Mrs de Koren does the same with Chicago, having first proved her descent from Massachussetts. Miss Marbury, and indeed all three, cannot refrain from an outburst of copy-book maxims. 'It is better to say nothing at all if you cannot say something nice,' is one of them. All these American memoirs are defeated by the necessity of the authors to prove their claims while claiming at the same time that it is not necessary to prove them. Mrs van Renselaer, after flaying the genealogy of the Astors and Vanderbilts, yet uses them against the Kahns and Rockefellers. Any aristocracy must disintegrate when it is not based on political power and territorial responsibilities. America, except before the revolution, and in the South, before the civil war has never had either – money must logically become the only criterion in a country where the rich have no natural piety, the poor no feudal ideas and where the army, navy, church and politics are all unfit for gentlemen. In France the feudal idea remains though the political importance has gone. In England both are breaking down but are still important enough. Lord Salisbury is grander than Lord Donegall. But in America there is no test except the social register. Yet after reading Boni de Castellane's[1] book, one can't help admiring Americans all the more, especially in his wails about his wife's refusal to realise the importance of the Queen of Naples, the King of Portugal, the contempt of Bourbon for Orléans and of both for Napoleon. Just as the vagueness of American social distinction makes everyone in a sense a snob, so the absence of admitted inferiority, the impossibility of being relegated to a definite rung on a single ladder, makes for the most unsnobbish rankfree people that there are.

1931

The essence of country life is waiting for the post.
The essence of marriage is £200 a month.
Love in a cottage, agony in the garden.
The acute boredom, the mental anguish, which I feel at settling down, at being in the country, seems to me only proof of my inherent restlessness, my horror of loneliness, my love of travel, of society, of a varied existence kept continually in motion, but if instead of feeling *l'ennui de la campagne*, I felt religious doubt, people at once would take care of me and reassure me. I would be perfectly certain that it was my duty to overcome them rather than indulge them. Their degree of intensity would prove the importance attached by the powers of evil to their victim, the complaints of mystics, the dark night of the soul would regale me as seen by countless predecessors and all the writings of the church would console me instead of only the uncertain scientific trifle that the appetite increases for the first three days of starvation and then begins to diminish.

---

[1] *Comment j'ai découvert l'Amérique* (1924), a dispiritingly candid account of an old-world aesthete and marquis successfully hunting new-world fortunes.

Proust-ridden

The artist is a member of the leisured classes who cannot pay for his leisure.

The want of money renders insipid every joy that money cannot buy.

> Give me back my nightmares
> cried the poet to the djinn.
> But alas a settled income
> came instead and settled him.

I have fallen out of love with myself and I don't want to let anyone in on the secret.

Solvency is a whole-time job.

A romantic converted to realism loses his faith not only in his creed but in himself.

Poverty, since the war, is a disgrace as well as a discomfort.

Disintoxication –

Wanted, a cure against preoccupation with money, contempt for the spirit and advancing years.

When one ceases to be liked, one must learn to get oneself lumped.

Surrealism is attractive because it teaches you how to be romantic without being sentimental, how to rediscover a universe which revolves round your own personality, and how to see visions in cities – *le paysan de Paris* to whom the gods appear.

One can get richer by one's friends getting poorer.

The Huxleys have added ten years to my life.

Spring

Paris or Venice?

If one could attain anonymity in Paris one might find onself.

And it is a metropolis.

While Venice is only a water escape.
Sleep: Prepare for life.
The Anonymous Voyage.

Four years elapse – *florebit amigdalus impinguabitur locusta dissipabitur capparis* [Ecclesiastes XII, verses 5 and 6, has the standard or unimproved version of this: 'The almond tree shall flourish, and the grasshopper shall be a burden, and desire shall fail: because man goeth to his long home, and the mourners go about the streets.']

Houses   *Lauriers Roses*
          France
          Deauville – Trouville. Paris (Bourgogne and Rue de
          Vaugirard)
          Dulverton
          Cavendish [i.e. Hotel]
          10 Wilton Mews November–March
          Spain Morocco Majorca
          Paris, Foyot's, Université
          Savoy
          3 Capener's Yard November–February
Greece.
Sicily – Capri.
Praia da Rocha. Lisbon. Cintra.[1]
Brighton.
Bayzehill House, Rottingdean. July, Aug
Juan Les Pins. Cannes. Cagnes.
Paris. Hotel de Bourgogne.
Royal Court.
312 Kings Road Jan 9–
          – Anes, vernal anes –

April 15th 1934
A l'an de mon trentiesme âge

We took Evelyn[2] to dinner last night at the Café Grill, mirrors,
banquettes, baroque warmth, bill 3.6.9. First asparagus of the year.
Hot night, hottest April 40 years, not seen Evelyn nearly two, face
thinner but broader, less flesh more bone – Evelyn very crusty and
charming – of Peter, 'Don't tell me he's trying to be a gentleman
now,' asked after Howard and Hendy.[3] He is our valued friend – so
mature and pithy, and religion apart, so frivolous. Made most of the

---

[1] Praia da Rocha 'was everything we had pined for – air and sun and huge breakers . . .
Finally we went north and settled at Cintra.' From Cyril's contribution to *Brian Howard:
Portrait of a Failure* (edited by Marie-Jacqueline Lancaster) p 353.

[2] Evelyn Waugh was younger than Cyril by only a matter of weeks. During the summer of
1931 he had stayed with the Connollys at Sanary. 'I did so much enjoy it,' he wrote to Jean
afterwards, 'and it was exciting meeting the Huxleys and going to St. Beaune and seeing the
brothels at Toulon. I rather hated Villefranche. Nina Seafield was living near and had
collected all the biggest bores on the Riviera.' (Letter, not dated, in the Connolly archive at the
University of Tulsa, Oklahoma.)

[3] Brian Howard, 1905–1958. Gavin Henderson, 2nd Lord Faringdon, 1902–1977.

people we see seem dowdy. He carouses with Teddy Jessel, oddly. Wants to join us visit Elizabeth Bowen 27th by liner Washington to Cork. Friday–Sat. Peter and Marcelle[1] to dinner. Marcelle passed out, put to bed, both stayed night and Marcelle stayed luncheon. She is a fine girl, the sexiest articulation, mouth like Betty Kemble's – a natural drunken Bohemian, discussed diseases – she has several times woken up with strange man in bed and remembered nothing of what happened – useful thing to know, naive, conceited, narcissistic, sweeping, alcoholic, big sweet clumsy puppy. Hates Stally [i.e. previous Mrs Peter Quennell]. Will Peter geld her into appropriate sitwelline mayfairina or will she cure him of hacking by the bottle? Higgins to dinner – her problem – why such a bore? is pretty, not stupid, classy tastes? Answer – too serious, no conversation, no touch, all painters are artisans – bricklayers. Left records – very reposeful, mother's breast kind of Berlioz and Bach. Thursday dined Wansboroughs[2] – lost thirty shillings bridge. Hyslop there. I hate him – he is my antiself, anticyril. A *novus homo*, mean, canny, sly, quiet, farseeing, never gives himself away, never says anything downright, or abuses anyone, *faber fortunae suae* [maker of his own fate], echoes flaccid buggery good taste, butters Jews, melts, kisses, obstinate old puss. Mulgrave to my Rochester. Octavius to my Antony.

To be born again, to be born again.

> Wives of writers all remind us
> we can leave our wives at home
> Go to places they can't find us
> Frig and fuck till kingdom come.
> Man of Letters, ere we part
> Tell me why you never fart?
> Never fart! my dear Miss Blight,
> I do not have to fart, I write.

Joe[3] said he was sterile but not impotent. That the best specialists in America could only explain it as a result of writing – he had written

---

[1] Marcelle Rothé. Her father was a Belgian diplomat, her mother was German. Peter Quennell's second wife.

[2] George Wansborough had been a contemporary in College.

[3] Joseph Hergesheimer, 1880–1954. From Philadelphia, where he was a friend of Jean Connolly's mother. Author of a score of novels, including *The Foolscap Rose*, published in 1934.

so many books as to atrophy his creative organs. 'They have a hard job anyhow to get me to take my pants off now,' he said, 'and if I do, I want to go straight to first base, and then I find myself thinking about my next book all the time.' He finds Mayfair very slow and stodgy compared to American society and London much more religious than New York. I like him a lot but he dissatisfies me in a non-stimulating way. Too rich, too highly paid. Gets on well with Bunny Garnett whom we find very lovable. How few people I love, only Christopher [Sykes]. He has been gone too long. Miss Higgins spends a hundred a year on being analysed every morning.

'You can't do this in here – not with your wife in the room,' said young man to Tommy[1] who was assaulting him. Tommy looked at him insanely, 'Cockteaser!' and continued. Peter detected Stally's unfaithfulness because she always put on her best black silk under-clothes to dine with Pulham[2] but burnt the evidence she gave him. Stally asked his cook if Peter saw much of 'his friend'. 'You mean the blonde young lady?' 'Yes, blonde – of a sort.'

Self
Am thirty now, am no longer young, but how humiliating if I was.

Daydreams, preoccupations etc.
Winning the lottery. The Emperor Makeamillion of Mexico. With money would buy houses – Thurloe Square, one in country, in South of France or Canaries. Great curiosity about Tenerife, passion to go there.
Favourite daydream – edit a monthly magazine entirely subsidised by self. No advertisements. Harmless title, deleterious contents.

It's delicious!
    Out on Monday
      MERIDIAN
      The magazine with a 'literary' flavour

---

[1] In *Memoirs*, Frances Partridge wrote of Stephen Tomlin that he had the profile of a Roman emperor on a coin. 'A destructive impulse in him had the effect that he couldn't see two people happy together without being impelled to intervene and take one away, leaving the other bereft. Or it would take the form of a direct bid for power over others – whether male or female, for he was bi-sexual – which he was well equipped to exert.'

[2] Peter Rose Pulham was a photographer and artist in vogue, briefly attracted to Nancy Stallybrass, then to Jean. For him and his attractions, see *With Love*, by Theodora Fitzgibbon.

Projects of the moment.
Get on with stories (The English Malady)
A Whig Anthology.
And paper on Congreve, Walpole, Beckford, Thack[eray], Firbank, Evelyn, Dornford Yates. The Prose of Hedonism. (A Defence of Pleasure.)

Feel well at last today after fortnight of flu, spring horror, and convalescence. Designed Summer costume – 1 pair of navy blue Kashmere shorts and ditto trousers to be worn with crash or linen cream tunic, cut like private soldiers or Dutch stingah shiftah with large pockets, horn buttons, slit armpits and dark blue stiff collar, closed when formal or chilly, widely open otherwise. No shirt or tie needed, and cold taken less easily.

Authors of the moment.

ROCHESTER

FIRBANK

Ackerley

Bêtisiers of the moment – Harold Nicolson's *People and Things* Lady Horner's Burne-Jones drivel,[1] Dornford. *Music* ballet, Chalmer and Fadas – Rumbas. *Art* 'off' at present. *Places* Tenerife.

People

Socially at the spring ebb, great desire to get out of London, nobody I particularly want to see. Mild dissatisfaction with sub-Bloomsbury. They never ask us back and are consequently a little guiltier and sillier whenever we see them. Barbara [Bagenal] was so fearfully tiresome at dinner the other night – she seems such a very careful little lady dog at moments. Julia [Tomlin] nicer because absent. B. a bluestocking, a policewoman, yet kissing everybody and terribly afraid of being disliked. Her most agreeable quality – that of living in the moment and keeping up a pert and sympathetic commentary on the film that unrolls before her – can be changed by drink into a series of chippy sillidities [sic]. She thinks people become themselves when drunk. I luckily think it is only the gin or whisky talking. She sees herself as Egeria? Bunny [David Garnett] can be a bore but his set gaze, they say due to paralysis of eye

---

[1] *People and Things* was published in 1931: Lady Horner's *Time Remembered* in 1933.

muscles is very stimulating – he 'fixes' one like the Ancient Mariner. I feel like a snake being mesmerised by a rabbit – but when tight he is a teddy bear. Wogan[1] too silly – too much the Tolstoy – inspired Moujik – the cracky and obstinate rebel but no intellect. Rosamond got across us by accepting and refusing and though all is forgiven she won't believe it – Patrick we liked seeing a lot, much improved by foreign travel and didn't highbrow me as he usually does, so we both could be modest at last. Elizabeth[2] fine; but so plain. D. Abdy really charming but he is difficult[3] and that means it must always be a party. Logan v. reliable.

Too much leisure – with so much leisure one leans too hard on everyone and everything and most of them give way.

> Her face is an erotic zone
> where all who look must stay
> like sailors whose escape is gone
> marooned on that sweet cay.
>
>   smiling vale
> the hills the woods the curving shore
> { they salute and know to be
> { the finer their gaze are spread
> { beyond the reach of oar and sail
> { and on their hands for evermore
> { their useless destiny
> { that proud and empty head

And now we are going to play to you a new number entitled 'Teenie weenie Peenie'.

17th.

Took my design for a summer linen tunic to Turnbull & Asser. They find it practicable. A warm day. The asphalt of London came out from winter sleep and began to heave and smell, and women looked fatter in their summer frocks. Joined Howard Hardy and [John] Banting in café late. Usual argument going on.

---

[1] Wogan Philipps, born 1902, 2nd Lord Milford. A Communist landowner. Married the novelist Rosamond Lehmann in 1928.

[2] In one of his earliest *New Statesman* columns (September 3, 1927) he had reviewed Elizabeth Bowen's *The Hotel*. The novel had prompted a very characteristic phrase: 'Imprisoned in an English rock-pool by the southward-flowing tide.'

[3] Sir Robert Abdy had married Lady Diana Bridgeman in 1930.

'It's no good looking so fat and sheepish, Eddie – artistically you're both finished. You belong to the last generation – to the ideology of Clive Bell – you look at pictures for quite personal reasons, you judge them by a purely private emotion – you and Clive and Roger Fry – if you took the trouble to read Herbert Read's article in the *Listener* you'd see it – you're both very charming – but Edwardian I'm sure Clive –'

'Heigh! Hoo! Clive! Roger Fry! I mean good God where are we – are we in London or are we on Lundy Island?'

'I can hear you quite well if you don't shout, John.'

'But what is going to take the place of their art criticism, Brian?'

'If you read Herbert Read's article in the *Listener*, Eddie, you will see – I don't know – I only know it will be some thing very much more exact and very much more difficult.'

18th. Logan around: said à propos of Lady Horner's drivelling book that allee samee she was clever woman – people not used to writing, however clever and cynical, could only tap the cesspools of their mind. Said could only read two of Peter's stories, found incurable faults of style – exasperation, lassitude, anaemia. He respected him as a man of letters, however (Evelyn thinks him a Francis Fribble, a distinguished hack).

Read sexy story by Dali: I could have known Crevel, Buñuel, Ernst, Tzara and Aragon. Why not? bad French, love of money and comfort and elegance (but elegant people don't know me nor Money comfort every fault).
Why don't I know Auden and Spender? I know so few people, and I don't like disputations any more. Most unpleasant memory of last six months was drink with Nicolson in Café Royal. He must have been trying to humiliate me. Is enemy and shall be considered so.

18th. Read *Walpoliana*. First volume and catty preface extremely intelligent. Out and met Noel took wine in Markham Sq. Betjeman said he most envied Kenneth Clark. Think how good we should all be at everything if we had so much money as Alan Pryce-Jones – he likes living abroad and he lives abroad. Bought Croker's *Johnson* though promised to Desmond. I don't like Johnsoniana. I only like high life in the eighteenth century. Robin and Barbara to dinner, Bunny forgot, 21 afterwards with Elizabeth. Dull.

ou se masturbira -t-on?
ou sodomisera -t-on?

Thoughts for prose of hedonism:

Two veins run through English literature, the cyrenaic and the epicurean (Walton Addison – Bacon – Lamb). Lucas and Flucas (Lucas Flucas) the cyrenaic: aristocratic, mature with the knowledge of excess and the fear of boredom, mundane and ecstatic (Rochester, Congreve, Walpole, Harvey, Beckford, Sterne occasionally, Thackeray). The other upper middle class, armchair naif and insipid: both based on the conception of leisure and both difficult in the employment of it, an incentive to one class, a sedative to the other.

The Cyreniac view is based on the happiness of the moment and the beauty of the passing moment is the *raison d'être* of this literature.

20th. Logan took us out to tea, afterwards we walked round Mayfair and went to bookshop. Logan charming and his usual embarrassing self in bookshop. 'Cyril, I don't believe you like Meredith.' 'No, I don't.' 'Well listen to this – and this of Browning – this of Matthew Arnold, "but for peace her heart was yearning and now peace laps her round".' He reads rising and falling on his toes with a swaying priestly movement and intones, the words like ether, going under after a few lines with thickening consonants and slurred vowels. He nibbled at a Herbert 2nd Edition.

'Don't you like Herbert, Sir?' 'What?' 'Don't you like Herbert, Sir?' 'Of course I like him. Why I've been to the place he was rector of. What's it called? Bemerton Logan, of course Bemerton – I remember I said to Lytton Strachey once, where's Bemerton? I don't know, he said, I've never heard of it. I don't believe you have Cyril, either, but still you'd think as a specialist in the 17th century he would have. O here's a delicious thing, let me read it you.'

Called on Peter afterwards, he had forgotten he had asked us. Marcelle rushed up to have a bath before going out with him – she wore a yellow sweater and looked more beautiful than ever. Peter said one should have a new house, new interests, new friends and a new lover every year and one would be always young. He certainly illustrates it and all the little marriage-boats in the harbour rock uneasily as the backwash of his new craft hits them.

21st. Visit from Molly Higgins who was charming, on to Robin's for sherry-in-the-dark. Rollo Hayes, rather tight, began doing his frog-into-bull act, this time about Lady Cunard. Sidney Beer arrived to fetch someone. I asked him about Salzburg. Peggy off. 'O are you an Austrian – how goody. I adore Austrian men.' Dinner with Robin and Colville, political arguments, very breezy. C. said he was only unhappy one week a year, Robin only happy same. C. said he would be a Tory if it was not that there was something stagnant about all Toryism which made the atmosphere impossible to breathe, instances, the *Spectator*, *Morning Post*, county families, Eaton Square. Robin admitted his communism wore thin in England, hated English communists so; besides nobody cared. Could see no future for England except increasing and painful de-industrialisation, leading to ultimate pastoral bliss. Inclined slightly to Bertrand Russell and Lord Allen, liberal reasonableness. C. said that if there was something unbreathable in Toryism, there was something pedantic and dowdy about liberalism, even if it was still alive. Preferred Whigs, of dead causes. Colville blamed Whigs for industrial revolution, rise of middle classes, USA free trade and everything awful – it appeared he was the sub-editor of Oxford and Cambridge and the argument dissolved in ribaldry. Walked home through the vernal tart-strewn streets. Ridiculous uniformity of British parks. Looked in vain for mackintoshed ladies, extra high shoes, long hair, short hair, furs, gloves, breeches, busts, corsets, and in fact any signs of healthy fetichism – only regional changes apparent, the women being plain and mousy in Bloomsbury, brazen in Piccadilly Circus and Shaftesbury Avenue, point-to-point in Sackville Street, hardened old Belgian *poules* in Bond Street and the same sequence in reverse as far as Hyde Park Corner.

22nd. Wet day – spent in bookshops. Bought several, coveted more and nearly stole first edition of Thackeray's English humourists. Eventually wish a library to consist of:
1. Selected French books
2. Shelf of Greek and Latin
3. Detective stories: *sottisiers* (D. Yates etc)
4. Special period 1680–1740 English
5. Modern novels, poetry and pamphlets (the 20's)
6. Travel
7. Whig memoirs from Harvey to end of Greville
8. Albums and works of pornography and reference

Jean's library – one shelf of Victorian novels

must buy 4 Pope Swift Dryden Loves of Poets, Harleian miscellany,
    Harvey
    5 *Lost Lady Fiesta Antic Hay Foxhunting Man Waves*[1]
    Pirelli English Humourists
    7 Greville Creevey
    1 Céline

My father to dinner: at his best, made Jean read out to him obituary
of her grandfather from family bible of sorts.

'He has not enjoyed good health for months and last Monday
morning he was attacked by a serious ailment of the bowels.'
'That's what's going to get me worse luck' –
'which the physicians, Dr L. D. Wilson and others, could not battle
with successfully'
'damned doctors – don't get any for me, never do any good'
'He was born in 1820'
'just like my grandfather – he was born in 1820'
'and died seventy-five years of age'
'just like my grandfather – he would have been a hundred and
fourteen, the old fool'
'In 1860 Mr Paxton was elected President of the North Western
Bank of Virginia.'
'and my grandfather was elected Rector of Bath, damn him'
'Mr Paxton was a public spirited citizen and will be remembered for
the beautiful gift he made the city, a number of years ago, the costly
Paxton fountain in the city building square'
'Mine spent £50,000 on restoring Bath Abbey. The damned old
idiot. I hate him. I hate him. When you realise what we might have
had'
'No man in those trying days was more devoted to the government
of the state and it would be a fitting testimonial to his name if a
public monument were erected to his memory.'
'Poof. Moo. They gave him a rood-screen – mind you I'm not
grumbling old boy – but when I think – poof. moo. well – damn
him.'

---

[1] 'After the falseness of *Orlando*, she produced a masterpiece in *The Waves*,' according to
Enemies of Promise. Cyril concluded that it was 'one of the books which comes nearest to
stating the mystery of life'. To Virginia Woolf, this was 'cocktail criticism'.

Joe [Hergesheimer] was at first terrified of his secretary, a Miss W., niece of the peer, she was so stern and upper class and British. He noticed, however, that a girlfriend called for her every evening and that she looked paler every morning and finally went to sleep while he was dictating. He finally said, 'Now look here Miss W., I don't care if your poppa had a crack at you or how you got that way but you've got to lay off that girlfriend if she's going to take it out of you. I pay you to listen to me, besides, you'll get cancer with all that friction.' She said nothing at the time and he thought she was going to report him to the police but as she was leaving she said very meekly, 'Can you really get cancer?'

> 'Love the most generous passion of the mind
> That cordial drop heaven in our cup has thrown
> To make the nauseous draught of life go down.'

Sunday

Read Roger's *Table Talk*, half Trevelyan's *Early History of C. J. Fox*, some of the Devonshire House book, and some Selwyn and *Walpoliana*. To go to the cinema after a day in the 1760's is like a nightmare. Reading these memoirs brings out how corrupt I am, or else how crazy the human race is. For the political vices of Walpole and Holland, the social vices of gambling, drinking, and wenching of Fox, Porson and Queensbury, seem the natural employments of mankind when they get the chance to, as sane and mature as the poetry of Rochester or the reprehensible dilettantism of Horace Walpole. To a *pourri* it is fascism, communism, buchmanism, pelmanism, etc that seem insane, and the corruption of a life of pleasure that seems sensible – and to a lover of beauty the contrast between elegance in men and women and what they look like today, between the appearance of dandies and the people who wish to change them, between the melancholy wisdom of excess and experience and the pedantry or embarrassing egotism of religious or romantic reformers, does nothing to speed conversion.

Told Robin all poets were snobs, to which he said, 'What about Milton, Marlowe, Shelley and Keats – and Blake?' C. answered that three died young, one was blind and one mad, otherwise they would have been. Logan to tea. Discussion on Lady Harvey, Horace Walpole's parentage, etc. Agreed with Robin on the total lack of glamour of intellectual life in London after Paris, compared to our drunken conversations in the night restaurants of Montmartre. The

Café Royal etc are simply places where one shelters from the general inclemency and drinks, like tropical administrators, because whisky is an excellent germicide.

> So when my days of impotence approach
> and I'm by love and wine's unhappy chance
> Driven from the pleasing billows of debauch
> on the dull shore of lazy temperance.

Monday. Book hunting. Eddie [Sackville-West] to dinner and café – lunch talk of Horace Walpole, Pope and first editions. Rain.

The prose of hedonism.

Analyse the defects, from this aspect, of Arlen, Nicolson, Hinks.[1]

Arlen comes very near it but cannot exclude orientalism from his style nor snobbery from his attitude to his characters, in short vulgar.

Nicolson 1) cannot exclude the sense of duty, the worship of action and 2) writes from the apologetic armchair epicurean angle, in short a flatfoot.

Hinks in letters to N.R-S develops second rate Walpolism, is posing always as a fastidious blade, a museum rake, and shows a certain lack of confidence in the impersonation.

The truth is, that in no department of writing is it truer to say *le style c'est l'homme* than in that where the unliterary temperament of someone who prefers acute sensations to cerebral effects, attempts to fix them on paper that perilous medium. Quote Hemingway on Huxley from *Death in the Afternoon*.[2]

No-one probably so well read or so un-literary in regard to quotations metaphors etc as our heroes Congreve, Walpole, Beckford, Waugh and Firbank and Smith.

---

[1] Roger Hinks, a British Council aesthete, with the looks of a Toby Jug, according to his obituary tribute in *The Times*. The book referred to here is *Pictures and People*. Subtitled, 'A Transatlantic Criss-Cross between Roger Hinks in London and Naomi Royde-Smith in New York, Boston, Philadelphia'. (1930).

[2] On pp 181–3 of *Death in the Afternoon*, Hemingway criticises Huxley for creating characters rather than projecting living people from his experiences. He concludes, 'A serious writer may be a hawk or a buzzard or even a popinjay, but a solemn writer is always a bloody owl.'

Contents of such a style.

Irony, maturity, grace, grace being what is called 'merely lyricism'

(n.b. how many pejorations lyricism has now come in for. Clark on Grant. Nicolson on intellect without creative action is a mere gaudy thing).

Irony + grace − maturity = epicurean prose of Walton, Lamb and the middlebrows

irony + maturity − grace = Hemingway, *The Waves*

irony = contrast (Rylands and Eliz. Trag. preface)

Begin.

No cause is so lost today as that of pleasure. The philosophy, the temperament and the means by which men were supplied with the most wholesome of all bases of existence are unobtainable.

Poets, though I sincerely believe, they all, if lyrical, are of this persuasion, I will not refer to as living for pleasure because they often have such very odd ideas of it.

There is an integrity in true worldliness which a saint would envy.

Wednesday Dinner party.

Joe [Hergesheimer], Violet [Mrs Hammersley], Deirdre Balfour, Richard and Freya [Elwes], Peter and Joan Eyres-Monsell, Evelyn, afterwards Patrick. A double magnum of pop. This one of the best and most typical of our dinner parties but it is too late to remember

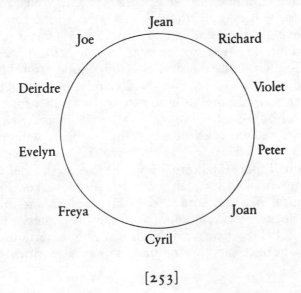

much about it. Joe particularly awful – terrible all the way through and Evelyn consequently very aggrieved.

Joe cross at not being the centre of the party – complained that it was too big – that Englishmen talked too much. Violet huffy at hearing that her American tenants had given a party without her and had the Prince of Wales. Peter did his best with Joe but only got his knuckles rapped. Evelyn happy to see Deirdre Balfour but furious with Joe's appalling remarks – the best was, after the ladies had withdrawn, to boast about how hard he worked, today he had written 7,000 words before lunch and who knows – eyeing Peter and Evelyn – that some of it is imperishable prose. Attacked Logan backed up by Peter. Logan defended by Violet and us. He left fairly early with Deirdre and was subjected to general censure. Finally went on to Florida, with Peter, Elwes and Joan. Found her very attractive and sweet. Talked about Alan, whom she says won't marry her without a grand wedding. We all got tight at the Florida. Altogether a very pleasant balmy evening, a young party with two really pretty women. Terrible hangover next day though amiable, tipsy and Eyres-Monsell-conscious in the morning. Lunch with Logan. Jane Clark there – amazing to see how from a pretty governess she has made herself a real *femme du monde*, beautifully dressed, assured, waiting to be amused, her voice two keys lower, a severe, agreeable, natural distinction. Very ill afterwards. Eddie to cocktails.

Finally got away and felt better over Rye Highs on the Washington. Much titivated by bevies of American beauties and would willingly have continued to New York. [H. G.] Wells on board. Long wait for tender. Everything American on boat, food, drink, money, above all the broad round, with a few Latin exceptions, American skull. The men are certainly a rough lot. Queenstown pretty and foreign. Long motor drive from exotic littoral by green fields, stone walls, and dirty villages. Ireland quite derelict, empty and down at heel. Elizabeth's house lovely but rather forlorn. The country so cold, as usual. Owing to rural torpor increased by the relaxing climate all literary effort is here impossible so will only summarise briefly. Next day (Sat) go to have tea at Anne's grave. Woolfs arrive. He small spare intellectual Jew, she lovely, shy and virginal. They seemed shocked by Jean's dress (Virginia asked Elizabeth what unnatural vice was) and talked only of plans and motoring. Occasional flickers of animation over the boringness of Arthur Waley and Bob Trevelyan, and the difficulty of entertaining (why should drink be necessary?). Virginia Woolf gave a satirical description of G. B. Stern.[1] We agreed that we could not like people if we didn't like their books. They left next morning.[2] Visit from perfect Bulldog-Dornford young woman who said of unsatisfactory P.S. [?] 'I'm afraid he's a nasty piece of work. In love with big brother as is often case with Sapper's women.' Tea at Mallow Castle, dingy and discrete, Monday in Cork – rather disappointing. Comic dinner party, seedy, knowing, Eton and New York young heir of Mallow, Sapper girl Nasty Piece and his (much nastier) keeper – 21 afterwards – flirtation between Sapper girl, 28–9, no juice, pert, and given to 'philosophising' black hair, red cheeks, brown eyes, 'Irish' colouring rather paddyish nose and mouth and faded Bordighera – Chateau D'Oex evening dress. Keeper small hunchbacked ex-soldier in flyblown tux.

Keeper: 'Going to be here this summer?'

Sappergirl: 'No alas I'm going to Scotland.'

Keeper: 'Going to slaughter a few grouse?'

Sappergirl (with little brown-mouse ogle): 'No – I'm going to take my little bow and arrow and try and get a twelve pointer.'

The Nasty Piece was amusing and grateful to get some conversation. Knew Piers [Synnott].

Tuesday Went to Mitchelstown and sat by lake. Castle quite demolished, trees felled, lake the local *jardin publique*, nothing but the almshouses and Great-aunt Anna's grave left of the glory of the

---

[1] G. B. Stern 1890–1973, prolific lady novelist.

[2] 'There we spent one night, unfortunately with baboon Conolly[sic] and his gollywog slug wife Jean to bring in the roar of the Chelsea omnibus.' That was written, with the fine sensibility of feeling and expression for which Virginia Woolf is celebrated, in her diary, under the entry for Monday April 30, 1934 (see *Diary*, Vol IV, p 210). In a letter to her sister Vanessa Bell on May 4 1934 (see *The Letters of Virginia Woolf*, Vol V, p 299), she kept to her refinement. 'We spent a night with the Bowens, where, to our horror we found the Connollys – a less appetising pair I have never seen out of the Zoo, and the apes are considerably preferable to Cyril. She has the face of a golliwog and they brought the reek of Chelsea with them.'

These opinions of hers were a matter of common knowledge. 'If you want to be malicious about Cyril, the last word was said by Virginia Woolf: "I do not like that smarty-boots Connolly,"' the philosopher A. J. Ayer said in the streets one night in 1941, to hear Cyril replying from the darkness, 'Not so loud, Freddie.' (See his autobiography *Part of my Life*, p 248.)

Smarty-boots sounds too contemporary from her, and whether or not she said it cannot be authenticated. 'I think not and somehow it seems unlikely,' her biographer Professor Quentin Bell writes to me. Evelyn Waugh's *Black Mischief* (1932) introduces General Connolly, Duke of Ukaka, whose soldiers eat their boots, and whose duchess is Black Bitch. Waugh habitually spoke of 'Boots' Connolly.

Lycidas Kings and the Earls of Kingston. Dinner alone and talk of nephews with Elisabeth.

Wednesday Walk by Blackwater, and Listowel's ruins – a noble river, parks with wooded cliffs, choughs nesting and leaping salmon.

Thursday. Flight. Drove car from ruins of Spencer's castle at Kilcolman.

Friday. Into Cork, Lunch at Castle Hyde, miss Dublin train, sleep at Youghal.

Saturday. See Raleigh's myrtle grove at Youghal. Congreve's college, Cork's tomb, lunch at Dungarvan, dine at Waterford in gloomy expensive hotel, cross by Fishguard. Delighted to get back to London where one is not constipated, stupid, and irritable and can live up on one's nerves again and keep irregular hours. Lunch at Victor – on and see Joe.

Joe told us Evelyn had been round to warn Ronnie Balfour about him and said he shouldn't let his wife go out with people like that. Dinner in café grill with Peter and Marcelle joined afterwards by Joe. Marcelle depressed and rather sweet and naive, she coughed a little which irritated Peter. 'O for God's sake stop coughing. All my married life seems to have been punctuated by a woman coughing – Akeffa – keffa – keffa,' he mimicked. Joe told Marcelle she was too old to be a film star and too soft to be a gold digger. Peter said she didn't care about clothes, trampled on them etc. 'Don't be simple – she cares all right – she just doesn't care for the clothes she's got.' – 'God how I hate a poor woman,' he added.

London now completely summer. Trees, tawdriness spreading west from Tottenham Court Road, evening pavements crowded with aimless sex. V. Woolf asked Elizabeth what unnatural vice was – 'I mean what do they *do*?'

Lord Hymen – Castle Hymen – the Bride of Ballyfaghty.

Have absolutely outgrown Ireland, the climate Boeotian, the charm a nuisance, the West of all points of the compass the least suggestive, in fact nowhere in Ireland seems to have any *raison d'être*, any focus, the ruined demesnes along the valley of the

Blackwater bear witness to an extinct society – but Elizabeth's house, for instance, was built to be near Mallow – well, so it is. Comparison with the Southern States of America – Faulkner etc but without the niggers, drink and tropics.

Ireland must be the least homosexual country in the world.

Monday spent in facing enormous bills, the hosts of Midian, buying books, good dinner and later, a visit from Marcelle. Talk of abortions and pregnancies. M. lost her virginity to an actor at 17, he never saw her again, says she is sterile. On Wednesday Peter is to have his co-respondent and we discussed whether she would mind if he had her. Stally wants to marry a rich man and keep Pulham as a lover – Becky Sharp, without the charm. It amused me to hear Peter laughing at Evelyn's 'provincial little Arnold Bennett *arriviste* appearance'. Evening at Café typical of London, delicious after country – The mirrors and baroque cherubs, the empty hock bottles, Joe, Peter, Marcelle, and the near vulgarity of the King of Greece. It is odd to think of Peter's affairs stretching backwards through these diaries to earliest letters at Oxford, just as Joe knows more of Jean's father than she does. The life of everybody living in London is a series of fortuitous meetings, temporary connections, arranged round a kernel of hard matter – The people they have to see, family, business partners, wives, mistresses and cronies. Sooner or later everyone else drops away and these nuclei are formed very early and admit very few of the later accumulations. Thus Bloomsbury remains a family business. Thus Wogan and Rosamond will go on seeing Barbara and Bunny and not us, just as Eddie sees Brian and spotted John,[1] or Violet Hilda – whom do I see? Peter, Logan, Christopher and the people they collect round them. They are the people who would be asked for our address.

The King's Proctor Blues. Urinal Stomp.

Reading: Spence's anecdotes. Finished. Death scenes with Bolingbroke very moving. 'Pope was a whig and would have been a Protestant if his mother had died.' Wharton? The interest of Pope, Addison and their circle is that they are the first modern literary group in England. Their quarrels and their attachments are those of men of letters anywhere, yet they are still bathed in the radiance of

---

[1] John Strachey, known as 'spotted' to distinguish him from his namesake, the politician.

Great Charles and the periwig. Addison the first person to write for the middle class, hence detestable. Pepys a middle classman of course – but the literary society from Marlowe to Dryden was composed of amateurs or professionals who passed their time between the tavern and the patron's mansion. With the Augustans arose the choice dinner parties in villas which were just the same up to Gosse. With Gray-Johnson the bourgeoisie become, in letters, supreme.

Virginia Woolf told us she hated the Regency – that the circle of the Prince Regent's Pavilion, Creevey etc, was the vulgarest period in English history. Logan came round and read out some remarks of Mrs Warre-Cornish, of which the best was told him by Sir Denis Bray, retired Anglo-Indian. 'She said the most extraordinary things – once after I had been singing, she said, "O Sir Denis you should never have come down from Monte Rosa."'

> What are the gay parterres, the chequered shade
> The morning bower, the evening colonnade[1]
> but soft recesses for uneasy minds
> to sigh unheard in, to the passing winds?
>
> So the struck deer in some sequestered part
> lies down to die, the arrow at his heart,
> he stretched unseen in coverts hid from day
> Bleeds drop by drop, and pants his life away.

The only beauties of the 17–18th century who seem beautiful to me are the Duchess of Marlborough and Nell Gwynn.

Delighted to find that Congreve tried to purchase a picture of Rochester: first fact that bears up my theory that C. based his heroes on R. tradition, hence in fact his ceasing to write when wenching went under to politics in 1700. He stands half way in, half out of the Augustan age, taken up too early by older men.

Fascinated only in National Gallery by a Highmore 'gentleman in murrey brown velvet'. Surely must be a Hervey.

---

[1] From Alexander Pope. 'Early in the 1930's I had copied out his lines on Lady Mary Wortley Montagu,' Cyril wrote, when he came to choose *The Evening Colonnade* as the title of his last collection of essays and reviews. 'Is not my work compact of columns, in this case all that's left standing from some five hundred of them?'

(Waller on Rochester)

He is rather pleasant, then arch. He is comparatively reserved; but you find something in that restraint, which is more agreeable than the utmost exertion of talent in others.

Once, upon Mr R's filliping a piece of bread into a blind fiddler's face, it held him in an excessive fit for half an hour, which returned whenever the thing was only mentioned afterwards. (Spence on Marquis of Blandford.)

Oddly enough I have never been in London for the summer for seven years. So far the heat is bracing, women better dressed, shops brighter, a recurrence of dandyism.

Life for me, Lady Winifred, is one long Paul Jones.

There is something wrong with a world in which one meets Mrs Lowinsky and Roger Hinks and Mrs Royde-Smith. They smell of middlebrow.

Friday. Angela's wedding,[1] embarrassed in church by absence of tails, at reception by Rosa Lewis, ''ere's the man wot owes me money. Bobbie give 'im a writ' – we had to slink out very quickly, on to see Patrick rather poorly, he has seen the Richards'[2] at Chagford. They spend whole days in their room, without seeing anybody. Poor Nigel – ah woe is me to see what I have seen, see what I see.

However wise we are, we are only worldly wise for others.

Nicolson's review of Firbank in *Daily Telegraph* 'arresting figure', 'life dealt in porcelain hints. The timidity inseparable from such epicene gigglings has discouraged me from becoming an admirer of Ronald Firbank – cachinnations of Ronald Firbank – a literary curiosity – Beardsley in plus fours' – 'I question whether such a reputation will prove durable.'

How he would have enjoyed that.

---

[1] Angela Sykes married Lord Antrim. The story of Rosa Lewis presenting this unpaid bill has been told so often and so well that this entry alone recovers it from fiction.

[2] Nigel and Betty Richards. *The Rock Pool* was written around him. In a preface to the 1981 Oxford University Press edition of the novel, Peter Quennell speaks of Nigel Richards' 'amatory mishaps'. In 1946, Cyril explained in a postscript to the novel that Nigel Richards' 'extraordinary beauty' had to be ruthlessly suppressed for purposes of the narrative. Also he had 'died in the black winter night above Germany'.

'As an antidote to the febrile flourishes of Ronald Firbank I warmly recommend *The Age of Reason* by Professor R. B. Mowat, etc etc.'

How stale, fatigued, third rate, is the vocabulary of defamation – gigglings, cachinnations (for laughter) epicene (a pejorative noise) flourishes – I question whether – what a rusty outfit with which to drag someone down, journalist and debater's outfit.

Restoration beauty.

A fine, easy clean shape, light brown hair in abundance; her features regular, her complexion clear and lively, large wanton eyes, but above all a mouth that has made me kiss it a thousand times in imagination, teeth white and even, and pretty pouting lips with a little moisture ever hanging on them, that look like the province rose fresh on the bush, ere the morning sun has quite drawn up the dew.

(The Man of Mode cp. Love for Love)

While one can, by introducing, be responsible for a few happy couplings, in London as a rule there is always a reason why two people don't know each other already. Never introduce contemporaries.

'Thus then were these remains of the best set of actors that I believe were ever known at once in England, by Time, Death, and the Satiety of their hearers mouldering to decay.' Webber of Betterton and Co.

Story of Mrs Warre-Cornish and Desmond, at that time a cautious young man afraid of giving himself away. She stopped him as he was leaving after weekend. 'Did I tell you about my young French friend, who came to England for the first time, and was asked what he liked best – a dish of cold crumpets he'd had at a tea party. Goodbye.'
Mrs Warre-Cornish asked if she'd heard of homosexuality.
'O indeed, it's an ancient, aristocratic, traditional vice here at Eton, but quite unknown in the sanitary linoleum schools.' Lady Ponsonby said she was selfish and would never admit her husband was dying, that Molly and Desmond found her a great strain; she had been present at lunch where Mrs W.C. had been consistently brilliant but they had never even smiled. Such is the truculence of consanguinity.

Kenneth to lunch. Dinner Blakistons. Dorothy Warren's party. This very interesting as the *reductio ad absurdum* of entertaining – about

16 people, each of whom knew not more than three others, standing about in evening dress and drinking tepid cup. No-one introduced to each other. It seemed a little like the Hollywood idea of a typical evening in an English country house, all that goes with evening dress and the temperature the same at eleven o'clock as at one. Mostly nobody talked, the men were bored with the people they knew, apprehensive of those they didn't, and it was left to the wives to get along.

Wed. Hangover without the consolation of having earned one, matinée of Miss Enters, after a brandy at the Ivy. Very moving performance, especially byzantine dance in which an ikon comes to life and expresses her simple archaic faith in a few gestures – bad men go below, good men up sky. This means YOU! and after blessing, denouncing, cradling, and lying in effigy, the world as she knows it, she returns to her niche again. Also the boy cardinal, in which she expresses every refinement of vanity, lechery, cruelty, and grace; the corrupt imperious boy, irritably blessing when occasion requires, superstitious and pompous in face of the altar, pauses in his red robes to slowly wipe his face while his narrow eyes above the handkerchief solicit the congregation. There was nothing literary, nothing Firbank or Beardsley in the urchin's dance, it was the beauty of selfishness and vice, the natural lubricity of adolescence, the romance of nepotism.

Thursday. Pretentious lunch with Lady Bonham Carter – Madame de Margerie[1] like a nightmare, hotted-up Lady Colefax. 'I tell you who fascinate me – your Scotch mystics of the 18th century – I am mystic myself and can tell when a room has been used by Böchine or Gerald Manley Hopkins. I tried to make Charlie du Bos read him.' Lady Cunard says – John Hayward says – Lady Londonderry says – George Katawi[2] says. Hinks there and also the Chelsea Christ and Perownes. Elizabeth [Bowen] looks in for a moment in the evening, delight at seeing her.

---

[1] Wife of Roland de Margerie, First Secretary at the French Embassy, 1933–1939.

[2] Egyptian-Jewish diplomat, aesthete, author. In a number of respects, his French prose style included, he modelled himself upon his friend Marcel Proust. His *L'Amitié de Proust* was published in 1935. He preferred to spell his name as Georges Cattaui.

Friday. Work on stories, book hunting. Logan comes in, talk with Hyslop – then smokey evening.

> Blessed be the great for those they take away
> and those they left me; for they left me gay
> left me to see neglected genius bloom
> neglected die, and tell it on his tomb:
> of all thy blameless life the sole return
> my verse, and Queensberry weeping o'er thy urn.

> A waving glow the bloomy beds display
> Blushing in bright diversities of day.

> Another age shall see the golden ear
> imbrown the slope and nod on the parterre
> Deep harvests bury all his pride has planned
> and laughing Ceres re-assume the land.

Logan talked of the vulgarity of the great world, apropos of Madame de Margerie 'Is she a goose?' he had asked Hopey, 'well aren't they all?' He described Henry James tearing to pieces a Mrs Clifford who was supposed to be an exquisite hostess of her day and him saying to H. James, 'Well don't you think Madame Geoffrin or Mrs Montagu were much the same?' James said he was afraid they were. Logan thought Holland House must have been terribly dull, he had met in his youth one of the survivors of that world where conversations consisted of long monologues which displayed your general knowledge and reading (in the survivor's case it was the route of Alexander's Indian expedition). While all the other old gentlemen sat round waiting for the first cough, I read him *Trilby* on the upper classes which he admired. Decided Madame du Deffand was different. Of modern hostesses he said Lady Colefax had the gift of getting people who all wanted to meet each other but she then insisted on talking herself. Lady Cunard alone managed general conversation which she got by shouting something preposterous. 'Sex plays no part in modern life.' Logan described the Duke of Connaught's attempts to grasp the idea.

Dinner the *reductio ad absurdum* of entertaining, like the Trotters' theological parties. All four drank solidly; Marcelle began by saying how badly we had behaved at the Bon Viveur, where we removed a few mistakes from the bill, and conversation continued heatedly on this merry theme. When it changed to books or people she plunged her head in her hands and gloomed for the rest of the meal. Peter told good story of Rosa Lewis saying to Katawi, 'O I remember you,

you was a great friend of King Edward, wasn't you, and a terrible one for the women.' After vainly protesting he was led upstairs to meet Stally, 'the best little thing she had ready at present'. Marcelle returned as soon as she had gone upstairs with Jean and began to fight; this new departure in etiquette annoyed C. considerably and Marcelle also was irritated by the obvious dispensability which we felt for her. Took her upstairs where she gloomed some more, went up on the roof and collapsed on one sofa while Jean, after a Keramon, went to sleep and began to snore on another. In these circumstances, we conducted a three-cornered conversation with Elizabeth [Bowen] on the awfulness of women writers and the nastiness of her friend Mrs Woolf, both topics introduced by Peter. Marcelle disappeared for some time with occasional plug pullings to remind us of her and finally came back to leave with Peter. Pleasant chat with Elizabeth. M. will not recur.

Friday. Car conscious. Gloomy cinema. Saw Brian [Howard]. Saturday. Cars, my father to dinner.

'I'm very much worried. I think we ought to give Germany back her colonies. I don't think we ought to have taken them – we ought to give them all back. Except Tanganyka. That's the only one that's worth anything.'
Logan to lunch Sunday, afterwards (evening) pleasant pub crawl. Peter and Marcelle on best behaviour.

Logan talked of Edith Wharton, how she'd always get what she wanted – of her terrible rudeness, shyness, loyalty to friends etc how glamorous all the people in her autobiography sounded till you came across someone you knew. Not a success in England because she lived for the salon, the small group of people (H. James, Sturgis, Bourget, Blanche, Norton etc) doing everything together, and in England people preferred a more social more vulgar existence.

Weekend with Cox on sailing barge to Rochester.
Amusing dinner here. Peter, Tony P. [i.e. Powell], [David] Gascoyne,[1] Howard (USA) and Elizabeth [Bowen].

---

[1] In an entry dated October 13, 1936, in his *Journal 1936–1937* (Enitharmon Press, 1980) David Gascoyne writes, 'In the evening, after a street corner meeting in Twickenham, went up to a party at Esmond Romilly's. Drink, talk, smoke, a gramophone playing. Cyril Connolly and Jean, surprisingly, were there. And Arthur Calder-Marshall and his wife.' Gascoyne had just had his twentieth birthday, he says of himself, and had joined the Communist Party.

Evening in Eiffel – at Sutro's – day at divorce court – dinner and party James Strachey's.

Weekend Violet's, bought car, too busy on stories to write much in this. Much excitement over car. Down to Patrick's for weekend with it. Evelyn there. Evelyn's new locutions – cinematograph, 'sock' (the Eton slang). Cocktail party, Betty Maclaren, Gladwyn there. Trotters afterwards. They fulminate about the sub-tenants, 'Eddie Gathorne-Hardy, Brian Howard and Mr Banting – worthless, no talent, homosexual sewer rats.' Brian Howard the worst and most hated. Philip Trotter: 'We can't let our artists down.'

Misunderstood.

The now retired
profession of the calamus.

O yes decidedly
having a sense of humour and a past
one will amuse oneself decidedly

Movements
Visit to Sledmere
to Rosamond where attacked the ancient mariner
to my cousins
my mother in England
Jean's mother in England
the CAR
Abbotsbury
September in Cornwall. Ham Manor – Salcombe – Fowey – St Ives – Truro – Boscastle – Tavistock – Chagford, Peter and Marcelle at Chagford.

The Abdy's home, new things from America. Books, silver, the genette. Jean goes to nursing home.

He has the journalist's inability to read or to listen.

Nov 1st. Day of sun and frost
        Sleep before evening.

Dead. Roger Fry – Sligger – Joyce Turner
        accident   – illness – suicide

George Wansbrough's sister put her car in the station yard at 8 pm. Put herself under the train at eleven. What did she feel in those three hours?

Joyce had already taken an overdose of veronal in New York and been brought to by a stomach-pump. She wrote a lot of letters first. Poor child, a Cassandra, her lyrical fluttering quality so suited to enjoying life, to living in the moment, yet condemned by excess of sensibility, courage, distinction of heart to suffer a perpetual kind of adolescent brainstorm of passion and disappointment – a Russian egotist – perhaps trying to prove the genuineness of her feelings to herself, perhaps carried away by their genuineness, a tragic subject.[1]

The vulgarity of living – pretences on the telephone, with Patrick, Nancy, and Peter of not being quite sure it is her. 'How *awful*, must find out – anyhow we meet on Thursday, don't we?' Suicide such a censure, a pathetic minority report on existence. What loneliness, wretchedness or exaltation, decision and indecision must have been going on – a girl of twenty-five with mother, father, a brother and two sisters.

The Spears family – a neurotic missionary side coming out unexpectedly to cripple the plans of the hard American socialite success-worshippers.

Joyce, Comfort and Emmie in Addison walk, at tea.
Mary, Susan and Emily
with their large round mouths laugh he-he-he.

Russian, *Constant nymph* household – Joyce's face like the singing women in the National Gallery's.
Piero della Francesca.
What happens to people?

May Spears – woman of exquisite elegance and chic simple cordial, ironic, a flower of capitalism – now writes potboilers about the Holy Family.

---

[1] An undated letter from Joyce Turner at Naworth Castle must have been written soon after Cyril's marriage. 'I am getting old and lazy and long to marry someone like Jean – but she may be congratulated for marrying Connolly and I envy you and her the epicurean future and if you find a house with white columns (inside and out) I should settle there.' She also wrote, 'It seemed very queer for Connolly to have found security in the U.S. so delightfully, so emphatically.'

Joyce, frail, thin and tiny, painting and writing poetry, warmly American and yet with so strong a flavour of Emily Brontë, growing into a plump sexy communistic co-ed in New York, a slattern in England with dirty clothes and servants' stockings, and married men and abortions in the air and then social work – unity, happiness and death.

most people are dead to us anyhow
but that poor child –

Jean's pills contain essence of the gland which leads to social success. The slims.

> O Osbert father Osbert
> to whom the young men pray
> a Sitwell voice and Sitwell face
> bestow on me this day,
> and teach me in society
> to cleave to what is best
> and ogle, flatter, boast, till I
> may stink like all the rest.

Us he devours. I live and she is dead.
Let nothing be done to break his spirit, the world will accomplish that business soon enough.

Party before Christmas, very good landmark of 1934. Diana Cavendish, Diana Selby Lowndes, Joan Eyres-Monsell, Evelyn, Henry and Dig Yorke, Patrick, Alan, Roy Harrod, afterwards Bunny Garnett, Kenneth [Rae], John Sutro, Christopher and Freya and Richard [Elwes].

Torn between world of people who think and feel – world of literary action, and the last of the dandies. No use any more for middlebrows, or Tories.

Return of Christopher, Logan.
Dinner for Christopher and Robert Byron[1] at Boulestins. Joined by Freya and Richard. Salmon trout, breasts of chicken with asparagus, wood-strawberries Romanoff. Iced sherry, muscadet, Chateau D'Issan, champagne nature rose, armagnac. Afterwards café and visit to Frisco.

---

[1] Christopher Sykes and Robert Byron had been travelling in Persia.

Entry into our lives of Isherwood and Pamela Johnson. Revue victims.

And the little People.

Rejection of *Rock Pool* by Fabers.[1]

Desire for literary intrigue, power, influence, struggle. And more poetry to read.

A dinner party in heaven.

Christopher, Freya, Evelyn, Robert, Patrick, Peter and Marcelle, Joan, Penelope [i.e. Mrs John Betjeman], Betjers, Brenda, Renée, Rosamond, the Abdys, Raymond, Logan, Desmond, Violet, Rachel, Brian Howard, the Lees, Bobbie, but it would be a failure.

A 'literary' party. Tibullus, Propertius, Catullus, Horace, Rochester, Congreve, Dryden, Horace Walpole, Flaubert, Baudelaire, the Duke of Queensberry [sic], Firbank, Norman Douglas, Scott Fitzgerald, Auden and Isherwood.

A sexy party. Lesbia, Delia, Cynthia, Chloe, Phyllis, Jeanne Duval, Albertine, Gilberte, Joan Crawford, Jean Harlow, Robert Heber-Percy.

Liked David Cecil very much, a charming, open-minded human person. When people really like literature all envy and competition should of rights be banished and sunk in the interchange of affec-

---

[1] The book was considered obscene. Cyril ascribed the infirmity of its moral tone to the education which had taught him to enjoy the classics. In the summer of 1935 Jack Kahane came to London, learnt of the manuscript and its history, and accepted it for the Obelisk Press, which he ran in Paris without regard to moral tones. Later he complained that it was 'a disgrace to his list', so little salacious was the novel, though in his *Memoirs of a Booklegger* he called it 'as sweet a piece of writing as ever I have seen, the work of an exquisite'. (A general account of Kahane is to be found in Hugh Ford's *Published in Paris*.)

'Any first book is always in the nature of a tardy settlement of an account with the past, and in this case my debt is with the nineteen-twenties. It was a period when art was concerned with futility, when heroes were called Denis and Nigel and Stephen and had a tortured look,' Cyril wrote in the introduction to the Obelisk Press edition. Also, 'I think I may claim to have created a hero as futile as any.' Naylor in the novel bore much the same relation to himself as the setting of Trou-sur-mer did to Six-Fours and Sanary and Cagnes, where he and Jean had dawdled away one summer after another. *The Rock Pool* was planned to extend to a trilogy with two further novels, *The English Malady* and *Humane Killer*. The latter existed as a fragment, amounting to nine pages when it was published in the *London Magazine* Vol 13, Number 3, August/September 1973. Cyril apparently had intended to sign himself 'Lincoln Croyle', a not quite perfect anagram of his name. One or two extracts from this journal were incorporated, notably the verses on p 243 starting 'Wives of writers', though this was improved to 'Wives of great men'.

tions and ideas. Attempts to score off each other and to establish personality are marks of a charlatan, or adolescent growing-pains.

Sunday – picnic – Hindhead, Liphook, Midhurst, Goodwood, Chichester, Selsey. Dylan Thomas,[1] Kay,[2] David Gascoyne. At lunch on beach threw stones at bottles representing Edith Sitwell, Virginia Woolf, John Lehmann, Michael Roberts, Engels. Back by Arundel, Amberley, Pullborough, Leith Hill. Dylan stays night.

Jokes, sprung – realism. Percy my pillion-proud, my camber-conscious.
Norman Cameron calls Spender 'the Rupert Brooke of the Depression', Wyndham (forgotten man) Lewis.
Hemingway and Michael Arlen? Merry as a grigson.

> If you don't like my erotic play
> why then all I can say
> If you don't like my erotic play
> is 'I don't like your erotic play.'

> M is for Marx
> and Movement of Masses
> and Massing of Arses
> and Clashing of Classes[3]

> The Evening Colonnade
> Colonic lavage
> Caveat Empson
> Haverstock Eliot
> 'Design for a Sex' by Haberstock Eliot

---

[1] Dylan Thomas was then twenty, and had not been long in London. Constantine Fitzgibbon, in his *The Life of Dylan Thomas* (p 149), describes a dinner given for him about this time by Cyril. Other guests were Waugh, Robert Byron, Anthony and Lady Violet Powell, and Desmond and Molly MacCarthy.

[2] For Kay Hime, see David Gascoyne's *Journal 1936–1937*. On page 12 there, he writes that Julian Trevelyan from Cambridge had first introduced him to Kay Hime at a party in Montparnasse during his first visit to Paris in 1933. She had just left school and was supposed to be studying French. 'She was a radiantly healthy blonde with a style of dress and coiffure that now appear to me to have been peculiarly typical of the Thirties, and it was not long before I "fell in love" with her,' he writes to me in a letter. Referring to this expedition, his letter continues, 'At some point during the first stage of our journey, when everyone seemed to be in light-hearted mood, Kay suddenly decided to amuse her fellow-passengers with her repertoire of Irish stories told in what seemed to me a pretty good imitation of a broad Colleen accent; whereupon Cyril, rather to my surprise, turned round with a wholly unamused expression and told her that if there was one thing he could not bear, it was the sound of that kind of Irish voice.'
Lawrence Durrell's poem, 'The Death of General Uncebunke', (1938) is dedicated to her.

[3] Incorporated into *Where Engels Fears to Tread*.

When writers meet they are truculent, indifferent, or over-polite. Then comes the inevitable moment. A shows B that he has read something of B's. Will B show A? If not, then A hates B, if yes, then all is well. The only other way for writers to meet is to share a quick pee over a common lamp post.

Peter works from 10–6, in the evening writes articles.

Who'll toll the bell?
'I,' said Marcelle,
'I'll toll the bell.'

Who'll collect his works?
'I,' said Geoffrey Faber,
'It will be a love-labour
I'll collect his works.'

Who'll correct his proofs?
'I,' said John Hayward,
'His syntax was wayward
I'll correct his proofs.'

Who'll take his wife?
'I,' said Kit Hobhouse,
'Send her down to the club house
I'll take his wife.'

Who'll take his place?
'I,' said Bill Empson,
'I like the *New Statesman*
I'll take his place.'

Who'll finish Byron?
'I,' said Montgomery Belgion,
'If there's anything I don't know
I'll ask Hector Bolitho
I'll finish his Byron.'

Who'll read his will?
'I,' said Sacheverell,
'To Sutro he leaves his guarantee
and to Simon his obituary.
To Cyril he leaves the novels
and to the Sitwells his travels.
Robert gets his job on Shell
and Patrick takes Marcelle.'[1]

Let us never forget the fine distinction between the dead and the buried.

perils of authorship
marriage, mayfair, drink, drudgery, reviewing, advertising, log-rolling, over-production and sterility.

---

[1] He wrote another more formal epitaph for Quennell.
'A copywriter in the carnal part,
Yet still a proud Augustan in his heart.
Here in this simple bed I lie alone,
No longer plagued to placate and to please
Capricious women, annexed for vulgar cash,
At last, thank God, a Gentleman of Ease!'

The seven month child.

I raise myself upon an awkward elbow
and mourn their promise by the open window
those two who fell at Pressan Ambo.

The morning bowel and evening colon-aid
the strong sour smell of the early Thirties
inter-luptious intelluptions.

Dylan when drunk I can imagine you
vomiting in the porter's lodge
of some obscurer college
among the gowns and bicycles.
And generally drunk you are,
anything that goes down your throat you say
and 'hell I would have fucked her stiff and dry'
and 'some of us must starve, let buggers starve'
and then too, you show off
diddling with words like any Oxford boy
a tiger in his tea-cups.

And sober with a solemn hangover
and plastered eyes above the broken tooth
the jitters take you over
though seriously one can talk with you a little
of trends and tendencies
but soon your master claims you.
Shaking the limbs, congesting lungs, and rolling stomach above all
in the head.
There the caged alcohol still fumes and frets
peers out at eyes, or ventures on the breath
to join its brother in the bottle.
And I remark how you come in a room
like a small animal – palm civet or toddy cat.
Tasmanian devil
your brown eyes blinking at the unaccustomed cleanliness
of guest and collar.
Will they be friend or foe.
Will they support your ego?
You small Welsh sailor.

But when I read your book, my lubrique scholar
the almond-blossom of your early promise
the bloom the beauty the obscure precision
we'll do our best to foul it — So why blame you
for joining in the fun.

All pirates are dead pirates
All fascists are dead fascists.

Powells to dinner, very nice. He asked for opinion on him and
Evelyn. I said I thought Tony had more talent and Evelyn more
vocation. Tony is likely to dry up and Evelyn to make mistakes, but
you can learn from mistakes, you can't learn from drying up.

Lunch Diana Boothby, Patrick, Hamish [St. Clair Erskine], Mary
Sewell.
window shopping afterwards.
Cocktails Lady Hastings, met charming Soviet girl, Irena Ehren-
burg.
Brian's stag-cocktail party, Eiffel and Frisco's with them and David
Herbert. Very nice evening.

Wed. 20th Ballet with Jean. *Sylphides — Presages, Boutique*. Went
on from Betty MacLaren's cocktail party. Momentous evening
—*Sylphides* made me feel the importance of concentrating on the
lyrical, making it the essential characteristic of my work, more
moral beauty, more ephemeral [sic], more style.

Baranova in *Presages*, Toumarova in *Boutique*.

I said to Robert Byron that *Presages* was pure Hemingway. He
replied, 'I don't agree — it's pure Dante, I think.' Afterwards to Café,
met Dick Wyndham. His Dinka photos.

Summer journey in car.

Calais — Beauvais — St Germain-Paris (Harmsworth) — Orleans —
Bourges — Beaulieu sur Dordogne — Albi — Carcassonne — La
Nouvelle — Perpignan — Tossa. Tossa — Rocafosca — Palamos —
Figueras — Port Vendres. Port Vendres — Béziers — Aix en Provence —
Sanary — Hyères — Saint Tropez — Sainte Maxime (Beauvallon) —
Cannes — Juan les Pins — Cap d'Antibes — Nice — San Remo —
Stoporno — Genoa — Mantua — Padua — Venice (Mary Baker,
Rodds, Hamish) — Venice — Ragusa (Romney Summers) — Ragusa —

Trieste – Celje – Balaton – Budapest. Budapest – Vienna, Vienna (Alan Pryce-Jones, Pollocks) – Linz, Munich. Munich – Lindau – Constanz – Freiburg – Cézanne – Paris (Kahane, Miller). Paris – Soissons – Mons – Brussels. Brussels, Bruges, Ostend, Calais.

Words
burbot, a fish
bummaree, a middleman
bulimy, bulimia, morbid hunger
bryologist, moss expert
breast summer, bressummer, cross beam.

Friends
1935 Christmas
Christopher, Freya, Quennells, Betjemans, Violet, Nancy, Joan, Logan.

1937	Dead	Basil Murray
		Stephen Tomlin (no go no more wheatsheaf eiffel)
	Friends	Peter Q
		Christopher
		Pierre [i.e. Peter Watson]
		Ray
		Patrick and Angela,[1] Jennifer [Fry], Betjemans
		Wiz? [i.e. W. H. Auden][2]

1936	Food Tour. Harry [Sir Henry d'Avigdor-Goldsmid], Betty [Fletcher-Mossop]. (Calais – Bordeaux – Irun – Saragossa – Paris)
	Tickerage (Harry, Betty, Raymond, Roger Senhouse, Joan [Eyres-Monsell], Barbara, Christopher etc.
	Party

---

[1] Patrick Balfour was to marry Angela Culme-Seymour.

[2] In a letter postmarked November 15 1938, Auden congratulated him on *Enemies of Promise*, 'a brilliant and also solid and moving book . . . the best English book of criticism since the war . . . you really write about writing in the only way which is interesting to anyone except academics, as a real occupation.' In the same letter Auden mentioned that 'that fascist shit Longden', now headmaster of Wellington, had forbidden him from setting foot in the grounds of the college.

Summer. Calais, Cologne, Annecy, Cannes. Joan, Peggy [Bainbridge], Tony [Bower][1] Kitzbühel. Accident. Bad Gastein, Salzburg, Munich, Paris.
Party. Harry = Marcelle Christopher = Camilla[2]
Spain 2nd Food Tour (Harry. Marcelle) Paris, Lyon, Vienne, Boisy, Spain.
Peggy lives here. Leaves.

1937   Spain again with Ran [Lord Antrim]. Paris
        London diary
        Budapest, Tirol, Paris
        Party
        Glenarm [Lord Antrim's house in Northern Ireland]
        Normandy, Paris, South Annecy, St Moritz, Austria etc
        Peter

Decay of Friends

Patrick, a Fleet Street tough, Angela a sly boots

Mark a yegg

Peter, an advertising man, 'smooth'

Christopher a much married journalist

Tony [Bower] a queen

English Law

Where there are two alternatives: one intelligent, one stupid; one attractive, one vulgar; one noble, one ape-like; one serious and sincere, one undignified and false; one far-sighted, one short; EVERYBODY will INVARIABLY choose the latter.

---

[1] Tony Bower, American art critic. The Connollys had met him in Majorca on their honeymoon, and afterwards conducted a bickering Rock Pool friendship with him. In 1940 on the editorial staff of *Horizon*. Eventually found murdered in New York.

On the back of the agreement between the proprietor of *Horizon* and its publisher, Cyril composed a long poem playing on several friends, beginning:
   'I make two classes, the animal sweetmen
   the slant-eyed Tonis, with their gifts of betrayal,
   the spaniel-lovers who lumber over their masters
   fawning with wet paws, till they smell a rabbit
   and away to the burrows of the night, or the ruthless chase
   for the Holy Grail of a gold cigarette case.'

[2] Christopher Sykes married Camilla Russell in 1936.

PIERRE's unpopularity due to not being completely able to conceal his superiority to the company he keeps.

A group of people always denies the good quality of each individual; each individual prefers to be in a group.

Conversations.

Audrey amusing about pylon boys. All three boosting themselves as great men and at the same time saying how the other two are 'finished'. 'Christopher's finished – he's gone hetero etc.' Finds Tony a repulsive character. Stephen and Inez[1] faring badly – The Homintern.

---

[1] 'We both saw marriage as a solution of temporary problems,' Stephen Spender writes of his first wife, Inez, in *World Within World*, p 206.

EPILOGUE

Where to live, in what style? That gentleman's Georgian dream-house, stucco and pillars inside and out, or Dorset cottages, Almuñecar, a Vernonesque castle in Ireland, even a yacht? Could hedonism be reconciled with the self-denying ordinances of art?

At the outset of their marriage, Cyril and Jean had gravitated to the south of France, arriving there after a honeymoon in Majorca (where the correct thing, Jean wrote to her mother, had been to call on a villa inhabited by three American lesbians and some uneasy young men, 'to swim in the oily pool, stay for buffet luncheon and play vingt-et-un all afternoon'). Les Lauriers Roses, the house they rented for a year, was at Six-Fours, by Sanary, within range of Cassis and Bandol and Toulon. Two bedrooms, a garden, a pergola, a view. Rose of England and other ferrets and lemurs became part of the way of life.

'Through the dark evening I used to bicycle in to fetch our dinner, past the harbour with its bobbing launches and the cafés with their signs banging,' Cyril was afterwards to describe it in *The Unquiet Grave*. 'I would bowl back heavy-laden with the mistral behind me, a lemur buttoned up inside my jacket with his head sticking out. Up the steep drive it was easy to be blown off course into the rosemary, then dinner would be spoilt. We ate it with our fingers beside the fire – true beauty-lovers – then plunged into advertisements in *Country Life*, dreaming of that Priory at Wareham where we would end our days.' The lemurs wormed their way to the bottom of the bed. The ferret lived in a coop in the garden, until one day it strayed and was beaten to death by ignorant peasants, 'filthy-hearted women'. On the money Gladwyn Jebb had given them as a wedding present, a raccoon was bought; it escaped, never to be seen again.

'I hate to think of you still picturing your son-in-law as one of those bloated young men that dine out a lot and work in museums in

New York or London. I got so fat because Maryland cooking took me that way,' Cyril wrote to Mrs Warner, Jean's mother. 'Of course I am still just as greedy but I don't get the same chances. We bathe such a lot, play so much ping-pong and eat so little breakfast that I look quite myself again. Jean runs the house excellently though it only consists of one servant who goes away in the afternoons . . . Now the winter is coming on and we shall probably regret being so far out in the country.' Jean liked food and drink, she cooked well. They dined in Toulon and Marseilles, in the best restaurants, returning to Six-Fours on the Omnibus du Soir. Once married, Cyril was never thin again. By means of the increasing bulk, enjoyment and self-reproach became intimately connected, and he was not going to deprive himself, except intermittently, of either.

Literary expatriates on the Riviera included Somerset Maugham at Cap Ferrat and Edith Wharton at Hyères, but the Connollys could scarcely expect to be taken up as equals by them. To Peter Quennell Cyril wrote that he did not feel cut off as people were always turning up, but, 'I very much miss having no male friends here. I don't at all like the French and Aldington and A. Huxley, the only English people I have met, have both gone south.'

Aldous and Maria Huxley had emerged from a period of travelling far and wide, and were then living at Sanary. Also a scholar of Eton and Balliol, Huxley had been only nine years ahead of Cyril, but his reputation had formidably survived there. Had his eyesight allowed, he would have served in the war, and so seemed to belong to an altogether older and even remote generation. In any case he had become a model of possible achievement. His sequence of novels leading up to *Point Counter Point* blazed a contemporary trail. Such fiction as Cyril was then attempting, or was to attempt in the future, also amounted to social commentary or satire. Like Huxley's, his characters were mouthpieces for an attitude or an idea, and their names – Pennywise, Dingyman, Persimmon, Goldprick, to give examples from various bits and pieces – made plain what they were supposed to stand for.

Just as Cyril had fallen before into an unconscious imitation of Pearsall Smith, so he hoped now to learn from the Huxleys how to pull off the trick of success. Undoubtedly the Huxleys had public and private glamour; there was even Maria's lesbianism. But anything exemplary about Huxley – even his friendship – foundered upon divergence of temperament. Huxley's ambitions were matched by capacity to work. And he was writing *Brave New*

World. As Sybille Bedford, herself a witness of life at Sanary, records in *Aldous Huxley: A Biography*, the Connollys, dropping in, would be interrupted by Maria with the words, 'Aldous is *working*.' Nor did the Huxleys find the Connollys' style romantic. 'Eating your dinner with your fingers reading before the fire meant leaving grape skins and the skeletons of sardines between the pages. The ferrets stank; the lemur hopped upon the table and curled his exquisite little black hand around your brandy glass. Your *brandy glass* – exactly: liqueurs after luncheon.'

Early in December 1930, Edith Wharton brought these neighbours together in her house at a luncheon party. 'It consisted of Aldous and Maria Huxley, Jean and Cyril Connolly, our hostess and the painter, Robert Norton, a charming dilettante and great friend of Edith Wharton,' Cyril wrote thirty years later, but still smarting from the recollection. 'Logan had arranged the introduction for us, and the Huxleys, with whom we were on terms of profound ambivalence, drove us over in their red three-seater Bugatti: Jean and Maria Huxley were highly suspicious of each other and Aldous was quite unaware that my deep admiration for him – which was responsible for us settling in Sanary – had curdled.' The Connollys felt snubbed by the Huxleys' conversation. At lunch Mrs Wharton (née Jones of New York in 1865), had enquired into Jean's Baltimore and Pittsburgh origins, deciding that she was 'an awful lump', and writing so to Bernard Berenson's confidante Nicky Mariano, who told Mrs Berenson, so publicising and eventually recording in her memoirs the entire non-incident.

Unable to shrug off such things, Cyril instead enveloped himself in them, exploring in his imagination every shadow and nuance, until convinced of the reality of failure. According to the single line in his journal (page 241), in which he summarised his experience of them, the Huxleys had aged him ten years.

Catching up with the gossip, Pearsall Smith wrote to Cyril on December 14 1930, 'I feel that you somewhat mismanaged that scene at Mrs Wharton's – from what you say it is plain that she was *terrified* of you all – thought that you regarded her as an old has-been and Mrs Humphrey Ward, and that she put on, as she does to protect herself, her masque of wealth and worldliness.' On January 4 1931, he returned to the topic, 'I hear via Florence that you were a great success with Mrs Wharton. If she asks you to stay with her, remember that she is a demon for *tidiness*, but the food makes it worthwhile.' By September he was teasing

Cyril that Mrs Wharton was said to be writing a novel about him.

By then the Connollys had left Six-Fours for England. In London they stayed at Rosa Lewis's Cavendish Hotel, or with friends, or in a house rented in Wilton Mews. Jean was persistently unwell, and in pain, apparently as a consequence of the abortion earlier in Paris. She had to undergo an operation which meant that she could never have children. There were other symptoms too. She began a letter to her mother about her health, but left it unfinished. 'I have been to see Dr Giekie-Cobb who is supposed to be one of the best doctors in England chiefly about glands. He says my glands are very disarranged but that the particular trouble is that I have over-strained my heart. It isn't in the least serious if I take it in hand. I am to go to the country quietly with Cyril (to avoid the expense of nursing home – no visits), and live on fruit and vegetables, no drink and no smoking, no coffee or tea, bed at 9.30 or 10, and as late as possible in the morning. Apparently I can't digest anything richer than a grilled chop.'

Neither Jean nor Cyril could keep to such a schedule for a moment. Had Jean been in better health, and had they become parents, Cyril felt afterwards, they would have been happier, and their marriage might have turned out differently. The obvious incentive to home-making had been removed from a naturally undomestic couple. And Jean's disarranged glands swelled, and fattened her unattractively. Regular cures had to be undertaken, mostly in summer at Brides, in central France, in the company of her mother, exchanging letters with Cyril about overweight.

In February 1933 Cyril took Jean off for a long stay in Greece, to recuperate. In Athens they encountered Brian Howard and his German lover Toni, with whom they adventured into the low life of the Piraeus. They journeyed in the Peloponese, and to some of the Aegean islands. In April all four sailed by way of Sicily to Lisbon (see page 242, footnote 1). 'The most awful thing happened in Lisbon before we left,' Jean wrote to her mother. 'We had come in to dine with Brian Howard, Toni Altmann and the Girouards . . . and went to our usual bar. We sat there until it was time to get the bill. Cyril, Toni and myself had had three ginfizzes each, the others two, but the bill was for eighteen.' High words followed. 'The chucker-out grabbed Cyril's arms and I grabbed his. He turned around and swung at me and I slapped him. He gave me a good blow on the cheek and everyone turned into maniacs and hit him and the waiters who hit back and it was a charming free-for-all.' Brian Howard slipped away to telephone the British ambassador. A joke now, she concluded, it had been no laughing matter at the time.

The death of Jean's father in 1932 had provided her with a little capital, much less than anticipated; her share of his furniture had been shipped to London; house-hunting began in earnest during the summer of 1933. On the back of one agent's list, which he stuffed into a pocket and so preserved, Cyril scribbled a couplet:

> What death does by the bed so wide
> we all can do ourselves, outside.

The flat they leased, in native Chelsea, had as its address 312a, King's Road, and was above a shop; two bedrooms, with a large studio suitable for entertaining. Behind the kitchen was another room for a couple, who were to be cook and butler. The first couple had a child who seemed to be perpetually wailing. Their successors, Cyril once wrote to Jean, were as usual 'whining for their wages', and besides, the man was caught dressing up in Jean's clothes.

312a King's Road was paid for out of Jean's inherited income, approximately £1,000 a year, depending on the exchange rate of the dollar. Mrs Warner also paid her a separate clothing allowance, and she settled expenses such as holidays taken together, or the summer cures at Brides. Cyril earned a few hundred pounds more through his contributions to the *New Statesman* (The Tattyman, in their language), or to other periodicals such as the short-lived *Night and Day*, as well as from advances for *The Rock Pool* and *Enemies of Promise*. Complain of poverty as he might, he was in fact well off by the standards of the day, and could afford to live as he chose, independently, without a regular job. Few writers of his generation enjoyed such fortune; the knowledge of it also served to inflame dissatisfaction. What were expectations in other people were impositions to him. It was almost as if he were under an obligation to spoil near-ideal conditions by ingenious contrivances for wasting time and resources. Books, silver, the genette: extravagances ran him into debt. Also party-going and party-giving, with each of the King's Road guests selected, in Cyril's phrase, as carefully as instruments in an orchestra.

At the back of her address book, Jean pencilled a list, for one of the parties perhaps: Eddie Sackville-West, Brian Howard, John Banting, Patrick Balfour, John Sutro, the Betjemans, Piers Synnott, Nigel Richards, the Blakistons, Peter and Nancy Rodd, the Henry Yorkes, followed by others with a question mark against them.

Clive Bell, Rachel Cecil, Comfort Hart-Davis, Evelyn Waugh, Francis Birrell. This was a milieu as select as it was cohesive. In that address book there were no outsiders except for Jean's Harley Street specialists and doctors, no foreigners except for schoolfriends from her American childhood, no nonentities. Generally speaking, the Connollys and their friends took for granted not only the possession of talent but also the right to express it as they saw fit. They were accustomed to doing as they pleased. The opinions of the day were coloured by their articles and books, their humour and morals and conduct. Struggle in this circle was less about careerism or status than a matter of striking an appropriate style, and to that extent it was a microcosm of the wider struggle of the Thirties – that they also had the freedom of so many available choices was the real nature of their privilege. The Brian Howards among them, too erratic to maintain a coherent or constructive style, turned themselves into living cautionary tales.

The writing of *Enemies of Promise* saved Cyril from becoming another Brian Howard, and justified his position among his friends. Once on paper, his cautionary tale served constructive purposes, however negative the apparent implications. Through the book, debts were repaid to his King's Road period, just as *The Rock Pool* had signed off his 1920s. And at one and the same moment he had founded his reputation as the author of something both topical and memorable, while presenting arguments that he was really a failure because his writings were not more and better. The evidence provided was carefully paradoxical and inconclusive about where the truth lay; he wanted a verdict of heads-I-lose tails-you-win. Yet it stood to reason that a man whose powerful and confidential analysis of his failure was actually a great success could only be engaged in making myths about himself.

When Mrs Q. D. Leavis came to review the book in *Scrutiny*, she attacked its 'cosy social homogeneity'. Cyril unconsciously revealed, she thought, 'the relation between knowing the right people and getting accepted in advance of production as a literary value'. In plain English, she meant that Cyril and his like were a lot of moneyed snobs engaged in promoting one another to the exclusion of Mrs Leavis and her like. Passing opinions on a book in terms of its author's supposed social standing is a rather fatuous form of gossiping, indicating envy moreover; no doubt Mrs Leavis guessed more or less correctly which names she would have found in that address book of Jean's. Under the group-confidence to which Mrs

Leavis was objecting lay the truism that talented people as a rule seek each other out, which is not at all the same thing as being exclusive. And 'right people' can in the end amount to nothing, just as outsiders develop into 'right people'.

Among those who came to 312a King's Road were Dylan Thomas (page 268) and George Orwell, both individualistic and neither of them 'getting accepted in advance of production as a literary value'. Orwell had fought hard for his style. In 1935 Cyril had favourably reviewed his novel *Burmese Days* in the *New Statesman*, pleased and a little astonished that someone he had known in such very different circumstances was capable of such work. Though they shared potential old-school loyalties capable of arousing Mrs Leavis's suspicions, this was actually a conspicuous example of how Cyril did not accept anyone's literary value 'in advance of production' — on the contrary, if anything he was much more likely to use personal knowledge to condemn out of hand, in the manner of Mrs Leavis herself. 'When Orwell came back from Burma he did not care for the Oxford and Cambridge intellectuals, the easy livers, "the pansy Left" as he called them,' Cyril was to recall later with due self-consciousness. 'His greeting was typical, a long but not unfriendly stare and his characteristic wheezy laugh, "Well, Connolly, I can see you've worn a good deal better than I have." I could say nothing for I was appalled by the ravaged grooves that ran down from cheek to chin. My fat cigar-smoking persona must have been a surprise to him.'

Twice in 1936, and again in January 1937, Cyril travelled to Spain (as itemised at the end of the journal, pages 272–3), much aroused by civil war in a country which he knew well, and whose language he spoke. In a dozen diary pieces, reports or book reviews in the *New Statesman*, he dealt with this war. Hope that the Republican government would defeat Franco, sympathy for the Anarchists, shifty compromise towards the Communists — his opinions tallied with those of the *New Statesman* or 'the pansy Left' in general.

Suddenly a jargon of anti-fascism and *salon* marxism jarred his prose; period hysteria too, about bombers and atrocities and red-flag heroes crying 'Salud! Kamarad!' over the graves of the fallen. Spain, he wrote in the *New Statesman* on January 16 1937, had swung 'the few remaining ivory tower-holders' like himself to the Left, though for mixed motives, not only consciousness of social injustices but to be better rewarded for their talents or to save their skins.

This was mimicry of the kind earlier displayed towards Pearsall Smith or Aldous Huxley; it did not stem wholly from conviction. In whatever pose, he remained unable to cheat himself to any great extent, and so could not cheat others. To his categorisations of the new converts to this cause of the Left, for instance, he added truths which were bound to offend them. 'There is the typically English band of psychological revolutionaries, people who adopt left-wing political formulas because they hate their fathers or were unhappy at their public schools or insulted at the Customs, or lectured about sex. And the even more typically English band, and much larger, of aesthetic revolutionaries; people who hate England for romantic reasons, and consequently the class which rules it.' Orwell was to put his finger on the wish to stay fashionable when he wrote to Cyril with gentle sarcasm, 'A pity you didn't come up to our position and see me when you were in Aragon. I would have enjoyed giving you tea in a dugout.'

'We had a fairly typical time in Spain,' Cyril wrote to Peggy Bainbridge on his return from his 1937 trip, in the company of Lord Antrim. 'Requeña, (the good-looking tough from the propaganda), met us with a car at Puigcerda and took us to Aragon, Lerida and Barcelona. The Majestic is a much nicer hotel than the Continental. The first night there was an air-raid alarm and we ran into a refuge but nothing happened. It was much more social than before – Spender was there and Christina Hastings and an awful American called Muriel Draper and a man we all hated called Catlin and Auden and Basil Murray and a horde of journalists, English clergymen, French deputies etc. We went over the university and went to a trial and went to the Hostal del Sol and the Shanghai and the Euzkadi and made friends with a very nice young barrister who was fighting with the anarchists on the Aragon front. Green was away. We motored to Valencia and there things began to go wrong.' He continued, 'Ran was given a terrible grilling by the communists – what did he want in Spain, what did he do etc? It shook him very much as he had never been treated except as a peer before. They wouldn't let him go to Madrid and I didn't want to go with those awful women whom I called the menopause revolutionaries, so we went instead to Alicante and Murcia. Very lovely but Ran had the jitters by that time.' (T. C. Worsley's *Behind the Battle*, published in 1939, had a passage about Cyril at that stage 'drinking and sexing his way round Europe', but this was removed from the proofs. Worsley, in the Connolly memorial number of the magazine *Adam*, published in 1975, regretted that he had been 'in those days a fanatical left-wing prig' but what he had actually written, he thought, had been a mild approximation of this phrase, and anyhow allotted to a character with a different name.)

Sensation-hunting through Spain, sensation-hunting through lovers: both counteracted similarity of experience, as well as boredom and complacency. Jean in her wisdom encouraged him to have affairs if he cared to, in order to get them over and done with all the sooner. On the first of his Barcelona trips in 1936 she had accompanied him, but not on the journey with Peggy Bainbridge and Tony Bower (mentioned in the journal, page 273) to Kitzbühel, Bad Gastein and Salzburg. An accident smashed up the car and prevented them from reaching Budapest, which had been their destination.

The Connollys had met Peggy Bainbridge in the south of France. Her husband had recently become a Mosleyite fascist, and she had separated from him as a result. Addressing her as '*Ma chère petite Vetséra*', Cyril wrote to tell her how 'I walked up to Montparnasse thinking about you and over-excited myself so I went into a brothel and picked out the girl who looked most like you and rushed upstairs with her. No sooner was the door closed than I saw it was no good and would not really make you nearer and so I paid her, put on my coat and rushed out again while she screamed "*Ce n'est pas correcte — soyez plus correcte monsieur — je ne suis pas si laide*" etc. Then I walked home again. Last night was better because we talked about you all through dinner.' (One of his maxims: 'In a couple, the first one to be unfaithful is the one who is going to mind it more.')

In the spring of 1937 a long poem 'West Bahnhof Blues' was written for her, with this final stanza.

> We shall have much to remember when it is too late
> The meeting in the *bois* the drive in the fog
> The *gams* the Casanova and the Bauer
> The pernod at the violet hour
> and on my birthday in Nancy
> the sad presentiment of my fate
> and the blackbird singing by the Gellert Gate.
> 'I need you more than he. You need him more than me.'
> He will have his exhibition in the spring.
> My loveless jobless spring that won't mean anything
> I shall spend in avoiding you, in regretting the day
> I fed on honeydew, regretting the wind that blew on the rock above
>   the bay

regretting your beauty and the meaning of life that was given and taken away.

To Jean he was to assert, 'I believe that two people make a third thing.' His pet-name for her was Yomps, meaning a strange intractable monster. He affirmed how much he loved her, confessing, resolving, analysing, squaring up to the future and backing away from it, while he could not make up his mind. His faults were laid at her door, her faults were his responsibility. Like Grannie Connolly before her, Jean was reproached for not having disciplined him, for having spoiled him. Time and again he repeated that his besetting sin was pride, hers was sloth, when the reverse was more nearly the truth. If she went out with someone else, he became jealous, frantic. Love was imperfect because he was not working enough; work was imperfect because he was not loving enough.

The points of marriage were listed like so many prescriptions.

1. Wife must live with and for husband not through him or against him.
2. Must either have a career or help him in his career.
3. Couple can only prosper if both work or both have a common cause (entertaining is not a common cause).
4. Wife must try to follow husband in his spiritual peregrinations.
5. Late hours and rival friends (friends who make similar demands on a wife as the husband) must go.

Turning a blind eye to his own signals, late in 1937 he had met and fallen in love with 'Miss Triangle', as he and Jean called her, or more simply △ in their letters (*Triangles* was another of the writing projects which never advanced beyond the title). Her tolerance strained, Jean increasingly spent her time in Paris – in Pansyhalla, according to Cyril, because her friends there included Peter Watson, the American Denham Fouts, and a circle of young men around them. Peter Watson, son of the inventor of margarine, had a house in the rue du Bac where he kept the modern pictures which he liked to collect. Jean often stayed there. Cyril remained in London with △.

From Cassis, in the old south of France haunts, Cyril wrote to Jean in April 1938 about this new relationship. 'I know it is ending and will have to end, but I am really very fond of her, also sorry for her and responsible, and I don't like to lose anyone who is so fond of me. She is going to stay here for ever as far as I can make out; I would love it if you could send me £50 at the end of the month.'

Inability to be decisive allowed them to drift. Hurt feelings hardened. Positions came to be taken in a way which neither Cyril nor Jean would necessarily have wished. The King's Road flat became superfluous, too expensive, and it was given up by the end of 1938. Cyril wrote to Jean, 'You must think of me not as a "little-of-what-you-fancy-does-you-good" fancier but as someone determined to become a great writer sufficiently near to middle age to wish to gradually break himself of the habits of youth which end in tears if carried on over that period, with an absolute horror of footling, footlers, and footle-carriers, and weak enough to cling hard to any means of escape, anyone who seems to help me to work and free myself from the ivy round my trunk – late nights with their correspondingly wasted days, extravagant tastes etc. My own fat is to me the outward symbol of moral and mental fat and that is why I dislike it.'

Afterwards he was to draw up his brief calendar of these events.

1937 autumn – cut out by △
1938 spring – flat
1938 summer – Cassisphobia
     fall   – near thing. △'s ill (?)
     winter – Mégève, abroad
1939 spring – △ troubles
     summer – J troubles

          chased round by H
     fall   – J troubles.

Jean declared that she would not return until he was ready to live with her whole-heartedly. On July 10 1939 he answered, 'I have been thinking about the other times we nearly separated, and the reasons. Trouville 1930, when American Jean was too much for English Cyril, but thawed in the polka-dot dress. Sanary, when you went to the hotel, and the time we got on badly because American Jean was out of hand (Formentor, Cannes with the Lizzies) and I see another four days would be necessary to discuss them. And tears, that I thought I could never manufacture again – machinery exhausted, plant obsolete – reappear, because I see how our marriage is not just a marriage but the whole youth of two people.'

'Facts stand out,' he continued.

    1. C.C. never had enough fucking. Except for tarts he had never been to bed with women until he met you. You were the first

equal he went to bed with, who was like Bobbie . . . Sooner or later he was bound to have affairs, to try to find out more about women, both as a man and as a writer. You should have helped him, as you will see that you are perhaps having the same desire to find out more about men.

2. Jean's operation. Horror upon horror, it made you fat, and it made the consciousness that you couldn't have children discontent the deep natural repose of our love. It was like cutting a ring of bark off a healthy tree. Then came Greece, Portugal, Rottingdean, Cagnes, Royal Court and King's Road. I began to be unhappy quite soon in the King's Road, and I was unhappy because I was doing nothing, and we were doing nothing either – and all the time, even when I have done something, *Rock Pool*, *Enemies of Promise*, and many articles, *WE* have still done nothing, we have talked, quarrelled, drunk and laughed a great deal, and made love – but constructed nothing and not even really helped our friends – our only creations, Tony Bower and Nigel Richards.'

Telegrams, plans, aborted reconciliations, more recrimination, bad dreams, 'each post came down like a rubber truncheon'. He asked, 'How can I love an exquisite little Arab pony when I am used to titanic struggles with my big black intractable mare?' He pleaded, 'Without your help, advice, love, and enthusiasm I am a mutilated person, a genius without a cause – and with your active indifference, or opposition, I am a genius who is sick and miserable.' Staying at Glenarm, Lord Antrim's house in Northern Ireland, he wrote laments:

> Kitzbühler Horn pray for me
> Sierra de Contrariesa fight for me
> Generalife Gardens, bring back my dark sweet
> Jean, my sleek sea otter, my close-clipped Jean.
> O summers and autumns, years and places
> Bring her back to me
> Hope of David, Star of the Sea, O Rue Delambre,
> Rue de Vaugirard, Rue de Sèvre, remind her of me.

As August 1939 drew to its close, and public events were finalising private matters, Cyril wrote to Jean, 'It seems to me that this week is very crucial, more even than next, and that we will be at war or not next Monday. I am afraid Mr Heetler (*sic*) is forcing you back into a man-made world. I find the German-Soviet Pact very funny, and enjoy the bewilderment of the Communists and the despair of the Capitalists who suddenly find an alliance between Communists and Fascists a frightful betrayal, piece of cynicism etc but see nothing cynical in a military alliance between Chamberlain and Russia. What you must decide, darling heart, is whether you want your war in your adopted country with the man of your ex-choice, or whether you would rather go to America, which you probably still could, or whether you want to stay in Paris with your friends there. I shall stay in England and try to get an interesting job avoiding London till the air-raids blow over (and I think they will be ghastly ones, with the new bombs that created such panic in Barcelona) and you may never see your poor ex-husband again.'

The declaration of war, he wrote next, had made London gloomy, and as for a job, 'I am determined to get something, as it will be intolerable to be only pink cannon fodder by the time the days draw in – if we're all back at school one must be a prefect.' Soon afterwards Jean returned to England, as did several of her Anglo-American Paris companions, including Peter Watson. Like Cyril, he too was looking for something to do. Innocent-minded, impulsive, flattered by the opportunity to become a generous sponsor and patron, he was prepared to finance Cyril's favourite day-dream of a magazine of 'harmless title, deleterious content'. It was a worthwhile way to spend the war. During September 1939 *Horizon* took shape during a series of discussions, until on October 18 a contract was signed by Watson, whereby as proprietor he undertook to pay £33 a month to subsidise 1,000 copies of the magazine. Its opening issue appeared in January 1940.

1940 spring　– H & △ in way
summer – J, △ & H

Rather than live with him, Jean preferred to stay with friends in the country, doing some work as a land-girl, going on a bicycle tour of Wales. Meetings with Cyril were not a success. On May 9 she drafted a will bequeathing him what she owned: 'I also request my mother most urgently to continue while she lives to give to my husband half the allowance she so kindly made me and on her death to bequeath to him the capital necessary to maintain this income.' Then, via Ireland, she sailed for America, writing to Cyril from the Shelbourne Hotel in Dublin, on June 14, 'It is beginning to sink in how very far I am going and for how very long. I think I have been mad to leave but perhaps this is the beginning of good sense.'

The marriage was over; and the Thirties had quite run out on him.

1940 fall	– v. near thing H
winter	– △ & Lys
1941 spring	– △ & Lys
	v. near thing
summer/fall	– d. near thing. Ditched by △
winter	– KL on scene.

Lys Lubbock was one of the assistants at *Horizon* – others included Diana Witherby and Sonia Brownell who was to marry Orwell just before his death. In a quip very much of its period, Sonia and Lys were said to be 'Lend and Lease'. Changing her name by deed poll to Connolly, Lys Lubbock was with him during the angst-ridden years in which he was incubating *The Unquiet Grave*. Published at the moment when war was turning into an exhausted peace, the book was immediately recognised as something original in English literature. It was a hymn to his ego, to be sure, in the major key celebrating pleasures that lay behind him and were perhaps never to be repeated, in the minor key grieving over the separation from Jean for which he felt to blame. There was hope in survival, however, and to be saying so, in such a way at such a point, brought out a universal element.

Through *Horizon*, values which mattered to Cyril were sustained. He published what he liked without bothering about collective improvement. Politically Cyril wanted to fight and win the war, and had no patience with the Audens and Isherwoods who were in America, and whose news he was receiving in detail from Jean. But he saw no reason to dissimulate either his tastes or his complaints. Had there been no war, the contents of *Horizon* might have proved much the same. The editorial personality of the magazine remained thoroughly idiosyncratic. Leftists felt as betrayed by his failure to follow the party line as once homosexuals had done by his abandonment of the Homintern. As a rule, critics were suspected of envy, well-wishers of insincerity, which in either case served to justify doing what he would anyhow have done.

Number after number contained contributions from writers who had caught Cyril's fancy, and if some were known, others were flashes in the pan, not heard of afterwards, men given their chance at a certain moment. Like all editors, he sought for any new voice, but he also tried to turn the page, having reached the specific conclusion that the Thirties had been a failure. (He said so in a broadcast reprinted in *Talking to India*, a collection edited in 1943 by Orwell. 'The literature most typical of those ten years was political, and it failed both ways, for it accomplished none of its political objects, nor did it evoke any literary work of lasting merit. When a future generation comes to study the names of those ten years they will be baffled to account for the esteem in which most of them were held.') His own Comments, prefacing each issue, amounted to an extended personal check-up, exploring and delineating what the future held, and some of them contain the most resonant things he wrote, not to be forgotten whatever the rest of *Horizon* might be. 'The great marquee of European civilisation, in whose yellow light we all grew up, and read or wrote or loved or travelled, has fallen down; the side-ropes are frayed, the centre-pole is broken, the chairs and tables are all in pieces, the tea-urns empty, the roses are withered on their stands, and the prize marrows; the grass is dead.' Anxiety plus inspiration plus elegy equalled *Horizon*.

Cyril became famous. His was now one of the names most in esteem. Invitations, dinners, platforms, literary functions – and after the war, prestigious trips to newly liberated Paris, to Switzerland, to America. Articles and interviews. *Happy Deathbeds* is the title of a lengthy piece of writing, still unpublished, and more reportage than fiction. In it, he portrayed a successful editor by the name of Brinkley. 'The French journalist stuck her face out at him. "*Et maintenant* (he knew what was coming) *M. Brancolee, qui sont les jeunes?*" Green-orange hair: orange eyebrows: imitation tortoise shell glasses with boot-button eyes behind – radish mouth and orange-black face: all of these he took in as he slid down the nursery slopes of his profession. "Henry Greed, Philip Baldpatch, John Gaspar," he rattled. "*Ils sont très forts.*" The pen-pencil swung across her page. "*Et qu'est-ce qu'ils font maintenant?*" She heaved. Everything was discreet about her except her expensive scent of tuberose and cape-lobster. Brinkley made a charm-face, his eyes twinkled (how does one manage that?) mouth budded and so forth into an expression of infantile disloyalty. He was forty-four. "*Mais des choses très importantes, Madame Scampi-Loetschberg – des romans – mémoires – livres de genre – un peu de tout, enfin – Ils sont très jeunes.*" She took it on the nib. "*Bowldpotch – et comment ça s'écrit?*" For ten years now he had been giving this answer, to the French, to the Belgians, the Dutch, the Americans ("They're very strong") and lately even to Germans and Italians. He sometimes wondered what translations, articles and further interviews flowed from his statement.'

As for Jean, she had settled in New York, in the literary circles of

Partisan Review and *The Nation*, where she published occasional art criticism. Regularly she corresponded with Cyril, she remitted him money. 'Mother is here,' she wrote to him one day during the middle of the war, 'and has just informed me that she can no longer keep me in the style to which I am accustomed. She is therefore cutting my allowance to $350 instead of $480 and leaving it up to me what I send you. I can't I'm afraid make it more than $100. Could you manage on that?' In another letter she told him that Mara Andrews had committed suicide, a sad *envoi* which found its way into *The Unquiet Grave*.

Late in 1945 she asked for a divorce; she wanted to marry Laurence Vail. A writer and an artist specialising in collages, Vail had lived in Paris in the Twenties. He had married first Peggy Guggenheim, and then the writer Kay Boyle, and had six children for whom he built a chalet-cum-studio in Mégève. Jean was therefore becoming a stepmother to a large family. 'He is not very young, but he is not the burnt-out end of dreary candlesticks you seem to imagine,' she told Cyril on November 20, 1945, when he was still resisting divorce, 'and I am not so young myself. A dim railway station light is still my most becoming.' She went on, 'And don't please have fevers or be so ill. Sleep well and dream pleasures. You are a great successful man now. Not for you a middle-aged, poorish American expatriate on-the-town girl, romantic, insufferable. You are well out of it.'

Soon after, in a letter of December 10, she remarked that she loved *The Unquiet Grave* (which had just been published) 'but it makes me too sad to talk about'. The divorce went through. In a series of letters lasting until 1947 he explored schemes for meeting and reconciliation, saying that he was like a clock with a broken mainspring, and that 'to my mind factors like Lys and Vail are irrelevant.' But Jean's ill-health caught up with her. In July 1950, while visiting Paris with Vail, she suddenly had a stroke, and died just one month before her fortieth birthday.

Matthew Connolly had died in his sleep on March 27 1947, at the end of a particularly severe and protracted winter. His usual room in the Naval and Military Hotel was 'terribly cold', Cyril found, its gas-fire never lit. Some money and furniture, his collections of shells and minerals, had to be distributed. To his mother in South Africa, Cyril described what dispositions he had made. The funeral had been at Bath during such a blizzard that the hearse stuck in the snow. 'It was like being left as a little boy at a new school, I thought – such a final hopeless parting. It is particularly sad when one thinks of what a dismal life Daddy had, chiefly I think because his parents forced a life on him to which he was quite unsuited. He should have been a scientist and never gone to Haileybury or Sandhurst and I am not sure if he ever should have married. Of course his love for you was the great emotion of his life but I think he would have been happier without the conflict between his love of a living person and his hoarding, collecting, cataloguing, passion for dead objects. If he had made science the whole of his life and not his main hobby I think he would have realised himself more but his "military" personality got in the way of it. I always felt he had some terrible *fright* as a child which had warped him.'

On January 11 1949 he was writing to commiserate with his mother on General Brooke's death (Maud Connolly lived on in South Africa until her death in 1964). Cyril continued, 'Before Christmas we gave a wonderful party here – about seventy people nearly all in evening dress, a barman and lots of champagne, many literary lights like Maugham, T. S. Eliot etc and many beautiful women, Lady Moore, Lady Rothermere, the Duchess of Westminster etc, a terrific success.' He also confided his hopes of marrying, now that he was free to do so – but not Lys, although 'she is so devoted to me and belongs to all the every-day part of my life.' Like Jean before her, Lys was to make her own way to America.

Horizon had lasted ten years, the magic span which a good book ought to have, according to *Enemies of Promise*. Looking back on the decade, Cyril thought that perhaps he had been a little crazy, and that the idea of decadence had hugged and haunted him. 'And then at Christmas 1949 the magazine did stop. That much was not a cancer of the soul or a disease of the imagination. We closed the long windows over Bedford Square, the telephone was taken, the furniture stored, the back numbers went to their cellar, the files rotted in the dust. Only contributions continued inexorably to be delivered, like a suicide's milk.' Another thousand subscribers and the magazine would have paid its way, but in any case Peter Watson was still prepared to make good the deficit. Arbitrarily Cyril decided that his editorial energy had been exhausted. He had lost interest. And the Forties had run out on him.

From 1950 to 1954 he was married to Barbara Skelton. In 1959 he married Deirdre Craig, and they had two children, Cressida and Matthew. The pram in the hall – dread symbol of servitude in *The Unquiet Grave* – ushered in more domestic contentment than he

[291]

cared to admit. It was appropriate that he had succeeded Desmond MacCarthy as the main reviewer on the *Sunday Times*. A twenty year stint of reviewing led to the description of himself as 'a hack in his element, hobbled', but there again he was romancing. When it came to researching, composing, and delivering his copy punctually on a Wednesday at the paper's offices, he was the thorough professional. In a weekly *causerie*, he expressed his personality, and the ideas and literature of the moment. The paper also commissioned travel articles about which he took immense care. Anyone who congratulated him on an article or a review was aware from his response that he knew the value of the work he was doing. He was gratified by it, though not fulfilled, on account of residual Oxford-cum-Bloomsbury naggings that originality alone mattered, and commentary was derivative, second-best, journalistic.

> At Eton with Orwell, at Oxford with Waugh,
> He was nobody afterwards and nothing before.

In this epigram, which he wrote into a copy of Virgil presented to Cuthbert Worsley, he cast himself to his own satisfaction as the great man *manqué*, the mythical role which he had come to prefer above all others, for it gave his imagination greatest play. Such a consummation was more attractive to the ego than acceptance of his position as the most influential critic in the country. But more than self-flattery was involved. His interest in himself was liable to flag through any kind of peace and quiet, and he was regenerating it. 'What Will HE Do Next?' by Rear-Colonel Connolly had been the title of one of his best turns in a *Horizon* Comment, but in fact it was a question constantly addressed to himself, always in the hope of an unexpectedly magical answer. Failure, as he imagined it in his case, at least was not boring.

In reality, he knew all the living authors whom he judged worth knowing, and made no effort to escape from the literary world at large. He did not seek after those seeking him, but the people he met and the places he visited remained all of a kind, reinforcing what had always been a narrow experience of life. Nothing very fresh was likely to happen to someone hunting those sensations long since proved safe. The search for the unstinting patron, for great houses and the Grand Tour, the finest collections, rare wine and exquisite food, a unique piece of china or silver, an unknown manuscript preferably by Baudelaire or Verlaine, might look like snobbishness or exclusivity, but more profoundly had become strategy motivated by the need to fend off boredom. His behaviour in this respect was like Evelyn Waugh's, and was yet another aspect of the Tweedledum and Tweedledee love-hate between the two. In the Waugh manner, he too could carry play-acting through in any company, either childishly sulking with those deemed inferior for whatever reason, or astonishingly rude to the great and powerful who for equally subjective reasons – meanness, lack of hospitality, stupidity – had failed to live up to the standards set for them. 'You write the worst cock of anyone I know,' Cyril opened a letter to one newspaper proprietor who had thought fit to criticise him about reviewing.

Anyone who makes a habit of turning jokes against himself is likely to be misunderstood, or more harmfully, taken at face value. 'Connolly's being funny again' seemed to have stood him in good stead ever since the age of eight, but of course straight-forward people often could not be bothered with the act in a grown-up, or had not enough perception to understand its underlying insecurity. ('Ugh!' for instance was the simple expletive reserved for him by Rupert Hart-Davis, writing to George Lyttelton after attending a large literary dinner party at which Cyril had been present – as recorded in their correspondence.)

As author of the bizarre tragi-comedy in which he featured himself always at a disadvantage, Cyril had only himself to blame. Of course those in contact with him formed a fascinated audience, ranging from the hostile and malicious to the amused and devoted, and containing some, to be sure, almost a claque, prepared to tolerate anything for the sake of that personality. Through the pages of dozens of books by contemporaries – Osbert Sitwell, Bowra and Waugh, Acton and Powell, Quennell, Julian Maclaren-Ross, Michael Wishart, Enid Bagnold, James Lees-Milne, Stephen Spender and John Lehmann and Cecil Beaton, Muggeridge ('We discussed parasiticism [sic] with special reference to Cyril Connolly.' Like It Was) – stumbles this character, then, in his solo performance, almost invariably worsted, outstaying his welcome, caught out equally as squanderer and money-grubber, untidy and 'not as good as he looks', lying all morning on his bed reading and writing wrapped in a damp towel after his hour-long bath, abdominous baby and semi-Falstaffian satyr, the genius indistinguishable from the clown. Whatever else, the last laugh was his.

In a notebook of mine, there is this entry, dating from November 1973.

'Quite right that Cyril Connolly's seventieth birthday dinner should be held on a day when the government declared a national emergency and the stock market slumped dramatically. Cyril is the motionless hub of a spinning wheel. He carries crisis, yet when the barbarians come, he will be caught just outside the city gates.

The Glenconners are giving this party for him in the Pinafore Room of the Savoy. It feels and looks like the Titanic at sea. Cecil Beaton, like an old milkmaid with a floppy tie, Diana Cooper, the Spenders and the Leigh Fermors, the Old Guard – and I, chosen by Cyril at the last minute, to fill a place, as though to be a survivor on a raft. *Te salutamus nos morituri.*

Christopher Glenconner rises up. "We are here among old friends to celebrate Cyril's birthday. We wish him many more years in which to enjoy his friends, his family and his *fem.*"

His *what*? screams Diana Cooper.

His fame.

Oh, his fame.

So Cyril stands. There are three things a man is supposed to want, he began, fame, friends, and love. Fame – he kicked the word away like a shoe in his way. No writer can bear his book two years after its publication.

What is he to do next? Not what he has done. And friends – he has seen too many of these at the fortieth birthday party which he gave in *Horizon*'s day. At his fiftieth birthday party his wife was sulking.

Comes Deirdre's voice, from the other end of the table, "Not me, the other wife!"

As for love, he once wrote that one of the world's excitements was to be on a southward-bound sleeper with a woman you love. Then he realised that many have the misfortune never to love a woman. So he changed it to read "on a southward-bound sleeper with someone you love". Realising that love affairs cause the torment of parting, he had a final version: "on a southward-bound sleeper with someone you are morally entitled to love". It lost the rhythm, he ended, but got the meaning.'

In the summer of 1974, while in the south of France, he was taken ill with a heart disease. Brought back to a nursing home in London, he lingered for weeks, developing secondary symptoms, until he died on November 26.

Enemies of Promise was reprinted in 1961 as a Penguin Modern Classic, with a howler in the blurb on the very first page, where he was described as Cyril Joseph Connolly. How he minded, rubbing salt into the wound — not only the irony that a Modern Classic author could not be correctly named, but the omission of Vernon, with its echoes going back to childhood. On the cover was the photograph which had come to represent his final self, a mug-shot of an intellectual desperado with a reward on his head, dishevelled, reproachful, his own wild ghost fugitive within the unhappy face.

'So it was you!' that face has seemed to be telling me, the voice as flat as could be. 'I have foresuffered all — why else do you imagine I had you invited to the last of my parties? A little extra mortgage on posterity. It was you after all, reading my papers, on the trail of my friends and lovers, finding out more than is good for them, more than is good for you, and certainly more than is good for me. Kindly conjugate for me an irregular verb: I performed, she loved, we escaped, you exposed, they laughed.

'Didn't I give you lunches at White's, and quieten sagging afternoons with cigars and confessions? I had you to stay, I opened Taittinger champagne for you, I asked you to look over the proofs of *The Modern Movement*. Think of the expeditions we made to second-hand book-shops, the Sundays spent working out anagrams and quotations in crosswords. Think of that tea-room in Tunbridge Wells where we formed a new literary movement, shouting "Down with Koestler! Down with Spender!" And now you dig out the secret shame of Crace's report that even when I was fourteen he could spot the Sunday journalist in the making.

'Spoiled, is it? Offered a choice of toys and preferring both? Stuck in Pop, as in the anal phase? Well — it was made easier than it might have been by all that. And certainly Logan inclined me to settle for the style to which he was accustomed. What if I'd been born with a million pounds? I might have lived in the style to which my gifts accustomed me. I might even have had the unique sensation of running through my million bidding at Sotheby's and Christie's instead of day-dreaming over catalogues.

'The rich entertained me because I entertained them. Any previous age would have had no difficulty understanding that. The rich, particularly rich women, exist to facilitate things. Yes, my Top Ten Play-Girls would be told in what order they ranked, so that they could exert themselves on my behalf and improve their standing. I wrote to one, "When I have money I never give your money a thought but when I haven't it is like toothache, one thinks only of the cure." I told her, "I used to think a house or a car or a villa would drop suddenly through the letter-box." A lot of pain and nuisance

[295]

might be avoided if the rich would only appreciate the point when love becomes money.

'Only two things are worth having – money which you have not had the trouble of earning, and irresponsibility. The artist has to be in a position to afford all possible choices all the time – that's what attracts so many to try to be artists, and drives the rest of the world to jealousy. So what if this is a rationalisation of love of pleasure? Love of pleasure is the reverse of fear of pain, and the more seductive and encompassing it is, the finer life becomes. You'll agree I got the best of it there. It *was* intoxicating to get away with being quite so free.

'Writers of my generation mixed together their social and literary aspirations. Behind the typewriter lay the engraved invitation to a ball in an Adam house. Our fathers were younger sons, majors or colonels at most, the titles in the family belonged only to great-aunts. To us, writing was a white-tie profession. We wanted to learn how it was done. Is that really the same as the worship of heroes, and the search for father-figures? According to you, I shouldn't have imitated young Bobbie, and Bowra, and old Logan and Sligger, and Huxley and Auden and the pylon boys. I should have been a bold bad tough. If I'd been as true to myself as Evelyn Waugh or John Betjeman were to themselves, I'd have done justice to my writer's vocation. Back to "character" again, as with those Eton ushers. Brace up, Connolly, you know you'll be swiped if you don't show up your masterpiece on time.

'As if anyone really cared! What are you working on now, even one's friends would ask, besides your reviews, I mean – when are we going to have another *Enemies of Promise*? That was their way of saying, why am I not as young as I was when first I read *Enemies of Promise* and heard about you? Friends can't resist the thrill of betrayal. They wouldn't stay the course with me, even if I was champion only of the one-yard free-style dash.

'All the books I didn't write went into the need to be loved. And which is better, to have been loved by many or to have taken up more library shelf-space? "*Le plus grand amour c'est l'amour d'autre chose.*" And what we perform is always inferior to what we imagine. If you're thinking of someone to miss, there isn't time for much else. "The past is the only dead thing that smells sweet."

'*Angst* isn't quite real because it's in the mind, is that what you're saying? All Prometheus had to do then was to make a pet of his vulture by feeding it nicely. You very well know that I had flesh-and-blood enemies; They hated me, They persecuted me. Culture for Them had something to do with barbed wire. What you call timidity, I'd call taking on protective colouring. Why should I have spent my life fighting angrily for my tastes, when I wanted only to enjoy them?

'Since the last war, envious women and embittered young-old men have dominated literary life. Their interest has been almost exclusively in the witch-like casting of spells against the act of creation of which they are not themselves capable. Preachers and commissars to the Left, bumsuckers to the Right. Critics and professors can write their books with mumbo-jumbo titles like *The Romantic Image* and *The Great Tradition*, they are paid by the tax-payer to sit in a library, but they are forgotten the day they retire. I had to keep myself safe from them. I had nothing but my talent – they had colleges, cliques, pensions, the party line. Born in Coventry, I'd have died in coventry if they'd had their way.

'Because I had something to say, I am read. So if it was an act, then at least it worked! A significant failure! We did what we could, always cleverer or deeper than the company we kept. Might the oak have greened more? *Perdidi diem*. There's no telling.'

INDEX

Abdy, Sir Robert & Lady, 246 & n, 264, 267

Acton, Harold, 44, 47, 58, 63, 112, 141n, 293

Acton, William, 58

Aldington, Richard, 276

Alington, C.A., 41, 42

Andrews, Martha (Mara), 118–20, 199n, 200n, 211–20, 290

Antrim, Earl of, 2, 59, 273, 282, 286

Ashbury, Helen, 118, 211

Ashton, Leigh, 130, 149, 191

Auden, W.H., 85, 247, 267, 272 & n, 282, 288

Ayer, A.J., 255n

Bagenal, Barbara, 245, 257, 272

Bagnold, Enid (Lady Jones), 221 & n, 293

Bailey, Cyril, 57, 171n

Bainbridge, Peggy, 272, 282–4

Bakewell, Anne (Mrs Davis), 117, 118, 123

Bakewell, Jean (Mrs Cyril Connolly), 116–125, 199n, 200, 201–4, 211–220, 229, 232n, 250, 263, 265n, 270, 284–7, 288, 289–90

– illness, 264, 266, 278, 286, 289

– at King's Road, 242, 279, 285

– marriage, 124, 284, 290

– at Sanary, 238, 242, 275–7

– travels, 222, 238, 242, 275–8, 284, 287

Bakewell, Tom, 117

Bakewell, William, 118, 257, 279

Balfour, A.J., 69, 207

Balfour, Deirdre, 253–4, 256

Balfour, Patrick, see under Kinross, Lord

Banting, John, 246, 264, 279

Baring, Maurice, 90, 92, 103, 130, 131, 144, 148–9, 180, 185, 188, 189, 193

Barrie, J.M., 43

Beach, Sylvia, 114, 203 & n, 209, 216

Beaton, Cecil, 30, 103, 185, 292, 294

Beazley, J.D., 66, 73

Beddard, Terence, 38, 41

Bell, Clive, 247, 279

Belloc, Hilary, 63

Bennett, Arnold, 183, 184, 185, 190 & n, 191, 200, 257

Berenson, Bernard, 95–6, 102, 103, 137–9, 277

Berenson, Mrs Mary, 95, 101, 102, 277

Berners, Lord, 142 & n, 143

Betjeman, John & Penelope, 141n, 152n, 247, 267, 272, 279

Bibesco, Elizabeth, 179

Bibesco, Princess Marthe, 182, 196

Binyon, Laurence, 103

Birrell, Francis, 180, 200 & n, 201, 215, 279

Bismarck, Prince & Princess, 182, 190

Blake, Mrs Harriet (Aunt Tottie), 19

Blakiston, Georgiana (Giana), 133 & n, 176, 190n, 279

Blakiston, Jack, 85–6, 164, 167, 168, 176

Blakiston, Noel, 38, 39, 41, 71, 77, 82, 85, 89, 96, 102, 117, 121, 124, 133n, 139, 145, 159, 168, 176, 190, 193, 201, 201, 211, 215, 235, 247, 260, 279

– portrait at Eton, 46

– *Romantic Friendship* quoted, 60, 85, 88, 94

Blanche, Jacques-Emile, 209, 219 & n, 228 & n, 263

Boase, T.R.S., 171 & n

Bonham Carter, Lady, 260

Boothby, Diana, 271

Boothby, Lord, 131, 132, 133, 153–5, 176, 178–80

Bowen, Elizabeth, 15, 111, 246, 247, – C stays with, 254, 257, 261, 263

Bower, Tony, 273 & n, 286

Bowra, Maurice, 64–6, 75, 77–8, 83, 96, 122, 236, 293

Boyce, Annie Gordon, 118

Brassai, 119

Brenan, Gerald, 92, 100, 176 & n, 177–8, 198, 204

Brett, Oliver (Lord Esher), 113
Bridgeman, Maurice, 43
Brooke, General Christopher (see also Mrs Matthew Connolly), 53, 55, 291
Brownall, Sonia (Mrs George Orwell), 288
Buchan, John, 74, 233
Buckley, C.D., 35, 190
Buschor, Professor Ernst, 73
Butterwick, J.C., 36
Byron, Robert, 44, 63, 175 & n, 266 & n, 271

Calder-Marshall, Arthur, 263
Cameron, Norman, 268
Carisbrooke, Marquess of, 171–2 & n
Cavendish, Diana, 266
Castellane, Boni de, 240 & n
Catlin, Professor George, 282
Cecil, Lord David, 114, 132n, 267
Charters, Jimmie, 120 & n
Chelmsford, Earl of, 29
Chichester, Ann, 186
Christie, R.N., 35
Churchill, Winston and Mrs, 103
Clark, Kenneth, 57, 61, 64, 84, 95, 106, 114, 176, 193, 247, 253
Clark, Jane, 95, 99, 176, 193, 254
Clausen, Miles, 58
Coghlan, R.L., 35
Cohn, Edgar, 59
Colefax, Lady, 90, 92, 110, 180, 261, 262
Connolly, Cyril – ancestors 15–6
– birth 17
– and Bloomsbury 91–3, 114, 146, 164, 202, 245, 257
– debts and money, 72, 79, 81, 113, 122, 123, 125, 216, 238, 279, 290, 295
– and England 84, 146, 173, 184–5, 194, 222–4, 230–5, 273, 282
– and Eton 35ff, 50; scholarship 32, school fees 30; Sunday journalism predicted 37; "Ugly" 36
– first writings 72, 80, 105ff, 115, 267 & n, 276–89
– Guide book to the Balkans, 88, 106–9, 174
– homosexuality, 40–1, 48–9, 58, 61, 67, 73, 76–7, 98–9, 122, 126, 145, 169, 177, 181, 218, 260
– King's Road flat 279, 285, 286
– influence of Eton, 38, 45, 47, 50, 57, 58, 64, 126
– influence of Ireland 19, 146–50, 165, 203, 254–7, 268n; as "Irish rebel" 28
– Jean 116ff, 121, 123, 201–4, 210–220, 223–3, 284–7

– and The Lock House 22–24, 60, 74–5, 86, 121
– and Robert Longden, 60, 69, 70, 71–2, 75, 76–7, 85, 104, 145, 148, 160, 164, 167–71, 174
– and love, 30, 40, 48, 60, 63, 98, 103, 118, 124, 131, 210–20, 280–7, 294
– marriage, 124, 240, 275–87, 291–2
– Oxford, 56, 58ff, 137, 141, 145n, 146, 187, 224, 249, 253; scholarship 42.
– parents, 16–9, 51–3, 60, 74–5, 79, 81, 117, 250, 290–1
– and Logan Pearsall Smith 86–93, 94, 95–8, 105ff, 158, 247
– parodies and spoofs quoted, 32, 39, 40, 112, 153, 195, 204, 205–6, 220–1, 225–8, 232, 247, 292
– reviewing 108–9, 111–4, 156, 199–200, 291, 293
– Saint Christopher's Bath, 20–1
– Saint Cyprian's Eastbourne, 23, 26ff
– self-portraits 11, 36, 46, 666–7, 94, 109, 112, 114, 115, 124, 160, 197–8, 229, 237, 244, 284, 287
– seen by contemporaries, 10–2, 43, 45, 57, 66, 78, 163, 176n, 190, 294
– Spanish civil war 272, 281–3
– stays with Berenson 95–6, 137–9; with Bowen 254; with Nicolson 142, 161, 163–7, 207–9
– visits Austria 88, 96; Corsica 120; Germany 54, 103, 121, 142–5, 163–7, 207–9; Greece 71, 88, 278; Hungary 54–5, 141; Italy 60, 69, 72, 96, 103, 137; Jamaica 80–4; Morocco 95; Portugal 242; Spain 64, 68, 71, 74, 104, 137, 202, 222; Tunis 70; Turkey 71, 78; Yugoslavia 140
– Yeoman's Row 101, 104, 108, 114, 149–50, 174, 185–6, 189, 193
– youthful poems 29, 39, 56, 58, 81, 82, 83, 98
– *Condemned Playground* 163n
– *Enemies of Promise* 9–10, 14, 16, 28, 30, 36, 40, 43, 50, 53, 250n, 272n, 279, 280 (reviewed by Q.D. Leavis 280), 286, 294
– *Evening Colonnade* 258n
– *Horizon* 273n, 288–291
– *Modern Movement* 295
– *New Statesman* 108–9, 111–4, 199–200, 267n, 291, 293
– *Previous Convictions* 132n
– *Rock Pool* 56, 145, 203, 259n, 267 and n, 279, 280, 286
– *Unquiet Grave* 11, 106, 123, 190, 275, 288, 290, 291

[299]

– *Where Engels Fears to Tread* 9, 268n
Connolly, Jean, see Bakewell, Jean
Connolly, Captain Matthew (died 1790), 15
Connolly, Admiral Matthew (1816–1901), 16
Connolly, Major Matthew (1872–1947), 16–18, 37, 51, 55, 86, 117, 250, 263, 290–1
– Christmas with C, 75
– half-pay, 22
– letters, 16, 17, 18, 26–7, 51, 79–80, 81, 88
– nicknamed by C, 51
– publications, 18
– separates, 17, 53, 291
Connolly, Mrs Matthew, see Vernon, Muriel Maud
Connolly, Mrs Matthew (Grannie), 19–21, 39, 77, 79, 284
Conybeare, A.E., 36
Cooper, Lady Diana, 131, 294
Costelloe, Frank, 101
Crace, J.F., 35, 36–7, 40, 42–3, 45, 48, 50, 60, 68, 171n
– portrait at Eton, 46–7
Crawford, Earl of (Lord Balniel), 69, 154
Crevel, René, 91, 247
Culme-Seymour, Angela, 272, 273
Cunard, Lady, 130–1, 192, 249, 261, 262

d'Avigdor-Goldsmid, Sir Henry, 6, 272
D'Costa, Charlie, 80, 81–4
D'Costa, Mrs, 80, 81, 84
Dannreuther, Denis, 38, 45, 46, 50, 52, 58, 59, 60
Dawkins, R.M., 66
de Margerie, Roland and Madame, 261 & n, 262
de Zoete, Beryl, 92
Delves-Broughton, L.R., 35, 45, 58
di Verdura, Fulco, 200 & n
Donegall, Marquess of, 192 & n, 240
Douglas-Home, Sir Alec (Lord Dunglass), 43
Draper, Muriel, 282
du Cros, Sir Arthur, 79
Dugdale, Mrs Blanche, 69
Duggan, Alfred, 43, 63
Duggan, Herbert, 43, 58, 59
Durrell, Lawrence, 268n

Eastwood, Charles, 35, 41, 45, 50, 74, 132 & n, 190
Ehrenburg, Irena, 271
Eliot, T.S., 67, 152, 198, 231, 268, 291

Elwes, Richard & Freya (Sykes), 195, 253–4, 266, 267
Empson, William, 268, 269
Erskine, Hamish St. Clair, 271
Essex, Earl of, 29
Evans, Sir Arthur, 73
Eyres-Monsell, Joan, 253–4, 266, 267, 272, 273

Fisher, Lady (Cecilia), 102–3
Fisher, Horatia (Racy), 102–3, 104, 114, 121, 129–34, 199, 147, 148–50, 158–9, 160, 167, 185, 192, 204, 211, 219, 231, 235
Fisher, Rosamond, 102–3, 131, 133 & n, 148, 231
Fisher, Admiral Sir William, 102
Fitzpatrick, Colin, 30
Fitzpatrick, Nigel, 30
Fletcher-Mossop, Betty, 272
Ford, Ford Madox, 111, 118
Forster, E.M., 110, 111
Foster, J.G., (Sir John), 35
Fouts, Denham, 284
French, Lily, 133, 176n, 188–9, 190, 193
Fry, Jennifer, 272
Fry, Margery, 99, 177, 247
Fry, Roger, 99, 177, 186, 264

Gardiner, Evelyn, 59; as Mrs E. Waugh, 227
Garnett, David (Bunny), 92, 107–109, 110, 135, 186, 244, 257, 266
Gascoyne, David, 263 & n, 268 & n
Gathorne-Hardy, Eddie, 264
Glenconner, Lord and Lady, 294
Gosse, Sir Edmund, 90, 113, 183, 258
Gow, A.S.F., 34
Graves, Allen, 179–80
Graves, Robert, 15
Greene, Graham, 57
Greenidge, Terence, 63
Grigson, Geoffrey, 268
Guinness, Bryan (Lord Moyne), 130
Guinness, Meraud, 172, 193
Gurdon, Robin, 43

Halliday, Edward, 168 & n, 171, 201, 217
Hammersley, Mrs Violet, 90, 92, 253–4, 264, 267, 272
Hardy, Howard, 246, 264
Hardy, Thomas, 137, 151, 231, 233
Harmer, Freddy, 38, 39, 41, 46, 50, 52, 74, 82, 88, 132 & n, 146, 176, 193, 222
Harmsworth, Desmond, 271
Harrod, Roy, 77, 266
Hart-Davis, Comfort, 265, 279

Hart-Davis, Rupert, 293
Hastings, Lady, 271, 282
Hayes, Rollo, 249
Hayward, John, 261, 269
Headlam, G.W., 42–2, 64
Heber-Percy, Robert, 267
Hemingway, Ernest, 111, 120, 204, 252 &
   n, 268, 271
Henderson, Gavin (Lord Faringdon), 242
   & n
Henderson, Roddy, 149
Herbert, David, 208 & n, 209, 271
Hergesheimer, Joseph, 117, 243 & n, 251,
   253–4, 256–7
Heygate, Sir John, 59
Higgins, Molly, 243, 244, 249
Hime, Kay, 268 & n
Hinks, Roger, 252 & n, 259, 261
Hobhouse, Christopher, 269
Hollis, Christopher, 46, 58, 63
Horner, Lady, 102, 207, 245, 247
Howard, Brian, 44, 57, 65, 77, 141n, 149,
   175n, 188, 242 & n, 263, 264, 267,
   271, 278, 280
Hudson, Nan, 90
Hussey, Christopher, 69
Hutchinson, Mary, 191
Huxley, Aldous, 47, 163n, 174 & n, 198,
   224, 238, 242, 252 & n, 276–7, 282
– "added ten years to my life", 241, 277
– Sybille Bedford, *Aldous Huxley*, quoted,
   277
Huxley Maria, 242, 276–7
Hyslop, Paul, 193 & n, 243, 262

Isherwood, Christopher, 267, 274, 288

Jebb, Gladwyn, 69, 104, 130, 132, 137,
   142–5 & 145 n, 146, 148, 149, 154,
   159, 162 & n, 173, 174n, 176,
   178–80, 185, 190, 191, 193, 207, 264,
   275
Jessel, Teddy (Lord), 43, 58, 59, 60, 243
John, Augustus, 73
Joyce, James, 114, 147, 150, 151, 152, 164,
   193, 198, 203n, 207, 216, 224, 228
– interview with, 203

Kahane, Jack, 277n
Kahn, Mrs Otto, 103, 239
Katawi, George, 261 & n, 262
Kemble, Harriet, 16
Kennedy, Margaret, 143
Kennedy, Richard, *A Boy at the Hogarth
   Press* quoted, 131n
Keppel, Colonel G. and Mrs, 103
Keynes, J.M., 102

King-Farlow, Denys, 38, 41
Kingston, Anna Countess of, 14, 19, 254–6
Kinross, Lord (Patrick Balfour), 64, 66, 70,
   76, 88, 94, 101, 103, 104, 108, 110–1,
   114, 123, 130, 131, 133, 139, 148–50,
   159, 160 & n, 174, 175n, 176, 182,
   186–8, 190, 193, 200, 201, 211, 246,
   253, 264, 266, 271, 272, 273, 279
Knebworth, Viscount, 43

Lascelles, Dan, 143 & n, 144, 161
Lauriston, Dorothy, 83
Lawrence, D.H., 124, 143n, 150, 152,
   201n, 224, 238, 239
Lawrence, T.E., 137–8
Le Fanu, William, 38, 74, 139
Lees-Milne, James, 293; *Harold Nicolson*
   quoted, 163n, 208n
Lehmann, John, 268, 293
Lehmann, Rosamond, 246 & n, 257, 264,
   267; *Dusty Answer* 151
Leng, Kyrle, 202 & n
Lewis, Rosa, 153, 259 & n, 262–3, 278;
   Cavendish Hotel, 242, 278
Lewis, Wyndham, 111, 152, 174, 193, 203,
   239, 268
Lindsay, A.D., 57
Lingerman, Eric, 162
Londonderry, Lord and Lady, 103, 261
Longden, Robert, 38, 57, 58, 60–2, 63, 64,
   66, 67–9, 71, 72, 74, 76–7, 79–80,
   84, 88, 89, 95, 96, 100, 102–4, 106,
   121, 130, 139, 145, 147, 148, 160,
   161, 164–7, 168, 169–71, 174, 176,
   184, 185, 190, 193, 211, 229, 272,
   286
– portrait at Eton, 60
Loxley, Peter, 38, 188
Lubbock, Lys, 288, 290, 291
Lubbock, Percy, 103

MacCarthy, Dermod, 149, 150
MacCarthy, Desmond, 90–3, 96, 100,
   107–8, 113–4, 122, 131n, 144, 163,
   176, 180, 185, 193, 195, 222, 247,
   260, 267, 268n, 291
MacCarthy, Molly, 91–3, 99, 100, 103,
   131n, 132, 148–50, 193, 260, 268n
MacCarthy, Rachel, 91, 102, 131 & n, 132,
   149, 176, 178, 231, 267, 279
MacGregor, D.C., 59
Mackenzie, Duncan, 73
Maclaren, Betty, 264, 271
Maclaren-Ross, Julian, 293
Macnaghten, Hugh, 41–2
Mariano, Nicky, 271
Marsden, H.K., 171 & n

Marsh, Sir Edward, 143, 172–3, 227n
Marshall, Elizabeth, 118, 219
Marten, C.H.K., 41, 42
Maud, John, 40, 187 & n, 188
Maugham, Somerset, 12, 276, 291
Mencken, H.L., 123
Messel, Oliver, 44
Messel, Rudolph, 58
Meynell, Francis, 107–8
Meynell, Godfrey, 35, 36, 38, 166
Meyrick, Mrs, 153 & n
Michonze, Gregor, 119, 203 & n
Milford, Lord (Wogan Philipps), 246 & n, 257
Miller, Henry, 119, 272
Milligan, W.C., 35, 52, 53, 190
Minns, C.E., 35
Mirlees, Hope, 110, 262
Mitford, Nancy (Mrs Rodd), 191n, 271, 279
Moore, George, 110, 130, 137, 150
Morand, Paul, 111, 139
Morgan, Evan (Lord Tredegar), 136, 191
Morrell, Lady Ottiline, 74
Morrell, Philip, 143n
Mortimer, Raymond, 163–7 & 163n, 174, 176, 178–80, 193 & n
Muggeridge, Malcolm, 293
Murray, Basil, 122, 272, 282
Mynors, Humphrey, 187
Mynors, Roger, 32, 38, 53, 58, 59, 60, 66, 74

Nicholls, Beverley, 163
– The Sweet and Twenties, quoted 142n
Nicolson, Harold, 103, 121, 142–5, 147, 152, 159, 161, 162, 163–7, 176, 179, 182, 185, 193, 207–9, 245, 247, 252–3, 259
– C stays with, 142–5, 161, 163–7, 207–9
– discusses Souls, 207–8
Noble, Cynthia, 159, 191n
Norton, Robert, 277
Novello, Ivor, 142–3 & 142n

Oakeshott, Walter, 57
O'Connor, H.M., 124
O'Dwyer, J., 35, 39, 41, 54
Orwell, George (Eric Blair), 26–30, 32, 34, 76, 281, 283, 288, 291
– C reviews Burmese Days, 281
– "curious communication", 44
Oughterson, Miss, 45

Panza, Mario, 142 & n, 143, 144
Pares, Richard, 63, 69, 78
Partridge, Frances (Marshall), 178 & n

– Memories quoted, 131n, 244n
Pearsall Smith, Logan, 86–93, 94, 96, 99, 101, 105, 107, 114, 117, 123, 132, 137, 158, 160, 176, 193, 201, 202, 215, 247, 248, 254, 257, 262, 263, 267, 272, 276, 277, 281
– allowance to C, 101, 114, 123
– "Down with Cyril Society", 97
– "enemies" of Virginia Woolf, 92
– opinion of C, 89–90, 108, 114–5
Perlès, Alfred (Fredl), 119–20, 211, 213, 217
Potocki, Count, 138
Powell, Anthony, 43, 44, 109, 263, 268n, 271, 293
Powell, Lady Violet, 268n, 271
Pryce-Jones, Alan, 9, 247, 254, 266, 271
Pulham, Peter Rose, 244 & n, 257

Quennell, Peter, 57, 108, 120, 122, 146, 152, 162n, 176, 180, 187, 190, 193, 196, 197, 204, 225, 232 & n, 243, 247, 248, 253–4, 256–7, 259n, 262–3, 264, 267, 272, 273, 276, 293
– epitaphs for, 269 & n.

Richards, Betty & Nigel, 259, 279, 286
Ritchie, Philip, 64, 65, 74, 77, 138 & n
Roberts, Michael, 268
Rodd, Peter, 191, & n, 271, 279
Romilly, Esmond, 263
Rothé, Marcelle (second Mrs Quennell), 243, 256, 257, 262–3, 264, 267, 269, 272
Rowse, A.L., 160 & n
Royde-Smith, Naomi, 252 & n
Runciman, Steven, 32, 130
Russell, Alys (Pearsall Smith), 99
Russell, Bertrand, 99, 249
Russell, Lady Victoria, 190
Rylands, George, 38, 225, 253

Sackville-West, Edward, 77, 209, 247, 254, 279
Sackville-West, Vita(Nicolson), 143n, 147 & n, 152, 159, 161, 193, 209, 233
Saklatvala, Shaparji, 153 & n
Sands, Ethel, 90, 92, 190 & n, 201
Scrope, Adrian & Petsy, 195 & n, 196
Seafield, Nina Countess of, 130, 131, 132, 149, 159, 192, 242n
Selby Lowndes, Diana, 266
Senhouse, Roger, 191 & n, 272
Seton, Ernest Thompson, 21, 31
Sewell, Mary, 271
Sharp, Clifford, 113, 159, 174, 190
Shaw, G.B., 147, 172–3, 200, 230

Sitwell, Edith, 74, 90, 152, 183, 268
Sitwell, Sir Osbert, 51, 74, 90, 152, 183, 293
– parody poem to, 266
Sitwell, Sacheverell, 74, 90, 110, 152, 183, 269
Skelton, Barbara, 291
Smith, A.L., 56
Sparrow, John, 96
Spears, General Sir Edward, 141n, 172, 185, 265
Spears, Lady (Mary Borden), 141n, 172, 185, 227n, 265
Spender, Stephen, 247, 268, 274 & n, 282, 293, 294
Squire, Sir John, 180, 195, 233
Stafford, Winny, 176n, 177–8
Stallybrass, Nancy (first Mrs Quennell), 120, 176, 190, 197 & n, 243, 244 & n, 257, 263
Stephen, Adrian, 101, 131n
Stephen, Ann, 101–2, 131 & n, 148
Stephen, Judith, 101, 131 & n, 148
Stephen, Karin, 101, 131n, 181
Stern, G.B., 225 & n
Stone, C.G., 59
Strachey, Barbara, 101
Strachey, Christopher, 101
Strachey, James, 264
Strachey, John, 257
Strachey, Julia (Mrs Stephen Tomlin), 186n, 245
Strachey, Lytton, 64, 110, 138n, 155, 191n, 248
Summers, Mrs Dorothy Mabel (Aunt Dot), 19
Summers, Montague, 85–6
Summers, Romney, 271
Summers, Walter, 19
Sutro, John, 264, 266, 269, 279
Sykes, Angela (Lady Antrim), 195 & n, 196, 259 & n
Sykes, Christopher, 131, 143, 195 & n, 208n, 244, 266 & n, 267, 272
– marries Camilla Russell, 273 & n
Sykes, Sir Richard, 104, 188, 195 & n, 196, 200, 211, 212
Synott, Piers, 74, 86, 88, 138 & n, 176, 255, 279

Talbot-Rice, David, 63
Tayeb bin Ahmed, 71
Taylor, Valerie, 201 & n
Thomas, Dylan, 268
– parody of, 270
Tihany, Lajos, 119
Todd, Dorothy, 180 & n

Tomlin, Stephen, 186 & n, 200–1, 204, 215, 244, 272
Trask, Carrick, 21
Trefusis, Violet, 103, 193, 200
Trevelyan, Hilda, 92, 130
Trevelyan, R.C., 92, 180, 254
Trotter, Philip, 143n, 191, 264
Turner, Joyce, 141 & n, 149, 158, 176, 193, 264–5 & n

Urquhart, F.F. (Sligger), 57, 59, 61–3, 71, 72, 75, 77, 80, 82, 85–6, 99, 101, 130, 160
– death, 264

Vaughan Wilkes, Mr & Mrs (Sambo & Flip), 27 ff, 53
Vernon, Edward, 17
Vernon, Mrs Edward (Granny Vernon), 23, 101
Vernon, Muriel Maud (Mrs Matthew Connolly), 16–8, 26, 51, 54, 55, 75, 79, 121, 122, 132, 186, 264, 290 1
– and General Brooke, 53, 291

Wales, Prince of, (Edward VIII), 130, 254
Waley, Arthur, 92, 105, 110, 140, 180, 186, 198, 254
Wansborough, George, 243 & n, 265
Warner, Daniel List, 117–8, 122
Warner, Mrs Daniel List (Gertrude Logan Paxton), 117–8, 123, 264, 275, 278–9, 287, 290
Warre-Cornish, E.C., 91
Warre-Cornish, Mrs, 91, 258, 260
Warren, Dorothy, 143 & n, 190–1, 260–1
Waterfield, Lina & Gordon, 138 & n
Watkins, A.R.D., 35, 45
Watson, Peter, 272, 274, 284,
– and Horizon, 287, 291
Waugh, Evelyn, 62–3, 65, 110, 112, 122, 192n, 227, 242 & n, 247, 252, 253–4, 255n, 256, 266, 268n, 271, 279, 291, 293
– Diaries quoted, 153n; A Little Learning quoted, 62
Wayne, R.S.J.C., 35, 190
Wellesley, Lady Dorothy, 147 & n
Wells, C.M., 41
Wells, H.G., 200, 230, 254
Wharton, Edith, 88, 263, 276–7
Wicklow, Earl of, 58
Wilkes, John, 58, 59
Williams, Sidney, 117
Willson, Terry, 30ff
Wilson, Paul, 59
Winn, Godfrey, 11, 185

Wishart, Michael, 293
Witherby, Diana, 288
Wong, Anna May, 190 & n
Woodall, Edward, 43
Woodward, Professor, 73
Woolf, Leonard, 92, 254
Woolf, Virginia, 92–3, 101, 130n, 143n,
    147n, 155–6, 180 & n, 183, 184,
    200n, 228, 254–5, 256, 258, 263, 268.

– *Orlando*, 180, 200, 250n
– "smarty-boots", 255n
Worsley, T.C., 282–3, 292
Wright, Frank, 30
Wyndham, Richard, 271

Yencken, Arthur, 179
Yorke, Henry (Henry Green), 44, 57, 266,
    279